Knowing Our Limits

Knowing Our Limits

NATHAN BALLANTYNE

OXFORD

UNIVERSITY PRESS

OXFORD
UNIVERSITY PRESS

Oxford University Press is a department of the University of Oxford. It furthers
the University's objective of excellence in research, scholarship, and education
by publishing worldwide. Oxford is a registered trade mark of Oxford University
Press in the UK and certain other countries.

Published in the United States of America by Oxford University Press
198 Madison Avenue, New York, NY 10016, United States of America.

Library of Congress Cataloging-in-Publication Data
Names: Ballantyne, Nathan, author.
Title: Knowing our limits / Nathan Ballantyne.
Description: New York : Oxford University Press, 2019. |
Includes bibliographical references and index.
Identifiers: LCCN 2019006877 (print) | LCCN 2019980862 (ebook) |
ISBN 9780190847289 (cloth : alk. paper) | ISBN 9780190847296 (ebook) |
ISBN 9780190847302 (updf) | ISBN 9780190847319 (epub)
Subjects: LCSH: Knowledge, Theory of.
Classification: LCC BD201 .B35 2019 (print) | LCC BD201 (ebook) |
DDC 121/.2—dc23
LC record available at https://lccn.loc.gov/2019006877
LC ebook record available at https://lccn.loc.gov/2019980862

For my family

My thoughts!—It is the building a house for them that troubles me.

—Joseph Joubert (1754–1824), *Pensées*, published posthumously

Every thing has its own limits, a little centre of its own, round which it moves; so that our true wisdom lies in keeping to our own walk in life, however humble or obscure, and being satisfied if we can succeed in it. The best of us can do no more, and we shall only become ridiculous or unhappy by attempting it. . . . An overweening vanity or self-opinion is, in truth, often at the bottom of this weakness; and we shall be most likely to conquer the one by eradicating the other, of restricting it within due and moderate bounds.

—William Hazlitt, "On the Shyness of Scholars," 1827

Vanity and vexation close every inquiry: for the cause which we particularly wished to discover flies like the horizon before us as we advance. The ignorant, on the contrary, resemble children, and suppose, that if they could walk straight forward they should at last arrive where the earth and clouds meet. Yet, disappointed as we are in our researches, the mind gains strength by the exercise, sufficient, perhaps, to comprehend the answers which, in another step of existence, it may receive to the anxious questions it asked.

—Mary Wollstonecraft, *A Vindication of the Rights of Women*, 1792

A man's got to know his limitations.

—Clint Eastwood, in the 1973 action thriller *Magnum Force*

Contents

Acknowledgments

While writing this book, I accumulated debts to many people for helpful conversations and written comments on draft chapters. There are too many people to thank, but let me mention a few names here.

I am grateful to Alex Arnold, Andrew Bailey, Matthew Ballantyne, Michael Bergmann, E.J. Coffman, Stewart Cohen, Sorana Corneanu, Thomas Crisp, Carlo DaVia, Dennis Des Chene, Peter Ditto, Joshua Dolin, David Dunning, William Dyer, Ian Evans, Marcello Fiocco, Bryan Frances, Daniel Greco, Stephen Grimm, Michael Hannon, John Heil, Terry Horgan, Daniel Howard-Snyder, Xingming Hu, Tim Kenyon, Nathan King, Hilary Kornblith, Charlie Lassiter, Keith Lehrer, Kirk Lougheed, Michael Lynch, Jonathan Matheson, Andrew Moon, Blake Roeber, Patrick Rysiew, David Schmidtz, Norbert Schwarz, Roy Sorensen, Mark Timmons, Justin Tosi, Greta Turnbull, Joseph Vukov, and anonymous reviewers. A number of friends, former teachers, and colleagues shared insightful feedback on the project as well as gestures of encouragement: Jason Baehr, David Christensen, Paul Gooch, Peter King, Klaas Kraay, Sydney Penner, Andrew Rotondo, and Jada Strabbing. And I ought to single out three people who read more rough draft material than is right or safe: Peter Seipel, Shane Wilkins, and Benjamin Wilson. Peter and Shane commented tirelessly on the manuscript, made it better, and were sympathetic to the project when I found myself wondering what on earth I had gotten myself into. Ben offered wise counsel, keen questions, and support from false start, to start, to finish. His writerly powers and comedic instincts are matchless among former Junior Resident Fellows of Massey College.

Draft versions of different chapters were tested out on audiences at Boston University, Bowling Green State University, Loyola Marymount University, Ryerson University, University of Arizona, University of California at Irvine, University of Connecticut, University of Southern California, University of Tokyo, and Washington University in St. Louis. Thanks to audience members for discussions during Q&A sessions.

While I was at work on this project, my research assistants at Fordham University helped me hunt down sources and scholarly curiosities. They are Johnny Brennan, Noah Hahn, Allysa Lake, Joe Morton, Justin Reppert,

Luke Schumacher, and Nicholas Sooy. Thanks to Alison Shea at Fordham's Law Library for her help cracking the case of the butcher jurors. For ad hoc translation advice, I turned to Carlo DaVia, Peter King, and Shane Wilkins. Johnny Brennan translated from German the Goethe epigraph in Chapter 8. Suzie Appenzeller and Margaret Donovan, who expertly manage the day-to-day affairs of Fordham's Philosophy Department, were invariably knowledgeable and kind whenever I needed help.

I taught graduate seminars at Fordham where my PhD students heard about some of the arguments that ended up in these pages. Thanks to all of my students for their questions and input, especially Samuel Kampa and Coran Stewart, who gave me sharp and detailed feedback on draft chapters. Sam took a careful look at the whole manuscript during the copy-editing stage and beat me in a contest to catch my typos.

I am grateful both to my editor at Oxford University Press, Lucy Randall, for enthusiastically supporting my project, and to Hannah Doyle for her guidance throughout the production process.

Earlier versions of a few chapters appeared elsewhere. Chapter 5 began life as "Debunking Biased Thinkers (Including Ourselves)," 2015, *Journal of the American Philosophical Association* 1 (1): 141–162. Most of Chapter 6 appeared earlier as "Counterfactual Philosophers," 2014, *Philosophy and Phenomenological Research* 88 (2): 368–387. Chapter 7 is based on "The Significance of Unpossessed Evidence," 2015, *The Philosophical Quarterly* 65 (260): 315–335. Chapter 8 is a lightly brushed-up version of "Epistemic Trespassing," 2019, *Mind* 128 (510): 367–395. For permission to reproduce some material from those articles, I acknowledge Cambridge University Press, John Wiley & Sons, and Oxford University Press. Thanks also to Warner Bros. Entertainment Inc. for allowing me to use as an epigraph an excerpt from the 1973 film *Magnum Force*.

My work was generously supported by the John Templeton Foundation, the University of Connecticut's Humanities Institute, and Fordham University. Thanks are due to Alex Arnold, Eva Badowska, John Churchill, John Drummond, John Harrington, Michael Lynch, and Michael Murray.

If I could sit at my desk and start again on the first blank page, I suspect I would do it all differently, except for the music that animated my writing sessions. I am partial toward "North German" music—Sweelinck, Schütz, Buxtehude, Bruhns, and Johann Sebastian Bach—as well as Canadian music—Oscar Peterson, Glenn Gould, Lenny Breau, Angela Hewitt, The Tragically Hip, Propagandhi, and The Weakerthans.

I am grateful to my whole family for their companionship and thoughtful-ness, and for forgiving me for the times when I should have been "there" but was working instead. My parents, Brenda and John, have been unfailingly supportive of my efforts in all things over the years and filled with love and enthusiasm. I also want to thank my grandmother, Betty Ballantyne-Brown, and my late grandfather, Frank Dicks (1932–2016), for kindness, generosity, and fishing trips.

I was confronted by my limits more than once while working on this project, but I didn't have to rely on my own abilities to keep going. My wife, Jennifer, and our daughter, Clara, cheered me on and kept me grounded. Jennifer was a judicious and patient sounding board for ideas and encour-aged me to cultivate the right attitude toward writing about academic epis-temology. Clara once asked me whether the book's cover could feature a picture of her riding a Stygimoloch. Her arrival on the scene prompted me to try to say something about my chosen academic field that I didn't know how to say. Without Clara, this work would have been completely different.

There's an old observation, attributed to Blaise Pascal, about authors and their books: "Certain authors, speaking of their works, say: 'My book,' 'My commentary,' 'My history,' and so on. They resemble middle-class people who have a house of their own and always have 'My house' on their tongue. They would do better to say: 'Our book,' 'Our commentary,' 'Our history,' and so on, because usually there is in their books more good from others than from themselves." This book owes so much to many people—but most to my family. I dedicate it to them.

Nathan Ballantyne
June 2019

A Note to the Reader about
the Book's Cover

The cover of this book takes inspiration from one of the most resonant epistemological images from the history of philosophy: René Descartes' analogy between our corpus of opinions and a building in need of repair. Descartes used his building image to introduce his method for placing human knowledge on stable foundations. Readers of Descartes can't miss the obvious: theorizing about knowledge is (at least for Descartes) a little like practicing architecture. If we want to conduct our intellectual lives well and attain secure knowledge, Descartes says we must begin with the right blueprint.

The photograph on the book's cover was shot in June 1949 and shows a lighthouse on iron pilings standing in water roughly ten miles from Key West, Florida. Built in 1855, the Northwest Passage Light continued operation until 1921 when it was decommissioned by the United States Lighthouse Service (USLS) and the light on top was removed. Later in the twentieth century, the lighthouse came to be known locally as the "Hemingway House on Stilts" on the basis of rumors that the writer Ernest Hemingway had purchased the house after the USLS deactivated it. Today, the Ernest Hemingway Museum in Key West displays a scale replica of the house on stilts. But Hemingway certainly didn't own the lighthouse—the USLS never sold off decommissioned buildings during Hemingway's lifetime. Nevertheless, Hemingway and his fishing buddies probably did use the house as a platform to cast for silver barracuda or as a stopover point on trips to the Marquesas Keys or Dry Tortugas. The lighthouse was destroyed, probably by arson, in August 1971. All that remains today are the old pilings.[1]

---

[1] Thanks to Brewster Chamberlin, Beth Crumley, Scott Price, and Russ Rowlett for answering my queries about the Hemingway Stilts.

1

Epistemology and Inquiry

It is good, from time to time, to view the present as already past, and to examine what elements it contains that will add to the world's store of permanent possessions, that will live and give life when we and all our generation have perished. In the light of this contemplation all human experience is transformed, and whatever is sordid and personal is purged away.

—Bertrand Russell, "On History," 1904

Epistemology is careful reflection on inquiry. When we inquire, we use evidence to answer questions. One inescapable fact is that we are all imperfect inquirers. We are often overconfident, prejudiced, muddled, and wrong. Improving our intellectual life takes work. But how should we direct our efforts? What can we do to become more reasonable and reliable? That is where epistemology figures in. We need guidance to overcome our intellectual shortcomings, and my central thesis in this book is that epistemology can provide that guidance.

An inquiry-guiding conception of epistemology has played an important role in the history of philosophy, though it is not so well represented today in the field of professional epistemology. Let me briefly describe two historical roots of the present work.

Some philosophers in early modern Europe played a central role in their world's intellectual affairs. After the gradual breakdown of the widespread religious and moral consensus of the Middle Ages, people faced a crisis. The sources of authority that had ordered human life for centuries had eroded. Many people found traditional values and ideas doubtful. Some philosophers tried to fill the intellectual vacuum by rejuvenating inquiry. They turned to questions about methods, knowledge, and reasonable opinion. They tried to build new foundations for science and medicine, challenge superstition and dogmatism, and draft blueprints for a more stable society. We now think of their efforts as ringing in the ages of "Scientific Revolution" and "Enlightenment." An important part of philosophers' work was what John Locke called the "first inquiry"—the attempt, as Locke put it, "to examine our own Abilities, and see, what Objects our Understandings were, or were not fitted to deal with" (1975 [1690], 7). Philosophers often saw themselves as using truths about inquiry to promote the sciences and human flourishing.

In Vienna during the early decades of the twentieth century, a small but influential group of European intellectuals met regularly to talk. They discussed philosophy, science, and society. They called themselves *Der Wiener Kreis*—the Vienna Circle. What united them was empiricism. By starting with the idea that experience is the only source of knowledge, they wanted to articulate and defend what they called the "scientific world-conception." Although some members of the Vienna Circle were academics, the group was not merely trying to settle scholarly scores; many of them hoped that philosophy and science would transform the social and political order. Some members took it as their goal to "unify" and coordinate the sciences in the service of effectively planning modern life. Reaching out in public lectures and writings, they conveyed the scientific world-conception to audiences. They hoped that their ideas could help counteract the rise of totalitarian regimes. After all, mistaken epistemological ideas threaten to usher in dangerous social consequences. During the 1930s, politicians and propagandists used ideas such as "highest duty" and "national community" to whip the masses into a frenzy and to launch armies of goose-stepping soldiers. Members of the Vienna Circle thought clear-eyed empiricism would eliminate such perilous nonsense and help to preserve civil society. One historian remarked that the Circle sought nothing less than "to help fulfill the promise of the eighteenth-century French Enlightenment" (Reisch 2005, 3).

There are many other examples of thinkers seeking to use reflection on inquiry as a tool to improve inquiry and thereby our lives. I offer this book as a modest contribution to the long tradition of what I'll call *regulative epistemology*—the kind of epistemology that aims to provide guidance for inquiry.

My path to writing this book has been roundabout. Here's one little habit that led me here. On a quiet afternoon, I like to choose a well-regarded academic philosophy journal from the library shelves and skim fifteen or twenty issues from the first half of the twentieth century. It usually takes me until dinner. I glance at articles by scholars whose names I have mostly never heard of. I wonder about the origins of now-forgotten theoretical agendas and debates. At high speed, I watch a great parade of philosophical research pass by. I have tried to fathom the quantity of the ambition and the striving represented by these many thousands of pages. How many late nights, how many waste bins loaded with crumpled-up drafts, did all of this take? Is this what it's like to view philosophers' lives from the outside? I'm confronted in these acid-free pages with questions about my own working days. One key-stroke at a time, I add a few more pages to the growing heap of work on academic philosophy. But what is the point of these efforts? Is it more than paying bills, or seeking promotion, or trying to eke out a place in a professional field?

So I've thought a little about what professional epistemologists do. In their work, they reflect on inquiry carefully. What is the purpose of their reflection? Which parts of inquiry matter to them? What is epistemology for? For me, these are disquieting questions. I bring no conclusive answers. Yet I am often moved by the idea that careful reflection on inquiry could have great value if it makes us less imperfect in our attempts to figure things out.

In the first three chapters of this book, I introduce regulative epistemology by examining its nature and scope, a brief part of its history, and its practical ambitions for guiding inquiry. The present chapter orients us toward the place of regulative epistemology within the contemporary scene. First, I describe some general trends in recent academic epistemology, explaining why the field often does not share the concerns of regulative epistemology (sections 1–4). Then I describe how regulative epistemology requires contributions from scientific and humanistic researchers who focus on inquiry. As I explain, there's a vital role for epistemologists to play in the project (sections 5–7).

1. What Is Professional Epistemology?

In 1986, a group of epistemologists met at Brown University to celebrate the seventieth birthday of a renowned practitioner of their craft, Roderick Chisholm (1916–1999). The philosophers sat together in a large seminar room and listened to presentations. Principles and arguments in premise-conclusion form were written in chalk on a blackboard. During Q&A periods, speakers and audience members went back and forth in critical exchange. One speaker joked that if a bomb had been dropped on the building where the group had met, the profession of epistemology in America would cease to exist. Professional epistemology has only ever been a relatively slight thing. Even today, all of the professional epistemologists would probably fit into the grand ballroom at a corporate conference hotel.

What do epistemologists do? In recent textbooks and encyclopedias, epistemology is defined as the branch of philosophy that investigates questions about the nature and scope of knowledge and reasonable belief.[1] The subject matter of contemporary epistemology is widely thought to be general, abstract epistemic concepts or epistemic states themselves. Practitioners aim to describe propositional knowledge, epistemically justified belief, and evidence. They puzzle over radical skeptical challenges and evaluate responses. They detail the character traits of virtuous thinkers.

But the vast majority of work in contemporary professional epistemology is not regulative epistemology. Although many philosophers in the past launched campaigns to repair our intellectual shortcomings, it would be a stretch to describe epistemology today in those terms. Today, little traffic flows from epistemology to other fields of research. Fields such as physics, biology, or computer science are paradigms of knowledge production, but they evolve with apparently no intervention from professional epistemologists. The same apparently holds for investigation carried out by laypeople. People asking questions about politics, morality, or religion don't ordinarily appeal to the relatively esoteric products of epistemological research to guide them. And when newspapers or magazines feature stories of truth-seeking gone awry—bias in scientific research, say—journalists don't ask epistemologists for a sound bite. Epistemology is not known as a field that trades in guidance.

2. The Drift

I've already noted that early modern and early twentieth-century epistemological projects aimed to guide inquiry. So what happened? As I'm concerned with it here, epistemology is careful reflection on inquiry. Professional

---

[1] Reaching over to my bookshelf, I find several introductory books on epistemology, and each one includes a terse statement about its subject matter: "The theory of knowledge, or epistemology, is the branch of philosophy that addresses philosophical questions about knowledge and rationality. Epistemologists are primarily interested in questions about the nature of knowledge and the principles governing rational belief" (Feldman 2003a, 1). "Epistemological questions involve the concepts of knowledge, evidence, reasons for believing, justification, probability, what one ought to believe, and any other concepts that can only be understood through one or more of the above" (Fumerton 2006, 1). "Epistemology is the philosophical study of knowing and other desirable ways of believing and attempting to find the truth.... Most of the central questions of epistemology, then, pertain to knowledge: What is knowledge? Is knowledge possible? How do we get it?" (Zagzebski 2009, 1–2).

epistemology involves such reflection and thus qualifies as epistemology in my sense. But the field has been dominated in recent generations by methods and preoccupations that have drawn it away from the ongoing business of inquiry. The practices and problems of real-world investigators do not normally shape epistemologists' work, though there are interesting exceptions. In general, the discipline has drifted away from inquiry in this sense: its products are not likely to direct anyone's intellectual efforts.[2]

To see what I mean, just reflect on situations where we need guidance. We often confront complex, mixed bodies of evidence. How can we determine what our evidence makes it reasonable for us to believe? Epistemologists could at this point provide us with stock theories of epistemic justification. Perhaps they tell us that *process reliabilism* is true: a belief is justified when it is produced by a process that generates mostly true beliefs (Goldman 1979). Or perhaps theorists report that *evidentialism* is true: a belief is justified when it is a fitting response to our evidence (Feldman and Conee 1985). Over the last few decades, hundreds of articles have been written on reliabilism and evidentialism, to mention only two popular theories. But, all on their own, do reliabilism or evidentialism offer guidance? These theories do seem to help if we need to distinguish between cases of justified and unjustified belief, where we happen to know all of the background details about the cases. The background details would include, for instance, facts about the total evidence or the belief-forming processes that produced some beliefs. But when we need guidance, we typically need something else. Learning about the nature of justified belief won't usually tell us how to gain or preserve justified belief when we're faced with complex bodies of evidence and ignorance about the specifics of our situation.

But let's be fair to the theorists. Their goal was not to guide. Instead, they aimed to describe the nature of epistemic goods or articulate reasoning for or against general epistemic principles. One possibility is that theorists need not explicitly aim to enhance inquiry in order for their efforts to accomplish precisely that. A theory that's good for one thing can also be good for another. So why not think epistemologists' labors already serve some regulative purpose or other?

---

[2] I am thinking of inquiry in a broad sense to include a wide range of practices where evidence is used to answer questions. We can say that *personal* inquiry involves one person asking herself what to think about a topic and how to go about gaining information to form a good opinion on that topic. In a *social* inquiry, there is some question about what a group or community should think about some question. A particular personal or social inquiry could take as its object some question about science, ethics, politics, history, religion, or the like.

That idea is charitable but implausible. Critics of recent epistemology have often explicitly denied that standard theories and theoretical investigations improve inquiry. For instance, Mark Kaplan, in an article criticizing research on propositional knowledge, tells epistemologists "to stop and face the unpleasant reality that we simply have no use for a definition of knowledge" (1985, 363). Michael Bishop and J. D. Trout write: "It is time for epistemology to take its rightful place alongside ethics as a discipline that offers practical, real-world recommendations for living" (2005, 6). Mark Webb asks whether epistemology can be "of any use to non-philosophers" and answers thus: "Not by doing what [epistemologists] have been doing for most of the twentieth century" (2004, 51). According to Susan Haack, "much contemporary work in epistemology is hermetic and self-absorbed" and can't help people who are seeking to inquire (2015, 3). And Stephen Stich piles on:

> On the few occasions when I have taught the "analysis of knowledge" literature to undergraduates, it has been painfully clear that most of my students had a hard time taking the project seriously. . . . They could recognize the force of the increasingly arcane counterexamples that fill the literature, and they occasionally produced new counterexamples of their own. But they could not for the life of them see why anybody would want to do this. It was a source of ill-concealed amazement to these students that grown men and women would indulge in this exercise and think it important—and of still greater amazement that others would pay them to do it! This sort of discontent was all the more disquieting because deep down I agreed with my students. (1990, 3)[3]

Theorists have not returned fire at their critics by asserting that standard theories improve inquiry. Silence does not imply the allegations are correct. But it's doubtful, I think, that standard answers to questions like "What is knowledge?" or "What is epistemically justified belief?" or "Is there a good response to radical skeptical arguments?" are likely to guide anyone's investigation.

If all professional epistemologists were to suddenly hang up their boots—or if, forbid the thought, their conference hotel was destroyed by a bomb—what would happen? The world would want for new articles and books in

---

[3] Thanks to Samuel Kampa for reminding me of this passage.

professional epistemology. But human inquiry would proceed mostly uninterrupted.

Here is my view of the matter. As the critics insist, abstract theories about inquiry don't, on their own, help imperfect inquirers. However, we should not leap to pessimistic conclusions about the potential usefulness of recent theories. Use is the best test of an idea's utility. I doubt theorists have put their ideas and methods to that test. They have not, in the main, tried to use their ideas to guide inquiry. Yet I think that many recent theoretical proposals can do precisely that. But not on their own. First, the proposals must be repurposed, salvaged for regulative aims, and fitted carefully within a new framework for theorizing.

3. Academic Specialization and Professional Epistemology

Before I say more about how regulative theorizing works, it will prove instructive to consider this question: why has contemporary epistemology drifted away from direct concern with inquiry? Thinking broadly about the nature of academic specialization will suggest a plausible explanation.

The field of epistemology is one branch of academic philosophy, and philosophy is itself one branch on the tree of academic disciplines. Epistemology's place on the tree seems to presuppose that epistemologists will not guide inquiry. That's just what we get with the organization of highly specialized research. Advances in organic chemistry will probably never help to answer questions about aeronautical engineering or Soviet political history. Academic epistemology is just one insular, specialized discipline among many.

Although epistemological research sometimes draws on ideas from the social and cognitive sciences, empirically-informed epistemologists have been a minority in the field in recent years. Knowing little or nothing about the sciences or the humanities does not impede most contemporary research, in part because knowing about inquiry elsewhere is not required. And practitioners do not seem to assume that progress in answering their questions would mandate changes in how other investigators do their jobs. Few professional epistemologists believe that their theoretical offerings— even if correct—will do much to help researchers elsewhere improve their store of knowledge or justified belief. Epistemologists have their own field to roam and they seldom stray from it. Even less often do outsiders drop by for a visit.[4]

If it's guidance for inquiry that people need, they will probably look elsewhere. The "logic" of academic specialization suggests why epistemology has drifted away from the wider world of inquiry. The evolution of academic fields depends on the making of distinctions. Over and over again, the world of knowledge has been broken into smaller pieces, like miraculously dividing loaves of bread. New distinctions create new disciplines, subdisciplines, and subsubdisciplines. The evolution of increasing differentiation and segmentation has produced professional epistemology. I return to this issue in Chapter 2, but it is enough for now to see that practitioners find within their field's boundaries a set of questions and answers that is largely for them alone. Their questions, or perhaps their answers, are apparently not of much relevance for the conduct of inquiry anywhere else.

4. The Vienna Circle, Sputnik, and Gettier

I've used some ideas about the organization of academic disciplines to describe how professional epistemology drifted away from real-world inquiry. Granted, these ideas are a bit abstract. We will see the drift more easily by considering a historical story. We can recognize epistemology's drift by noting some sweeping changes that made the field increasingly specialized through the middle decades of the twentieth century. I will tell the story in two parts: first, by describing the broad background conditions that led to the rise of "analytic" philosophy in the United States after the Second World War and, second, by looking at how one methodology became dominant in professional epistemology during the 1960s and '70s.

The story begins with the Vienna Circle in the 1920s and '30s. As I noted earlier, the members of the Circle used empiricism as a tool to articulate and defend the "scientific world-conception." They declared in a manifesto that "[n]eatness and clarity are striven for, and dark distances and unfathomable depths rejected" (Neurath, Carnap, and Hahn 1979 [1929], 89). Their

---

[4] Let me say what I don't mean. I don't deny that progress in academic epistemology leads to changes in how research is conducted in other philosophical subdisciplines, such as metaethics or metaphysics, where philosophers often wrestle with epistemological quandaries. I also don't deny that occasionally epistemological research could clear up confusions in fields far from professional philosophy. Neither do I suggest that academic epistemology could not pique the curiosity of researchers in other disciplines or interested people more generally.

empiricism led them to dump "the metaphysical and theological debris of millennia" (1979 [1929], 89). Their epistemological project was intended to resolve problems in philosophy and science, but it was also part of an effort to reorder social and political life.

The reception of the Vienna Circle's ideas on American soil occurred during an important transition in twentieth-century philosophy. During the first third of the century, American philosophy was a relatively eclectic enterprise where scholars explored broad questions about value, society, education, and metaphysics. Through the 1930s and '40s, the scene was transformed by the importation of ideas from Europe. These ideas challenged the methodological underpinnings of American philosophy. One idea, stemming from writings by Ludwig Wittgenstein (1889–1951), was that traditional philosophers were doing something meaningless and that philosophical work properly pursued would clarify meaning through careful analysis. The ideas of the Vienna Circle moved in these currents. At first, these new ideas reached U.S. shores in the form of articles, books, and home-grown philosophers returning from European tour, such as a young Willard Van Orman Quine (1908–2000). But then important Circle members fled totalitarian Europe for the safety of American teaching posts. For instance, Rudolph Carnap (1891–1970) moved from Europe to the University of Chicago and later the University of California, Los Angeles, while Phillip Frank (1884–1966) taught physics and philosophy of science at Harvard University.

Nevertheless, the bold vision and style of ideas from the Circle, sometimes labeled "logical empiricism," primed many American philosophers to reconceptualize the methods and problems of philosophy, even though many of them rejected logical empiricism. Looking toward the sciences, many philosophers found a new model for objectivity and value-free neutrality. Influential members of the profession increasingly regarded the hard sciences as the ideal and championed a new conception of scientific philosophy, which involved hostility toward metaphysical speculation, instead treating conceptual or linguistic analysis as the proper work of philosophers. Bruce Kuklick suggests that "[t]hese developments gave American thought worldwide honor in professorial circles, but came at great cost to the public presence of philosophy and even to its audience outside the academy. . . . In contrast to what philosophy had been . . . philosophy after World War II had narrow concerns" (2001, 199). American philosophy's humanistic roots began to wither. As Alexander Nehamas noted, philosophy in the United

States around mid-century "no longer saw itself as bearing a direct relation to the world." For most researchers, the field was "an essentially theoretical discipline" (1997, 212). As Quine confessed, philosophers have no "peculiar fitness for helping to get society on an even keel" (1981, 193).[5]

In the '20s and '30s, many members of the Vienna Circle had hoped their approach would renovate social and political life. So what happened in the United States? As George Reisch (2005) argues, the Circle's ideas and ambitions were "depoliticized" in America following the Second World War. The dark paranoia of the McCarthy years meant that many socialist and left-leaning academics were scrutinized and sometimes persecuted. These were the days of loyalty oaths and hunts for communists. The director of the Federal Bureau of Investigation, J. Edgar Hoover, had case files on Carnap and Frank, who were surveilled by agents in the '50s. Although logical empiricism in America was by no means an apolitical movement, as is sometimes asserted, the Circle's technical and methodological ideas— not its social or political ones—blossomed in the anti-communist soil. During this period, many believed commitment to one's academic vocation ought to be free from values and politics, especially radical politics. As Reisch notes, some academics thought "the path to intellectual success and integrity in any discipline and the path to job security and freedom from political attack were one and the same" (2005, 233). Analysts did not dream to remake their world. Their ambitions were more modest: they were building a professional field where conceptual technicians could solve theoretical problems.

These conditions in professional philosophy figure into wider trends that some historians call the "new rigorism" of the post-war university. Disciplines like economics, political science, and English literature also remade their goals using putatively objective tools. Like philosophy, these disciplines turned from many of the broad, synthetic concerns and value questions that had defined education and scholarship in earlier decades (Bender and Schorske 1997). Some observers at the time described a new style of modern American intellectual who had dispensed with "wide-ranging, curious, adventurous and humane study" and instead aimed to produce "results"

---

[5] Hans Reichenbach, an influential logical empiricist expelled from Germany by fascists before taking up a teaching post at UCLA, wrote in his 1951 book *The Rise of Scientific Philosophy*: "Those who ask the philosopher for guidance in life should be grateful when he sends them to the psychologist, or the social scientist; the knowledge accumulated in these empirical sciences promises much better answers than are collected in the writings of the philosophers" (quoted in Reisch 2005, 355).

(Reisch 2005, 349). The forces shaping mid-century academic philosophy came from both within and without.[6]

And so it was that professional epistemology began to find its life and purposes in the 1960s. The whole story here is complex and involves a large cast of characters and theoretical projects, ranging from Chisholm's work in the '50s on foundationalism to C. I. Lewis's work on the "given" (the sensory qualities we are immediately aware of in experience). But we can begin to see what happened in the field by zooming in on one particular episode.

It begins at a public university in Detroit, Michigan during the early 1960s, a few years before the city would descend into economic failure, "white flight," and postindustrial decay. John F. Kennedy was still president and the Philosophy Department at Wayne State University had recently hired a group of young philosophers. Some of these philosophers had turned down job offers from Ivy League universities. They chose instead to teach in the cinder-block buildings on Wayne State's urban campus.

These were peculiar days in the American academy. The Soviet launch of *Sputnik 1* into orbit in October 1957 precipitated a hiring bonanza across many fields. In response to fears that the United States was falling behind the Soviet Union in education, President Eisenhower's *National Defense Education Act* of 1958 flooded the country's universities and colleges with resources as never before. Historians have noted the dramatic changes to fields like physics (Kaiser 2006), but academic philosophy was also transformed. There were more teaching posts for philosophers than there were new PhDs to fill them. Some young philosophers had their pick of the available jobs.[7]

One faculty member in the Wayne State department, Keith Lehrer, had accepted a job offer from Brown University and then wriggled out of his contract to go to Detroit; another, Alvin Plantinga, chose Wayne over Yale. They went to Detroit on the promise of an intense intellectual community, persuaded by the department chair, George Nakhnikian. They weren't

---

[6] See Reisch (2005) and Isaac (2012) for more on the rise of scientific philosophy in mid-century America.

[7] This situation didn't catch professional philosophers by surprise. In the wake of *Sputnik 1*, a committee of the American Philosophical Association, chaired by none other than Roderick Chisholm, produced a report on the state of graduate education in American philosophy. The report notes that "a shortage of qualified philosophy teachers will probably become serious before 1965" (Chisholm et al. 1958–1959, 155, footnote 1). To increase supply to meet demand, the report recommends that philosophers "should investigate the possibility of making more extensive use of our total resources of teaching manpower, for there are certain groups we now tend to overlook. It may be, for example, that we do not now give sufficient encouragement to women, or to certain racial groups, or to people who have been working outside of the academic world" (1958–1959, 149).

disappointed. The philosophical gang met for nearly-nonstop discussion at a local coffee shop, interrupted occasionally by their teaching schedules. They practiced a style of philosophical conversation that involved detailed analysis of concepts and painstaking testing of proposed analyses by counterexamples. In departmental colloquium talks, they welcomed visiting speakers with tough objections. By the time of the 12th Street riot of July 1967, the cohort of gifted philosophers had largely disbanded. Commenting over a decade later, Roderick Chisholm remarked that "this brief period in Detroit constituted one of the brightest episodes in the history of American philosophy" (1979, 385).[8]

In 1963, one junior faculty member, Edmund L. Gettier III, published a three-page article in the journal *Analysis*. Gettier proposed two counterexamples to a time-honored analysis of knowledge. According to the analysis, a thinker knows a proposition p is true if and only if the thinker has a justified true belief that p. This appeared to be the traditional theory of knowledge.[9] Gettier's counterexamples feature thinkers who hold justified true beliefs only because of an accident—and, plausibly, these justified true beliefs fall short of knowledge.[10]

Gettier's article exemplified the Wayne State style, and it was to become the most famous single effort from the group. It started a craze in the coming years. Following Gettier's take-down of the justified-true-belief analysis, epistemologists began to devise ever more subtle analyses of knowledge to accommodate problematic examples of accidentally true belief, while their opponents shot back with ever more clever counterexamples in the spirit of Gettier's originals to refute the new analyses. A great deal of philosophical

---

[8] The coffee shop was located at 5470 Cass Avenue in Detroit, across the street from the old Wayne State Philosophy Department building. The cohort's ranks included Richard Cartwright, Héctor-Neri Castañeda, David Falk, Edmund Gettier, Keith Lehrer, George Nakhnikian, Alvin Plantinga, and Robert Sleigh. In an essay on the history of analytic philosophy in the United States, Scott Soames remarks: "Such was the abundance of available talent, and the enthusiasm of young philosophers entering the profession, that between 1955 and 1970 the philosophy department at Wayne acquired a reputation for precision, passion, and fierce analytical argumentation that had few rivals anywhere" (2014, 13). In an autobiographical essay, Plantinga recounts his time at Wayne State (1985, 22–29). (Thanks to Joe Morton for helping me figure out the address of the gang's hangout, and to Keith Lehrer and Alvin Plantinga for clues about its whereabouts.)

[9] Dutant (2015), among others, denies that the justified-true-belief analysis is the traditional account of knowledge. Plantinga notes that "[i]t isn't easy to find many explicit statements of a JTB analysis of knowledge prior to Gettier; it is almost as if a distinguished critic created a tradition in the very act of destroying it" (1990, 45).

[10] Unbeknownst to Gettier, Bertrand Russell had years earlier devised a similar example (2009 [1948], 91). Chisholm (1989, 92) noted that Alexius Meinong, in a 1906 book, suggested a pair of Gettier-esque examples. Scholars have also claimed that pre-modern Indian and Tibetan philosophers made up similar examples, but that claim is controversial (Stoltz 2007).

horsepower went into this project, but it has proven easier to conjure up counterexamples than a victorious definition that would withstand them.

What came to be known as the "Gettier Problem" was worked over in a big, technical, epicyclic literature.[11] Gettier's 1963 article has been cited several thousands of times. To this day, many epistemologists are intrigued by thought experiments involving lucky true belief, even when they're not trying to analyze knowledge in the classical style by defending a set of jointly necessary and sufficient conditions. On the fiftieth anniversary of the publication of Gettier's article, epistemologists met for conferences at the University of Edinburgh (*The Gettier Problem at 50*) and Swarthmore College (*Thinking about Knowledge: Epistemology 50 Years after Gettier's Paper*), and still more journal articles on Gettier-related topics soon appeared in print. Large expanses of the Motor City are now broken down and ghostly, but some heroes of Wayne State helped to modernize the infrastructure of contemporary epistemology.

Some may think this history sounds a bit triumphalist. For philosophers trained to practice a brand of epistemology that takes its models for good work from the ideas and intellectual standards fashioned during the heady years after Gettier's article, a celebratory tone in recounting the period is not so surprising. My own graduate training in the field encouraged me to regard with special seriousness, maybe even a touch of awe, this era when professional epistemology was formed in the darkness. But that is not how I have come to understand this period of epistemology's history. There are upsides and downsides. So let me release some air from the triumphalist's balloon.

While a comprehensive story of epistemology's development in the second half of the twentieth century is long and complicated, the origin of the Gettier Problem at Wayne State is a case study that reveals how broader institutional and economic changes helped turn epistemology into the relatively isolated, insular discipline it is today.

Once the counterexample method was used to test accounts of knowledge, many researchers were able to join a relatively well-defined research project and reap career benefits in the process. The assumptions undergirding the Gettier Problem helped to organize and unify the rapidly growing subfield. The goal was to describe epistemological concepts. Eventually, there were

---

[11] See Shope (1983) for a detailed introduction to the first two decades of the debate and Lycan (2006) and Rysiew (2018) for helpful retrospective discussion. Coffman (2017) discusses competing explanations for Gettier-style cases. Hetherington (2016) rises to the defense of the justified-true-belief analysis.

many new descriptive projects afoot and the popularity of these projects meant that professional training and incentives shunted fledgling scholars toward still more research describing epistemological statuses and principles. Graduate students were trained in the techniques of analysis and counterexample. Students gunning for careers in research could easily see the recipe for success: refute theories published in issues of *Analysis* or *The Journal of Philosophy*, do even better in the game of analysis, or analyze something else that makes a splash. Over the decades, descriptive theorizing became the field's dominant approach, passed on through new forms of training, conceptual tools, and professional enticements.

Crucially, success in the business of epistemological description doesn't require much familiarity with actual human inquiry. As the philosophical study of knowledge grew up, it came to have little to do with knowledge-seeking.

Following the glory years of the Gettier Problem, academic epistemology broadened out and now features many well-entrenched research topics: the nature of epistemic justification, testimony-based knowledge and justification, self-knowledge, the value of knowledge and its constitutive parts, the relationship between knowledge and action, responses to skepticism about the external world, epistemic paradoxes, the semantics of knowledge ascriptions, and so on. But even as epistemologists' topics and methods have changed, the basic goals of their theorizing have remained the same. The field's inertia has led most epistemologists to practice a kind of epistemology that has little to do with guiding inquiry.

5. Expansion

There is no deep or compelling reason why epistemology cannot or should not try to guide inquiry. My proposal is that professional epistemology's boundaries should be expanded to include greater focus on regulative issues. As I think about it, the field's boundaries are just the set of topics its members explore. These boundaries can look imposing and permanent, but they are contingent to some extent.[12]

---

[12] The field's boundary lines are far more rigid than lines in the sand we can easily wipe out and draw elsewhere. The field is structured by a powerful system of incentives that reinforces the dominant research agendas and methods. Researchers who pursue non-standard issues may risk their reputations and even careers. It's better to think of the boundary lines as being drawn in concrete, not sand. We can sometimes choose where to redraw the lines, but doing so calls for some noisy jackhammering and a cement-mixing truck loaded up with fresh concrete.

Other epistemologists have issued similar calls for expansion. In 1978, Alvin Goldman published an article in *The Journal of Philosophy*, "Epistemics: The Regulative Theory of Cognition." Goldman encouraged epistemologists to create theories that "seek to regulate or guide our intellectual activities" (1978, 509). He argued that regulative theories would need to draw on cognitive psychology. He said we discover the nature of our limitations by empirical means and that the idealized epistemological theories on the scene in the '70s did not provide limited agents with useful guidance. When Goldman raised and saluted the regulative flag, the Gettier Problem was still a central focus for the field. Goldman dubbed his project "epistemics," artfully avoiding the term "epistemology." He anticipated that his peers would say the regulative undertaking was not real epistemology.

Goldman's epistemics never really caught on.[13] But in the years after the article appeared, epistemologists fanned out and widened the field's topics. To take just one example, the bearing of the social world on knowledge and intellectual practices has become a central concern for researchers, due in no small part to Goldman's influence, especially his 1999 book, *Knowledge in a Social World*. Practitioners of social epistemology have explored questions about testimony, trust, disagreement, collective or group knowledge, and epistemic institutional design. In the 1980s and '90s, moreover, feminist epistemologists helped to inject social topics into the field by posing questions about how gender and power relations influence our efforts to know.[14] But the discipline has remained largely the same since the late '70s in one crucial respect: regulation is still not a common goal—with some exceptions I'll note soon.

Nearly three decades after Goldman's article on epistemics, two books appeared which made epistemic regulation their central preoccupation. These books represent examples of regulative theorizing, but neither one captures the broad approach to theorizing I call regulative epistemology.

Michael Bishop and J. D. Trout's book *Epistemology and the Psychology of Human Judgment* (2005) features a theory that takes its cues from scientific

---

[13] Notably, the spirit of Goldman's epistemics project animated later work by naturalized epistemologists, who theorize in view of the science of human judgment and reasoning. Later in this section, I discuss work by Michael Bishop and J. D. Trout. Another influential naturalist is Hilary Kornblith, who has noted that epistemological "ideals are meant to play some role in guiding action, and an ideal that took no account of human limitations would thereby lose its capacity to play a constructive action-guiding role" (2001a, 238). Kornblith says that epistemological ideals that don't guide us "fail to make sense of the interest of epistemological theorizing" (2001a, 238).

[14] Grasswick and Webb (2002) discuss the relationship between social and feminist epistemology.

research. Drawing upon some of the advice Goldman had imparted years earlier, Bishop and Trout say inquirers should be guided by findings from the cognitive science of reasoning and judgment and that the chief work of epistemologists is to explain how the science applies to real-world situations. The duo says their proposals are "normatively reason guiding and genuinely capable of benefitting the world" (2005, 7).

Bishop and Trout don't merely set out to do this. They also give their fellow epistemologists an earful. They write that "the normative issues raised by the psychological literature are interesting and important, but analytic epistemology does not have the resources to adequately address them. So we sat down to write this book" (2005, viii). Further, they say the field has "clearly failed to bring the potential benefits of epistemology to ordinary people's lives" (2005, 7).

What is the problem with contemporary "analytic" epistemology? Why can't it improve inquiry? According to Bishop and Trout, its goals and methods are "beyond repair" (2005, 22). They advocate a brand of "naturalism" that rejects the standard methodology of consulting intuitive judgments about cases in order to understand epistemic normativity. In addition, they "do not believe that constructing theories [of justified belief] is a fruitful endeavor" (2005, 116). Of course, the development of such theories is one central research topic on the contemporary scene, so following Bishop and Trout means turning one's back on a large part of the discipline, letting the dead bury their dead. An about-face is needed, they contend, because popular approaches to epistemology "will never provide effective normative guidance, and so [these approaches] will never achieve the positive, practical potential of epistemology" (2005, 22). And they admit to despairing sometimes "about whether most contemporary epistemologists have lost sight of this potential—and, indeed, of our obligation to seek it" (2005, 22). These are fighting words. Bishop and Trout's book expresses professional epistemology's equivalent of "Fifty-Four Forty or Fight!"[15,16]

---

[15] That was a political rally cry in the United States during the 1840s, when the Democrats asserted America's rightful ownership to territory in a boundary dispute with British North America concerning parallel 54° 40′ north.

[16] Bishop and Trout's saber-rattling rhetoric might unnerve epistemologists. But what is their argument for the idea that epistemology's methods can't help regulate inquiry? While they don't address that question directly, their remarks about standard epistemology's methods reveal their thinking.

Bishop and Trout argue that, as a normative endeavor, epistemology is dead on arrival: its methods can only secure descriptive, not normative, conclusions (2005, chapter 7). That means epistemology can't regulate inquiry in the sense of helping people recognize how they *should* inquire. I leave this

Bishop and Trout are not the only philosophers demanding changes to epistemology's boundaries. Robert Roberts and W. Jay Wood's book *Intellectual Virtues: An Essay in Regulative Epistemology* (2007) launches a different regulative project. Roberts and Wood's idea is that good guidance will help people acquire intellectual character traits such as humility, courage, caution, and love of knowledge. Their book describes intellectual virtues by drawing on literary and historical examples. Their regulative project seeks to improve people's epistemic conduct by providing rich descriptions of intellectual excellence, but it's easily extended to reflection on epistemic limitations and errors (Roberts and West 2015). Roberts and Wood see themselves as breaking sharply from the contemporary field:

> Given the central place of knowledge and understanding in human life, one would expect epistemology to be one of the most fascinating and enriching fields of philosophy and itself an important part of an education for life. We might expect that any bright university student who got all the way to her junior year without dipping her mind in an epistemology course would have to hang her head in shame of her cultural poverty. But the character and preoccupations of much of the epistemology of the twentieth century disappoint this expectation. (2007, 8)

idea to the side, as I doubt Bishop and Trout have shown that epistemology can't generate normative conclusions. (Conee 2008 criticizes Bishop and Trout's project on this score.)

Bishop and Trout also say that epistemology's methods are "shockingly conservative" (2005, 11). When epistemologists ask questions such as "What is knowledge?" or "What is an epistemically justified belief?" they typically assume what Bishop and Trout call the *stasis requirement*: correct accounts of knowledge or justification will "leave our epistemic situation largely unchanged" (2005, 8–9). In other words, epistemologists will judge that what is known or justifiably believed is the same before and after they theorize. Theorizing will not modify judgments about what we know or justifiably believe. (Of course, we shouldn't think the stasis requirement holds for our considered judgments about theories. That's because theorizing can, and often does, modify people's judgments about which theories are correct.) But if some method can improve inquiry, presumably it must be able to contribute to changing such judgments. Thus, epistemology can't improve inquiry, Bishop and Trout would say, in the sense that its products help people change their judgments.

This argument assumes that the stasis requirement, in any episode of epistemic theorizing, must cover the full expanse of our considered judgments (not including ones about theories), leaving those judgments intact after theorizing. But it's possible, I think, to use a subset of judgments to develop a regulative theory, and then use that theory to modify some of our judgments outside the subset.

Here's what I mean. Plausibly, epistemological reflection won't change our judgments concerning matters of commonsense and well-established science. But if we can use the subset of reflectively stable judgments to design regulative theories capable of scrutinizing our judgments outside the scope of commonsense and well-established science—say, our judgments concerning controversies about politics, economics, ethics, or metaphysics—then epistemology's standard methodology can help guide inquiry. (I am grateful to Klaas Kraay for questions here.)

Fighting words yet again. Roberts and Wood say that one problem with recent epistemology is the overriding concern to formulate necessary and sufficient conditions for knowledge and other epistemic goods such as epistemic justification (2007, 9–20). Practitioners should quit trying to define these things—a task that is "just an interesting theoretical challenge for philosophy professors and smart students" (2007, 21).[17] Roberts and Wood presume that many popular projects of contemporary epistemology do not advance their goal of guiding the life of the mind. They want epistemologists to start doing the "kind of epistemology [that] aims to change the (social) world" (2007, 21).

Roberts and Wood say they want a revolution. Do most epistemologists want to change the world? Probably not. Many of them are satisfied with the disciplinary status quo. Setting aside the question of whether epistemologists should be moved by the critics' attacks, it's unsurprising that most practitioners have not gone along. Try to see it their way. Many epistemologists enjoy their work. They have invested years in their field and its debates. Perhaps they see genuine value in trying to understand the nature of knowledge and other epistemic statuses, an illustrious project they trace back to ancient Greek philosophy. What's wrong with carefully following in Plato's steps, adding a little footnote here or there? And epistemologists may be unconvinced by the critics' arguments. At any rate, most epistemologists are not about to relocate to new lands. The critics' battle cries probably sound kind of annoying.

So I should distinguish what I call regulative epistemology from these other projects. Although Bishop and Trout and Roberts and Wood offer all-out regulative proposals in my sense, they call for dramatic shifts in epistemological research while at the same time disparaging the discipline's prevailing methods and preoccupations. Bishop and Trout mean to replace standard epistemology with a brand of cognitive-science-fueled philosophy; Roberts and Wood want epistemology to illuminate intellectual character, eschewing the common practice of developing sets of necessary and sufficient conditions for traits. These philosophers promote the idea that epistemologists should avoid certain methodological commitments—certain types of epistemic description or conceptual analysis. This is what I call *radical* regulative epistemology. I do not endorse those restrictions. Nor is accepting them required to practice regulative epistemology in my sense.

---

[17] For critical discussion of Roberts and Wood's "virtue anti-theory," see Battaly (2009).

I want to encourage a broad, inclusive research program that recognizes the value of ongoing research on "non-regulative" questions. I intend to practice *inclusive* regulative epistemology. As I see it, theorists need not settle all of their methodological debates before pursuing regulative projects.

My call for expansion of the field should not offend practitioners. For one, expanding the field's boundaries in one direction does not necessarily mean shrinking them in another. Indeed, regulative and non-regulative projects can be mutually encouraging and collaborative. Descriptive epistemology might benefit from attention to regulative matters—new regulative questions may call for new work for descriptive epistemologists to pursue. For another, we should not understand the value of the two projects in zero-sum terms. Learning that regulative questions are important is not a reason to think non-regulative questions are unimportant. A plurality of approaches may help to advance the regulative research program. As I see things, the field in its current form contains a wealth of normative ideas and conceptual tools that can and should be applied to regulative questions.

6. An Interdisciplinary Inquiry into Inquiry

Regulative epistemology is a broad approach to epistemological theorizing. In Chapters 5 through 9 of this book, I offer guidance for improving an important dimension of intellectual life: our beliefs about controversial matters. My proposals will not exhaust what regulative epistemology is or could be. The tent is big. I'll now say something about the whole program.

Regulative epistemology calls for contributions from researchers across the cognitive and social sciences and the humanities. At present, there is no "field" of regulative epistemology in any ordinary sense. There are no conferences, no specialized journals, no central research topics. But researchers in many fields all want to understand human inquiry and how it can be improved. To begin to see the far-reaching interest in regulative matters, witness a brief cavalcade of inquiry-focused research.

Cognitive and social psychologists study systematic biases in judgment and reasoning (Tversky and Kahneman 1974; Nisbett and Ross 1980; Kahneman 2011). Researchers in psychology, anthropology, and history explore the nature of ignorance and failures of metaknowledge (Dunning et al. 2003; Proctor and Schiebinger 2008). Scholars in many disciplines attempt to understand the effective teaching of "critical thinking" skills (King and Kitchener 1994; Kuhn 2005) and the content of "informal logic" used to evaluate arguments (Walton 2008). Virtue epistemologists describe intellectual excellences (Battaly 2008; Baehr 2011). Historians explain how various intellectual virtues have been central to some scientists' conceptions of scientific practice (Shapin 1994; Stump 2007; Corneanu 2011). Psychologists and philosophers of social science examine sources of bias in peer-review practices (Peters and Ceci 1982; Lee and Schunn 2011). Sociologists examine the social, institutional, and individual factors shaping the production of intellectuals' ideas and professional judgments (Gross 2008; Lamont 2009). Philosophers defend the viability of truth-aimed discourse and inquiry against anti-realist and "postmodernist" sentiments (Lynch 2004; Boghossian 2006). Feminist epistemologists study the ways in which prejudice can cause audiences to fail to give speakers credibility when credibility is due (Fricker 2007). Historians recount cases of intellectual dishonesty and fraud (Judson 2004; Reich 2009) while philosophers describe epistemic vices (Cassam 2016). Naturalized epistemologists give accounts of human knowledge by drawing on findings from the cognitive and social sciences (Kornblith 2002). Traditional and social epistemologists explore normative questions about disagreements (Goldman 2001; Feldman and Warfield 2010; Christensen and Lackey 2013).

How are all of these projects related? One idea arguably motivating them is that a better understanding of the ins and outs of inquiry can make people better at inquiry. From my perspective, these projects can help us clear pathways toward epistemic guidance.

Regulative epistemology's broad-based research program is prompted by a concrete problem: our intellectual imperfections. The problem is an old one, but regulative epistemology aims to attack it in a special way. Three perspectives normally disconnected must be joined together: descriptive, normative, and practical. Corresponding to each perspective is a general question. What are inquirers like? What should inquirers do? How can inquirers do more of what they should? The research program involves describing inquirers, understanding what they should do, and figuring out how they can better reach their epistemic goals. I will briefly describe each of the three perspectives.

Descriptive questions about our minds and the workings of inquiry are central to regulative epistemology's research program. How do judgment and reasoning work? What cognitive, social, and cultural factors influence inquiry? Do most inquirers possess intellectual virtues? How do particular technological systems influence investigation? What norms for inquiry are taken for granted by individuals and institutions? What are common and dangerous sources of intellectual failure, from biases to fraud? How do inquirers try to improve their knowledge and opinions? Insight into descriptive questions like these may come from fields such as psychology, cognitive science, the philosophy of psychology, sociology, anthropology, science studies, and intellectual history. Practicing regulative epistemology requires some understanding of the fabric of inquiry, because in order to develop good guidance, we need to know what we're trying to guide. We need to know about our mind's tendencies, because good guidance should allow us to manage or overcome our limitations. We need to know about the methods inquirers actually use, because regulative epistemology may try to modify them with better ones.

Descriptions of inquiry must be joined with perspectives that show us which actual and possible practices are appropriate. We must ask *normative* or *evaluative questions*. Powerful means for articulating and answering these questions come from contemporary epistemology, the history of epistemology, and the history and philosophy of science. To understand what success and failure in inquiry is, we need to explore questions about good and bad reasoning and inference, the goals of inquiry, the nature of evidence and explanation, and good and bad intellectual character. We need to know about the nature of these things and understand how they figure into appropriate investigation. What kinds of epistemic goodness or badness can beliefs, inquirers, and communities have? What goals can inquiry aim at? What goals do inquirers have the most reason to care about trying to reach? These questions fall within the purview of professional epistemology.[18] Without ongoing "basic" research on non-regulative questions about the nature of epistemic evaluation, epistemic statuses, and intellectual character traits, regulative research would be worse off. Regulative epistemology stands to gain from non-regulative research.

Finally, *practical questions* about implementing epistemic guidance are part of the broad project. To fulfill its purpose, regulative epistemology needs to help inquirers better live up to normative ideals. The normative perspective is idealized—it considers what should be done. The practical perspective

---

[18] That isn't to say these questions are not sometimes raised by social and cognitive scientists who are trying to evaluate judgment or reasoning. Some psychologists have welcomed help from philosophers to untangle knotty normative questions. See, for example, Nisbett and Ross (1980, 13–14) and Chinn, Buckland, and Samarapungavan (2011, 142–143).

sees how it can be done, and this can involve making suitable adjustments between ideals and realities on the ground. The practical concern is to understand how careful reflection on inquiry can transform inquiry. Here are some relevant questions: How can regulative ideas guide our search for truths? What are the most effective ways for regulative recommendations to be followed? What roles can groups and institutions play in the implementation of inquiry-guiding ideas? How are such ideas transmitted and acquired? How do our tools, from books to computers, play a role? What are effective techniques for teaching regulative ideas? On this front, psychologists, education researchers, sociologists, and philosophers of education offer resources for understanding how to implement regulative ideas.

What unites regulative researchers is a common purpose to use descriptive, normative, or practical perspectives to address the problems of imperfect inquiry. Three clarifications are in order.

First, I said that regulative epistemology aims to produce guidance for inquiry, but I didn't mean that everyone contributing to the wide research program must aim to do so. Many questions—descriptive, normative, and practical—can be addressed independently of the process of designing guidance. For example, anthropologists or historians might describe the activity of some inquirers while leaving aside normative or practical questions. But their descriptions can be used to craft guidance. Researchers can identify imperfect practices by joining together descriptive and normative perspectives. They can add to regulative epistemology in two ways: indirectly, by contributing information needed to develop guidance, and directly, by developing guidance itself.

Second, practicing regulative epistemology requires synthesis. When psychologists study biases, or historians of science describe failed scientific institutions, they add to the stockpile of insights that regulative epistemology can draw upon. When we use those insights to create epistemic guidance, we practice regulative epistemology. As I note in a later chapter, I am aware of the hazards of interdisciplinary research projects. Ideally, multidisciplinary teams of researchers could work shoulder to shoulder. They would evaluate the available insights with the goal of guiding some type of investigation. This synthetic craftwork requires a more flexible methodology than has been commonplace in recent professional epistemology, though there are some intriguing examples from the history of epistemology that I discuss in the next chapter. Careful description of normative states like knowledge or evidence will certainly have a place, but close-up work on normative matters must be joined with perspectives that show us what some inquiry is and how its practice can become more effective.

Third, I don't assume that epistemic guidance will take any form in particular. Anything that might help people become better inquirers is fair game. Take your pick: rules, principles, guidelines, instructions, checklists, detailed descriptions of inquirers' characters and practices, educational curricula, informative examples, institutional design plans, technological gadgets, environmental modifications, and more. In my view, it's an open question what kind of regulative ideas and practices will improve some inquiry, though Chapters 5 through 9 of this book explore some principles that help us reflect on our controversial beliefs. My focus on principles should not suggest that I believe principles are the most effective sort of regulative idea. Regulative epistemology is perhaps like medical research. It would be a mistake to pin all of our hopes on one experimental drug or novel surgical procedure. Diversity and competing approaches should be welcomed. We should tackle the problems of imperfect inquiry with any means available.

7. Regulative Epistemology among the Disciplines

If regulative epistemology were to grow up and find its place in the spreading tree of academic disciplines, where would it go? It doesn't fit neatly on the tree. Regulative epistemology aims to intervene throughout the tree of specialized knowledge. It tries to help specialists guard against harmful blight, fungus, and rot on their own branches. It shows them something about how to help their part of the tree flourish and grow.

Conceiving of epistemology in that way may signal a return to an old-fashioned idea: epistemology as "First Philosophy." Once upon a time, many intellectuals saw epistemology as laying the groundwork for inquiry and science. Investigators had to first settle epistemological questions before proceeding to gain systematic knowledge about the world. On this model, epistemology is like the roots of the tree from which science sprouts up. Contemporary epistemology does not embrace its heritage. The field is by specialists and mostly for specialists. As I am thinking of it, regulative epistemology is not First Philosophy in the grand old sense. And yet its practitioners need to be audacious enough to insist that sustained reflection on inquiry can benefit human inquiry. Epistemology in this sense isn't the sole potential route to improvement, but it is an important and neglected strategy.

Some people might resist any step toward epistemology as First Philosophy. Here's one way of digging in heels. Notice that the contemporary sciences have been eyepoppingly successful but not because of anything resembling First Philosophy. Doesn't that suggest regulative epistemology will not advance knowledge-seeking in established disciplines? That is an important question.

The rise of the sciences in early modern and modern Europe might naturally be viewed as gradually marginalizing epistemology to an autonomous, isolated branch on the tree of academic knowledge. Successful science over the years has featured less and less of what could be called epistemological reflection. Science has been a matter of getting out there and inquiring— shooting first, not asking epistemological questions later, or at any other time.[19] That's overstating the idea, but historians and sociologists of science tell us that the forces shaping scientific research are not ordinarily high-level conversations about epistemological ideals or norms. Careers and grant cycles move too fast. Science is propelled by social forces, institutions, material infrastructure, and money.

But the truth is that scientists may sometimes benefit from ideas not found in their disciplinary toolboxes, ideas crafted by regulative epistemologists. Within any scientific field, the accumulated knowledge and techniques can't make practitioners anywhere near perfect, as everyone will concede. Scientists err. Presumably, good guidance could help them do a little better. The real question is: guidance for doing *what*?

Here are two stories to suggest where regulative interventions could be useful. Imagine (if imagination is required) some scientists publish flawed results due to their biases and prejudices. The scientists' peers take years to uncover the errors, burning through precious resources in the process, endangering the public's trust in science. Or let's imagine some researchers are launched into superstardom and occupy public pulpits. These scientists

---

[19] The twentieth-century physicist Percy Bridgeman remarked:

> It seems to me that there is a great deal of ballyhoo about scientific method. I venture to think that the people who talk about it most are the people who do least about it. Scientific method is what working scientists do, not what other people or even they themselves may say about it. No working scientist, when he plans an experiment in the laboratory, asks himself whether he is being properly scientific, nor is he interested in whatever method he may be using as *method*. . . . The working scientist is always too much concerned with getting down to brass tacks to be willing to spend his time on generalities. (quoted in Shapin 2010, 37)

address general audiences and talk about issues, from politics to metaphysics, far beyond their own professional competence. Those scientists shape social policy and public opinion. They look and sound convincing to many people. But they spread confusions. Meanwhile, real experts must expend effort trying to right the wrongs in the popular mind.

Stories like these are familiar. In a better world, scientific fields might keep their members out of trouble. But how? It isn't necessarily in scientists' job description to know. Physicists study particles, not fraud; biologists study cells, not bias. Here is where a field like regulative epistemology could be of assistance to scientists and others. Epistemologists could try to devise better methods to root out biases and keep overreaching experts in check. While first-order science can be—and should be—left to the scientists, there are all sorts of matters at the "edges" of scientific practice that could be addressed with good guidance. I don't see why epistemology can't or shouldn't aspire to be a little more like First Philosophy.

Importantly, we should distinguish between regulative efforts to improve specialist and non-specialist inquiry. The task of improving people's beliefs about politics is different from improving a professional discipline like political science, for example. My proposal is not to launch a "general regulative epistemology" that sets down good guidance for use by every inquirer everywhere at all times. There is no one-size-fits-all fix for the problems of imperfect inquiry. Although I expect regulative researchers can generate lessons that apply fairly widely, they must address specific practices and local concerns. Regulative epistemology fights in the mucky trenches of inquiry, not in sky-high abstractions.

Take an analogy.[20] Philosophers in the twentieth century, many of whom had been influenced by logical empiricism, worked on "general philosophy of science." They developed abstract models of scientific reasoning, deductive-nomological explanations, the distinction between theory and observation, and so on. In much the same way that epistemologists during this period often sought to understand the nature of propositional knowledge, philosophers of science wanted to understand the workings of science at a high level of abstraction. But, arguably, the program failed. It was too general to do much good. One problem is that there is no "scientific method." Different sciences use different methods. Another problem is that general philosophy of science was not well-suited to capture the richness of

[20] Thanks to Andrew Bailey for suggesting this to me.

the evaluative, social, and historical ingredients of actual scientific life and practice. Gradually, general philosophy of science was superseded by more specific philosophies of sciences—philosophy of biology, of psychology, of physics, and so forth. Arguably, these more specialized efforts have been more fruitful than their general forebear.[21]

Intellectuals' discussions often swing from the concrete to the abstract and then back again. That swing can be seen in the philosophy of science through the course of the twentieth century. Something similar may happen to epistemology in the future. There are signs that a move toward the concrete is underway—recent work on social and virtue epistemology has cast light on intellectual life by drawing on an array of ideas about philosophical psychology and the power dynamics in human relationships. Regulative epistemology aims to understand better how our inquiry works, how it should work, and how we can do better. It's important to recognize that to create guidance we must balance the abstract and the concrete.

I believe that professional epistemologists can help make human inquiry less imperfect. Vindicating my conviction is another matter. And practicing regulative epistemology is not easy. For one, regulative epistemology is largely uncharted territory today. There is not much of a recent tradition to join. For another, the realities of professional epistemology may make regulative pursuits appear impractical and even quixotic. The familiar may appear essential and unchangeable—think of Alvin Goldman naming his regulative project "epistemics" in order to fend off the objection that guiding cognition is not legitimate epistemology. But if we want to see how epistemology could indeed be used to make inquiry better, what can we do? I suggest in the next chapter that history can teach us.

---

[21] I suspect that's true even if philosophers working outside of these highly specialized subfields tend to be more interested in the old-style general philosophy of science.

2

Regulative Epistemology in the
Seventeenth Century

We are here in the state of mediocrity—finite creatures, furnished
with powers and faculties very well fitted to some purposes, but very
disproportionate to the vast and unlimited extent of things.

—John Locke, "Of Study," 1677

Doth any man doubt, that if there were taken out of men's minds
vain opinions, flattering hopes, false valuations, imaginations as one
would, and the like, but it would leave the minds of a number of men
poor shrunken things, full of melancholy and indisposition, and un-
pleasing to themselves?

—Francis Bacon, "Of Truth," 1625

We are in pursuit of regulative theories and knowing something of
epistemology's past will shine light on the unfamiliar path ahead.
Seventeenth-century thinkers traversed similar trails and byways. They offer
us models, inspiration, and cautionary lessons. They show us what it means
to try to join together various bits of our knowledge—descriptive, normative,
and practical—for the purposes of improving intellectual life.

Recent contributors to the project of regulative epistemology have
sometimes noted historical antecedents for their ideas, in part because
latter-day regulative projects are thin on the ground.[1] As I will propose,

---

[1] Alvin Goldman (1978, 522–523) notes his regulative proposals are similar to ideas from
Descartes, Spinoza, Locke, Berkeley, and Hume. Robert Roberts and W. Jay Wood (2007, 20–23) discuss Descartes and Locke, saying their own project is Lockean in spirit. Hilary Kornblith noted how
he was drawn to epistemology by studying Locke's *An Essay Concerning Human Understanding* in a
college class:

> The idea that inquiry itself might be an object of intellectual investigation, and that an
> understanding of the very nature and limits of human knowledge might not only be

seventeenth-century intellectual history is a lamp unto our feet. Regulative epistemology is a research program aimed at developing guidance for inquiry, as I noted in Chapter 1. The program brings under its large multidisciplinary tent contributions from descriptive, normative, and practical perspectives. But today there is no "field" of regulative epistemology in any ordinary sense. There are no conferences or workshops, no well-established lines of research, no professional journals or edited collections.

Instead, we find researchers across numerous fields brandishing their tools to answer many questions about inquiry. Most of these researchers toil in the company of their disciplinary cohorts. Relative interdisciplinary isolation is the norm. Psychologists uncover systematic errors of judgment and reasoning with help from other psychologists. Sociologists join forces to study the social bases of trust and credibility. Epistemologists come together and try to pin down the nature of epistemic justification or intellectual virtues. But no organized academic field is responsible for sifting through all of the insights about how inquiry works and how it should work with the goal of telling us how it can go better. It is nobody's job to take the raw materials and craft from them a unified product: good epistemic guidance.

The realities of academic specialization make sense of the current situation, as I suggested in Chapter 1. Researchers concerned with improving inquiry are spread out across different academic fields. They ask different questions. They write and speak in different technical languages. They do not read each other's articles or books. This is how it is. Observers may say we live after the Tower of Babel: the tongues of scholars were confounded and then packs of scholars were scattered to the far corners of the earth.

Mythopoeic metaphors aside, we can try to "rewind the tape" of intellectual history's unfolding. The past shows us times when the things we now find separate and disintegrated were whole. Take the field of physics, for example. If we rewind the tape on physics through the twentieth century, we will reach Enrico Fermi (1901–1954), the Italian-born physicist who won a Nobel Prize in 1938. Fermi made major discoveries in both experimental and theoretical physics, a feat without parallel since. In his day it was possible—though not easy or likely—to become a "complete" physicist. One colleague described Fermi's work on the first atomic bomb:

> possible, but might aid in the conduct of inquiry, captured my attention. I had no doubt that this was a worthwhile project. . . . I also wondered what such a project would look like if it were informed by the science of our time rather than that of Locke's. (2008, 211)

The problems involved in the Trinity test ranged from hydrodynamics to nuclear physics, from optics to thermodynamics, from geophysics to nuclear chemistry. Often they were interrelated, and to solve one it was necessary to understand all the others. Even though the purpose was grim and terrifying, it was one of the greatest physics experiments of all time. Fermi completely immersed himself in the task. At the time of the test he was one of the very few persons (or perhaps the only one) who understood all the technical ramifications of the activities at Alamogordo. (Segrè 1970, 32)

There is no Fermi in contemporary physics. Knowledge and techniques in the field have expanded far beyond one person's comprehension. Over the years, the first physics-only journal in America, *Physical Review*, has divided into an array of "subjournals," reflecting the unrelenting ramping up of specialization. Graduate programs in physics now siphon eager students into experimental or theoretical physics, before setting them up with one or another micro-specialized research project. Historians of science note striking transformations in the way research was conducted through the twentieth century. Peter Galison comments on the nature of physics experiments:

Through the 1930s . . . most experimental work could be undertaken in rooms of a few hundred square feet, with moderate, furniture-sized equipment. But at Fermilab [a particle physics laboratory located outside Chicago] . . . a herd of buffalo actually grazes in the thousand-odd acres surrounded by the main experimental ring, and individual detectors can cost millions or tens of millions of dollars. (1987, 14)

Physics is now deeper and wider than ever before, but no one surveys the whole as Fermi once did. Fermilab replaces Fermi. An immense force of collective labor stands in for the complete physicist. Other disciplines have followed the general pattern of physics to varying degrees.

Here is why rewinding the tape on regulative theorizing is instructive. As we watch in reverse, we will see philosophers, psychologists, and others concerned with improving inquiry gradually coming into closer contact with each other, rubbing shoulders, talking in the same languages. At the end of the nineteenth century, for example, we will spot William James (1842–1910), a major contributor to both philosophy and psychology. Winding still further back, we will see many of our current disciplinary concerns and perspectives growing increasingly blurry and eventually fusing in the lives of single individuals. A scholar like Gottfried Leibniz (1646–1716) made innovations in fields from logic to geology, jurisprudence to mathematics. As we rewind and survey these quaint, long-gone intellectual worlds, we will notice how general knowledge in the past seems to us a compressed and relatively slight thing, compared to our densely packed and sprawling stockpiles of information. But watch closely. We will witness philosophers joining together descriptive, normative, and practical perspectives. A multidisciplinary effort will unfold before our eyes.

So I want to sit back, hit the rewind button, and consider an earlier age in regulative epistemology's life.

Do I mean to turn back the clock? No. Specialization has scored magnificent increases in knowledge, and humanity is better for it. For many problems, our best hope is specialized research. When I have an infection, give me my antibiotics, not dried squirrel kidneys from a seventeenth-century apothecary. The fact is, the kind of sophisticated knowledge that largely characterizes our science, medicine, and engineering is, by nature, specialized—and I gladly reap the benefits. But will the normal sort of specialized research resolve all of our important problems by itself? It seems not. Specialization may sometimes obscure questions that are unanswerable from inside any one discipline. The more serious the problem, the less likely any single professional field has the resources to solve it. Here we may think of problems such as anthropogenic climate change, epidemics, deforestation, poverty, weapons of mass destruction, and childhood obesity. Trying to address those problems with the resources of one field of knowledge isn't likely to pan out. The problem of imperfect inquiry is like that. It must be tackled with ideas and techniques from a range of fields.

I would like to understand how a multidisciplinary effort to enhance intellectual life could flourish in times like ours. Mimicking earlier thinkers is no way forward. Beginning to integrate our knowledge to produce epistemic guidance demands a reorientation toward the present. We need to see how specialized research could be a means, not only an end; we need to see the value of versatility and synthetic understanding. How can we change our ways of seeing? There is no better teacher than history.

Our discussion will reveal interesting questions about good epistemic guidance. We'll see philosophers deploying a range of ideas—rules, exemplars, duties, theories of human nature—in the service of their regulative aims. Most important, the ideas surveyed in this chapter will also let me distinguish between two broad approaches to regulative epistemology.

Regulative theorists have usually aimed to provide principles or rules for inquiry, on the one hand, or suggestions for the inculcation of an improved intellectual character, on the other. In this brief look at the seventeenth century, we will find on display both *principle-focused* and *character-focused* theorizing. I will consider René Descartes, Antoine Arnauld, and Pierre Nicole (sections 2–3) followed by Francis Bacon, Robert Boyle, and John Locke (sections 4–6) before concluding with observations about the relevance of this epistemological scene for current theorizing (section 7). But these thinkers are more than merely rough historical cohorts. Their efforts were shaped by a crisis that defined their times. Let me begin by setting the scene.

1. Crisis

During the early modern period, Europe experienced tremendous religious, political, and scientific upheavals. Many historians have called the era a time of crisis. They have described a fracturing and splintering of the relatively broad consensus of the Middle Ages. Historians have recognized the widespread uncertainty about how to put the broken pieces back together. The crisis affected everyone—learned and illiterate, rich and poor. But I want to focus on the tiny minority whose uncommon life circumstances allowed them to do work that can be called "intellectual." What was this period like for them?

In the year 1400, the majority of European intellectuals could have taken a lot for granted: the authority of the pope, a social and political system centered on the natural law, feudal forms of political organization, and the operations of the heavenly bodies, among many other things. By the year 1600, this was no longer the case. Certain important ideas and assumptions ordered intellectual life for a long time. Then they didn't. There are many fascinating studies of this age of crisis, but I will only gesture at a few elements that brought about the sense of uncertainty many thinkers experienced: (*i*) the emergence of modern "science," (*ii*) the Reformation and Counter-Reformation, (*iii*) reports from newly explored lands, and (*iv*) renewed interest in ancient skepticism. Such factors helped to push questions of proper intellectual regulation to the foreground in philosophical discussions.

In the sixteenth and seventeenth centuries, Europe was a battlefield. Some campaigns were waged by soldiers with sabers and arquebuses; others featured intellectuals with their books and public debates. In discussions of astronomy and natural philosophy in the early decades of the seventeenth century, for instance, thinkers quarreled over new theories, watched by the eyes of theologians, scanning for any sign of heresy. These battles were fought over ideas, but debates sometimes erupted in physical violence, as when books and their authors were committed to flames. From our current viewpoint, these may appear to be contests between enlightened prophets of rational empiricism and "science" and retrograde defenders of "tradition"—a clash between light and darkness. But the battle lines cannot be drawn so easily. Simple dichotomies do not capture the complexity of this intellectual world. One historian notes that theories about nature during this period "were developed in a convulsive flurry of changes that included studies of natural magic, witches, Paracelsus, and the enigmatic and obscurantist follies of those who claimed to represent divine or satanic interventions in human affairs" (Clarke 2006, 74).

What we now think of as the "science" of the period was produced through a tempest of cultural and mystical ideas as well as advances in techniques for understanding the natural world. These early paragons of "science" inhabited a world of ideas that was far more complex, fluid, and unsettled than we moderns are primed to expect. A scientist, an alchemist, and a mystic could talk shop. Sometimes they might be one and the same person, as we find with Paracelsus (1493–1541), an influential physician and botanist of the German Renaissance and founder of the discipline of toxicology. Paracelsus rigorously applied empirical methods in medicine and also toiled in the fields of astrology and the occult. Was Paracelsus a scientist? Yes. An occultist? Yes, he was that, too. From Paracelsus's perspective, science and mysticism fit together, mortar in pestle; they were how he made sense of the world. Even by the middle of the seventeenth century, Robert Boyle (1627–1691), who I discuss in more detail later in this chapter, was running groundbreaking experiments with his renowned air-pump while also practicing alchemy.[2]

This was a period of intellectual turbulence, when relatively little was established as a firm starting point. Here is a curious episode that hints at how much was up for grabs. In 1614, a document titled *Fama Fraternitatis Rosae Crucis* (The Story of the Brothers of the Rose Cross) appeared which told of the origins of a secret brotherhood purportedly founded in 1408 by a man named Christian Rosenkreuz. The document claimed that Rosenkreuz had acquired esoteric knowledge during pilgrimage to the Middle East and that

---

[2] For more on the "scientific revolution," see Shapin (1996) and Dear (2009).

the brotherhood had retained Rosenkreuz's wisdom, practicing in secret for generations. Now the brotherhood was preparing to reveal their knowledge to all, which would bring in a new age. No one knows who wrote the *Fama Fraternitatis*, but this hoax (or publicity stunt) caused a stir. The gossip mill got turning and several hundred discussions of the Rosicrucians were published in the following two decades. In Paris during 1623, placards were posted announcing the arrival of members of the brotherhood to the city, some of whom were reported to be invisible to the human eye:

> The representatives of our principal college of the brothers of the Rose Cross, who are visiting this city, visible and invisible, in the name of the Most High, toward whom the heart of the just is turned. We teach all the sciences without books, writings or signs, and we speak the languages of the countries where we live in order to rescue men, our equals, from error and death.[3]

Latter-day onlookers could be forgiven for finding all of this rather baffling. But it was a very real part of the Parisian intellectual scene in 1623.

The fracturing of old confidences and the birth of modern science were hastened in part by the Reformation and the Counter-Reformation, beginning in the early sixteenth century but emanating outward in time with significant changes to the social and political order.[4] When Martin Luther challenged the authority of the Roman Catholic Church, he posed deep questions about the sources of authority and morality and our means for discerning important truths. Indeed, Luther asserted it was legitimate for ordinary people to discern the truth for themselves. Open swung the door for new ideas and opinions. One slogan among German speakers in this period was "*die Gelehrten die Verkehrten*" (the Learned, the Perverted). The line was a bomb dropped in pamphlets and broadsheets, and Luther used it as rhetorical ammunition. The slogan encapsulated grassroots distrust of authorities high up in their ivory towers. One historian notes that it is "the exact formulation of a conviction hardened by a century of repression" (Oberman 1989,

---

[3] Quoted by Clarke (2006, 75–76). As Clarke notes, Descartes was accused by opponents of associating with Rosicrucians and an early biographer reported Descartes's response (2006, 78). To refute the claim that he was a member of the "invisibles," Descartes simply appeared in public!

[4] Merton (1938) argues, in the spirit of Max Weber, that modern empirical science arose with the Protestant work ethic. Schreiner (2011) discusses this period and its epistemological crisis from the perspective of the history of theology. (Thanks to Joshua Thurow for telling me about Schreiner's book.)

51). The end of the medieval consensus has been widely recognized as pre-
cipitating the early modern intellectual crisis.

The crisis was also kindled by contact between Europeans and civilizations
in the "New World." To take one example, we can see wide-eyed surprise at
foreign civilization in Michel de Montaigne's (1533–1592) popular *Essais*. The
Essais is a set of learned and personal writings that Montaigne revised and expanded over many years—occasionally wise and hilarious, almost always ram-
bling, often profane enough to shock your grandma. His essay "Of Custom, and
not easily changing an accepted law" reports (alleged) practices from faraway
lands. Portuguese and Spanish ships carried spices, precious metals, and human
cargo from the East Indies and the Americas, but explorers and merchants also
brought back tales of unknown peoples. Montaigne used these reports to try to
undermine the ethnocentric presumption that European culture is superior to
all others. In part, his essay is a believe-it-or-not catalogue of weird stuff; some
of the reports—either based on spurious information or Montaigne's artistic
license—we certainly should *not* believe.

Montaigne says that "there falls into man's imagination no fantasy so wild
that it does not match the example of some public practice" (1957 [1572–74],
96). He tells us there are places where

> they not only wear rings on the nose, lips, cheeks, and toes, but also have very
> heavy gold rods thrust through their breasts and buttocks. Where in eating
> they wipe their fingers on their thighs, on the pouch of their genitals, and
> on the soles of their feet. . . . Where they sleep ten or twelve together in beds,
> husbands and wives. . . . Where they fight in the water, and shoot accurately
> with their bows while swimming. . . . Where . . . the priests put out their eyes
> in order to communicate with their demons and receive their oracles. . . .
> Where they live in the belief, so rare and uncivilized, in the mortality of souls.
> Where the women bear children without complaint or fright. . . . Where chil-
> dren are four years nursing, and often twelve. . . . Where they kill lice with
> their teeth like monkeys, and think it horrible to see them crushed between
> the fingernails. . . . Where seven-year-old children endured being whipped to
> death without changing expression. (1957 [1572–74], 97, 98, 99)

I spare the gentle reader Montaigne's even more shocking examples.[5] With
a grab bag of weird practices in hand, Montaigne moves to his general

---

[5] Here I should mention Pierre Bayle (1647–1706), the Huguenot philosopher and footnote-writer
extraordinaire, who liberally filled his *Historical and Critical Dictionary* with stories of profanity

thesis: "there is nothing that custom will not or cannot do" (1957 [1572–74], 100). But if custom is so powerful a force, what does that mean for European customs? Montaigne admits he's unsure how to justify the observances of his own country (1957 [1572–74], 101). He likes to strike an ironic pose in his essays—unable to justify his own conventions but content to be conventional, more or less. One source of his doubts about the correctness of many European practices flowed from new reports of human diversity.[6]

Montaigne wasn't the only one feeling skeptical. A general climate of uncertainty had been encouraged by a blast from the ancient past. Sextus Empiricus, a second-century physician and philosopher about whose life we know little, wrote a compendium of skeptical stratagems called *Outlines of Pyrrhonism*. Sextus' handbook was translated from Greek to Latin in the 1560s. *Outlines* is a barrage of "modes" that help skeptics argue that for every argument there is an opposing argument. Skeptics thought these modes would induce suspension of judgment about whether we know anything at all. The Pyrrhonian's case for generalized intellectual paralysis had an important therapeutic purpose: agnosticism will bring us inner peace, as dogmatic opinions disturb the mind. The modes were supposed to help people chill out and be happy. In its various translations and editions, Sextus' *Outlines* was never out of print during the early modern period. Its skeptical arguments influenced many thinkers, including Montaigne, Descartes, Blaise Pascal, Pierre Bayle, and David Hume.[7]

During the seventeenth century, Western philosophy is often described as taking an "epistemological turn." Discussion veered away from metaphysical matters and collided head-on with perplexities about knowledge and proper opinion. I have noted some reasons for that turn. The inherited religious tradition was subject to dispute. The intellectual culture was fractured. Doubts

and moral depravity. (I wager that Bayle's *Dictionary* will shock your grandma even more than Montaigne's *Essais*.)

[6] What is Montaigne's argument against ethnocentrism? It is unclear. In fact, a common complaint from early modern authors about Montaigne's writing is that it displays insufficient argumentative clarity. For instance, Arnauld and Nicole in the *Port-Royal Logic* say that Montaigne "tells ridiculous stories, whose extravagance he recognizes better than anyone, and he draws even more ridiculous conclusions from them" (1996 [1683], 212; III, 20, ix). Montaigne seems to be aware of the problem. Invoking chamber pot imagery, he describes one of his essays, "Of Vanity," as "some excrements of an aged mind, now hard, now loose, and always undigested." He was unafraid to present himself raw. All that said, Montaigne's anti-ethnocentric thesis apparently has limits, for in his essay "Of Cannibals," he judges that cannibalism is morally wrong.

[7] Annas and Barnes (1985) translate and comment on some ancient Pyrrhonian texts. Barnes (1990) introduces and assesses ancient skeptical argumentation. Popkin (2003) offers a wide-ranging history of skepticism during the early modern period ("From Savonarola to Bayle").

about the very possibility of knowledge were in the air. Surely the rise of science itself was unsettling, too. Observers with microscopes and telescopes reported seeing marvels, tiny and vast, previously undreamt of in natural philosophical systems. All of this must have been overwhelming for some people. An orderly world had been disrupted.

Some thinkers hoped that epistemological theorizing would locate a safe port in the storm or help to uncover powerful truths about nature for humankind's benefit. Others aimed to unsettle their opponents' dogmatic complacency or smug confidence in the powers of reason. Many philosophers hoped that reflection on inquiry would change their world. What are the sources of error? How can one avoid falling prey to mistakes? How can we discern the truth when the truth is not obvious? What is the correct method for constructing knowledge? Many seventeenth-century thinkers raised questions about how to properly guide inquiry and regulate the life of the mind. Let us consider a few of their ideas.

2. Descartes on Method and Error

One lesson to take away from the seventeenth century is the need for methods. Dissatisfied with the state of natural and philosophical knowledge in his time, René Descartes (1596–1650) launched his epistemological project. Descartes' concern with intellectual regulation can be seen throughout his works, but I'll focus mainly on his *Discourse on Method*. The *Discourse*, published in 1637, is nowadays read as a standalone work, but Descartes wrote it as a preface for several essays on scientific topics—essays on mirrors and lenses, meteorological phenomena from snowflakes to rainbows, and geometry. The prefatory discourse was intended to summarize the Cartesian method, the use of which Descartes illustrates in the essays.

He begins the discourse by briefly recounting his early intellectual history prior to the discovery of his method. His classical education with the Jesuits gave him no means for distinguishing truth from falsehood, he says, though he adds that the indubitable reasoning of mathematics impressed him. As a young man, he desired to avoid common traps: the inevitable errors of drawing opinions from one's own culture and the risks of following arguments that fall short of delivering certainty. Descartes says he wanted "a clear and certain knowledge of all that is useful in life" (1985 [1637], 113; i, 4). His education had left him bereft. An interesting observation here is that

Descartes set for himself a far more ambitious goal than most epistemologists aim at today. He didn't seek to describe the nature of knowledge, justified belief, or any other epistemic state—he wanted to eliminate his mistakes and ignorance so he could act more effectively.

In the second part of the *Discourse,* Descartes narrates his initial discovery of his method. In 1619, a twenty-something Descartes seems to have been drafted into the Duke of Bavaria's Catholic army, temporarily based in Germany. Delayed by a snowstorm, he spent a full day thinking, alone in a "stove-heated room" (1985 [1637], 116; ii, 11). His thoughts, recounted years later in his discourse, reveal a young intellectual's angst. In a striking image, he likens his set of opinions to a building with a poor foundation in danger of collapsing (1985 [1637], 117; ii, 13). He wanted to tear it down and rebuild from the bottom up.

In a preliminary, ground-clearing step, Descartes explains how he cleansed his mind of dubious opinions. He subjected all of his previous beliefs to radical doubt: "I could not do better than undertake to get rid of them, all at one go, in order to replace them afterwards with better ones, or with the same ones once I had squared them with the standards of reason" (1985 [1637], 117; ii, 13–14).[8] Having stripped his cognitive house bare, Descartes explains how he rebuilt and redecorated.

He tells the reader he devised four rules that would allow him to reach his goal of certain knowledge, provided he "made a strong and unswerving resolution never to fail to observe them" (1985 [1637], 120; ii, 18). His first rule is designed to ensure that he accepts only what he knows as true—"to include nothing more in my judgements than what presented itself to my mind so clearly and so distinctly that I had no occasion to doubt it" (1985 [1637], 120; ii, 18). The second rule is to divide problems into smaller, manageable parts. A third rule requires him to order his thinking from simple matters to more complex ones. Finally, he says he set about to review everything carefully and completely so he could "be sure of leaving nothing out" (1985 [1637], 120; ii, 19). Descartes is trying to use his method to set aside what is distracting and misleading in intellectual life and to reveal what is essential for progress. The method calls for rejecting the confused and unreliable evidence from the

---

[8] Descartes elsewhere offers an analogy to explain this part of his method. If you have a basket full of apples and worry that some are rotten, your best strategy, says Descartes, is to dump them out and separate the good from the bad. So it goes with our beliefs, he says: we should "attempt to separate the false beliefs from the others, so as to prevent their contaminating the rest and making the whole lot uncertain" (1984 [1642], 324; 7, 481).

senses and the imagination: our minds must be lifted "above things which can be perceived by the senses" (1985 [1637], 129; iv, 37). Genuine knowledge of the world requires getting behind obscure sensory evidence and fanciful imaginations by using the intellect to seek "clear and distinct" evidence for our judgments. Equipped with his method, he says he was "sure in every case to use my reason" (1985 [1637], 121; ii, 21).[9]

The project of starting from scratch may impress us with its bold, unflinching commitment to getting things right. For good reasons, the *Discourse* and the *Meditations* are often used by philosophy teachers to introduce undergraduate students to philosophy. For one, the picture of radical doubt and of rebuilding from foundations is vivid and sometimes inspiring to students. This seems especially true of some college students in the United States near the beginning of the twenty-first century, who grew up being told that you can remake yourself into a better person just by putting your mind to it.[10] To such readers, Descartes' texts might have a "Western frontier" kind of feel. Here's this long-haired French guy, going it alone in an intellectual wilderness, bushwhacking new trails, finding riches. At any rate, Descartes plays well in introductory classes even when many teachers set up his arguments only to knock them down. And indeed, as many of Descartes' critics have insisted, the Cartesian methodological picture is doubtful—not philosophically defensible, not psychologically feasible.

But let us momentarily follow in Descartes' footprints in the snow to his stove-heated room and, like him, just ignore such doubts. Let us try to better understand his motivations for his radical method of cognitive cleansing. The four rules from the *Discourse* make sense in light of his view of error. His understanding of error and his method to combat error dovetail.

---

[9] The rhetoric of using reason in everything is misleading. Descartes' method tells a thinker how to construct knowledge by following rules, but these rules are not for guiding belief, generally speaking. They are rules for arriving at a body of propositions each of which has been certified as clearly and distinctly true or deduced from what has that status. In fact, Descartes proposed a "provisional moral code" for the regulation of opinion while he searched for the foundations of science. The first maxim of his code was "to obey the laws and the customs of my country" (1985 [1637], 122; iii, 23), which meant following the most moderate opinions of the most judicious people in his society as well as the dictates of his childhood religion. For more on the scope of Descartes' method, see Wolterstorff (1996, 181–218).

[10] Around the time I began writing this chapter, my daughter was occasionally watching a Richard Scarry *Busytown* video (circa the 1990s), in which the talking-animal characters sing: "You can be anything you want to be!" Such ideals go much deeper in U.S. culture than children's cartoons. In a 1979 speech announcing his candidacy for president, Ronald Reagan said to the American people that "we have it in our power to begin the world over again." Reagan was quoting Thomas Paine's words, originally addressed to General Washington's frozen troops at Valley Forge.

People are obviously sometimes led astray by errors. But how do mistakes happen? What are the mechanics of getting it wrong? That is less obvious. In his *Meditations*, Descartes proposes that errors stem from our judgments being out of sync with the clarity and distinctness of our ideas. Importantly, assent or belief for Descartes is under direct voluntary control: we choose what we assent to.[11] His idea is that our understanding is subject to much stricter limits than our willing. Our minds only see some matters clearly, but we can exercise our ability to accept or abstain from accepting claims in a much greater range of matters. His errors, he writes, are due simply to the fact that "the scope of the will is wider than that of the intellect; but instead of restricting it within the same limits, I extend its use to matters which I do not understand" (1984 [1641], 40; iv, 58).

According to Descartes, our will puts us at risk of error whenever we accept claims we do not clearly and distinctly perceive. To err is to have judged incorrectly. Given his account of error, it's unsurprising that he sets down strict rules designed to help thinkers determine when they do and do not grasp claims as clearly and distinctly true. By following Descartes' rules, we can hem in our wayward acts of willing and thereby inquire more effectively.

3. Errors of the Heart in the *Port-Royal Logic*

Descartes' methodological proposals and themes were influential, but even when other thinkers were in broad agreement with many of the rules he set down, they sometimes conceived of error and regulative proposals quite differently. Noticing these differences will illuminate regulative ideas and questions we don't find in Descartes. I'll turn to Antoine Arnauld (1612–1694) and Pierre Nicole's (1625–1695) *Port-Royal Logic*, the last edition of which appeared in 1683. Officially, their work is titled *Logic or the Art of Thinking* (*La Logique ou l'art de penser*), but the "Port-Royal" label has stuck because of their involvement with the religious community at the famous Port-Royal Abbey, a Cistercian convent outside of Paris. A few words about Port-Royal—the intellectual and spiritual home for the authors of the eponymous *Logic*—are in order.

In the middle of the seventeenth century, Port-Royal Abbey was a stronghold of Jansenism, a mostly French religious movement named after the

---

[11] Vitz (2010) discusses Descartes' understanding of the relationship between belief and will.

Belgian Bishop of Ypres, Cornelius Jansen (1585–1638). Jansen's posthumous book *Augustinus*, published in 1640, advanced a particular understanding of Augustine of Hippo's theology. The book immediately drew fire from Catholic authorities, who branded Jansen's ideas as a kind of Calvinism. Briefly, Jansen taught that God's grace cannot be resisted and that it doesn't require any human agreement or assent. When Jansenism was first attacked as heretical in the early 1640s, a young theologian, Antoine Arnauld, rose to Jansen's defense. The Port-Royal community had been transformed in earlier decades from a lackadaisical nunnery to a bastion of moral and intellectual seriousness by Antoine's impressive older sister, Marie Angélique Arnauld (1591–1661), and the convent soon became a hub for Jansenism.[12]

In their *Logic*, Arnauld and Nicole offer a broadly Cartesian approach to method.[13] Like Descartes, they propose that we should strive to make our ideas clear and distinct and to limit assent to what is found in them. But the Port-Royalists' discussion of errors is motivated by a far more interesting story about human beings than we find in Descartes' thought.[14] It's a love story.

The story has roots in the writings of Augustine (354–430) and was central to the identity of the Port-Royal community. According to Augustine, all human beings suffer for the penalty of the first man's disobedience. This is Original Sin.[15] Fallen humans are turned away from God and turned inward toward themselves. Their broken state is affective and volitional at its core, though the consequences are sweeping. The very nature of humankind has been altered by the Fall. Pride was present in the primal sin, according to Augustine, when "humans took delight in being their own masters rather than in God's power."[16] Human loves and wills are disordered—we love the wrong things and will what is wrong. Augustine taught that only divine grace can address our corruption by redirecting human loves and choices back toward God. Crucially, the Port-Royal community thought that humans are

---

[12] Marie Angélique was a sophisticated intellectual and, in the course of her radical reform activities at Port-Royal, wrote on topics such as virtue, predestination, and gender. Conley (2009) examines the intellectual and practical lives of nuns in the convent, largely through the writings of Marie Angélique and her sister Agnès, and their niece, Angélique de Saint-Jean.

[13] Nadler (1989, 34–44) summarizes Arnauld's methodological Cartesianism, and the chapters in Kremer (1996) explore aspects of Arnauld's thought. Finocchiaro (1997) suggests that the *Logic* is a precursor to the contemporary field of informal logic.

[14] See Corneanu (2011, 87–88) and Clarke (2006, 292).

[15] King (2007) describes metaphysical perplexities concerning Original Sin and the Fall during the medieval period, starting with Augustine.

[16] *Enchiridion* 13, 45. I have used King's (2007) translation.

entirely dependent on divine grace for salvation, denying the role of free choice in the acceptance of grace. For the Jansenists, this would lead to conflict with the Jesuits and other powerful Catholic authorities who taught that fallen humans could freely accept God's saving grace. Arnauld and Nicole's discussion of errors in their *Logic* is infused with the postlapsarian story of prideful rebellion and a disastrous fall.

That story adds a bleakness to their epistemology—and, to be honest, that's why I like it. The Port-Royalists were not afraid to deliver the reader a serious buzzkill. They say that people typically hold their opinions not because of the truth or for good reasons (1996 [1683], 204; III, 20, i). Instead, our opinions are often determined by our depraved heart—"the monster we carry in our bosom," as Nicole put it in an essay from 1677 (Schneewind 2003).[17] Self-love and corrupt passions drive the formation and revision of opinions by giving rise to many "sophisms," which "consist in transferring our passions onto the objects of our passions, and judging that they are what we wish or desire them to be" (1996 [1683], 205; III, 20, ii).

When you love yourself, you tend to love your opinions and will protect them; and when you dislike someone else, you tend to dislike her opinions and will dismiss or attack them. Self-love and inordinate passions breed poor reasoning, dogmatism, credulity, selective exposure to relevant evidence, quibbling pedantry, intractable disagreements, and (as Arnauld and Nicole could have said but sadly did not) Jesuitry. Like Descartes, the Port-Royalists also see a link between will and error. But whereas Descartes thinks the will is crucial for not accepting what fails to be clearly and distinctly perceived, the Port-Royalists see that our depraved will has fixed in our minds error-producing tendencies. Descartes sees the will as a tool that can be used well or badly; the Port-Royalists see it as inherently flawed.

---

[17] In his *Essais de morale* of 1677, Nicole offered this doozy:

> The word *self-love* is not sufficient to make us understand its nature, for one can love itself in many different ways. We must add other characteristics in order to form a true idea of it. These are that corrupt man not only loves himself but loves himself beyond measure, loves only himself, and relates everything to himself. He wants every kind of property, honor, and pleasure, and he wants them only for himself. Placing himself at the center of everything, he would like to rule over everything and wishes that all creatures were occupied with nothing but pleasing him, praising him, and admiring him. This tyrannical disposition, being firmly implanted deep in the hearts of all men, makes them violent, unjust, cruel, ambitious, obsequious, envious, insolent, and quarrelsome. In a word, it carries within it the seeds of all man's crimes and profligacies, from the slightest to the most heinous. This is the monster we carry in our bosom; it lives and reigns absolutely within us, unless God has destroyed its reign by filling our hearts with a different kind of love. ("Of Charity and Self-Love," translated by Elborg Forster, in Schneewind 2003, 371)

Arnauld and Nicole paint a gloomy picture. We suffer from many "illusions of the heart" and these are difficult or perhaps impossible for us to detect. Some of these illusions may remind us of contemporary ideas from cognitive and social psychology, with an important difference: latter-day psychologists typically posit "biased" cognitive processes to explain error, but the Port-Royalists diagnose a moral source for the mechanics of disordered thinking. For example, here is how Arnauld and Nicole explain the differences between a person's self-judgment and her judgment of others:

> The human mind is not only naturally enamored of itself, but it is also naturally jealous, envious, and malicious toward others. It allows others to have advantages only with difficulty, because it desires all of them for itself. Since it is an advantage to know the truth and bring insight to others, people develop a secret passion to rob others of this glory, which often leads them to criticize others' opinions and discoveries for no reason. (1996 [1683], 207; III, 20, vi)[18]

For Arnauld and Nicole, error grows from a twisted moral root. The wages of sin is epistemological death.

Their aim in the *Logic* is centrally in "educating our judgment and making it as precise as possible" (1996 [1683], 5; "First Discourse"). They identify some cognitive-cum-affective weaknesses that need correction, and they apparently think recognizing these weaknesses can improve our reasoning and judgment in science and everyday life. But how can we avoid the troubling illusions of self-love? It is unclear what the Port-Royalists would have us do.

Consider whether someone can be reasonably confident that he or she is not subject to illusions of self-love. From the Port-Royalists' Augustinian viewpoint, fallen humans are self-deceived about their moral condition. It's hard for us to know, for instance, whether we are acting generously toward our neighbor out of love rather than miserable self-interest. Whenever we face an open question about whether our judgment is inappropriately moved by passions, as opposed to good reasons, the Port-Royalists should worry about self-deception. Someone might *feel* confident that he's not moved by self-love, but how can he trust a heart which he believes is deceitful above all things? Insofar as it's difficult to diagnose correctly one's own moral

---

[18] Similarly, contemporary psychologists have found that people suffer from powerful ego-protective biases. We have a motive to see ourselves in a good light that is not extended to others so easily. I say more about these issues in Chapter 5.

condition, the Port-Royalists should be doubtful, to some potentially great extent, whether they suffer from the illusions of self-love, and thus whether their beliefs are based on good reasons.

Arnauld and Nicole's Augustinian anthropology sets limits for the effectiveness of regulative interventions or it at least places considerable weight on the role of divine grace to improve our intellectual affairs. Thus, the Port-Royalists show us that figuring out what good intellectual guidance is naturally introduces questions about human nature and cognition. Though we may think quite differently about the origin of imperfect inquiry, we can still recognize, along with Arnauld and Nicole, the importance of the attempt to escape the mess we are in.

This brief and selective discussion of epistemology in the seventeenth century has so far featured philosophers on the European continent. On the English side of the Channel, we also find philosophers engaged in similar reflection on inquiry. But whereas Descartes and the Port-Royalists reflected upon the individual inquirer, the English philosophers I discuss next had a special concern for the social dimensions of knowing.

4. The Character of Baconian Method

Francis Bacon's (1561–1626) significance as a proponent of inductive methods is widely recognized. I want to note some ways in which Bacon's reflections on method were, like Descartes', shaped by concerns about the origin of error. Bacon's understanding of our shortcomings and his proposals for improvements influenced many later English thinkers, to whom I will turn shortly. In Bacon's thought, questions about proper methods are tightly linked to questions about proper character.

Bacon was a man of considerable energy and wide learning. Late in the nineteenth century, *The Works of Francis Bacon* (edited by James Spedding) was published in fifteen beefy volumes, totaling 8,317 pages of text. Bacon's pen was rarely at rest. Although he left behind an immense body of philosophical writings and correspondence and participated in many experiments, he was only a part-time philosopher for most of his working life.[19]

---

[19] The arc of Bacon's career deserves at least a footnote, and not only because of this fact: to know something about his career is to feel we have been slacking off. He was educated at Trinity College, Cambridge, and subsequently studied law in London at Gray's Inn. The death of his father in 1579 left Bacon with a meager inheritance; the leisure of an established gentleman of wit and parts was not in the cards. He had to get a job. Choosing politics, he attained high positions of influence in

Bacon's hope for progress in natural philosophy was gargantuan. In his unfinished utopian novel, *New Atlantis*, he envisioned a curious state-funded scientific research institute, Salomon's House, where division of labor and specialization would enable researchers to tackle investigations too demanding for any single person or unorganized group. Bacon dreamed of a "great renewal" that was nothing short of a complete reboot and restructuring of learning and applied science. He wanted to understand how humans can overcome their failings due to the Fall posited by Christian theology, in an effort to prepare for the millennium of God's earthly reign. Just like Descartes, the Rosicrucians, alchemists, occultists, and others in this period, Bacon believed that the uncovering of natural knowledge would commence a New Age of prosperity and power over nature. He had caught, and also expressed, the excitement of the era.[20] What made Bacon different was his proposed means to the end of improvement and his explanations for why so little progress had been made thus far.

In *Novum Organum Scientiarum*—literally, "a new instrument of science"—Bacon compares the natural world to a labyrinth of dense and twisting pathways. Some people may have tried to act as guides through the labyrinth, but Bacon deems them lost (2000 [1620], 10; "Plan of the work"). The inherent complexity of nature is only part of what has delayed scientific progress. The human mind is also to blame. The mind is like a rough, unpolished surface that can't reflect the "true rays of things" (2000 [1620], 18; "Plan of the work"). In fact, this poor surface distorts the images that nature presents of itself:

Elizabethan and Jacobean England, partly with assistance from his powerful uncle, Lord Burghley, chief advisor to Queen Elizabeth for much of her reign. Bacon served as a member of the Parliament for thirty-seven years, as Attorney-General, as Queen's Counsel, and as a regular mediator between the Parliament and the Crown. His rise through inner circles of power was signaled by adornments of pomp and privilege: he liked to host lavish parties and kept a large retinue of servants, dressing them and himself with what one historian called "an ostentation verging on the unseemly." (Jardine 2000, viii). His debts were often a source of considerable anxiety and embarrassment. When his political career went down in flames in 1521, after he was discovered to have taken bribes, Bacon was permitted to retain his titles and property. Retiring in disgrace, he spent the last five years of his life on natural philosophical pursuits. In his final act, he sought to discover whether fowl meat would be kept fresh by freezing. He died of pneumonia following the icy experiment. (Beat that, slackers.)

[20] See Dear (2009) and Shapin (1996) for introductions to the history of the "scientific revolution." Bacon's aspirations are vividly represented on the title page of the first edition of *Novum Organum*. The cover illustration shows a sailing ship entering the Atlantic Ocean from the Strait of Gibraltar, the boundary of the Mediterranean, on the sides of which stand the smashed Pillars of Hercules, a traditional representation of the limits of knowledge. Bacon thought he could sniff the fresh breezes wafting from a "New Continent" of exploration awaiting scientific conquest (2000 [1620], 88; I, cxiv).

For however much men may flatter themselves and run into admiration and almost veneration of the human mind, it is quite certain that, just as an uneven mirror alters the rays of things from their proper shape and figure, so also the mind, when it is affected by things through the senses, does not faithfully preserve them, but inserts and mingles its own nature with the nature of things as it forms and devises its own notions. (2000 [1620], 18–19; "Plan of the work")

According to Bacon, our cognitive shortcomings begin with our lazy tendency toward speculation and overgeneralization: "the mind loves to leap to generalities, so it can rest" (2000 [1620], 36; I, xx). Once ideas have lodged themselves in our minds, however, the truth is sometimes blocked from entering (2000 [1620], 40; I, xxxviii). He describes four types of mental obstructions or "idols" (Latin: *idola*).

The *idols of the tribe* are "founded in human nature itself" (2000 [1620], 41; I, xli) and include imperfections in visual perception and other standard-issue defects, such as our tendency to disregard disconfirming evidence in order to "preserve the authority of [our] first conceptions" and to be "much more moved and excited by affirmatives than by negatives" (2000 [1620], 43; I, xlvi). The *idols of the cave* are based upon our individual particularities, not the shared features of human nature. "The human spirit (in its different dispositions in different men)," writes Bacon, "is a variable thing, quite irregular, almost haphazard" (2000 [1620], 41; I, xlii). Carved and painted by our upbringing and habits, idols of the cave decorate our "private worlds" and prevent us from recognizing the "great or common world." Bacon is also sensitive to the ways in which shared language can mislead us. Inquiry can be befuddled either by words that are not precise enough to carve nature at its joints, or by words that do not refer to real things (2000 [1620], 48–49; I, lx). He names these errors *idols of the marketplace,* appealing to the idea that language arises in commerce between speakers. Finally, *idols of the theater* are grounded in our mistaken theories. We project our theoretical inclinations onto the world. These fictitious images of reality promote blunders (2000 [1620], 42; I, xliv). Philosophers are like dramatists. Both have a knack for crafting stories that are a bigger hit with audiences than serious candidates for the truth (2000 [1620], 50; I, lxii).

Bacon hopes his fourfold division of idols will "give warning to the human understanding" (2000 [1620], 42; I, xliv). But how is that? Can we smash the idols? Bacon tells us:

There remains one hope of salvation, one way to good health: that the entire work of the mind be started over again; and from the very start the mind should not be left to itself, but be constantly controlled; and the business done (if I may put it this way) by machines. (2000 [1620], 28; "Preface")

The "machines" are the various parts of his methodological proposals— the means for repairing and retrofitting our minds. Like Descartes, Bacon intends to reset inquiry and start fresh, but the two philosophers have rather different approaches to rebuilding. Like Arnauld and Nicole, Bacon thinks the Fall has cognitive implications, but he's more upbeat about our prospects for self-improvement. Let me focus on two key Baconian ideas.

First, there is Bacon's "logic": his celebrated inductive method. Baconian induction requires apprehending particular facts and only then gradually moving to generalizations or axioms. He pitches his inductive logic as a replacement for the Aristotelian deductive logic of his day. Natural philosophy, he says, must be based upon painstakingly gathered "natural histories," which are sets of observations, not rumors or speculations (2000 [1620], 80; I, xcviii). His idea is that by moving from our sense experience to the development of detailed natural histories, we can infer axioms or propositions concerning the unobservable, inner causes of things. Compiling a Baconian natural history for any subject is a monumental undertaking, and Bacon foresaw the necessity of collaborative effort. Unlike Descartes' method, which was for disciplining an individual's reasoning, Baconian method calls for well-organized collective labor. Bacon's vision made him a hero, centuries later, to champions of "modern science."

A second, less well-recognized, feature of Bacon's method is that it was intended as a "regimen" for the mind.[21] It's not just a method to guide people in drawing conclusions from evidence, but a method for healing their sick minds. In his "Letter and Discourse to Sir Henry Savill, Touching Helps for the Intellectual Powers," written sometime between 1596 and 1604, Bacon articulates his concern for a kind of practical education of the intellect. It is widely appreciated, Bacon says, that people can be responsive to education. Underwater divers are taught to hold their breath for a long time, children are trained to walk a tightrope, and so on. But he thinks philosophers have neglected education's power to shape the mind.[22]

---

[21] Corneanu (2011) and Gaukroger (2001) emphasize this point.

[22] Bacon's concern is mirrored in recent efforts by philosophers to bridge the fields of epistemology and education. See Baehr (2013) and Kotzee (2013).

He distinguishes the kind of education at issue from the traditional disciplines of logic and rhetoric, and then he notes that "the motions and faculties of the wit and memory may be not only governed and guided [by the rules of logic and rhetoric, for instance], but also confirmed and enlarged, by custom and exercise duly applied" (1996 [1596–1604], 114). What exactly is "custom and exercise duly applied"? Bacon explains with an example. There is a difference between properly aiming and shooting a bow, on the one hand, and developing the strength and balance needed to properly aim and shoot it, on the other. And so it goes for logic and rhetoric, thinks Bacon: those arts are different from the practices that help someone properly use logic or rhetoric. Thus, one of Bacon's concerns is to understand how to build up the strength of the mind—"by custom and exercise duly applied"—so that the mind will be prepared to use intellectual tools well.

Bacon's goal is to improve inquirers' characters by purging imperfections from their minds and hearts.[23] To take just one example, Bacon notes that to avoid the idols of the cave—idols grounded in an individual's particularities—thinkers must resist two extremes: admiration of antiquity and love of novelty. This proves difficult because "few have the temperament to keep to the mean without criticizing the true achievements of the ancients or despising the real contributions of the moderns" (2000 [1620], 47; I, lvi). Reformation of character is a central concern of Bacon's theorizing about method. Reliably discovering new truths about nature requires us to become new people.

5. Boyle on Trust and Credible Knowledge

In the decades after his death, some of Bacon's ideas and themes were taken up by new hands. This would become a chapter in what was later called the "scientific revolution." I want to look at some of the methodological ideas that developed among Bacon-influenced philosophers, but I will focus on Robert Boyle. We'll see how questions about character and social comportment ended up being central to some natural philosophers' thinking about knowledge.

These days, we tend to think of objective scientific methods as providing a kind of external check on inquiry by obliterating scientists' distinctively personal traits. As Lorraine Daston and Peter Galison note, "To be objective

---

[23] I follow Corneanu (2011, chapter 1) and Gaukroger (2001, 11–12) on this point.

is to aspire to knowledge that bears no trace of the knower—knowledge un-
marked by prejudice or skill, fantasy or judgment, wishing or striving" (2007,
17). But natural philosophers' methods during the early modern period were
not designed to fulfill any such aspiration. Their methods hinged on human
character. Like Bacon before them, they sought to attain a kind of objectivity
by reforming or correcting character.

Consider some contours of the story.[24] Around the middle of the seventeenth century, Bacon's ideas helped to form the bedrock for the Royal
Society of London. The society, conceived as "a Colledge for the Promoting
of Physico-Mathematicall Experimentall Learning," was founded in 1660
and received a charter from King Charles II two years later. Its members
were devoted to the study of nature. Prior to the Royal Society's launch, a
few groups of thinkers apparently met in a similar fashion. One group, with
Robert Boyle among its leaders, called itself the "Invisible College," alluding
to an image promulgated earlier by Rosicrucians. Boyle and his associates
hoped that science, rightly pursued, could bring the promised benefits of esoteric arts with none of the hocus pocus. By grasping truths about the world
through experimental means and using that knowledge to control nature,
they believed that philosophical investigation would make good on the lofty
promises of alchemists and occultists.

These experimental philosophers spared no effort in uncovering nature's
secrets. Boyle's famous air-pump removed the air from inside a large glass
sphere while the sphere's contents could be observed. Boyle experimented
upon creatures great and small, watching and waiting to see how long cats,
mice, frogs, and bees could survive in the airless space. But gentlemen in
powdered wigs didn't do all of the hard work. The Royal Society's technicians
would sometimes dissect live animals in experiments to understand the operation of nerves, lungs, and intestines; they would sometimes load foodstuffs
inside an air-pump to determine the rate of putrefaction; they injected ale,
wine, and opium into dogs, which Boyle noted led to "suffering, vomiting,
intoxication and I fear death." Clean-up couldn't have been fun. The pages
of the *Philosophical Transactions of the Royal Society* report on the details of
many experiments, but we learn little about the technicians and staff who
had to deal with some devastating messes. We should remember them with
sympathy.

---

[24] I draw on Shapin and Schafer (1985), Shapin (1994), and Corneanu (2011).

The Royal Society sometimes needed human test subjects. In November 1667, a meeting of members witnessed a blood transfusion from a sheep to a man, among the earliest animal-to-human transfusions. The volunteer for the procedure was one Arthur Coga, a poor and eccentric divinity student from Cambridge—"cracked a little in the head," according to one gentleman's diary entry. Coga's reward was a Guinea (twenty shillings). Incredibly, Coga survived and returned for another sheep-blood transfusion, proving beyond a doubt that graduate students since at least the seventeenth century have been willing to suffer for improper compensation.[25]

This may sound like mayhem. But was it? Was a meeting of the Royal Society akin to a gang of unpleasant kids, setting off baking-soda-and-vinegar volcanoes in public toilets, torturing rats with hacksaws, and pulling the wings off of flies? No, this was sober inquiry into the nature of things. One should imagine Boyle near the air-pump while a technician adjusts a valve, gradually suffocating a dog. Boyle takes down notes, records the time, as the witnesses assent to the measurements, carefully jotting down details in their own books. This was the scientific life for seventeenth-century English elite, not a field day for delinquents.

But how did these philosophers think investigation should be pursued? What was their method? Generally, Boyle and his associates aimed to establish knowledge that would not be subject to squabbles and dissent. Mere armchair speculation about nature had proved a dismal failure. Boyle thought the various proposals of Aristotelians, Cartesians, Paracelsians, and others had not delivered credible natural knowledge. According to him, experiments were the key. If truths could be revealed by a machine like the air-pump, and trustworthy observers could witness the experiments, then claims about nature would stand on firm footing—certified by the good character of the witnesses.[26] Boyle's writings often articulated the kind of trustworthiness at issue. For him, the problem of knowledge was in part the problem of whom to trust—and the problem of whom to trust was, at its core, a moral and social problem.[27]

Boyle had a name for the ideal natural philosopher: the "Christian Virtuoso." Boyle crafted the Virtuoso by combining preexisting cultural ideas and roles to create a striking new figure. The Virtuoso's character is a blend of

---

[25] For more on the early history of blood transfusion, including Arthur Coga's xenotransfusion and Boyle's intoxicated dogs, see Learoyd (2012).

[26] See Shapin and Schaffer (1985).

[27] The next paragraphs summarize details from Shapin (1994).

the wealthy gentleman, the (Protestant) Christian, and the scholar. He looked more than a little like Boyle—son of one of England's wealthiest men—and Boyle's well-heeled colleagues. The amalgam of identities and roles was crucial for Boyle's purposes; these traits were designed to give the Virtuoso a trustworthy character that would be publicly recognizable as such.

In Boyle's day, neither the gentleman nor the scholar was a suitable candidate for the role of experimental philosopher—the likes of these could not be trusted to speak on behalf of reality. This is worth explaining. In early modern English society, gentility was often identified with pleasure. The gentleman's life was devoted to hunting, hawking, gambling, and social calls, none of which was befitting a serious philosopher.[28] Common portrayals of professional scholars—the "gown-men"—inspired even less confidence. The scholarly lecture and disputation, inheritances from the medieval period, were set in "a rhetoric and theater of warfare, combat, trial, and joust," historian William Clark observes (2006, 75). Clark says the early modern professional scholar was a member of a "juridico-ecclesiastical academic order"—a sort of prophet and warrior (2006, 76).

Scholars could cut an impressive figure at least some of the time, in formal academic settings like lectures or thesis defenses. But later many of them would loosen their belts and take their fill of food and drink at college dinners.[29] An observer in 1654 described the scholastic academic culture in England as "a civil war of words, a verbal contest, a combat of cunning craftiness, violence and altercation."[30] (Readers acquainted with modern-day academic philosophy conferences may have some sense of what this was like.)

---

[28] Shapin (1994, 170–175). As Blaise Pascal noted in his *Pensées*: "Vanity: gaming, hunting, visits, theater, false perpetuity of name" (2004 [1670], 164; S561/L628).

[29] Clark (2006) quotes an early twentieth-century historian commenting on Cambridge University during the eighteenth century:

> [the Fellows] stand accused of wasting their time and opportunities. . . . But the Fellows can be reproached with more than lack of scholarship and industry. Far too many of them led frankly self-indulgent lives and did not trouble to conceal their shortcomings. . . . Indeed the pleasures of the table loomed large in their lives, and, even when they did not grossly exceed, they were disinclined to curb their appetites.

Then Clark chimes in, noting that the eighteenth century is usually thought to be the low-point of Cambridge's history and Oxford's, too, and adds: "I suspect, however, that the college fellows of the sixteenth and seventeenth centuries were given neither less to leisure and pleasure, nor more to work and study" (2006, 24). A friend of mine, who once studied at Cambridge and asks to remain unnamed, assures me that many college fellows there today have carried these proud traditions into the twenty-first century.

[30] Quoted by Shapin (1996, 122). See also Shapin (1994, 171).

Boyle thought the natural philosopher needed to be a different brand of person altogether.[31]

Part of the trouble is that identities and interests can bias inquiry. Tracing the problem back to the Fall, Boyle writes that "our Understandings are so universally byass'd, and impos'd upon by Wills and Affections."[32] Like Bacon, Boyle saw the human mind as cluttered with "idols" and prone to poorly regulated assent. For example, professional scholars were enamored with their own ideas, eager to defend their turf and advance their reputations. And members of the merchant class, like chemists or medical doctors, might easily be moved to bend the truth for financial gain or keep findings to themselves to ensure future profits.

Boyle's reaction to these epistemic-cum-moral failings was to envision an appropriate type of inquirer: an intellectual exemplar. The Virtuoso's makeup was supposed to guard against such failings. The Virtuoso enjoyed a kind of intellectual independence that scholars and merchants lacked. He was disinterested, detached, impartial, and free to tell the truth. As a gentleman of respectable birth and means, the Virtuoso had no need for material advancement and thus would not be moved by pecuniary interest; he could share his useful findings for the benefit of humankind. Tied to no profession in particular, he would not be biased by obligations to organizations of experts or professional institutions. As a Christian, the Virtuoso was committed to sincerity and modesty of mind—and, as a Protestant, he wouldn't owe fidelity to the Bishop of Rome. Moreover, Boyle thought careful experimental inquiry would help to cultivate "modesty of mind," which is for him a matter of being wary of hasty assent, forming tentative conclusions, remaining open to new information, and being ready to revise one's thinking in light of new evidence, even when this means changing cherished opinions.[33]

The Virtuoso was the straight shooter. He would never be bought. He was eminently deserving of trust. He would ensure the experimental findings would stand firm. In the drama of experimental philosophy, the Virtuoso was cast into a social role Boyle expected other actors would easily bungle. My suggestion is that Boyle's proposals concerning the Virtuoso were a kind of epistemological theorizing—not regulative theorizing about rules or

---

[31] Why should we think that the adversarial method of disputation actually makes scholars untrustworthy? Boyle took himself to have some insight into the operations of biases. I return to the topic of judgments concerning biases in Chapter 5.

[32] Quoted by Corneanu (2011, 122).

[33] See Corneanu (2011, 125).

principles, as we find in Descartes, but an attempt to illuminate the character and comportment of the ideal natural philosopher. We find in Boyle's writings an effort to describe the life of a trustworthy inquirer.

Of course, some people nowadays may feel cynical about this "virtue" business. Isn't Boyle's Virtuoso out of step with reality? Gentlemen have biases of their own. Furthermore, Boyle's conception of the Virtuoso apparently excludes from natural philosophy vast swaths of society: women, the poor, Catholics, infidels. And why should we accept that veracity is guaranteed by virtue? Today, we place trust in scientific experts, their moral character notwithstanding. So I expect some contemporary observers will find it doubtful that Boyle's vision of virtue could help explain what gives science its objective oomph. They will say that science's reliability is not a matter of anybody's good character. Indeed, as philosophers and sociologists of science sometimes suggest, ferocious competition among scientists for resources, prestige, and other professional rewards can promote reliable inquiry. Scientists can be self-interested and yet, collectively, do well at getting the truth—if the social incentives and institutional arrangements are right. Success hangs on a well-balanced system of reward and punishment, not the impartial or dispassionate pursuit of truth.

But the significance of these reservations about Boyle's emphasis on virtue and trust should not be overstated. Boyle got something right. Effective science needs trust and trust calls for virtue. We won't understand the virtues exactly as he did, but we should leave room in science for virtue.

To see why, notice that we are appalled to learn that scientific "findings" have been faked. Our contemporary techno-scientific culture reserves special honor for scientists, but they are banished to outer darkness for known deception or dishonesty. Experiments may fail and research programs may fizzle out, but scientists should never knowingly sin against accuracy and truthfulness. The halls of scientific shame are filled with portraits of shysters. Jan Hendrik Schön, a German physicist working at Bell Labs in New Jersey, claimed he had created transistors using organic materials, making possible a leap from silicon-based electronics to organic microelectronics. Then in 2002 Schön was revealed to be a con artist. Marc Hauser fabricated data in his studies of primate cognition, resigning in disgrace from his position at Harvard University in 2011. And the once-celebrated Soviet biologist Olga Lepeshinskaya claimed to have vindicated the "spontaneous generation" of living cells from non-cellular matter. She persuaded others by filming the death and decomposition of cells and then playing the films in reverse.

These are well-known cases of misconduct, but one meta-analysis of studies of scientific fraud found that around 2% of scientists quietly admitted to having fabricated, falsified, or modified results; nearly one-third confessed to having used questionable research practices (Fanelli 2009). When asked about the behavior of others, nearly 15% of scientists wagged an accusatory finger at fabricating colleagues and 72% said their colleagues had used questionable practices. Blind review and peer scrutiny do not always catch the corner-cutters and charlatans.

Boyle's Virtuoso has something to teach contemporary investigators. Boyle's concern to guide inquiry using character may still resonate with all of us as we try to bring our own intellectual affairs into better order.

6. Locke on the Education of the Mind

The early Royal Society was an important institution for bewigged virtuosi. Some of their names remain with us: Robert Hooke, Edmond Halley, Christopher Wren, and Isaac Newton. But I want to turn instead to another one of Boyle's famous contemporaries: John Locke (1632–1704). Boyle informally served as Locke's scientific mentor at Oxford, where Locke was exposed to the new experimental philosophy, and the two men remained lifelong friends. Locke was elected as a Fellow of the Royal Society in 1668. Whereas Boyle reflected on the moral and social underpinnings of reliable testimony in the economy of natural philosophy, Locke theorized about how to root out the problematic opinions of his fellow citizens and make them— both the opinions and the citizens—more reasonable. By considering Locke's epistemological thought, we will see how the pursuit of good guidance can aim at social and political goals.

Locke studied medicine at Oxford and, by a chance meeting, became personal secretary and medical doctor to the First Earl of Shaftesbury (Anthony Ashley Cooper), a significant political figure and founder of the Whig party. One day in 1671, Locke met with five or six companions in his room at Shaftesbury's residence in London, Exeter House. The friends' discussion touched upon matters of morality and religion, and Locke says in *An Essay Concerning Human Understanding* that the friends "found themselves quickly at a stand, by the Difficulties that arose on every side" and perplexed by doubts (1975 [1690], 7).[34] This experience prompted Locke to reflect on

---

[34] Woolhouse (2007, 97–105) describes the conversation at Exeter House and the initial trajectory of Locke's thinking about human understanding.

epistemological questions in candid hope that inquiry into inquiry could resolve important disputes.

Locke's theorizing about the proper regulation of assent was part of his vision to rehabilitate society. In the wake of the disintegration of the medieval consensus following the Reformation, European intellectuals by Locke's day could survey a spread of well-entrenched but incompatible frameworks of thought concerning philosophy, politics, and religion.[35] But Locke did not simply want to throw in his lot with any particular tradition. He needed a new guide for opinion.

Finding a new guide was a matter of great urgency for him. When he was ten in 1642, a civil war broke out between King Charles I and the Parliamentary army; Locke's father served with the Parliamentarians. Violence and political strife would scar the national scene well into Locke's adulthood. He lived as a political exile in Holland and the United Provinces for most of the 1680s. His personal letters sometimes reveal a sadness and anxiety about the conflicts and a longing for political stability. He knew how clashing convictions about politics and religion could lead countrymen to tear each other apart. Locke perceived the role of polemical writers in fueling conflict. He accused "the pens of Englishmen of as much guilt as their swords," noting that "furies, war, cruelty, rapine, confusion . . . have been conjured up in private studies" (1997 [1660/61], 5; "Preface"). Citizens following conflicting traditions would come to blows.

Locke penned works on political ideals like liberty and toleration, trying to discern the social and political principles and structures of a stable society. He also reflected on the kind of intellectual character citizens would need to safeguard such a society. Though Locke thought citizens would need human reason as their guide, he knew this would not be easy. To follow reason, citizens would need to compensate for their weaknesses. This is a central theme in a posthumously published work, *Of the Conduct of the Understanding*.

To begin with, Locke says the human mind is in a deplorable state:

> There are several weaknesses and defects in the understanding, either from the natural temper of the mind or ill habits taken up, which hinder it in its progress to knowledge. Of these there are as many possibly to be found, if the mind were thoroughly studied, as there are diseases of the body, each

[35] Wolterstorff (1996, 1–8).

whereof clogs and disables the understanding to some degree, and therefore deserves to be looked after and cured. (1996 [1706], 187; §12)

As I noted, Locke was trained as a physician: he doubtless found the comparison of diseases of the understanding to bodily ones congenial. He points out
the need for a Baconian "natural history" of the mind's maladies and makes
a start on the project himself by describing a few. For instance, we tend only
to seek out arguments that support our opinions (1996 [1706], 189–190; §15)
and often settle on our opinions before inquiry has concluded or even begun
(1996 [1706], 169; §3).

Our intellectual imperfections can be overcome by conscientious self-
governance and industry, says Locke. To try to improve is our God-given
duty and reason is our main instrument.[36] It is our "touchstone" for recognizing the difference between truth and mere appearances, "substantial gold
from superficial glitterings" (1996 [1706], 171; §3). Reason dictates that we
apportion our assent to our evidence.

But following reason is not just a matter of being taught rules for reasoning.
As Locke observes, people are no better off for knowing the rule that assent
should be regulated by evidence. Though they know the rule, they often form
opinions on the basis of slim evidence, no evidence, or even against their evidence. Merely knowing rules for reasoning is not sufficient to regulate assent:

> Nobody is made anything by hearing of rules, or laying them up in his
> memory; practice must settle the habit of doing without reflecting on the
> rule, and you may as well hope to make a good painter or musician ex-
> tempore by a lecture and instruction in the arts of music and painting, as a
> coherent thinker or strict reasoner by a set of rules, showing him wherein
> right reasoning consists. (1996 [1706], 175; §4)

Possessing rules for reasoning is not sufficient for well-regulated opinion
and the reason for that is simple, Locke thinks: our intellectual and moral
constitution is sick and infirm. In matters of assent and inquiry, we human
beings are a vain, obstinate, lazy, and reckless bunch. Our assent is not often
enough guided by reason; we are enslaved by the ailments of our minds. To
liberate ourselves, Locke says, we must discern our weaknesses and rigorously train our minds. Whipping ourselves into better shape takes self-denial

---

[36] Corneanu (2011, 145).

and continual effort. As one of Locke's friends, the poet John Dryden, once wrote: "the wise, for cure, on exercise depend."[37]

Locke was a no-nonsense epistemological doctor. Consider a few of his orders. We naturally love our opinions and wish for them to be true. Our tendency should be curbed by "a perfect indifferency," which gives us the freedom to apportion our opinions to the evidence (1996 [1706], 211–213; §34). Being indifferent or impartial is for Locke not a matter of being apathetic, but of loving the truth above all—more than our reputations, possessions, or preconceptions.[38] Locke also prescribes a dose or two of impartial self-examination in order to root out "the prejudices imbibed from education, party, reverence, fashion, interest" (1996 [1706], 184; §10). Prejudice "dresses up falsehood in the likeness of truth, and so dexterously hoodwinks men's minds" (1996 [1706], 184; §10). To recognize our prejudices, Locke says we must watch for signs. Our inability to listen patiently to our opponents in debate, or our strong feeling that we are correct even prior to hearing the other side, signals our prejudice (1996 [1706], 184; §10). He thinks we can expose our biases by rigorous self-study. This seems overly optimistic, though. Locke's debiasing technique will not always help if our powers of self-examination have limits—and surely our powers are limited, just as the Port-Royalists would no doubt remind us. If our self-judgment on some matter is clouded by prejudice, for instance, we may think we are listening to our opponents even when we're actually tuning them out.[39]

To effectively heed reason's guidance, Locke says we must vigilantly attend to our evidence. Unsurprisingly, he diagnoses some disorders of attention (1996 [1706], 223–227; §45). Sometimes our passions redirect our attention toward trivial distractions—Locke uses a "scrap of poetry" as an example. (For a more modern example, suppose you need to be listening to a lecture or reading a book, but you can't stop yourself from obsessively checking for messages on your electronic gadget.) Locke compares the "enchantment" of distraction to being hidden away in a "secret cabinet" where we

---

[37] The line is from Dryden's "Epistle to John Driden of Chesterton" of 1700. Let me add that I follow Corneanu's reading of Locke here. She sums it up as follows:

> the rightful conduct of the understanding for Locke will take the form not of a prescription of formal rules of reasoning but of a remedial regimen of exercises for the mental powers, aimed at training the mind to curb its vanity, master its forwardness and its sluggishness, regulate its assent, and govern its desires. (2011, 154)

[38] Corneanu shows that in Locke's writings the character of "the lover of truth" plays a role much like the Christian Virtuoso in Boyle's.

[39] I discuss recent psychological research on debiasing techniques in Chapter 5.

are mesmerized by the dance of a puppet (1996 [1706], 224; §45). To break the spell and restore our attention to its proper objects, Locke instructs us to counterbalance the meddling passion with another one, "which is an art to be got by study and acquaintance with the passions" (1996 [1706], 226; §45). Intellectual self-improvement requires us to understand our psychological mechanisms and to practice compensating for our poor temperament.

From one angle, Locke's emphasis on willful exertion may sound a bit Cartesian. Both Descartes and Locke think effortful choosing has a place in regulating inquiry. But they put different emphases on where we should make an effort. Descartes thinks we have the ability to directly control our believing; his rules are designed to help us control our assent. Locke denies we have any such doxastic power: "to believe this or that to be true does not depend on our will."[40] On his view, we must attend carefully to the evidence and train up our characters to help us do so by reflex and routine.

Locke's designs for epistemic health are not just for intellectuals like him and his friends. Intellectual self-improvement is the duty of all who are able. Nicholas Wolterstorff observes that, on Locke's view, European people "would have to be tutored differently in the use of their belief-forming dispositions if the cultural crisis was to be overcome—the crisis, namely, of a people schooled to consult tradition who now find their tradition fractured" (1996, xix). Locke approaches epistemological questions as a "culturally engaged philosopher," as Wolterstorff notes (1996, xix). Guiding people's assent by reason has profound cultural importance for Locke. One consequence of assent without evidence is that people are more easily subject to dangerous "enthusiasms," sweeping them up into misguided religious and political movements. Political freedom, one of the central themes in Locke's political writings, is thus bound together with the duty we all have to educate our minds and use them properly.

"Our business here is not to know all things," Locke writes in his *Essay*, "but those which concern our conduct" (1975 [1690], 46; I, i, 6). After taking stock of our public and private roles, we will need to investigate certain political, professional, and religious questions. We will need to know enough to give informed assent, rather than get dragged along by the crowd or blinkered by our biases. That sounds taxing, but Locke tries to downplay the challenge: "He that will enquire out the best books in every science, and inform himself of the most material authors of the several sects of philosophy

---

[40] *A Letter Concerning Toleration*, 1689.

and religion, will not find it an infinite work to acquaint himself with the sentiments of mankind concerning the most weighty and comprehensive subjects" (1996 [1706], 173; §3). Even if educated gentlefolk in the late seventeenth century could have done that hard work, we may wonder whether it is feasible for many of us today. At any rate, we should not doubt that leading the sort of intellectual life Locke envisions would be an arduous undertaking indeed.

7. Making Sense When Things Don't Make Sense

Thus concludes our look at seventeenth-century epistemology. There are other episodes of regulative epistemology from Europe during the same age, to say nothing of other places and times. I said nothing about Nicolas Malebranche or Baruch Spinoza, William Whewell or John Stuart Mill, Pierre Duhem or Bertrand Russell. I leave their ideas aside for now.

I described how a cultural and intellectual crisis engulfed Europe and how philosophers were provoked to reflect on questions concerning epistemological guidance. It was desperately important to them to learn how to rehabilitate inquiry and curate knowledge. Unlike many recent professional epistemologists, they were not satisfied to merely describe knowledge or justified belief, or to refute skepticism about the external world, or to resolve epistemological puzzles and paradoxes. These seventeenth-century philosophers faced an urgent practical problem of clearing away intellectual rubbish and confusion and finding out what was essential for progress, because so much new information about the world was on hand, because old certainties were imperiled, because strange ideas were on the rise, because dogmatic convictions were igniting social unrest and violence. All of these thinkers were at some level wrestling with a simple question that is exceedingly hard to answer: *What will we do with all of this?* Epistemological theorizing in the seventeenth century was part of an attempt to bring order to inquiry and to life. The projects I've noted reveal questions about method, the bearing of human psychology and anthropology on cognitive regulation, the connections between method and character, and the broader social and educational purposes of regulative theorizing.

From our vantage point, we may be impressed by the "multidisciplinary" nature of what these thinkers were trying to do. They mixed together conceptual work, armchair reflection on human psychology, theological doctrines, and careful consideration of the business of inquiry itself. But this was not an attempt to step outside of any "discipline." Indeed, the relevant disciplinary boundaries had not been invented. For these thinkers, it was natural to seek to understand the world using any available means, no holds barred. They hoped their proposals would create a better world. They often pursued their theorizing with enthusiasm and optimism—ignoring the Port-Royalists, bless their pessimistic hearts.

Our historical examples illustrate two different approaches to regulative questions.[41] Philosophers sometimes tried to formulate correct rules or principles for seeking the truth and avoiding error. This is where we find Descartes and the Port-Royalists. Other times philosophers tried to articulate character traits that promote more effective inquiry, perhaps also describing how people can acquire those traits. Here stand Boyle and Locke. Ambitions to generate reliable, truth-conducive rules and ambitions to direct character formation have led to different epistemological proposals. Typically one ambition is emphasized over the other. But Bacon planted a foot firmly in both camps, suggesting how both ambitions can be joined in a single theory. In the next chapter, I say more about the principle- and character-focused approaches and explain how my own regulative recommendations coming up in Chapters 5 through 9 could deliver both sound principles and improved character.

The historical examples also reveal a subtle difference between theories that aim to control the disordered inquirer and ones that aim to remake the inquirer anew. Self-control and self-development are distinct ambitions. Arnauld and Nicole, for example, think we have been ruined by Original Sin and the Fall and so the best we can do is try to follow rules that limit the intellectual lawlessness within our hearts and minds. On the other hand, I find a somewhat more optimistic spirit in philosophers like Bacon and Locke. They seem to presume that regulative ideas can construct a more perfect self. The division is driven in part by differences of opinion on anthropology, theology, and politics.[42] But whichever problem it is that regulative theories seek to remedy—our need for intellectual self-control or our need for better selves—we should not ignore the difference.

---

[41] Wolterstorff (1996) underlines the distinction in his comparison of Locke and Descartes. See also Roberts and Wood (2007, 20–23).

[42] For details on the influence of these broader perspectives on seventeenth-century epistemological theorizing, see Corneanu (2011).

Finally, this historical excursion shows us an argument for a conclusion concerning the present day. We have seen that when society is in the throes of a certain sort of crisis, intellectuals have reason to create regulative ideas. Today—no less than in the seventeenth century—our complicated, uncertain, and interconnected world faces problems concerning knowledge and reasonable belief, trust and authority, method and character, expertise and ignorance. We live in an age of crisis. Like our forebears, we have compelling reason to seek epistemic guidance.

3

How Do Epistemic Principles Guide?

We take the opinions and the knowledge of others into our keeping, and that is all. We must make them our own. We are just like a man who, needing fire, should go and fetch some at his neighbor's house, and, having found a fine big fire there, should stop there and warm himself, forgetting to carry any back home. What good does it do us to have our belly full of meat if it is not digested, if it is not transformed into us, if it does not make us bigger and stronger?

—Michel de Montaigne, "Of Pedantry," 1572–78

For the real environment is altogether too big, too complex, and too fleeting for direct acquaintance. We are not equipped to deal with so much subtlety, so much variety, so many permutations and combinations. And although we have to act in that environment, we have to reconstruct it on a simpler model before we can manage with it. To traverse the world men must have maps of the world.

—Walter Lippman, *Public Opinion*, 1922

I am sorry to observe, that reason and duty together have not so powerful an influence over human conduct, as instinct has in the brute creation.

—Mary Wollstonecraft, *Thoughts on the Education of Daughters*, 1787

Regulative epistemology aims to guide inquiry. We observed in the previous chapter that some regulative theories may focus either on principles or on character. My own proposals in Chapters 5 through 9 feature principles. Using these principles will reveal when some of our beliefs are unreasonable, thereby helping us better know our limits. But first we must turn to important questions. Can principles guide us? If so, how?

It is easy to doubt the power of philosophical principles and reasoning to guide people's thinking. Suppose you wanted to change someone's mind but had only two kinds of tools at your disposal: philosophical principles or social incentives. Principles are written in books or journal articles, and we think about them. Social incentives—from peer pressure to professional inducements, media influence to governmental policies—are woven into our everyday lives. To change someone's opinions, which kind of tool would you choose?

For readers who picked principles, the history of philosophy provides cautionary tales. In *Discourse on Method*, Descartes professed his intention to follow his reason in everything (1985 [1637], 121; ii, 21). For him that meant abiding by rules, one of which is to make careful, exhaustive reviews of evidence so he could "be sure of leaving nothing out" (1985 [1637], 120; ii, 19). Declarations notwithstanding, the truth is that Descartes was often uninterested in studying works by other scholars. Friends, admirers, and critics often sent him copies of books and manuscripts. Usually he ignored them. One biographer noted that "throughout his life he read few books, and he consistently avoided as much as possible the company of those who were regarded as learned" (Clarke 2006, 68). Descartes' inspection of the available evidence was a bit less exacting than the letter of his method might suggest.

The Frenchman is not the only philosopher to have difficulty following principles. In a well-known section from *A Treatise of Human Nature*, David Hume said he had been driven to skeptical doubts after reflecting on the "manifold contradictions and imperfections in human reason" (1.4.7.9). His philosophical thoughts pushed him to reject all of his beliefs, inducing a kind of intellectual paralysis: "Where am I, or what? From what causes do I derive my existence, and to what condition shall I return?" (1.4.7.9). Hume was confounded by these questions, but his crisis was short-lived. After a dinner out with friends and a game of backgammon, his spell of "philosophical melancholy and delirium" had been cured. His doubts were not dispelled by arguments or reasoning. It's just that, once he left his study, his skeptical reflections ceased to grip him. To borrow Hume's words from elsewhere, his own skeptical arguments "admit of no answer and produce no conviction."[1]

As these stories imply, approving of principles (or at least claiming to approve of them) is insufficient to be guided by them. Descartes seemed

---

[1] *An Enquiry Concerning Human Understanding*, 12.15 ("Of the Academical or Sceptical Philosophy"), footnote 32. Hume is commenting on George Berkeley's "merely sceptical" arguments.

to endorse a method he didn't follow often enough. His conduct revealed hypocrisy—saying one thing, doing another. Hume may have suffered from a kind of *akrasia*—believing one thing ought to be done, yet doing another. The prevalence of intellectual failings like hypocrisy and *akrasia* pose a practical problem for regulative epistemology. "Non-regulative" theories do not face a similar problem. They are successful on their own terms when they accurately describe facts about the nature of knowledge, epistemic justification, evidence, and so forth. Non-regulative theories are not supposed to accomplish anything practical. But regulative epistemology seeks to impart normative guidance for inquiry that's practically binding.

For this reason, regulative epistemology faces a challenge. Epistemological theories are abstract things. They are expressed in words or symbols and reflected on during quiet moments. But judgment and inquiry saturate our waking life. We are opinionated, busy, distractible, and animated by the subterranean forces of our nature. Regulative theories are supposed to influence judgment and inquiry, but how can they do that, given the nature of those theories and the vicissitudes of our lives? What must regulative theories be like in order to reliably guide creatures like us? The viability of regulative epistemology depends on good answers to these questions.

As I explained in Chapter 1, we need to take up regulative epistemology's practical perspective and ask how to implement regulative guidance to make actual inquiry better. We must draw on findings from psychologists, education researchers, sociologists, and others to understand how regulative ideas and practices can modify the behavior of flesh-and-blood inquirers. The practical challenge demands an answer. After all, a regulative theory nobody can use is a bust—if it doesn't work in practice, it's no good in theory either. An unusable theory may represent a lofty ideal we would like to live up to, but the point of regulative epistemology is not to articulate unfollowable ideals. Lest we forget why we are here, recall that we want theories to ameliorate intellectual imperfections—that was also the goal of the seventeenth-century thinkers. Ironically, if our regulative theories cannot exert some influence or control over us, then the kind of imperfections that call out for improvement from epistemology may also threaten to make regulative theorizing a pretty pointless business.

Regulative theories come in many forms: principles, rules, guidelines, instructions, checklists, informative examples, detailed descriptions of intellectual virtues and vices, and more. Whatever could improve inquiry is fair game. Consequently, there is no fully general answer to the practical challenge. Questions about how to implement each type of theory will need to be considered one at a time. Since my proposals in Chapters 5 through 9 advance a regulative theory featuring principles, I only consider what principles would need to be like to guide us.

Before I begin, I should air some self-conscious pessimism. I want to understand how epistemology could guide us even though I am unsure whether we can follow along in most of the situations where we should. Why these doubts? One reason is that the failings of Descartes and Hume seem so profoundly ordinary. Intellectual hypocrisy and *akrasia* are the norm, not the exception. Our human nature is not easily reasoned with. Out of the crooked timber of humanity, no straight epistemic agent was ever made. I tend to doubt that our powers of reflection, self-knowledge, and self-control will allow us to reliably follow our principles when we need them—and, regrettably, I don't know of a proven plan, regimen, or twelve-step program for becoming the sort of thinker who can reliably follow epistemic principles.

And yet I hope that social and behavioral scientists will one day identify effective means to implement regulative theories. For now, we should develop theories and try to use them to drive out what John Stuart Mill called "the fogs which hide from us our own ignorance" (1984 [1867], 239). Regulative epistemology is not at present a dazzling sun to lift the fogs, but I believe it can at least illuminate the mists and clouds that surround us. The regulative ideas I'll describe in this book begin to show us our limits.

In this chapter, I discuss the value and nature of regulative principles (section 1). Figuring out how to implement principles calls us to reflect on human cognition. We can't know how principles guide without knowing what they are supposed to guide. To that end, I draw on a standard "dual systems" account of judgment, arguing that principles must be used or deployed by fast, automatic, and unconscious cognition—not only slow, deliberate, and conscious thought (sections 2–3). Then I describe two possible models for how principles could guide us (sections 4–6) and suggest how regulative epistemology might fit into the fabric of our lives (sections 7–8).

1. Epistemic Judgment and Objectivity

Human beings are an opinionated bunch. Some of our most important beliefs involve epistemological claims. "We know it." "Her argument conclusively settles the matter." "This newspaper tends to be more reliable than that one."

"Nobody could possibly know that." "He has no idea what he's talking about!" "I can't trust any of his reports about the meeting, and you shouldn't either." "You still haven't proved your point." "Here's proof!" Every day we make scores of judgments, both explicit and implicit, about the reasonableness of people's attitudes, the weight of the available evidence, the overall balance of complex bodies of evidence, the reliability of belief-forming methods, the strength of arguments, and the like. Epistemic judgments are central to how we reach our opinions and try to make sense of them to ourselves and others.

Being judgmental on such matters comes naturally to us—always getting it right does not. An important job for epistemology is to articulate and defend principles (or rules, norms, or guidelines) that can improve the accuracy of our epistemic judgments. We need to improve our naïve, untutored epistemic judgments with principles that withstand reflective scrutiny. One consequence is that regulative theories don't necessarily add something completely new and different to inquiry. Consider what I mean. When we develop regulative theories, we may seek to augment ideas and habits already in place. Here's the idea expressed in Baconian or Cartesian rhetoric, with a "Western frontier" twist. Before the epistemologists' wagons rolled in, there was in these parts a dilapidated shantytown, no pristine wilderness range. The old town was a mess of plywood, rusty sheet metal, and bricks—all of the unreliable practices and unreflective assumptions behind our unaided inquiry. The Baconian and Cartesian ambition is to rip down the slapdash construction, recycle what's helpful, and use sound methods to raise up some respectable buildings.

Inquirers desperately need good principles for making epistemic judgments. That isn't to say there are no justified epistemic judgments prior to justified principles.[2] The idea is more modest than that. In many cases, drawing upon good principles will make our epistemic judgments more reasonable—based on good reasons—and more reliably formed—accurate over a long run of trials—than they would be otherwise.

To begin to see why, note that we are naturally prone to err on many significant epistemic judgments. When our personal and emotional investments get tangled up with our thinking, fair-mindedness may be difficult. If we expect or desire that a proposition p is true, then our judgment about whether

---

[2] Roderick Chisholm (1973) used "methodism" to name the thesis that there can't be justified judgments prior to justified principles. He argued that methodism induces widespread skepticism. The alternative to methodism, Chisholm said, allows at least some epistemic judgments to be justified in advance of recognizing justified criteria for justified judgments, a thesis he called "particularism."

we reasonably believe or know p may be based on our expectation or desire, not merely the relevant evidence or recognized facts (Kunda 1990; Ditto and Lopez 1992; Nickerson 1998). But whether an epistemic judgment is correct or reasonable does not hinge on what we consciously expect or feel. (We can set aside cases where our expectations and desires are relevant to the correctness or justification of the judgments.) Basing our epistemic judgments on something other than evidence is normally going to be an unreliable route to the truth. Ideally, epistemic principles drive a wedge between our prior beliefs and expectations concerning p, on the one hand, and our epistemic judgments concerning p, on the other. Principles help to ensure that our epistemic judgments are sensitive to our evidence, rather than irrelevant factors. Good principles are not a foolproof way to eliminate errors in epistemic judgment, but they are often the best we've got.

I witnessed an illustration of the value of abstract principles some years ago. I sat in the audience for an academic philosophy lecture, near the back. The speaker began by writing some simple-looking reasoning on the blackboard. Curiously, the speaker said nothing about his main thesis—he didn't even note the topic of his talk. After explaining the reasoning, he paused to ask everyone a question: Did we all agree that the reasoning had established its conclusion? Almost everyone appeared to sign on, though a few audience members were loath to either agree or disagree without knowing what was coming next. But the speaker felt he'd reached something like a consensus, so he finally unfurled his main thesis—an explosively controversial claim about political philosophy. The reasoning we had just endorsed could be used in an argument against a popular political view. Looking around the seminar room, I saw some audience members were stunned. They felt they'd been tricked. They seemed to believe it was illegitimate for the guest speaker to have scored a key premise in his argument without first saying what it was for. Maybe they had a fair complaint, but probably not.

Surprise! When we come to the table already invested in opinions, it's helpful for us to appeal to general, abstract principles and to *try* to momentarily ignore the opinions that might be threatened by the principles. Sometimes that may be impossible—and some of us may feel annoyed by the guest speaker. But if we are unwilling to subject our views to this sort of scrutiny, how is intellectual life more than a dog and pony show?

Principles can prevent our prior opinions from dogmatically calling the shots in our intellectual life, but they may also serve other ends. Sometimes we lack settled opinions about a topic; principles may draw our attention to what's relevant for making up our minds. Sometimes we discover a tension or conflict in our set of beliefs, and principles may help us determine how to react. In general, good epistemic principles bring us clarity about which epistemic judgments are correct. They promise us a measure of impartiality.

The benefits of accuracy and reliability in making epistemic judgments are clear. Supposing we are responsive to reasons, when we recognize that our well-supported principle implies that one of our beliefs is unreasonable, we will drop that belief. We can improve our judgments in general by improving our epistemic judgments in particular. If we are guided by good principles, we can bring better order to our sometimes untidy intellectual affairs.

Hopefully, regulative epistemology can deliver principles that guide us in a wide range of situations. Here is one commonplace type of situation where the principles I develop in this book are meant to apply. Commonly, we recognize that many of our confident, firmly-held beliefs are controversial. We are deliberating about how we should believe. We wonder whether we are reasonable, whether anyone can know the right answers, whether our opponents know something we've missed. How can we figure this out? What sort of facts should we take into account? Good principles will help us reach more reasonable and reliable judgments.

Before I say more about how we can be *guided by* principles, it's worth clarifying the basic idea a little. Let's consider regulative principles that require or permit a particular doxastic attitude (belief, disbelief, or suspension of judgment) or response under particular conditions. In particular, think about principles that say someone should have an attitude in particular circumstances. To a first approximation, we can say that someone is guided by such a principle only if the causal reason why she has the attitude in those circumstances includes her holding or taking for granted the principle. Suppose you have the attitude in those circumstances because you are biased. If you did not have that bias, however, you would not have held the attitude then and there, despite the fact that you hold the principle at issue. In such a case, your attitude perfectly conforms to the principle's recommendation, but there is no meaningful sense in which you are "guided by" the principle. The fact that your attitude fits the principle's advice is a fluke. Being guided by your principle means, at the very least, that you do what it advises because you hold or take for granted the principle, not because of accidental or irrelevant influences such as your biases. The idea here is similar to a common distinction from moral philosophy: conforming to a moral rule versus merely acting in accordance with the rule. The notion of being guided by a regulative theory can be sharpened, but what I've said will suffice for now.

2. Two Sources of Epistemic Judgment

Regulative principles promise to make our epistemic judgments more accurate and reliably formed. Better epistemic judgments can improve inquiry. But recall the worry we began with: How can an abstract thing like a principle influence us? To make sense of the question, we must think about human cognition.

Psychologists and cognitive scientists commonly divide cognitive processes into two systems, normally called System 1 and System 2.[3] System 1 involves fast, automatic, and unconscious processing, whereas System 2 processing is slower, deliberate, and conscious. We lean hard on System 2 while solving brain-teasing puzzles, balancing our monthly budget, and studying philosophy books. System 1 allows us to rapidly and effortlessly categorize faces as friends or strangers, throw a beach ball, and track objects in our immediate environment. Cognition is more than what we are aware of in reflective episodes. It also includes a labyrinthine underworld that is unknown to us by reflection alone (Wilson 2002). Crucially, the divide may be bridged: System 1 can influence System 2, and vice versa, and skills that once required System 2 processes can with practice become part of System 1 processing.

Some readers may feel that the dual-systems lingo is a bit boring. Is there a more vivid way to talk about the mind's twin powers? Jonathan Haidt offers some alternative language. The mind is divided, Haidt tells us, like a rider on top of an elephant: "The rider is our conscious reasoning—the stream of words and images of which we are fully aware. The elephant is the other 99% of mental processes—the ones that occur outside of awareness but that actually govern most of our behavior" (2012, xxi). Haidt notes that the rider is perched atop the beast and appears to be the boss. Don't mess with this mahout! But the rider is outmatched by the mighty elephant. In conflicts over which way to go, the rider normally loses. All of us are familiar with situations where our elephant lords it over our rider—we tried and failed to break a bad

---

[3] Kahneman (2011) offers an accessible introduction to the dual-systems framework. For a more technical discussion, see Evans and Stanovich (2013).

habit, or felt nervous about public speaking, or couldn't stop from bursting out unbecomingly in laughter. Blaming some of our failings on a headstrong pachyderm may feel gratifying. In fairness, though, the creature is often good at moving its feet where the rider wants them to go. The rider may catch its attention—with a whip, heel-kick, or tug on the ear. The rider can set a new course or train the elephant to react differently to the path. But, as we will soon see, the elephant also influences the rider.

A dual-systems picture of cognition helps us think about the origin of epistemic judgments. System 1 and System 2 each produce epistemic judgments. This model allows us to distinguish between two broad types of epistemic judgments by noting their origin in each system.

Epistemic judgments are sometimes produced in part by System 2: slow, reflective, deliberate cognition, the rider. *Reflective epistemic judgments* result from reasoning that makes use of epistemic principles (or norms or rules). These reflective judgments require us to consciously consider evidence, make inferences, and reach a judgment. At least one conscious step is required for an epistemic judgment to count as reflective. For instance, we could explicitly take into account relevant information and then infer a conclusion (the epistemic judgment). Sometimes reflection on a principle can license the inference from our information to the epistemic judgment. But reflection on the principle is not strictly required; a principle may also license a thinker's inference from information to epistemic judgment even when the thinker does not consciously reflect on the principle during reasoning (Pollock and Cruz 1999, 128).

System 1, the elephant, also produces epistemic judgments. These judgments "suddenly appear" in our consciousness without any explicit reasoning or reflection. These are *intuitive epistemic judgments*. They are accessible to consciousness, but the processes that give rise to them ordinarily are not; at any rate, intuitive epistemic judgments are not the result of explicit reasoning. Without any reflection or deliberation, most of us can come to judge that we know or reasonably believe many things. Intuition is an important source for epistemic judgments because we often have to make epistemic evaluations in a hurry.

I leave to the side the question of whether our epistemic judgments are *typically* or *for the most part* produced by reflection or intuition. Instead, I want to understand how to design regulative principles we can reliably follow, given that epistemic judgments are produced by both reflection and intuition.

3. Two Systems Are Better than One

Let's play a little association game. When I say "philosophical principles,"
what do you think of? Probably things like reasoning, deliberation, and reflection. The very idea of principles seems to be tied up with System 2 processes, and so it may be surprising that both System 1 and 2 are required to
implement regulative principles. As a matter of fact, without both sources
of epistemic judgment in our corner, we won't be able to follow our principles consistently. Regulative epistemology must say something about how
principles are connected to habits, abilities, and intellectual character. Let me
explain.

Imagine that all of our epistemic judgments were reflective—ones formed
by conscious reasoning, deliberate weighing of evidence, teasing out the
implications of our principles. This slow, effortful work would get burden-
some. Just recall the central place of reason and reasoning in the theories of
early modern thinkers such as Descartes. For better or worse, Descartes may
not have followed his method as studiously as he let on—apparently, he often
ignored his rule to review everything carefully and completely so he could be
sure of omitting nothing. Maybe he could have done better by his method.
But how? What could he have done differently?

Here's where a little counterfactual history comes in handy. Imagine that
Descartes had regularly followed his rules and that doing so had become
"second nature" to him. Let's envision him regularly applying the rules to
intellectual problems and receiving feedback on his success and failure to
do so. Whenever he fails, he redoubles his efforts to do it right. Eventually,
Descartes no longer needs to reflect explicitly on the rules in order to use
them. In this alternative history, Descartes' elephant—System 1 processes—
becomes trained to stop from wandering from the methodological high road
and rolling over in a ditch. Descartes might have better abided by his method
if both types of cognition had been cooperative partners.[4]

John Locke recognized how non-reflective cognition could help us
follow principles. He wanted to make following epistemic rules a matter of
habit, denying that conscious reflection on rules can properly regulate assent: "practice must settle the habit of doing without reflecting on the rule"
(1996 [1706], 175; §4). Translated into dual-systems lingo, the Lockean idea

---

[4] Descartes could accept the point. He notes in *Discourse on Method* that "in practicing this
method my mind was little by little *getting into the habit* of conceiving its objects more rigorously and
more distinctly" (1985 [1637], 121, ii, 21, emphasis added).

is that System 1 underwrites the good character needed to reliably follow rules and System 2 underwrites the practice needed to form such a character. Practice demands consciously reflecting on the rule, but the well-tempered reasoner will follow the rule without being mindful of it.[5]

Some intellectuals may be quick to disdain intuitive, automatic cognition. (If we decide to point out the irony, let's at least be nice about it.) But System 1 keeps inquiry and judgment humming right along. Our powers of reflection and deliberation help us with investigation because System 1 primes us to respond appropriately to the situation. We can breathe a sigh of relief—our epistemic affairs are complex and we couldn't possibly reflect on all of the details all the time. Moreover, System 2 is fallible and liable to make mistakes, but a well-trained System 1 may prevent some of those errors. Generally, System 2 alone is not up to the task of managing an intellectual life. The rider may think she runs the show, but it's the elephant that moves the rider to reflect and deliberate when the moment is right. System 2 needs System 1. A similar lesson was recognized by Blaise Pascal: "Reason acts slowly, and with so many perspectives, on so many principles, which must be always present, that it constantly falls asleep or wanders, when it fails to have all its principles present. Feeling does not act in this way; it acts instantaneously, and is always ready to act" (2004 [1670], 202; S661/L821). We all place considerable responsibility for normal operations upon intuitive cognition. System 1 is the unsung beast of intellectual burden.

The importance of System 1 suggests that regulative theorists should propose harnessing the power of fast, automatic, and unconscious processes to influence epistemic judgments. How could regulative theories make use of System 1 processes? It's helpful here to compare principle-focused regulative projects with character-focused ones. In some sense, the comparison is inapt, because character theories may not be designed to directly guide what I've called epistemic judgment. Even so, character theories assign both reflective and intuitive cognition a natural role to play. For instance, many philosophers, historical and contemporary, have claimed that a trait such as the love of knowledge (or of truth) is part of the virtuous mind. Love of knowledge is grounded in fast and automatic processes, though that trait also implicates slower, reflective processes. Love of knowledge disposes us to consciously reflect and deliberate in certain circumstances, but

---

[5] Compare to Aristotle's account of moral habituation discussed in Burnyeat (1980). For discussion of the notion of habit in psychology, see Wood (2017).

reflection and deliberation may help us acquire the trait of loving knowledge. Character theorists have a natural way to join together System 1 and System 2 processing.

How can principle-centered theories enlist help from both cognitive systems? One possibility is that regulative principles can shape intellectual life only through explicit, conscious reasoning—that is, by producing reflective epistemic judgments. If that were correct, the usefulness of regulative principles would be seriously limited. We would lack sufficient resources to use principles as often as we need them; time and attention are in short supply. Using our powers of reflection to control or constrain the high-pressure outflow of our epistemic judgments is like trying to catch a rainstorm in a bucket. Inevitably and often, we form epistemic judgments without the luxury of pausing to reflect on what we are doing. While sitting in a café, you absentmindedly overhear a heated political debate; you casually judge that these people have dubious political beliefs. This is an entirely common sort of situation. If regulative principles were only able to correct epistemic judgment through reflection, then our epistemic judgments would be beyond improvement a great deal of the time.[6]

So if reflection is an essential ingredient for following principles, then principles won't offer us broad enough help in many ordinary situations. Principles won't bear the weight of regulative epistemology's practical burden. Abstract principles may help during quiet moments of contemplation, when we are like Hume in his study. But how can principles assist us in the midst of life's hustle and bustle, when we are out on the town reveling in a game of backgammon?

4. Mirroring Principles

Lucky for us, conscious reasoning about principles is not the only way for principles to guide. An analogy will suggest why. Consider how grammatical

---

[6] The point here is related to Alvin Goldman's observation that epistemologists' rules are normally "idealized," specifying courses of doxastic action which most people will be unable to carry out. Goldman says regulative theories must provide rules that can be executed "given only some minimum of resources all normal humans possess" (1978, 513). My suggestion is that the actual range of our epistemic judgment in ordinary life far surpasses the scope of the explicit reasoning we could engage in, and so if regulative principles can only influence judgment through explicit reasoning, they won't be executable in Goldman's sense.

rules are related to judgments concerning the grammaticality of sentences.[7] A child competent in grammar is no grammarian. She need not have heard her parents or teachers state the rules, and she need not be able to work out the rules on her own. Yet the grammatical rules still guide the child's competence in some sense. She has some implicit grasp of them. When the child grows up and explicitly learns the grammatical rules, her judgments will ordinarily be guided by the rules in an automatic, unconscious way. She will spot an ungrammatical sentence without consciously thinking about the rule or rules that have been violated. The crucial point is that our grammatical competence is underwritten by a variety of cognitive states only some of which require conscious reflection on grammatical rules. Regulative epistemologists can learn something useful from the analogy. I'll argue that regulative principles, not unlike grammatical rules, can guide our epistemic judgments even when we do not reflect on them.[8]

Epistemic principles contain information. The information can be encoded or expressed in the world in many forms. It may be printed in a book, spray painted on a brick wall, sung in plainchant, reflected upon in conscious awareness, or captured in short-term memory. When a principle's information is encoded in cognitive states, those states become what I will call "mirrors" of the abstract principle. The information encoded in cognitive states may mirror the principle's information to some greater or lesser extent, and so we can talk about degrees of correspondence between the mirror and the principle. Mirroring can also explain the child who is competent in grammar. Her mind's cognitive states mirror grammatical rules, even though she can't yet formulate those rules.

Here is what mirroring gives us. When we consciously reflect on a principle, it is mirrored by a conscious state. Conscious states provide one type of mirror, but there are others, as we find in the cognitive states underlying various kinds of memory. Importantly, a principle can be mirrored by cognitive states that do not involve any conscious reflection on the principle. Once a principle is mirrored, its information may play a role in cognition even when we aren't reflecting on the principle. Thus, we should not assume that since epistemic principles are expressed in words or symbols, they can

---

[7] This sort of analogy is commonplace in discussions of the relationship between various kinds of judgment and rules: see Churchland (1996, 100), Pollock and Cruz (1999, 128), and Webb (2004, 56–57).

[8] Here I am indebted to Horgan and Timmons (2007). They defend the centrality of moral principles in moral judgment by making a similar point about the relationship between moral principles and embodied information in cognitive systems.

shape cognition only through conscious reasoning. Our principles can guide epistemic judgments even when we are not reflecting on them.

So far, so abstract. Let's get concrete. What sorts of cognitive states encode principles and enable the mirrored information to influence inquiry, all without requiring us to consciously reason or reflect on the principle? I think there could be such states, but what could they be like? I will describe the dispositions that undergird two types of mirrors.

5. Intuitive Expertise

The school gymnasium is packed with precocious preteens and parents swelling with pride. Fifty chess boards on little tables are neatly arranged in a circle. Everyone is here to watch a chess grandmaster play fifty students from local schools—simultaneously. Students focus sternly on their boards, maybe trying to look brainy. The grandmaster shuffles around the tables and moves one piece at a time. Quickly glancing at another board, she pushes her pawn, unceremoniously adding, "Checkmate in five." Five moves later, the first ankle-biter is done. A few hours later, the grandmaster has beaten them all. A few students fight to hold off tears.

The chess grandmaster is an astonishing sight to behold. But there is nothing mystical or otherworldly about her, as the cognitive and social scientist Herbert Simon observed: "The situation has provided a cue; this cue has given the expert access to information stored in memory, and the information provides the answer. Intuition is nothing more and nothing less than recognition" (1992, 155). Simon studied chess expertise and became convinced that a grandmaster's feats use the same type of cognitive powers we all have. Without furrowing our brows, we can solve new problems using our prior knowledge and experience.[9]

Locke said that practice would let us acquire the habit of following epistemic rules. Chess is no different. Simon says: "A large part of the chess master's expertise lies in his or her intuitive (recognition) capabilities, based, in turn, on large amounts of stored and indexed knowledge derived from training and experience" (1992, 156). In other words, fast, automatic System 1 processes can be trained up so that the rules guiding chess play, as well

---

[9] The "Dreyfus and Dreyfus" model of skill acquisition aims to explain the development of intuitive expertise. Dreyfus (2004) applies the model to learning chess.

as knowledge of good strategies, get to be "mirrored" in various cognitive states. The chess master's long practice transformed her into what psychologist Daniel Kahneman calls an *intuitive expert*. As Kahneman notes, accurate "intuitions develop when experts have learned to recognize familiar elements in a new situation and to act in a manner that is appropriate to it" (2011, 12). Intuitive experts can make reliable judgments about issues in their wheelhouse without conscious reasoning.

Inquirers may gain intuitive expertise in the use of epistemic principles. They may spontaneously recognize what their principles recommend in some situation without any reasoning or reflection on the principles. Practice regimens can train up their cognitive dispositions to "mirror" their principles. Once the principles are encoded in System 1, the relevant information can be prompted or cued in the right situations. Then the mirror states can guide the intuitive epistemic judgment.

Intuitive expertise has some drawbacks. For one, the process of encoding or internalizing information in System 1 processes must respect our cognitive limits. We can't become intuitive experts when the principles are too complex for us. Chess masters gain intuitive expertise with traditional moves in chess, but few or none could manage to do so for a chess-like game with cumbersomely awkward rules. Take the following rule I just made up: on Monday through Wednesday, a Queen moves any number of vacant squares in any direction, but on Thursday and Friday it may only move four squares diagonally, and on Saturday only three horizontally, and on Sunday only four vertically. (Got that?) A game with mixed-up, hydra-headed rules like that will foil aspiring intuitive experts, because those rules can't be grasped and applied using ordinary feats of working memory. The same goes for epistemic principles. Inquirers can't become intuitive experts with just any principle. Thus, to mirror principles successfully, we need to take into account inquirers' cognitive capacities.[10]

A second drawback is that intuitive expertise may look from the inside a lot like unreliable intuitive judgment-producing processes. Consider an example. Cognitive psychologists have discovered the "affect heuristic" which produces intuitive judgment directly through feelings of liking or disliking (Slovic et al. 2002). Disliking a person may incline you toward negative intuitive judgments about his or her epistemic capacities as an inquirer. But your judgment produced by the (sometimes unreliable) affect heuristic can

---

[10] Goldman (1978) underscores the need to accommodate regulative theories to our limitations.

be hard to distinguish from the manifestation of your (highly reliable) expert epistemic intuition. What is the difference from your perspective? To address this sort of problem, you might compare your intuitive judgment to your reflective judgment, calibrating the former by the latter. Unfortunately, sometimes your intuition-skewing biases will not be readily apparent to you, and so you won't know you need to calibrate.[11]

Intuitive expertise is imperfect, but it offers a way to implement regulative principles in situations where we do not reflect on principles. Let me turn to a different way to follow principles.

6. Epistemic Pictures

When the real things are not around, we make do with representations and substitutes. Perhaps you wonder what the San Rafael Valley in southern Arizona looks like. You are nowhere nearby and have never been there yourself, but photographs of that magnificent high desert valley can satisfy your curiosity. Or suppose it is my daughter's birthday party and I want the John Coltrane Sextet, circa 1965, to perform. They can't make it. But one of their recordings (*Live in Seattle*), turned up suitably loud, is a substitute. Representations help us make the most of our limits. When we can't reflect on our epistemic principles, a kind of representation may come in handy.

As I have noted, cognitive states can encode a principle's information to a greater or lesser degree. A principle can be "mirrored" by states that only partially capture its information. A partial mirror is not a perfect copy of the principle, but it is a fair approximation. In many situations, partial mirrors

---

[11] How does the process of calibration work? It's fairly clear in the case of the chess grandmaster. Watch her defeat her tween opponents in the "simul" match. Her intuitive expertise is well-calibrated; otherwise she wouldn't be victorious. She became well-calibrated by repeated practice with feedback on her performance. But what about the would-be intuitive epistemic expert? If he has no forum to prove his mettle, his intuitive judgments may fall wide of the mark without anyone knowing it. What he needs, then, are concrete situations to test his epistemic judgment. For instance, suppose the would-be intuitive expert could render judgments, intuitive and reflective, on many determinate cases where his principles happen to apply. If we had a baseline of correctness to appeal to, then we could measure the accuracy of both his intuitive and reflective judgments. With practice and feedback on his performance, the would-be intuitive epistemic expert could come to calibrate his intuitive skill.

All of this calls for further exploration. What norms of correct judgment can we appeal to? How do we calibrate "in the wild"? If a permissive response to evidence in some situation is permitted, in the sense that multiple attitudes are justified, how does calibration work? Such questions fall squarely within regulative epistemology's purview, but I won't take them up here. (I am grateful to Peter Seipel for prompting me to say more about calibration.)

are similar enough to the principles to help guide us, and they accomplish this without requiring any actual reflection on the principles. I call these cognitive states *epistemic pictures*.

Here is an example. Looking back on his early years as a professional philosopher, Peter van Inwagen wrote:

> I can remember having a picture of the cosmos, the physical universe, as a self-subsistent thing, something that is just *there* and requires no explanation. When I say "having a picture," I am trying to describe a state of mind that could be called up whenever I desired and was centered on a certain mental image. This mental image—it somehow represented the whole world—was associated with a felt conviction that what the image represented was self-subsistent. I can still call the image to mind (I *think* it's the same image), and it still represents the whole world, but it is now associated with a felt conviction that what it represents is *not* self-subsistent, that it must depend on something else, something that is not represented by any feature of the image, and must be, in some way that the experience leaves indeterminate, radically different in kind from what the image represents. (1994, 35)

For van Inwagen, a picture is a representational state. I presume a picture can be a mental picture, involving "seeing with the mind's eye," but it need not involve any visualizing or sensuous mental imagery. A picture can be a "conceptual metaphor," where the abstract is concretized in something we more easily grasp—such as thinking about politics within a nation state in terms of a "strict father" or, alternatively, a "nurturing parent" (Lakoff 2002). A picture can come rapidly into consciousness when we deliberate or when a non-deliberative cue is triggered. A picture is not constituted by conscious reasoning, though someone who has a picture may reason about the picture to determine whether it is consistent with particular claims. We do not acquire a picture because of our reasoning either; we can get it without proceeding through any inferential steps. A picture's worth a thousand words, but those words need not be in our minds.

Van Inwagen's picture was of "the whole world," but pictures may represent many other things besides. For example, many people have a picture of humankind's current-day technological power; the environmental impact humans have had on some place; the terrifying power of a rip current pulling you out into deep water; and so on. Pictures are intertwined with our practical lives; they allow us to act and choose. But they also play a role in philosophical discussions from ethics to metaphysics. Philosophers normally set in the foreground reasoning and arguments, effectively ignoring the pictures that hide in the background. It is our pictures that often make us feel that particular premises and tacit assumptions are compelling or dubious.

There is more to say about pictures, but here's how they can help address regulative epistemology's practical problem. Just as a desolate high desert valley can appear in a photograph, regulative principles may come in picture form. What I call epistemic pictures represent or stand in for principles. They are not exact copies. Pictures lack the informational richness of the principles they mirror. Pictures are like easy-to-use principles—stick shift is to automatic transmission as principles are to epistemic pictures. What's crucial is that pictures can be encoded in our cognition in ways that do not require reflection on the principle itself. Consequently, pictures can guide our epistemic judgments even when we are not reflecting on principles. And so in situations where principles would offer us recommendations, we may be directed by the pictures instead. They can "pop" into mind when our fast, automatic, and non-deliberative cognition detects relevant situations. Cognition may be trained to prime us to have the right picture at the right time.

The lines from van Inwagen suggest how a picture could encode a broad metaphysical framework—namely, that the cosmos is all there was, is, and ever will be. But what sort of picture encodes an epistemological principle? Here are two examples to illustrate. Take the principle that the justification for believing a proposition p that someone receives by testimony cannot increase when she further propagates p through testimony. Leaving aside the question of whether this principle is correct, here's a corresponding epistemic picture. When a testifier tells you that some claim is true, some epistemic juice is poured into your glass; but when you pour that juice into your friend's glass, you can't pour a greater amount than you were initially given— indeed, you might accidentally spill some and leave your friend with less than you had originally.[12] As a second example, consider a principle suggested in G. E. Moore's anti-skeptical writings, summed up by Thomas Kelly: "in resolving conflicts among one's beliefs, one should always favor those beliefs of which one is more confident over those beliefs of which one is less confident" (2005b, 191). A picture of that principle might involve some horses racing

---

[12] Andrew Bailey shared this example.

toward a finish line; the horse that crosses the line first is the one you should favor. Importantly, these are brief descriptions of pictures, not the pictures themselves. Pictures are mental representations. But the descriptions naturally suggest representations that can be more readily brought to mind than the principles to which the representations correspond.

Once an epistemic picture is fixed in our mind, it can produce intuitive or reflective epistemic judgments. We might consciously entertain the picture but form the epistemic judgment immediately or non-inferentially; it's not reflection on the picture that gives rise to the judgment.[13] Or we may explicitly reason about the picture and then infer the epistemic judgment. Either way, a picture influences our inquiry through rapid access to some of the principle's information. Like intuitive expertise, a picture is another way to encode information from a principle without reflecting on the principle. But unlike intuitive expertise, which is a judgment-producing process, a picture is a kind of representation. As such, multiple pictures of the same principle can differ in the detail they represent.

Just as we found with intuitive expertise, pictures can have drawbacks. For example, since a picture does not include all of the principle's information, it will prove unreliable in certain situations where a more subtle, information-rich response would be best. Sometimes only the real thing will do. But inquirers can be trained to recognize the limits of their pictures and switch over to reflection as needed.

In Chapters 5 through 9, I defend various epistemic principles. What I'll say about these principles will suggest to readers some epistemic pictures to which the principles correspond. But I can't fashion suitable mental representations—the pictures themselves—in anyone's mind but my own. Getting those representations requires reflection and effort. That said, I want to address two relevant questions. How in general do we become intuitive experts with principles? And how do we acquire pictures of principles? These questions concern human behavior and interventions that modify behavior. They bridge the disciplines of epistemology and education.

As I proceed, let me remind the reader of the puzzle I opened this chapter with. It is easy to doubt that philosophical principles are powerful enough to guide us. But suppose we want to change someone's opinion. Would we

---

[13] This case is similar to intuitive expertise, except in the following respect: the basis in cognition for the epistemic judgment is a mental representation (the picture) rather than unconscious processes.

choose to use principles or social incentives such as peer pressure or monetary inducements? The answer I prefer is decidedly ambivalent: both.

7. Bedtime Stories and Behavioral Interventions

Fred Dretske once remarked that "epistemology is ten bedtime stories."[14] An insightful contributor to the field, Dretske was affectionately poking fun at epistemologists' practice of devising fanciful examples to test their analyses and principles. Take just two:

> Jones owns a Chevrolet van, drives to Notre Dame on a football Saturday, and unthinkingly parks in one of the many spaces reserved for the football coach. Naturally the coach's minions tow Jones' van away and, as befits such lese-majesty, destroy it. By a splendid piece of good luck, however, Jones has won the Varsity Club's Win-a-Chevrolet-Van contest, although he hasn't yet heard the good news. Smith asks Jones what sort of automobile he owns; Jones replies, both honestly and truthfully, "A Chevrolet van." Jones' true belief that he owns such a van is true just by accident . . . , however, and hence does not constitute knowledge. (Plantinga 1997, 141)

> A person takes a pill from a bucket of 10,000 pills. One of the pills induces blue-green color reversal—that is, it makes blue things look green and green things look blue—while the rest of the pills are inert. The pill-taker knows this. As it happens, he takes an inert pill that leaves his color perception mechanisms undisturbed. He looks at a blue patch and forms the belief that it is blue. We may well be inclined to count him as knowing that he is seeing a blue patch. And we will of course count him as knowing that the patch he is seeing looks blue. But we will be far less open to the suggestion that he can deduce and come to know that the pill he took was inert. (Hawthorne 2004, 4)

Are these bedtime stories? I attempted to test Dretske's hypothesis. First, I randomly sampled epistemology examples from recent articles and books. The examples I collected feature the usual suspects: a man with ten coins in his pocket, an observer looking at barn façades in a farm field, visitors to a zoo

---

[14] Mark Timmons is my source for this quip from Dretske.

looking at a mule cleverly disguised to look like a zebra, two diners at a restaurant who disagree about how to split the bill correctly, and a lonely brain-in-a-vat. For several weeks, I read the examples to my young daughter before her bedtime. I wanted to disguise the examples, so I slipped them in alongside old standbys like *Goodnight Moon* and *Brown Bear, Brown Bear, What Do You See?* and *Little Red Riding Hood*. None of the epistemology examples passed the test. My daughter asked for "good stories" instead. Tough crowd.

Dretske still got it right. Epistemologists spin bedtime yarns. Although the proper demographic target market for bedtime stories—children like my daughter—is unimpressed and not falling asleep, let's ignore that. I am going to take Dretske's endearing little portrayal of epistemology and explain how it may turn out to be the literal truth about regulative epistemology.

Ancient Stoics sought to lead good lives by following regimens of philosophical training. Some of them told themselves bedtime stories. They tried to meditate on the day's activity in the light of their principles and ideals. Seneca the Younger (4 BCE–65 CE), the Roman philosopher, statesman, and orator, reported that his teacher, Quintus Sextius, would meditate on questions at the end of each day: "What bad habit have you cured today? What fault have you resisted? In what respect are you better?" Like his teacher, Seneca practiced nightly self-examination:

> When the light has been removed from sight, and my wife, long aware of my habit, has become silent, I scan the whole of my day and retrace all my deeds and words. I conceal nothing from myself, I omit nothing. For why should I shrink from any of my mistakes, when I may commune thus with myself? (1928, 341; "On Anger," III)

The Stoics used storytelling and reflection to bring philosophical principles to bear on life.

In the long tradition of regulative epistemology, the Stoic idea shows up in various guises.[15] Descartes in the *Meditations* describes himself as "withdrawing into solitude" (2000 [1641], 104; I.18), a monk retreating to the desert of the self. He invited his readers to follow him. Historians observe that Descartes was reusing elements from religious exercises he had learned as a

---

[15] For discussion of practices designed to repair imperfect minds in early modern English philosophy, see Corneanu (2011). Roberts and Wood (2007) use stories or at least story-like literary techniques to characterize intellectual virtues.

young student in the Jesuit college at La Flèche. The founder of the Jesuits, Iñigo López de Loyola (1491–1556), wrote a sort of devotional handbook, *Spiritual Exercises*, which was designed to help spiritual directors guide their charges through a set of contemplative exercises. In Descartes' writings, the themes of meditation and solitude are no accident. Descartes wanted his audience to do more than just read words on a page: he intended them to grasp his principles and arguments through mindful reflection and study of the self. As historian Anthony Grafton noted, "Descartes mastered and internalized the Jesuits' technology of self-scrutiny" (2000, 17).[16]

As intellectual life rushes past, we are often unable to reflect on our principles. To benefit from them, I have suggested we develop intuitive expertise and epistemic pictures, or some other way to mirror principles. The trick is to understand how to attain the cognitive dispositions that underwrite mirrors. A long history of exercises and regimens testifies to the fact that good intentions or sheer willpower won't transform us into principle-following inquirers. We must summon processes that shape and sustain cognitive dispositions. We need appropriate rituals, regimens, and relationships. What we need is culture—the manifold signs, images, and practices we use to make sense of ourselves and our world—and society—the bonds and associations tying us together. We must conscript culture and society into the service of our epistemological ends.

How can these processes make us into thinkers who follow principles? Seeing that culture and society construct people is far easier than knowing how to harness these forces to remake ourselves. But oftentimes culture and socialization are consciously used to forge people's characters. These efforts can have astounding effects. Consider chess grandmasters, avant-garde jazz musicians, longline trappers in northern Canada, or war-zone doctors and nurses. These lives do not appear from nowhere. They are made, to borrow Francis Bacon's expression, "by custom and exercise duly applied" (1996 [1596–1604], 114).

My concern is to understand how culture and socialization can be the crucible in which we can become principle-following inquirers. Where shall we begin? A first point is that, obviously, this happens. Principles are mirrored in

---

[16] Vendler (1989) and Grafton (2000) discuss Descartes' debt to Jesuit spiritual exercises. Hatfield (1986) recognizes Descartes' Jesuit influence and also shows how an Augustinian tradition of cognitive exercises is in the mix. In his *Confessions*, Augustine of Hippo had designs to eliminate sensory things from the mind in order for it to rise to God. Hatfield explains how this radical "purging" of the senses informed Descartes' project.

all sorts of domains. So why, the reader might wonder, can't we just go ahead and emulate the Stoics, pursuing epistemic self-examination through bedtime stories? Why not steal away to a stove-heated room for our latter-day Cartesian meditations? Won't this give us the right cognitive dispositions?

The trouble is that the effectiveness of such practices, if they were ever effective at all, is unlikely to translate across the ages. We can't quiz ourselves with a few questions before bedtime and then one morning awake as Stoics, any more than we can become chess masters by gazing idly at a chessboard for an hour each day. If Stoic bedtime stories were effective for the making of Stoics, that was because the stories were woven into a tapestry of ideas, habits, and influences. Becoming a Stoic in the Greco-Roman world meant being rooted in a specific community, surrounded by conversation, role models, important texts, and social inducements. As Pierre Hadot notes, "all [ancient] philosophical schools engaged their disciples upon a new way of life" (1995, 104). These schools would use training and exercises to stimulate disciples to rebuff culturally predominant values like wealth, honor, and pleasure, and instead to pursue contemplation and virtue. John Cooper says the philosophical schools used exercises as "ways of self-transformation" (2012, 20), to fix the meaning and implications of philosophical arguments "in one's mind and make oneself ready to apply them smoothly to situations of life as they may arise" (2012, 402).

I don't deny that contemporary variations of Stoic or Cartesian self-study techniques could help some people follow their epistemic principles. But these techniques must be set inside a broader matrix of culture and socialization, and I am unsure what forms that could take. One thing is clear, however. The practical challenge of guiding inquiry with principles calls for behavioral interventions. To become better inquirers, we need interventions to reconfigure how we live and thereby turn us into thinkers who follow our principles more than we do now. Scientific research is needed to identify the most effective interventions.[17]

Here we could benefit from an influential and successful paradigm in contemporary psychology stretching back to work in the early twentieth century by Kurt Lewin and others. This paradigm takes people's interpretations and stories about themselves and the social world as central to understanding

---

[17] The possibility of interventions raises questions about the ethical and political implications of changing people's dispositions. Just because we can make people into principle-followers does not necessarily mean we should. I set these matters to the side for now.

their behavior. The paradigm also recognizes that revising and rewriting our stories is possible. "Story editing" is what psychologist Timothy Wilson calls the process of redirecting people's narratives in ways that change their behavior. Wilson says that "in order to solve a problem, we have to view it through the eyes of the people involved and get them to redirect their narratives about it" (2011, 25). Controlled studies can help us understand how to modify the conduct and character of oncologists, college students, long-haul truckers, and recovering alcoholics.

Well-intentioned behavioral interventions may not work out. For instance, in the 1970s, a state prison in New Jersey started a community outreach program that soon spread across the United States. The program was designed to deter juvenile delinquents from further criminal activity by showing them what lies in wait down dark alleyways. The at-risk teens received a guided tour of the slammer, courtesy of some apparently civic-minded inmates. The inmates described the bleak conditions of the jail in distressing detail. They ridiculed the teens. They screamed obscenities while smoking cigarettes. All of this was supposed to "scare 'em straight."[18] The program backfired catastrophically. As Wilson notes, "not only do scared-straight programs fail to reduce the likelihood that kids will commit crimes, they actually *increase* criminal activity" (2011, 137). Studies have shown that the programs lead to greater average rates of delinquency than no intervention at all—teens in the programs are more likely to commit crimes than at-risk teens that aren't. Scared-straight programs make crooks.

Whether we intend to keep at-risk teens out of juvey or help inquirers follow their principles, our starting point must be empirical insights. Our ideas about how to implement regulative theories may seem to work well for us, but we should ask whether models and theoretical paradigms from empirical disciplines would support, or advise against, what we are doing. Ideally, well-designed studies should probe our interventions before we invest too heavily in them. We need not sit for hours in our stove-heated room if that intervention makes no difference, or leaves us worse off than before. The question is: what does make a difference? It is difficult to know unless we look at actual inquirers. As I noted in Chapter 1, the program of regulative epistemology requires contributions from social and behavioral scientists.

---

[18] This perhaps needs to be seen to be believed. For better or worse, it can be seen. A documentary film, *Scared Straight!*, was filmed in the New Jersey prison and won an Academy Award in 1978.

Indeed, implementing good epistemic guidance in a wide range of situations depends on scientists' insights.

While I await advice from scientists about what actually works, I'll be telling myself some bedtime stories.

8. Epistemology and Social Change

This chapter has considered what principles must be like in order to guide inquirers. Here are my main proposals in brief. Regulative principles need to influence epistemic judgment not only through conscious reflection on principles but also through fast, automatic, and non-reflective cognition. That can happen if principles get "mirrored" in cognition as the dispositions underwriting intuitive expertise and epistemic pictures. As a result, following principles calls for a type of character. So my proposals here uncover an important connection between principle-focused regulative theories and character-focused ones. But there are open questions about how we can acquire the right sort of intellectual dispositions. I noted that psychologists have methods to test the effectiveness of behavioral interventions. To follow our principles, we need the right character; but to develop the right character, we need the right interventions. The possibility of empirical investigation into possible interventions gives me hope that regulative epistemology's practical problem will one day be better understood and managed than it is at present.

My proposals here may seem to suggest the audacious idea that regulative epistemology aims at social change. Is that correct? Yes, and doubly so. First, it seems doubtful that most of us mirror our principles as effectively as we could. Like Descartes and Hume, we may suffer from intellectual hypocrisy and *akrasia*, sometimes failing to abide by the principles we apparently endorse. By fine-tuning our ways of life, behavioral interventions give us our best shot at getting the dispositions we need. Second, the presence of good regulative ideas in a society may improve widespread attitudes and practices. Let me explain the second point with an analogy.

Regulative epistemologists are like professional nutritionists. The job of nutritionists is to synthesize a great deal of research about food and health. They tell us about the diets and lifestyles that will conduce to long-term health. Physiologists and cardiologists could lay out all of the grisly consequences of consuming too much fried chicken and beer. But the nutritionists can explain why we need fiber, protein, and vitamins, and how to get these things into our diets and in what quantity. Nutritionists' insights into health only reveal what is *possible*, not what is easy, and certainly not what most people are going to accomplish. And yet nutritionists influence society nonetheless. Their ideas can shift prevalent attitudes. Governments require food packaging to include serving size and nutrient information. School board trustees instruct school cafeterias to stop serving barbecue chicken wings, chocolate donuts, and jujubes. Even the menu at McDonald's has changed a little from when I was a kid eating a "Happy Meal"—today, the tyke-sized meal comes with apple slices and a smaller serving of French fries. Nutritional research has somehow changed our complex relationship with food.

Regulative epistemology promises to reveal what is *possible* for those of us who desire to regulate our inquiry. Let me be the first to say that few people would care to follow the guidance brought forward by regulative epistemology's research program.[19] But in the same way that attitudes toward nutrition and eating habits have changed among millions of people who would flunk a nutritional science exam, regulative epistemology could generate ideas that catch on far from the academic crowd—in classrooms and workplaces, in newspaper editorials, in the popular mindset. Regulative epistemology is the pursuit of understanding how inquiry goes, how it should go, and how it can go better. I find no reason to doubt that this pursuit could one day advance commonplace attitudes about inquiry and the practices of many inquirers.

---

[19] Who are the envisioned "end users" of the regulative recommendations found in this book? Are these recommendations intended for people with no relevant background knowledge? No. In the same way that journal articles and monographs about nutrition science aren't *directly* helpful for neonates or elementary school children, this book can't help the vast majority of inquirers. It is a fairly abstract elaboration and defense of ideas—sort of like a "proof of concept." That said, if any of the regulative ideas on offer here happen to be worthy of refinement and development, I suspect they can be "translated" or "repackaged" into different formats and used by inquirers for whom this book could have no direct relevance. But I don't know how that translation or repackaging process would go, except that it would call for the kind of multidisciplinary effort described in Chapter 1.

4

How to Know Our Limits

I approached him in a humble spirit: "Mr. Edison, please tell me
what laboratory rules you want me to observe." And right then and
there I got my first surprise. He spat in the middle of the floor and
yelled out, "Hell! there ain't no rules around here! We are tryin' to
accomplish somep'n!" And he walked off, leaving me flabbergasted.
　　　—Martin André Rosanoff, a Russian-American chemist who
　　　　　　　　　　　　　　　　worked for Thomas Edison

[D]oubt is not a fearful thing, but a thing of very great value .... And
it is of paramount importance, in order to make progress, that we
recognize this ignorance and this doubt. Because we have the doubt,
we then propose looking in new directions for new ideas.
　　　　　　—Richard Feynman, *The Meaning of It All*, 1963

Confusion will be my epitaph.
　—King Crimson, "Epitaph," *In the Court of the Crimson King*, 1969

We do not ordinarily question the truth of our beliefs. Our beliefs are like
windows: we gaze through them and trust what we see. But things are not
always as they appear. That is an old lesson, but it's hard to live by, and part
of the problem is that we naturally presume that our beliefs reflect the world
as it is. This has been called naïve realism, the tendency to assume that our
doxastic windows give us an accurate, undistorted view of reality (Ross and
Ward 1996).

Naïve realism should not satisfy us, because we know some of our
beliefs are imperfect. Unfortunately, our general knowledge of our own
imperfections is a feeble thing. It can't effectively counteract or undermine
our naïve realism: we are naïve realists who know full well that we are imperfect. How can this be? Knowing we have limits is different from knowing

what our limits are. In other words, recognizing that some of our beliefs are mistaken is different from recognizing, of some particular beliefs, that they are mistaken. Armed with general knowledge that we are imperfect, we may furrow our brows and interrogate our minds, trying to discern which of our beliefs are defective. But we will be fooled by the window-like nature of belief. Attending directly to one of our beliefs, we will see it appears crystal clear—looking through it, we seem to apprehend the world outside.

By merely recognizing that some of our beliefs are imperfect, we won't overcome our tendency to presume that our beliefs afford us an accurate, unbiased viewpoint. What can we do to find out our imperfections? How can we know our limits?

We need a method. More specifically, we need a *metacognitive* method— a method to think about our thinking. Cognitive scientists study metacognitive rules and perspectives, and some metacognitive strategies improve inquiry. For example, psychologists prompted subjects to follow the rule "consider the opposite" and observed that the subjects avoided some biases more effectively than when abiding by rules such as "be as fair as possible" or "be as unbiased as possible" (Lord, Lepper, and Preston 1984). In another study, subjects were able to reason more effectively when psychologists cued them to think about personally significant issues from "a distanced perspective," as if they were remote observers (Kross and Grossmann 2012). Various metacognitive strategies have been recommended for avoiding biases and improving reasoning. What we also need is a metacognitive method that helps us know our limits as believers. In the present chapter and subsequent five chapters, I describe such a method.

Philosophers have discussed the limits of human knowledge for a long time, and Chapter 2 noted some early modern philosophers' efforts to grapple with regulative questions. The regulative impulse has always been to develop guidance for knowing the difference between what we should and should not believe. As John Stuart Mill put it, we need a way to draw "the line between what we know accurately and what we do not" (1867, 224). Roderick Chisholm thought epistemology raises "Socratic" questions such as the following: "How can I distinguish those things I am justified in believing from those things I am not justified in believing?" (1989, 1). Answering that question, in one special domain, is basically what the method I describe is for—it shows us the difference between beliefs we have good reason to doubt and those we don't. And the method can help us determine when we are not well-equipped to gain reasonable beliefs or knowledge. It consists in a set of epistemic principles as well as observations about ourselves as inquirers and the worlds we investigate.

The principles can be expressed in conditional form: *if* we have reason to think we are in particular conditions, *then* we should have doubt concerning some of our beliefs. We can know the principles are true even if we don't know we are in the conditions set down in the principles' antecedents. That is why we need observations about our intellectual lives. To apply the principles, we must know about the circumstances we are in.

In Chapters 5 through 9, I describe the principles and show how they apply to our lives. These chapters develop a cumulative or additive case for sometimes adopting what I call *doxastic openness*—a doubtful or unsettled mindset toward a special class of beliefs, a mindset contrasting with one where our views are settled. The present chapter outlines my approach.

I will begin by noting one challenge for regulative methods. Regulative epistemologists have often traded in methods that may appear bold if not grandiose. They've wanted to improve human knowledge and opinion in the vast domain of inquiry—the practices of answering questions using evidence. In that domain, we find scientific techniques, our informal reasoning abilities, tools for evaluating deductive validity, and so on. How can we improve inquiry in general?

It is a daunting question, but that has not stopped some philosophers from weighing in. As I noted in Chapter 2, for instance, Descartes in his *Discourse on Method* sets down four rules. He tells us the rules were designed to help construct certain knowledge about topics from mathematics to meteorology. But not everyone has been as impressed with the Cartesian method as its namesake was. The German polymath Gottfried Leibniz parodied Descartes' rules with a paraphrase: "Take what is needed; do as you ought; and you will get what you wanted."[1] Those rules are apparently not good for much. Take what is needed—*check!* Do as we ought—*check!* But if inquirers hope to answer any particular question well, what is it that they need and what ought they to do, exactly? The rules remain silent. They won't get us what we wanted.

Perhaps Leibniz's parody of the Cartesian method may strike us as unfair. The real rules in the *Discourse* are subtler than the parody. Furthermore, Descartes set down a more complete account of his rules in the unfinished *Rules for the Direction of the Mind*. But Leibniz's parody reveals an insight.

---

[1] Quoted in Broughton (2003, 4).

Janet Broughton observes: "I imagine that most [early modern] readers who learned something from Descartes about how to tackle problems in mathematics and physics found his actual explorations of specific problems much more helpful than the very general maxims of method" (2003, 4). Insofar as statements of methods aim for soaring generality and application to each and every situation where we seek knowledge and reasonable opinion, they risk being platitudinous and unusable in our ordinary inquiries. Regulative epistemologists must try to avoid the dangers of cliché and practical worthlessness.

Recall that regulative epistemologists aim to grasp how inquiry works, how it should work, and how we can bridge the gap between the two. To accomplish that, they must balance the abstract and the concrete. On one hand, Descartes' method (or at least Leibniz's parody of it) sets down rules that supposedly guide inquirers in all of their knowledge-constructing efforts, but it doesn't appear to help anyone. Descartes may have leaned too far in the direction of the abstract. On the other hand, too much concreteness brings other difficulties. If a regulative theory applies only to one special, highly specific situation, it won't make much contact with the practices of actual inquirers. Regulative epistemologists should aim to devise theories that apply fairly widely and offer good guidance that inquirers do not already take for granted. That is what I will try to do.[2]

1. The Method Miniaturized

I offer a method for helping us discover whether our controversial beliefs are epistemically unreasonable. It consists in principles as well as observations that guide us in applying those principles. The principles say that a thinker has reason to doubt an opinion in particular contingent circumstances. If the thinker can be sensitive to when she is in those circumstances, she

---

[2] The point that regulative theories must give inquirers advice they don't already take for granted illuminates a suggestion I made in Chapter 1: that standard theories of epistemic justification, such as reliabilism and evidentialism, won't serve regulative purposes all on their own. These standard theories tell us what epistemically justified belief consists in. But in order to determine, in a specific case, whether someone's belief is justified, we may need to know a great deal about the world. Reliabilism and evidentialism can more easily guide when we know in advance facts that are typically unknown or uncertain to us—such as whether a belief is formed by a reliable process, or whether some belief is a fitting response to our total evidence. That said, theorists could seek to "apply" standard theories to particular problems of inquiry, attempting to learn what normative guidance those theories impart to inquirers. (I am grateful to Jason Baehr for discussion here.)

will become aware of reasons to change her mind. The method can help us improve our stock of beliefs by showing us when particular beliefs are unreasonable.[3]

When do we need the method? Consider a characteristic situation. A student arrives on a university campus at the dawn of adulthood. She confidently believes that atheism is true—there are no supernatural beings. The student enrolls in an Introduction to Philosophy course and learns about arguments for and against the existence of God. She comes to reflect carefully on the fact that some intelligent and informed people reject her atheism. Agnostics argue that the overall evidence does not support either belief or disbelief in God; they claim we should suspend judgment concerning God's existence. Theists and other supernaturalists argue that God, or something like God, exists. The student comes to see that her belief in atheism is controversial in a special sense: she knows that some people reject her belief, even though they are apparently no less well-informed or well-disposed to evaluate the available evidence than she is. Accordingly, she wonders: Is my belief unreasonable?

We all engage in doxastic reflection. Sometimes we have already formed a belief and ask ourselves whether we should hold it. Other times we are sizing up our options for adopting a belief. We need to know how we should think. And we regularly know that there's controversy: the beliefs we hold, or could hold, are rejected by informed and intelligent people.[4] Controversial beliefs may seem somehow insecure, uncertain, and doubtful to us, at least on occasion. Doxastic deliberation on our controversial views may bring us second thoughts and maybe even some sleepless nights. Why do intelligent, informed people reject our beliefs? Are we missing something? Is it even possible to know which views are correct? *Are our controversial beliefs unreasonable?*

One reaction is to roll up our sleeves for some old-fashioned investigation. Such work may vindicate our controversial views. We may examine our opponents' best arguments and find them wanting. Or perhaps we will learn that our opponents' thinking is subject to biases. But the extra effort may humble us instead. Perhaps we will realize that we are missing some crucial

---

[3] If the method had an informative name, it might be something like the *Method of Recognizing Competence Defeaters for Our Controversial Beliefs*. But that is a mouthful, so I call it "the regulative method" or "the method."

[4] Although I hereafter talk about doxastic reflection concerning our actual beliefs, everything I say applies to situations where we prospectively consider beliefs to hold.

evidence our opponents have and that if we possessed that evidence, we might agree with them. To be sure, when we face questions about the epistemic status of our controversial beliefs, more investigation may be right and proper. But intending to explore an issue in the future won't tell us what we should think about it right now. Our original question will not go away. *Are our controversial beliefs unreasonable?*

As naïve realists, we may fancy that our controversial beliefs are reasonable and correct. Even if it's often acceptable to assume that how things appear to us is the way they really are, the fact that our beliefs are controversial should prompt serious deliberation. We naïve realists should not be impressed by the feeling that our views are accurate and unbiased. *Of course* we think our opinions are correct. But so what? Why should that fact figure into our deliberations? Our rosy impressions of our own powers distract us from the real trouble here. We are reflecting on our controversial beliefs. To judge whether they are reasonable or count as knowledge, we should consider facts over and above whether they have the singular distinction of being ours. We must appeal to evidence and information that helps us deliberate in a manner that gives us some independence from the "our-ness" of our beliefs.[5]

Thinking about non-controversial topics is characteristically different than thinking about controversial ones. Reflection on our controversial beliefs can put us in an existential mood. We don't merely judge our beliefs. We judge ourselves. Our self-conceptions, our social standing, our values, and our hopes are entangled with many of our controversial views. To come to see our controversial beliefs as unreasonable is to be confronted by our own shortcomings, and not in a merely abstract or theoretical way. To learn that our beliefs are unreasonable may change not just our minds, but also how we live, how we understand ourselves, and who we are.

The method aims to help us judge ourselves more circumspectly. It enjoins distinctive patterns of thought and attention. These patterns are guided by epistemic principles. The method draws our attention to evidence about our competence as inquirers and this evidence helps us determine whether our controversial opinions are unreasonable.

---

[5] Compare to David Christensen's "independence-based conciliationism" (2007a, 2011). I say more about Christensen's ideas in Chapter 5.

That brief description may make the method sound about as useful as Leibniz's parody of the Cartesian method. *Get wise to whether your opinions are unreasonable!*

Not quite. My goal in this chapter is to describe the method at a high level of abstraction. I explain how it operates in our intellectual economy, deferring discussion of its specific content for the following five chapters. There I introduce the principles and observations about intellectual life that are the lifeblood of the method, hopefully dispatching any lingering sense that the method is platitudinous. As I noted in Chapter 3, we need to internalize the method—to encode it in our minds so we can use it in everyday life. If we are guided by the method's principles, we manifest an intellectual virtue: a sensitivity or attentiveness to the marks of unreasonable beliefs. That virtue allows us to regulate our opinions about controversial questions.

To sum up, we need a method to determine whether our beliefs are reasonable, and such a method will help us judge ourselves and assess our competence to inquire into controversial questions. So far, I've described the method without elaborating on the key ideas. In the remainder of the present chapter, I introduce crucial concepts and terminology used in the arguments in Chapters 5 through 9: belief and controversial belief (section 2); unreasonableness and defeaters (section 3); positive epistemic status (section 4); competence defeaters (section 5); and the "doxastically open" mindset we may be enjoined to adopt if we are guided by the method's principles (section 6). I conclude by looking ahead to the next five chapters (section 7).

2. Belief and Controversial Belief

We represent reality to ourselves by holding the doxastic attitudes of belief, disbelief, and suspension of judgment. To *believe* a proposition is to hold a positive attitude toward its truth—not *wanting* it to be true, but *thinking* it is true. To *disbelieve* a proposition is to hold a negative attitude toward its truth. To *suspend judgment* concerning a proposition is to hold an attitude that is neither positive nor negative toward the proposition, but is instead counterbalanced between positive and negative attitudes. We can think about this attitude as a kind of settled resistance to either believing or disbelieving the proposition (Friedman 2013). Suspending judgment arguably requires having grasped or considered the proposition as well as the other doxastic options toward it, though I take no view of that matter. But merely failing to believe the proposition because you have never thought about it isn't equivalent to suspending judgment on it. Unless otherwise noted, what I say about belief applies to disbelief and suspension of judgment. I also use the terms *doxastic attitude, opinion*, and *view* to refer to any of the three doxastic attitudes—believing, disbelieving, and suspending judgment.

Beliefs admit of degrees of confidence. I believe I exist. I also believe my daughter collected shells at the beach on a frigid day in February 2017. But I am more confident in the first belief than the second. I am disposed to believe upon reflection that the first belief is more likely correct than the second. (Was that frigid day in February or March? Or January? I am pretty sure it was February, but I'm less sure of that than of my existence.) Typically, our beliefs do not have specific or explicit degrees of confidence, or if they do, we are not in a position to know them. Sometimes, however, we have degrees of confidence in our beliefs—for instance, when we play games of chance or assess the risks of medical interventions. But that is not the norm. As Richard Foley points out, if all of our beliefs were finely qualified with respect to their degree of confidence, we would be "overwhelmed if we tried to deliberate about complicated issues on the basis of them" (1992, 122). We can more easily determine our confidence in a belief relative to some another belief, but then only in a fairly rough-hewn way.

To a first approximation, what I call a *controversial belief* is any belief in an answer to a question over which there are recognized disputes between intelligent and informed people. Across great expanses of our intellectual world, controversy is commonplace.

Here are just a few examples of controversial questions. Is capital punishment morally justified? Are gun control laws morally permissible, or do they infringe on citizens' rights? Does foreign aid effectively relieve poverty in the developing world? What led to weighty historical events such as the French Revolution, the First World War, or the collapse of the Soviet Union? Are human actions free, causally determined, or both? Are human beings wholly material things? Do theories in physics give us true descriptions of things in the world? Is nuclear power the best alternative to fossil fuels? Is liberal democracy at risk in Europe and North America? Are there good arguments for or against the existence of God? Should speech on college and university campuses be free, and in what sense? These questions arguably divide intelligent and informed people. Controversial beliefs express answers to controversial questions. I'm invoking the idea of controversial belief to focus our attention on the type of belief to which the method applies.

I have so far used the term "controversial" in a fairly ordinary sense, but I will make the idea a bit more precise by stipulating a definition. Our belief in proposition p is controversial when the following three conditions are met: (*i*) the belief is rejected by thinkers (*ii*) who have evidence concerning p that's at least approximately as good as ours and (*iii*) who are at least approximately as good at responding to such evidence as we are.[6] By extension, questions are controversial whenever the beliefs we hold about them are controversial. Importantly, (*i*) is satisfied even if we and other thinkers have the same doxastic attitude but have a different degree of confidence.[7] Notice that conditions (*ii*) and (*iii*) can be met even when other thinkers have different evidence, and different skills for responding to the evidence, than we do. The notion of controversial belief is thus distinct from the idea of epistemic peerhood, which involves *equality* of evidence and intellectual skills between thinkers.[8] Furthermore, our beliefs can be controversial even when they are accepted by our epistemic peers. Suppose that all of our peers agree with us on some topic, but some of our superiors disagree. Here our belief is controversial because our superiors have evidence and abilities for responding to their evidence that are at least approximately as good as our evidence and evidence-responding abilities.

Sometimes our beliefs are controversial, but we are unaware of it. The method can help us when we recognize that some belief is, or may be, controversial. Consider two reasons to believe that many of our beliefs are controversial in the stipulated sense. First, we hold views about many questions about which we knowingly lack expertise. We have opinions about ethics, economics, law, politics, religion, history, metaphysics, and science, while recognizing we are outclassed by people who investigate these topics with great care, intensity, and sophistication. We often learn that some of these experts reject our views. These experts do not fail to have evidence that's approximately as good as ours, nor do they fail to be at least approximately as good at responding to the evidence as we are. They are our betters. Second, even if we happen to be experts on some topics, we will likely recognize that other

---

[6] Compare to Michael Bergmann's (2015) characterization of epistemic peerhood.

[7] I suspect the best version of condition (*i*) includes a qualification to explain why cases in which people have the same doxastic attitude but differ ever so slightly in their degrees of confidence don't involve a controversy, strictly speaking. I won't get into the details here. (Thanks to Blake Roeber for discussion.)

[8] For discussion of disagreement between epistemic peers, see Kelly (2005a), Feldman (2006), Christensen (2007a, 2009), Feldman and Warfield (2010), and Christensen and Lackey (2013).

people are experts, too—and some of them probably disagree with our views. We should think these topics are, at least for us, controversial.

At the same time, intelligent and informed people agree on many issues. That is, many questions are uncontroversial. Intelligent and informed people will all believe the continents are in motion; that there is presently life on Earth and that there was life on Earth millions of years ago; that the Earth is not flat; that smoking cigarettes causes cancer; that Billie Holiday sang the blues and Charlie Parker played the alto saxophone; that motorized vehicles in North America drive on the right side of the road; that Pronghorn antelopes run faster than tortoises. There is no real controversy about any of this.[9]

The lines between controversial and uncontroversial questions are movable. What is controversial for us today may be uncontroversial for us tomorrow. In 1912, German scientist Alfred Wegener put forward the idea that the continents are in motion. For decades afterward, Wegener's proposal was repudiated by most informed scientists. Today, the thesis of continental drift is regarded as settled fact—no informed scientist doubts or denies it. At any moment, what is controversial or uncontroversial may not always be easy to know, and the claim that one issue is or isn't controversial can itself be subject to controversy among intelligent and informed people. But, for most people, many questions are controversial.

---

[9] But haven't some philosophers defended radically skeptical claims about commonsense and well-established science and history that the vast majority of intelligent and informed people readily accept? Well, yes. Some philosophers apparently doubt they exist and that there are other minds, for instance. Does it follow that our beliefs about such claims are controversial? I doubt it, but I am of two minds about why doubt is in order here.

First, whether we should treat a question as controversial depends on our evidence. Do we have reason to believe that radical skeptics, who reject our basic views about commonsense and science and history, are no less well-informed and well-disposed to reasonably evaluate the relevant evidence than we are? In some moods, I am inclined to say that if some philosophers genuinely believe, on the basis of philosophical arguments, that they do not exist, or that our beliefs about such things are unreasonable, then good luck to them. They don't satisfy (*ii*) or (*iii*) or both.

On the other hand, I am sometimes inclined to doubt that condition (*i*) is satisfied. Why should I accept that some philosophers actually fail to believe they exist or genuinely suspend judgment about the existence of other minds? I like the following observation from the *Port-Royal Logic*. The opinions of Pyrrhonian and Academic skeptics, write Arnauld and Nicole, "were games and amusements for idle and clever people. But they were never views that they inwardly endorsed and on which they tried to act" (1996 [1683], 228; IV, 1).

There are further questions about how the method might lead us to view radical skeptics, but I leave that discussion for another time. Briefly, and speaking only for myself, radical skeptics either do not appear to be reliable judges of the matters on which they judge, or they do not actually disagree with the views of informed and reasonable people everywhere, or both, and so I doubt their disagreement is sufficient for controversy. Thus, I do not apply the method to my deliberation concerning beliefs about commonsense and well-established science and history—or if I do apply the method to such cases, the method won't lead me to change my thinking in significant ways.

3. Unreasonableness and Defeaters

The method will help us reflect on whether our controversial beliefs are unreasonable. But what is *unreasonableness*? As I use the term, it is one kind of epistemic status or evaluation of beliefs. Unreasonable beliefs are defective in a particular way, in light of various goals we may have to acquire the truth, avoid error, and make sense of the world. To a first approximation, our beliefs are unreasonable whenever we possess a sufficient reflective reason to doubt they are true. Not being properly based on evidence isn't sufficient for unreasonableness, as I use the term here.

It will take some work to fill out that initial sketch. By *reason* I mean an indicator that some proposition is true or evidence in favor of believing that proposition. A reason to believe may be an experience, an argument, or another belief.[10] A *reflective reason* is a reason that is accessible to us on reflection, in the sense that it's available to us from inside our perspective on ourselves as believers and inquirers. An *unreasonable belief* is one that we have a reflective reason to doubt, but the belief need not lack all other merits. An unreasonable belief can be true. It can be formed by a reliable process that is highly likely to produce mostly true beliefs. And it can be held on the basis of truth-conducive and non-misleading reasons. Again, an unreasonable belief is one we have reflective reason to doubt is true. An unreasonable belief— even when true, reliably formed, or based on truth-conducive evidence—is problematic from inside our perspective on ourselves.

To give us a firmer grip on unreasonableness, here is a further idea. A *defeater* is a reason for giving up a doxastic attitude we hold toward a proposition. In slightly different words, a defeater is a reason that threatens to eliminate a belief's positive epistemic status. I use the term to pick out reasons, evidence, arguments, experiences, or beliefs that a thinker has, not some fact in the world that's inaccessible to a thinker from her perspective on herself.

Following the late John Pollock, we can distinguish between two main types of defeaters.[11] Suppose you believe some proposition *p*. *Undermining*

---

[10] I mean to ignore differences between theories on which only propositions are evidence, others on which only facts are evidence, and others on which only mental states are evidence. For discussion, see McCain (2014, chapter 2).

[11] Pollock introduced the distinction in his 1974 book and developed it in later works, including Pollock (1986) and Pollock and Cruz (1999). Sturgeon (2014) examines Pollock's theory of defeaters. For other helpful discussions of defeaters, see Plantinga (2000, chapter 11), Bergmann (2005 and 2006, chapter 6), Thune (2010), and King (2016).

defeaters are reasons that attack the connection between your belief in *p* and reasons that support it. An undermining defeater is consistent with the truth of *p*, but it removes or neutralizes your reasons for believing *p* and, as a result, believing *p* to one degree or another becomes unsupported by your reasons and thus unreasonable. *Rebutting defeaters*, on the other hand, attack *p* itself. Rebutting defeaters for believing *p* are reasons to disbelieve *p* to one degree or another.

It's useful to think of a defeater as a *prima facie* threat to a belief. Although a defeater may at first appear to challenge the epistemic status of a belief, the challenge can be rejected, in which case the *prima facie* defeater is not an *on-balance* or *ultima facie* defeater.

How could the challenge to a belief posed by a *prima facie* defeater be rejected? Simply put, defeaters can defeat other defeaters. Suppose your mathematics textbook states that a particular theorem is proven. You believe it is proven. A trusted informant then tells you the textbook has a typo—it should state that the theorem is *not* proven. Now your reason for believing that the theorem is proven is defeated, let's say. But the defeater can be defeated if, for example, you learn that your informant was just messing around and had no clue whether the textbook has a typo. In general, it's possible for one defeater to defeat another defeater because defeaters can be *prima facie* reasons to give up a belief. But a defeater does not amount to an *on-balance* or *ultima facie* reason to give up a belief when it is defeated itself. We can thus talk about *defeated* and *undefeated* defeaters.[12]

A further distinction among defeaters draws our attention to the strength of a defeater. A defeater's strength concerns its power to change what a thinker should believe. Assuming they are undefeated, *full defeaters* for believing *p* make any belief in *p* unreasonable, no matter its degree of confidence, whereas *partial defeaters* permit some lower degree of confidence in believing *p* to be reasonable. This distinction between full and partial defeaters will prove important for applying the method.

I can now describe unreasonableness in greater detail. A belief is unreasonable if we have an undefeated defeater for it. Defeaters either undermine our grounds for believing or rebut the proposition believed. Undefeated

---

[12] Following helpful distinctions from Peter Graham (2006, 92), I assume that a *prima facie* reason is not eradicable or conditional, unlike an *on-balance* or *ultima facie* reason. Here is what that means. A *prima facie* reason gives us an *on-balance* reason only when it is not defeated. An *on-balance* reason is conditional in the sense that it requires we have no undefeated defeaters. But we have a *prima facie* reason regardless of whether we have undefeated defeaters. Though a *prima facie* reason can be defeated and so fail to provide us with *on-balance* reason, it can't be eradicated.

full defeaters require us to stop holding a belief altogether, whereas unde-feated partial defeaters only require changing our degree of confidence in our belief.

Let me illustrate the idea of unreasonable belief with an example. You are viewing what appears to be a monochrome green painting in an art gallery. You believe this artwork is a "subtle and vigorous" green painting. Turning to leave the exhibit, a gallery docent mentions to you that the painting is ac-tually white but appears green because it's illuminated by carefully hidden green lighting. The docent is not joking, lying, or deluded, so far as you can tell. You now have a rebutting defeater for your belief that the painting is green. For you, it's now unreasonable to believe the painting is green, though you should certainly believe it *appears to be* green.

Encountering defeaters for our beliefs is a ubiquitous experience. When we can't defeat a defeater, we should either adjust our confidence in our beliefs or change our minds because our views are unreasonable. I will offer many examples of defeaters in Chapters 5 through 9. For now, I only want to observe that the notion of unreasonableness is common in recent epistemo-logical theorizing. It's widely thought by theorists to be an epistemic status or state that eliminates knowledge, justification, warrant, and rationality. This fact plays into the design of the method. If I give principles that help us recognize when our beliefs are unreasonable, the principles will look viable from standard theoretical perspectives.

4. Positive Epistemic Status

I have characterized defeaters as threats to the "positive epistemic status" of a belief. What is that? To say more, I must at least mention recent debates in analytic or descriptive epistemology. These debates often astonish onlookers, myself included. In his review of theories of epistemic justification in the second half of the twentieth century, Alvin Plantinga observes "a wide and indeed confusing assortment of alternatives" and calls the theoretical scenery a "blooming and buzzing confusion" (1990, 46, 48). William Alston, in his review of theories of justification, notes that "we are confronted with a wildly chaotic picture of an enormous plurality of incompatible views as to what it is for a belief to be justified, and as to what further conditions are re-quired for a belief's having that status" (2005, 21). Epistemologists have been in the business of describing many types of epistemic states and statuses, and the results may prompt feelings of bewilderment, even among practitioners themselves.[13]

All this talk of chaos and confusion may suggest that epistemological debates are a kind of conceptual demolition derby—and fun for the whole family. Alas, the hair-splitting fastidiousness of epistemologists at work isn't quite as entertaining as people crashing cars. Epistemology does not make for good drama. Mercifully, I can proceed without entering into debates over epistemic states and statuses. That's because standard theories all recognize the normative status central to the present regulative undertaking: unreasonableness. The field reached what we might call an overlapping consensus about the importance of unreasonableness as an epistemic status, at least in the sense of the term I'm working with here. Though popular theories diverge about what generates positive epistemic status, all accord in saying that defeat takes it away.[14]

Why do standard theories all recognize unreasonableness but clash over the nature of knowledge, warrant, and justification? Here is a short answer that recounts some debates over these terms.

In his 1963 article, Edmund Gettier set out to refute the theory that knowledge is justified true belief, as I noted in Chapter 1. Gettier aimed to show that a standard analysis of knowledge was mistaken and he gave two counterexamples to do the job. In professional philosophers' discussions

---

[13] For some discussion, see BonJour (1985), Goldman (1988), Plantinga (1993a, 1993b), Fumerton (1995), Lehrer (2000), Kornblith (2001b), Feldman (2003), Alston (2005), Bergmann (2006), Lyons (2009), Graham (2010), Greco (2010), Henderson and Horgan (2011), Evans and Smith (2012), and McCain (2014).

[14] A few epistemologists have rejected the standard view about unreasonableness, arguing instead that defeat doesn't eliminate justification and knowledge. In other words, a thinker can have justification to believe proposition p and know p even if that belief is unreasonable in the sense I described earlier in section 3. Are anti-defeater views compatible with the method on offer in this book?

I think so. For a start, notice how it's plausible that these anti-defeater views just move a bump in the rug. Supposing a thinker has a defeater for a belief, anti-defeater views deny a normative defect *in the thinker's belief* but instead locate a defect *in the thinker's character*. Something is normatively amiss, though the belief is in the clear. One advocate of that sort of idea is Maria Lasonen-Aarnio (2010, 2014), who suggests that someone's defeated beliefs can be justified and known, even though such a person is being *unreasonable* in holding those beliefs. (For discussion of anti-defeat views, see Williamson 2011 and 2014, Horowitz 2014, Baker-Hytch and Benton 2015, and Brown 2018.) I suggest that anyone sympathetic to anti-defeater views can interpret the method as a way to help people better recognize when their characters (not their beliefs) are in some sense unreasonable.

Further, notice that on anti-defeater views, not changing one's belief when it's defeated is a distinctively epistemic character defect, and so it appears that a thinker exhibiting that defect over the long run will accumulate many false and unreasonable beliefs. Even if defeaters don't eliminate our justification and knowledge in some cases, ignoring defeaters is a policy that will tend to have bad consequences for our beliefs. As far as I can tell, proponents of anti-defeat views can still embrace the method as a long-term strategy to avoid false and unreasonable beliefs. (Thanks to Daniel Greco for helpful conversation here.)

around that time, the term "justification" was not fashionable. Gettier fixed his term's meaning in readers' minds in two ways: "having adequate evidence" and "the right to be sure." Gettier asserted that on either reading of "justification" his two counterexamples feature thinkers who have justified true beliefs but not knowledge. To the earliest readers, Gettier's use of a fresh theoretical term to name the status or state that helps make the difference between merely true belief and knowledge would have seemed unextraordinary. In 1963, nobody would have predicted that the term "justification" would become so central to professional epistemology in the decades to come.

The so-called Gettier Problem challenged epistemologists to understand the constituent parts of propositional knowledge. Virtually all theorists have agreed that *belief* and *truth* are necessary for knowledge.[15] Although Gettier had refuted the idea that "justification" together with true belief could be sufficient for knowledge, he did not challenge the idea that justification is necessary for knowledge. Once theorists were in the business of coming up with the correct analysis of knowledge, they realized that imprecise conceptions of justification—"having adequate evidence" or "the right to be sure"— wouldn't cut it.

Epistemologists wanted a sure grasp of the nature of knowledge, and so they typically devised accounts of epistemic good-making features that could plug the gap between true belief and knowledge. They often asserted these epistemic good-making features were, together with true belief, sufficient or nearly sufficient for knowledge. But it's not at all obvious that theorists have been interested in the same good-making features, even when they've called these features by the same name. For one, consensus about the right account of what makes the difference between true belief and knowledge has been elusive. For another, some observers have argued that the pursuit of such an account is quixotic, a search for something that doesn't exist, and that disputes over "justification" are merely verbal.[16]

Nevertheless, the field of epistemology was transformed in the late twentieth century because its members began to examine various types of

---

[15] Even when theorists have denied that belief is necessary for knowledge, they have typically replaced it with some belief-like representational state (though see Radford 1966 and Myers-Schulz and Schwitzgebel 2013). For example, Keith Lehrer (2000) argues that a state he names *acceptance* is required for knowledge. What one accepts is whatever is used as background information in thought and inference. Acceptance for Lehrer is a kind of functional state in the sense that what one accepts is a matter of what one would reflectively judge to be true were one seeking truth and avoiding error. Like belief, acceptance allows knowers to represent the world.

[16] For more on this theme, see Alston (1993, 2005) and Cohen (1995, 2016).

epistemic good-making features—which, for simplicity's sake, I lump together and refer to as *positive epistemic status*. Epistemologists working on the Gettier Problem had begun with one topic—knowledge—and then found another. The analysis of knowledge begat the analysis of positive epistemic status. By the late 1980s, Jaegwon Kim could say "it is evident that the concept of justification has come to take center stage in our reflections on the nature of knowledge" (1988, 382). Many theorists have defended subtle accounts of what positive epistemic status is and how beliefs can have it. But there's no widespread agreement concerning its precise nature.

Debates over positive epistemic status tend to divide epistemologists roughly into two camps: *internalism* and *externalism*. According to internalism as it's usually understood, what determines a belief's positive epistemic status—whether evidence, reasons, coherence, the fulfillment of an epistemic duty, or something else—must be accessible from inside the believer's reflective perspective. To put the idea differently, internalists typically say the requirements for positive epistemic status are such that a normal thinker has "special epistemic access" (in a tricky-to-pin-down sense) to whether those requirements are met. Positive epistemic status depends on what we can determine by reflection on our own minds. To know whether some belief of ours has positive epistemic status, what matters is internally-accessible evidence and reasons. Externalism denies internalism: positive epistemic status requires some states or properties that connect a thinker's belief with the world in the right way, but at least some of what determines positive epistemic status is external to, or outside, a thinker's reflective perspective. Externalists say that at least one of the necessary conditions for positive epistemic status is *not* such that a normal thinker has "special epistemic access" to whether it is met. Whether some thinker's belief has that status depends on facts beyond the thinker's ken.

Despite their disagreements, internalists and externalists agree about one necessary condition for positive epistemic status: what has been called the "no-defeater" condition. The no-defeater condition is satisfied by a thinker's belief if and only if the thinker does not believe, and would not believe upon reflection, that her belief is unreasonable (Bergmann 1997).[17] In other words, a belief cannot have positive epistemic status if we have an undefeated defeater for it. Internalists and externalists think about positive epistemic status differently, but agree on at least this: unreasonableness eliminates it.

---

[17] For a thoroughgoing defense of the no-defeater condition, see Bergmann (2006, chapter 6).

No matter what properties actually determine a belief's positive epistemic status, that status is imperiled when a thinker has an undefeated defeater.

Internalists say that what determines a belief's positive epistemic status is internally accessible to a thinker, and so it's unsurprising they embrace the no-defeater condition. When a thinker does believe, and would believe on reflection, that her belief is unreasonable, that belief lacks positive epistemic status. Externalists also accept the no-defeater condition, because the epistemic standing of a thinker's belief sometimes appears to be sensitive to what the thinker believes, or would on reflection believe, about her belief. That's so even though positive epistemic status does not require the thinker to have access to whether each of the necessary conditions is in fact satisfied. We can see that by considering an example.

You are in the art gallery again, and you come to believe that a particular monochrome painting is green. If your belief has positive epistemic status, externalists will say that is due to an appropriate connection between your belief and the world. Crucially, that connection need not be consciously accessible to you in order for it to confer positive epistemic status on your belief. Proponents of reliabilism, for instance, will say that your belief has positive epistemic status when it's produced by a reliable process even if you are unaware of that fact. Now imagine the gallery's docent tells you that the painting is actually white but illuminated by green lighting. As it turns out, the docent fooled you—the painting is actually green and there's no tricky lighting. Your initial belief was true and was produced by a reliable process. Even so, externalists will typically say that your belief's epistemic status has changed as soon as you learn of the docent's report. After all, the docent's report is a reason to doubt the truth of your belief that the painting is green and so its positive epistemic status is diminished to some extent. In general, if a thinker has an undefeated reason to doubt her belief is true, she should reduce her confidence or give up the belief altogether, even when various external conditions for that status are satisfied.[18]

Here's how these ideas tie into the main thread of this chapter. The no-defeater condition is embraced by all sides in debates over positive epistemic status, and so unreasonableness is common ground for theorists. Unreasonableness is one important criterion by which we judge whether beliefs have positive epistemic status.

---

[18] Grundmann (2009), Greco (2010, chapter 10), and Beddor (2015) examine the compatibility of the no-defeater condition with reliabilism.

Recall that I am describing a method to help us determine whether our controversial beliefs are unreasonable. Controversial beliefs are ones we recognize are rejected by other people who appear to us to be no less informed and skilled at evaluating the relevant evidence than we are ourselves (section 2). And unreasonable beliefs are ones that, from inside of our reflective perspective, we have reason to doubt are true—we have undefeated defeaters for those beliefs (section 3). When we find out, or even just suspect, that some of our beliefs are controversial, we'll be prompted to reflect on them.

Are our controversial beliefs unreasonable? The question is simple to pose but harder to ponder seriously. I will not offer a simple, clear-cut answer in this book. Instead I offer ways and means to grapple with the question more meaningfully. As I'll explain next, epistemic principles promise to reveal the marks of unreasonable beliefs to us by drawing our attention to a special kind of undermining defeater.

5. Competence Defeaters

Two questions arise if we want to know whether our controversial beliefs are unreasonable. First, *what is our evidence?* To reach an answer, we may return to evidence we have considered already. Or we may seek out and assess new evidence, especially if we doubt that our earlier investigation gave us a good sample of the total available evidence. But, as David Christensen notes about cases of controversy, "we know that simply looking over the arguments and evidence again, no matter how carefully and conscientiously, cannot be expected to disclose our mistakes to us" (2013, 90). Double-checking can occasionally show us our mistakes, but it can easily just reconfirm our initial view. This observation should not be surprising, for we know we are often prone to error, especially on controversial topics. When we are deliberating about a controversial belief, it's not always enough to revisit the evidence we have. So, we may ask a second question instead: *Are we competent to form a belief based on our evidence?*

The two questions lead us to deliberate in different ways. The first turns us "outward," toward evidence we have that's directly relevant to answering the controversial question. The second aims us "inward," toward evidence concerning ourselves and our abilities to form beliefs in light of our evidence. Answering these two questions calls for different types of evidence. The outward question requires *first-order evidence*—evidence that directly supports an answer to a question. In contrast, the inward question requires what I call *competence evidence*—evidence about our abilities and dispositions for responding effectively to that evidence.[19]

First-order evidence indicates the correct answer to some controversial question whereas competence evidence indicates whether we are well-equipped to answer that question using our first-order evidence. Are there good arguments for or against God's existence? The first-order evidence includes the relevant arguments of which we are aware—for instance, cosmological and "fine-tuning" arguments, on one side, and arguments from evil and "divine hiddenness," on the other. The competence evidence includes any considerations that bear on our ability to evaluate those arguments reliably—any information concerning our ability to assess and balance the arguments for and against God's existence. Suppose you find out you had evaluated these arguments while under the influence of cognition-impairing prescription drugs. That is competence evidence, because it provides reason to doubt whether you evaluated the arguments effectively.

When we are trying to determine whether a controversial belief is unreasonable, both first-order and competence evidence are relevant. When we deliberate about a controversial question, we want evidence concerning its right answer *and* evidence concerning whether we're able to answer the question effectively using that evidence.

Obviously, we should care about first-order evidence, but why does competence evidence matter? In short, it's a bad policy to ignore competence evidence. The policy could lead us to say curious things: "My first-order evidence supports my answer to the question, but I have no idea whether I am good or bad at using my evidence to reach my answer." Ideally, if we take a firm stand on a question on the basis of evidence, we will accept, at least on reflection, that our first-order evidence supports our answer and that we have some competence evidence for believing we can manage the first-order evidence. If we come to have competence evidence that raises doubts about whether we are good at managing the first-order evidence, we will take that

---

[19] Why don't I call competence evidence "higher-order evidence"? By definition, any evidence that tells us something about a body of first-order evidence is higher-order evidence. Competence evidence, which tells us how competent we are at responding to some first-order evidence, is one type of higher-order evidence. But not all higher-order evidence is competence evidence. For instance, evidence that indicates that a batch of evidence is testimonial evidence, or that it's evidence we obtained two years ago, or that it's evidence only left-handed people have, is higher-order evidence but not competence evidence.

into account in revising our thinking. As Richard Feldman (2005) puts it, we should "respect" both types of evidence.

An example will make these points more concrete. During the early years of magnetic resonance imaging (MRI), physicians and medical technicians didn't know how to interpret all of the information MRI provided. As it turned out, if the raw data that compose an MRI image are sampled incorrectly, the image will feature misleading artifacts. Between 1987 and 1990, clinicians viewing scans sometimes noted a prominent dark line appearing in patients' spinal cords. The line was a mere artifact of the scan, but clinicians sometimes interpreted it as a disease: a fluid-filled lesion called a syrinx. Many patients were misdiagnosed and treated for the disease. Eventually, someone with a background in both medicine and physics recognized the error and helped usher in new clinical techniques to correct the problem.[20]

Pretend it's the early '90s and you have been feeling back discomfort. You tell your doctor about the pain. She suspects you have a fluid-filled lesion in your spine and schedules an MRI. (Lately, you have been going to a lot of punk rock concerts, vigorously crowd surfing, and you expect this explains the pain; but you are too embarrassed to tell the doctor, who probably doesn't even know what a mosh pit is.) As it happens, your doctor knows of some credible competence evidence indicating her MRI scan interpreting skills are unreliable, but she believes all is well—just look at how many patients she has saved from life-threatening spinal lesions!

If you were to learn all of this, you would find a new doctor. The reason is that you think people should pay heed to available competence evidence, especially when it raises doubts about their ability to handle the first-order evidence. You judge that any doctor who "respects" the competence evidence will reduce her confidence in her clinical judgments based on MRI scans once she learns that her interpretative skills are unreliable. In general, people

---

[20] See Baird and Cohen (1999) for more about the episode along with images of scans showing the spurious artifact (known as "Gibbs ringing").

What happened to the patients misdiagnosed and treated for a syrinx? Aggressive treatments included inserting a tube into a patient's spinal cord to drain the supposed syrinx, a complicated and dangerous procedure that could lead to infection. An even more extreme treatment would have been a laminectomy (removal of the bones of the spine), in order to take suspected pressure off the spinal cord. Did any of these patients die? I wrote to ask Mark S. Cohen, a neuroscientist, and he informed me that death from these procedures was unlikely but possible. Cohen remarked that it isn't easy to know the consequences of the misdiagnosis, as "malpractice morbidity seldom reaches the medical literature" (personal correspondence in June 2017).

should evaluate their first-order and competence evidence while deliberating about what to believe.[21]

The method draws our attention to competence evidence. Sometimes competence evidence indicates we're perfectly capable of forming a reasonable, justified, or warranted belief on the basis of the first-order evidence. But this type of evidence can also raise doubts. I call doubts raised by competence evidence *competence defeaters*. These are reasons to doubt whether we are well-positioned to form a belief having positive epistemic status on the basis of our first-order evidence.

Here's how the method can help us deliberate about our controversial beliefs. The principles and observations about intellectual life draw our attention to *prima facie* competence defeaters. Some of these defeaters will be undefeated, because the *prima facie* threat is not neutralized. Thus, we have reason to doubt some of our controversial beliefs. The idea is that if the principles show us undefeated defeaters, we can recognize that some of our beliefs are unreasonable and thereby better know our limits as inquirers.

As I have noted, defeaters are full or partial reasons to give up a belief. So, which kind of defeaters does the method present for our controversial beliefs? In order to answer that question, we need to consider what makes one defeater full and another partial.

You might think the type of defeater, be it full or partial, is determined wholly by its intrinsic features. But that isn't correct. To explain why, I'll focus on how a belief's positive epistemic status changes once a defeater is acquired. A defeater is a *prima facie* threat to a belief. If the defeater is undefeated, it changes the degree of positive epistemic status the belief has. Suppose a defeater brings about a minor drop in the belief's positive epistemic status. That may be consistent with the thinker properly holding the belief *even after acquiring the defeater*. For example, suppose I ask nine meteorologists whether it will rain later today. Each one reports that rain is highly likely and

---

[21] I do not say that people should *always* consider competence evidence while deliberating doxastically. Such a requirement appears impossible to satisfy, given the threat of a vicious regress. For any belief you form about your competence, you'll be required to consider more competence evidence. But that can't go on indefinitely—eventually, the dizziness-inducing complexity of the beliefs concerning your competence to form beliefs about your competence will mean you can't meet the requirement. (For detailed discussion of this sort of point about vicious regress, see Bergmann 2006 and Kornblith 2012.) Thus, I assume that you should consider competence evidence when you have some question or doubt about your competence to evaluate the first-order evidence—and perhaps when you *should* have some doubt, including cases where the competence evidence becomes especially salient in your deliberation, so that failing to consider it would be an oversight. (Thanks to Peter Seipel for discussion.)

I believe them. When a tenth meteorologist reports that rain is highly un-likely, I acquire a *prima facie* defeater for my belief. Supposing the defeater is undefeated, we may imagine it would only call for a relatively minor drop in positive epistemic status. In this case, I'd still be permitted to believe rain is highly likely, though now my degree of confidence would be lower. In a dif-ferent situation, where I start out with weaker grounds for my belief before acquiring the defeater, an equally small drop in positive epistemic status may call for abandoning my belief altogether. Thus, a defeater does not change a belief's positive epistemic status wholly because of facts about the defeater. A defeater is not full or partial unto itself.

In general, whether a defeater is full or partial depends on the interaction between the defeater, the targeted belief, and the thinker's evidence or sup-port for the defeater and the belief. To put it differently, whether some defeater is full or partial for us depends on facts about our evidence for the defeater and our evidence for the targeted belief. And thus to know whether a defeater is full or partial, we must know about our broader epistemic circumstances. In still other words, we should not think of a defeater for a belief *simpliciter*, but always of a defeater for someone's belief. For simplicity's sake, I'll say a defeater is full or partial relative to our total evidence. A defeater is full if we add it to our total evidence and, as a result, we have reason to give up the be-lief altogether. A defeater is partial if we add it to our total evidence and, as a result, we have reason to lower our degree of confidence in our belief.[22]

Thinking about defeaters and defeat in this way has significant implications for the method. The method may deliver full defeaters, partial defeaters, or both. Suppose we are deliberating about a controversial belief of ours. Guided by one principle and associated observations, we may recognize a partial defeater for the belief. Using other principles and observations, we may come to see a distinct partial defeater for the same belief. One possi-bility is that the principles and observations only yield partial defeaters. This does not mean that using the method can't defeat a belief fully. Several partial defeaters, in the aggregate, can do precisely that. Full defeat by multiple par-tial defeaters is a fact of intellectual life. What we believe and how we change our minds over time is, or at least should be, sensitive to many bits of evi-dence, drawn from many sources. This is especially true when it comes to controversial matters.[23]

---

[22] Compare to Feldman (2009), Lackey (2010), and Kelly (2013).
[23] Nathan King (2016) describes a framework for understanding the cumulative impact of higher-order evidence.

6. Defeating Closed Minds

Let's take stock. We are in the midst of examining key ideas and definitions that play a role in the regulative method. The method uses principles and observations about intellectual life to identify *prima facie* competence defeaters for our controversial beliefs. If those defeaters are undefeated, our beliefs or our confidence in those beliefs are unreasonable. The principles help us regulate our controversial opinions. But we can't learn the principles and then promptly forget about them. The principles must guide us, in the special sense I described in Chapter 3. We need to gain cognitive dispositions that allow our inquiry to be guided by our principles even when we aren't consciously reflecting on them. To discover good techniques for equipping inquirers with principle-following dispositions, I noted that we must wait for insights from scientists. In the meantime, as I suggested in Chapter 3, we can try to develop exercises patterned after ancient and early modern philosophical "meditation" techniques. Some of the examples and "thought experiments" I present in Chapters 5 through 9 will suggest to the reader how these exercises could go.

For the time being, let's assume we are guided by the method. Where will it lead us? What happens to our controversial beliefs? The matter is not straightforward. In fact, while writing this book, I changed my mind about the consequences of following the method.

Now is a good time for a confession. This book had a couple of false starts.[24] Originally, I set out to defend epistemic principles which would deliver *undefeated full competence defeaters*, spurring people guided by the principles to suspend judgment in response to controversial questions. I had meant to defend a kind of mitigated or limited Pyrrhonian skepticism. Here was the basic idea. Truths about controversial matters are usually hidden from our view by the haze of competence defeaters—we have evidence indicating that we aren't well-positioned to answer controversial questions. Uncontroversial matters can be known more easily, however, so we need not become radical skeptics and doubt everything. In the end, defending the neo-Pyrrhonian position required more nerve—more skeptical bravado—than I could muster or fake.

The neo-Pyrrhonian approach faltered in two ways. First, although I could accept as an abstract possibility that everyone who gains the *prima*

---

[24] I mention another false start in Chapter 11.

facie competence defeaters also has *on-balance* defeaters and thus should suspend judgment, I didn't see a good argument to bridge the gap between *prima facie* and *on-balance* defeat. What if some people have evidence that defeats the *prima facie* defeaters? Couldn't such people maintain reasonable controversial beliefs while they are following the method? I couldn't see why not. Second, I came to believe that the neo-Pyrrhonian idea was not tough enough on thinkers who already suspend judgment about controversial matters. Why shouldn't they, just like believers and disbelievers, learn something new from the method? I couldn't see why not.

My initial thesis exploded on the launch pad. But all was not lost. As I kept writing, I recorded observations about my changing plan in a black notebook. I occasionally reviewed my notes. Sometimes I would be stuck at my computer's keyboard, wondering why in the world I was indoors on a quiet summer afternoon. I would seek guidance from the notebook. It contained lines from Pascal's *Pensées*: "discourses about skepticism are a source for assertion to the assertive. Few speak . . . doubtingly of skepticism" (2004 [1670], 167; S539/L655). I returned to Pascal's thought over months and years, committing and recommitting myself to the idea of writing doubtingly of skepticism.

The method described in these pages is designed to help you know the limits of your reasonable beliefs. My ill-fated neo-Pyrrhonian thesis laid down the limits explicitly—everyone who has the *prima facie* competence defeaters should suspend judgment concerning controversial issues. But that is not my thesis. I won't pretend to know anyone else's limits.

I offer principles and observations about intellectual life. I don't tell you how they should change your thinking. They may lead you to suspend judgment on many controversial topics, or not. Here is an analogy. You borrow a map from me and then head off on your travels. The map depicts some perilous mountain terrain. If you want to avoid danger, I can't tell you what steps to take. I would need to know where you are on the map and where you want to go. But how could I know that? The map, all by itself, will not tell you where to go, nor will it require you to seek any destination in particular.

The method is like a map. Suppose it gives you *prima facie* competence defeaters for some of your controversial beliefs. Now choose at random any one of those beliefs. Will the defeaters produce full defeat or partial defeat, or will they be defeated themselves? The correct answer depends on your total evidence, as I've explained. Knowing how *prima facie* defeaters should change your mind requires knowing what is in your total evidence.

The evidence that's relevant to any one of your controversial beliefs may be a simple *modus ponens*, or a complex battery of inductive arguments, or even certain perceptual experiences. But your total evidence is unknown to me.

It is here I find a chasm between you and me. Here I must write doubtingly of skepticism. Who are you? What evidence do you have? Since I don't know, I must remain silent about exactly how the method should influence your thinking. Whether it dictates that you suspend judgment depends on at least two things: whether you have reason to believe you satisfy the conditions set down by the principles, and what's in your total evidence. I offer you the method without telling you where it must lead.

But where *could* the method lead you, me, or anybody else? That's a question I can answer. The method can encourage us to doubt which beliefs are reasonable for us to adopt. It can induce a mindset that is more open, unsettled, and neutral than most people will typically have concerning controversial matters. Let me explain.

Imagine we witness a debate in a public park. Is capital punishment morally justified? Three opponents are seated behind a table covered with a precariously patriotic tablecloth and decorative runner. The case for believing that capital punishment is justified is offered by Believer. A second disputant, Disbeliever, defends disbelieving the proposition. Finally, Agnostic argues for suspension of judgment about it. We listen to the arguments, replies, and counter-replies. We weigh the evidence as judiciously as we can. As the debate concludes, we hear a little explosion somewhere behind us and then a cloud of confetti showers all around. Now the disputants want to know: *What do we think?*

The debate scenario lets us examine the mechanics of our deliberation concerning the three potential doxastic attitudes. It clarifies our options. Most obviously, we can declare one disputant the victor. For example, we can express our belief in the proposition at issue—that capital punishment is morally justified—by siding with Believer. Or we can follow Agnostic by declaring our settled resistance to either belief or disbelief.[25] But that's only one way to respond. Others are less straightforward and easy to overlook during deliberation. We may have significant doubts about which disputant made the strongest case. We may waver over which answer to the question is most reasonable for us to adopt. We may adopt one answer while feeling

---

[25] Here I follow Jane Friedman's (2013) view of agnosticism or suspended judgment as an attitude that expresses settled neutrality concerning believing or disbelieving a proposition.

conflicted and drawn toward another one. The prospect of having to choose any side at all may perplex us. What's the rush? Can't we just think about things for a while?

Envisioning our response to the debate illuminates different mindsets that reflect *our stance toward the three doxastic attitudes*. I want to model how we contemplate the prospect of adopting any of these attitudes, even if we do not end up holding one of them. Think about it like this. While we are listening to the arguments during the debate, and immediately after it's finished, we have a perspective on the question. Maybe our minds are made up; maybe our minds are open. What is the difference? That is what I want to describe. Sometimes our stance toward the three doxastic attitudes is relatively open. We survey the three options and feel unsettled and neutral. On the other hand, our stance toward the attitudes is sometimes relatively closed. We feel resolved and unequivocal. We are partial toward just one attitude.

We are *doxastically open* when we have some significant doubt about which attitude toward a proposition is reasonable for us to hold given our total evidence. We are *doxastically closed* when we do not have any significant doubt about which attitude is reasonable on our evidence.[26]

The debate scenario can help me illustrate these ideas. In uncomplicated cases, we hear the debate and side with one disputant. We do not significantly doubt which attitude is reasonable for us to hold. We are doxastically closed. A closed mindset does not imply any negative normative evaluation of our opinion, however. We are closed about many things—and so we should be. When I consider the three doxastic options concerning the proposition that I exist, I can only believe. I am closed. You are closed about the matter that you are reading a sentence right now. Geologists are closed about whether the continents are in motion. We are closed about the wrongness of chattel slavery. Notice that we can be closed even when we suspend judgment: if we're asked whether the last book we read has an even number of words, we'll have no doubt that suspension of judgment is the appropriate attitude. In many cases, we lack any significant doubt that our attitudes are reasonable given our evidence. And so we should be closed.

Other times we are doxastically open. Back in the debate scenario, imagine you are rather confident that siding with Believer is an unreasonable

---

[26] There are interesting questions about what doubt is, but I won't need to commit myself to any account of doubt's nature. For useful discussion, see Lee (2018). I follow Howard-Snyder (2013), Lee (2018), and Moon (2018) in the idea that doubts are reasons that can rebut or undercut reasons someone has for a belief. As I put it earlier in this chapter, doubts defeat.

response to your evidence. At the same time, suppose you're unsure whether your evidence points in favor of Disbeliever or Agnostic. You seriously doubt you can tell whether key pieces of evidence support disbelieving rather than suspending judgment. The matter is kind of slippery, and so you do not believe you are well-positioned to evaluate the evidence concerning the appropriateness of disbelieving or suspending judgment. Thus, you can't see your way to adopting either attitude. Perhaps the view you adopt is an attitude toward a higher-order proposition: you suspend judgment concerning whether disbelieving or suspending judgment concerning the first-order proposition is reasonable on your evidence. You remain doxastically open toward those two doxastic options.[27]

Try a second example of doxastic openness. Imagine that before the debate in the park begins, you take a fast-acting allergy medicine that makes you disoriented. The medicine makes you unfit to evaluate the subtle arguments given by the disputants and you know it. At the debate's end, you declare that you abstain from holding any of the three attitudes. Agnostic pumps her fist in victory while Believer and Disbeliever appear crestfallen. But they've missed your point. You explain that your abstention is not equivalent to suspending judgment concerning the proposition that capital punishment can be justified. Plausibly, your abstention can be understood as suspending judgment about a more complex, higher-order proposition: that for any of the three attitudes toward the first-order proposition, your total evidence makes it reasonable for you to adopt it. Your attitude toward that higher-order proposition distinguishes you from Believer, Disbeliever, and Agnostic, each of whom believe, or would believe on reflection, a higher-order proposition about the reasonableness of *their own attitude* toward the proposition that capital punishment is justified. Unlike them, however, you doubt that any of the three attitudes is the appropriate response to your evidence. You remain doxastically open toward the three attitudes.

If we adopt an attitude toward a proposition, are we doxastically closed? Not always. We can hold an attitude while at the same time significantly doubting that our attitude is reasonable given our total evidence. This can happen in various ways. Sometimes we are "of two minds" and hold one attitude while simultaneously feeling pulled toward another. We may waver

---

[27] Notice that you are doxastically closed when it comes to attitudes toward the higher-order proposition—unless you have significant doubts concerning whether suspending judgment is a reasonable response to your evidence.

between two or even three attitudes. Mental conflicts are part of our native condition. The French playwright Jean Racine, a Jansenist educated at Port-Royal, encapsulated the ambivalence of human love in a question: "Ne puis-je savoir si j'aime, ou si je haïs?" (Am I not able to know whether I love or hate?).[28] In more than just relationships, we are conflicted, indecisive, and unsettled. "Inconsistencies," as Samuel Johnson noted, "cannot both be right; but, imputed to man, they may both be true."[29] Our doubts can make us confused, perplexed, and mystified about many topics, perhaps especially controversial ones. But our opinions can only survive so much doubt. As a normative matter, doubts can make opinions unreasonable—doubts defeat. Doubts come in degrees and greater doubts tend to call for greater doxastic openness. As a psychological matter, doubts can extinguish our opinions; if we greatly doubt that an attitude is a reasonable response to our evidence, we may fail to qualify as having that attitude. Doxastic attitudes can coexist with significant doubts, but only up to a point.

If we are open with respect to some proposition, we are not closed. If we are closed, we are not open. Doxastic openness and closedness sit on a spectrum. Being closed places us at the furthest end of one side; being open puts us somewhere on a line of states of relatively greater or lesser openness. Picture a door.[30] There's just one way for the door to be closed, but the door can be open in ways that are more or less open. Doxastic openness is like that. For example, we can be open because we have significant doubt whether belief or suspension of judgment regarding a proposition is appropriate, or we can be open because we have significant doubt whether any of the three attitudes toward a proposition is appropriate.

Importantly, being closed does not imply that we have a high or maximal level of confidence in our attitude. When we're closed about an attitude, we don't have any significant doubt whether it is appropriate. We can be closed about an attitude held with low or modest confidence, if we judge that precisely that level of confidence is reasonable given our evidence. Suppose I normally have modest confidence about my perceptual beliefs concerning medium-sized objects viewed from a short distance away. I spot what appears to be a cottontail rabbit. My confidence that it's a rabbit is not high or maximal here, but I can be closed in my belief that it is a rabbit. I am closed here,

---

[28] *Andromaque* (1667), Act V, Scene I.
[29] *The History of Rasselas, Prince of Abissinia* (1759), Chapter 8.
[30] Michael Bergmann suggested this analogy.

because I don't have any significant doubt that my belief is a reasonable response to my evidence.

Being doxastically open and closed are different mindsets toward the three attitudes we can take toward any proposition. These stances can be thought of as attitudes toward higher-order propositions about the epistemic status of attitudes toward a first-order proposition.[31]

I have modeled doxastic deliberation as a response to an imagined debate between three points of view—believing, disbelieving, and suspending judgment. The model illuminates how our minds can be made up or unsettled. It also shows how doubts can keep us doxastically open. The model helps us recognize where the method could lead us—though where we go depends on our total evidence. The method reveals to us *prima facie* competence defeaters, which are reasons to doubt our controversial beliefs. If the competence defeaters are undefeated, they can make us more doxastically open about controversial matters than we would be otherwise.

7. Looking Ahead

In developing the regulative method contained in this book, I intend to follow a philosophical tradition that uses principles, dialectical methods, and arguments to open minds. Here are three examples that have stirred and inspired me.

In Plato's dialogues, Socrates' interlocutors often begin with great confidence in their knowledge. But after a few rounds of relentless questioning, Socrates has pinned his interlocutors against the ropes. Socrates floats like a butterfly and stings like an electric eel.[32] His interlocutors are stunned and

---

[31] Even greater heights of doxastic openness await thinkers who abstain from the three attitudes toward the higher-order proposition. To see why, consider a thinker who doesn't take one of the three attitudes toward the first-order proposition *or* the higher-order proposition concerning the epistemic status of attitudes toward the first-order proposition. She could do this by suspending judgment toward a third-order proposition concerning the epistemic status of attitudes toward the second-order proposition. Feeling dizzy yet? Try an example. Imagine you listen to a debate between advocates of each logically coherent combination of different all-or-nothing attitudes one could take toward *both* the first-order and second-order proposition. If you are confused and unable to side with any partisan, you may suspend judgment concerning a proposition at the "third" level—that is, you suspend judgment whether your evidence makes it reasonable for you to adopt one of the three attitudes toward either the second-order or first-order proposition. (Still not dizzy?)

My point is simple. We can describe increasingly "deep" doxastic openness about what people should think, at least insofar as human beings can grasp the increasingly complex propositions. If there is an upper limit for openness, that is total confusion—not just about what we should think but also about what we should think about what we should think.

[32] In Plato's *Meno*, Meno says to Socrates:

stupefied, cartoon halos of stars and birdies circling their heads. Now they feel *aporia*—a state of perplexity or doubt. Now they know that they didn't know what they thought they knew. The conversation with Socrates has made them more doxastically open, at least for a moment or two.

Michel de Montaigne was a kind of skeptic. Unlike ancient Greco-Roman skeptics, he did not confess "I don't know" or "I am ignorant." His watchword was "Que sçay-je?" (What do I know?) (1957 [1575–80], 477; "Apology for Raymond Sebond"). That question captures Montaigne's hope for calm ambivalence, a shrug of the shoulders in the face of the world's complexity and mystery. Fittingly, Montaigne did not commit himself to any general skeptical thesis, though he deployed skeptical modes of argument in his essays to strengthen and refine his judgment. He wrote:

> I like these words, which soften and moderate the rashness of our propositions: "perhaps," "to some extent," "some," "they say," "I think," and the like. And if I had to train children, I would have filled their mouths so much with this way of answering, inquiring, not decisive—"What does it mean? I do not understand it. That might be. Is it true?"—that they would be more likely to have kept the manner of learners at sixty than to represent learned doctors at ten, as they do. (1957 [1585–88], 959; "Of Cripples")

Montaigne was trying to keep his doxastic options open.

In 1910, Professor Gilbert Murray, editor of *The Home University Library* series, convinced Bertrand Russell to write a new title for the series. Murray encouraged Russell to "communicate his thoughts to shop-assistants." The following year, Russell took eight weeks to write *The Problems of Philosophy*, what he called his "shilling shocker."[33] In the concluding chapter, Russell addressed the value of philosophy. Although philosophy is not good for securing knowledge of the correct answers to its questions, he said it can

---

[I]f a joke is in order, you seem, in appearance and in every other way, to be like the broad torpedo fish, for it too makes anyone who comes close and touches it feel numb, and you now seem to have had that kind of effect on me, for both my mind and my tongue are numb, and I have no answer to give you. (1997, 879; 80a–b)

Contemporary readers likely know the fish in question as the electric eel. (For a fascinating historical study starring the electric eel, see Turkel 2013.)

[33] Schwerin (1999) describes the development of Russell's *The Problems of Philosophy* and the influence of Lady Ottoline Morrell on Russell's discussion in the final chapter of the value of philosophy.

suggest many possibilities which enlarge our thoughts and free them from the tyranny of custom. Thus, while diminishing our feeling of certainty as to what things are, it greatly increases our knowledge of what they may be; it removes the somewhat arrogant dogmatism of those who have never travelled into the region of liberating doubt, and it keeps alive our sense of wonder by showing familiar things in an unfamiliar aspect. (1997 [1912], 157)

I don't know what the shop-assistants made of this. But I remember when I first read Russell's words years ago and they have never ceased to delight me.

If we are guided by the regulative method, how will we think about controversial questions? Perhaps we will feel *aporia* more than we would otherwise. Perhaps we will wonder more often whether our beliefs are reasonable and seek to hedge against our instinctual rashness in judgment. Perhaps we will push deeper into the region of liberating doubt. If that is indeed where we go, we travel in good company.

I opened this chapter by comparing our beliefs to windows. We assume that our beliefs, like clear windows, reveal the world outside as it really is. But we know in general that our beliefs can mislead us, and we have reason in particular to reflect carefully on our controversial beliefs. Why do intelligent and informed people think differently than we do? *Are our controversial beliefs unreasonable?* The method I'll describe in the following chapters can show us how our controversial beliefs are smudged, distorted, and cracked— unreasonable. If we are guided by the method's principles, we will manifest the skill or virtue of being sensitive or attentive to the marks of unreasonable beliefs. Our judgments about what's reasonable for us to believe will be better attuned to relevant competence defeaters. The principles may deliver reasons to doubt our controversial beliefs, prompting us to be more open and unsettled in our thinking. The method can teach us to resist our natural tendency to assume that our own views are accurate and unbiased.

Regulative epistemologists face special occupational hazards. Aiming to improve inquiry, they risk floating up and away into stratospheric methodological abstractions, disengaged from the real challenges of inquiry and the imperfections of inquirers. I hope to stay tethered to the ground. At the same time, I want to offer principles that could assist inquirers in many situations. How could that work? How do I intend to avoid proposing merely theoretical abstractions while at the same time offering proposals that apply fairly widely to intellectual life?

As I've said, the method consists in principles and observations about intellectual life. The observations highlight features of situations we commonly experience. For example, we often learn that other people reject our beliefs, but then we dismiss them as biased. We recognize that if history had been different, we would know about powerful objections to our best arguments for our controversial views. We learn about vast bodies of evidence relevant to our beliefs found in books and articles we have not read. We recognize that answering controversial questions sometimes calls for expertise drawn from several specialized fields, but our training and background is fairly narrow. We know we depend on experts' testimony to understand the world, but the experts sometimes disagree among themselves.

As I'll contend in the next five chapters, each situation offers us competence evidence if we know how to find it. The method helps us sift through our experience and recognize competence defeaters for our controversial opinions. It is a cognitive tool for making sense of our experience as limited thinkers in a profoundly complicated world. Following the method promises to help us know a little better how limited we are.

5

Disagreement and Debunking

Our eyes see nothing behind us. A hundred times a day we make fun of ourselves in the person of our neighbor and detest in others the defects that are more clearly in ourselves, and wonder at them with prodigious impudence and heedlessness.

—Michel de Montaigne, "Of the Art of Discussion," 1585–88

The rule is perfect: in all matters of opinion our adversaries are insane. When I look around me, I am often troubled to see how many people are mad.

—Mark Twain, *Christian Science*, Book I, Chapter V, 1907

Don't talk to people who don't think you're decent. Don't read books, don't read articles, by writers who don't think you're decent, who don't think those who are like you are decent. Their writing is based on a false assumption. It's skewed, distorted. Your thought must be founded on truth, the truth that you are a decent person.

—Wallace Shawn, *The Fever*, 1991

Most of what we believe comes to us from the word of others. Our picture of the world would be unimaginably impoverished if we didn't have testimony from other people. But we do not always believe what we are told. Sometimes we reject thinkers' reports by attributing biases to them. We often reason in that way when we disagree with what others tell us.

Reflecting on our own experience reveals that we often engage in this kind of reasoning. Perhaps we think that some climate science researchers have been biased by powerful financial incentives from the oil industry and so we regard their reports about climate change as untrustworthy. Or perhaps we hear a smart but hotheaded talk show host who is biased by disdain for her political opponents; we take ourselves to have reason to reject her statements about her opponents' views and personal lives.

It's commonplace to observe other people dismissing their interlocutors by appealing to biases. For example, Hilary Putnam and Robert Nozick disagreed about political philosophy. According to Putnam, he and Nozick had talked extensively about politics, but—despite their patient, open-minded discussions—the dispute was never resolved. Putnam asked: "What happens in such disagreements? When they are intelligently conducted on both sides, sometimes all that can happen is that one sensitively diagnoses and delineates the source of the disagreement" (1982, 164). Putnam's diagnosis of Nozick's error came to this: Nozick had a certain "complex of emotions and judgments" that prevented him from enjoying a "certain kind of sensitivity and perception" about politics (1982, 165). Putnam thought his colleague was subject to "powerful forces of a non-rational kind [that tend] to sway our judgment" (1982, 167). Putnam didn't change his political views in light of the disagreement at least in part because he regarded Nozick as biased.

Here's one striking example of this sort of reasoning. At a psychiatric hospital in Ypsilanti, Michigan between 1959 and '61, three paranoid schizophrenic patients met for conversations. Each patient believed that he alone was Jesus Christ. The meetings were arranged and tape-recorded by a psychologist, Milton Rokeach, who intended to examine some theories about belief-change and to cure the patients' delusions. Rokeach hoped to observe how the three patients would react to having their delusional beliefs challenged. If they engaged with others who claimed the same messianic identity, would they "return to reality" or would they retreat further into delusions? Over two years of daily conversations, each patient persistently dismissed the other messiahs. One Christ claimed his rivals were just patients in a mental hospital and that he alone was God. Another Christ steadfastly denied the other two were even alive; he insisted they were in fact dead bodies animated by machines. The third said the others claimed to be Jesus Christ out of prejudice, jealousy, hatred, and a desire for prestige. The patients' conversations were often heated and sometimes ended in physical altercations. As Rokeach observed, "The three Christs were, if not rational men, at least men of a type we had all encountered before; they were rationalizing men."[1]

---

[1] For an account of the three Christs of Ypsilanti, see Rokeach (1964). Rokeach wrote an afterword to his book in 1981 by which time his reflection on the experiment had humbled him: "[W]hile I failed to cure the three Christs of their delusions, they had succeeded in curing me of mine: of

In cases like these, someone attributes a bias or some type of unreliability to a disagreeing thinker and then downgrades the testimonial evidence the thinker has offered. The testimonial evidence may have had an impact on someone's attitude—for instance, we may have changed our mind about climate change once we listened to the industry-funded researchers, or Putnam may have changed his political opinions in light of Nozick's disagreement, or the paranoid schizophrenic patients could have reconsidered their messiahship. But any downward push in confidence is prevented or diminished, at least to some extent, by debunking or discounting the testimonial evidence.

The significance of this sort of reasoning has been noted in epistemologists' discussions of what has been called the *Problem of Peer Disagreement*. Does learning that we disagree with an epistemic peer—that is, someone roughly equally informed and competent to answer some question—*always* give us reason to reduce our confidence in our view? So-called conciliationists think it does, but nonconciliationists argue that some cases of recognized disagreement between peers allow at least one of them to retain confidence.[2] But both conciliationists and nonconciliationists agree that attributing biases to those who disagree is one important strategy for reacting to disagreements. Theorists in both camps think that if we have reason to regard another thinker as biased, we can sometimes demote that thinker from peer status. The thought that we can, and do, reasonably attribute biases to others and thus prevent their dissent from lowering our confidence in our views is widely affirmed by epistemologists theorizing about disagreement.[3]

I call this *debunking reasoning*. To understand it better, I will address four main questions in this chapter: What is debunking reasoning? (section 1) What are good reasons to debunk testimony from thinkers who disagree with us? (section 2) How do people tend to make judgments about biases? (section 3) How often do we have good reasons to debunk testimony from thinkers who disagree with us? (section 4) And I will defend the following thesis: although debunking reasoning promises to preserve reasonable belief in the face of disagreement, debunking often won't be reasonable for us once we realize what it demands and once we know how people tend to make

my God-like delusion that I could change them by omnipotently and omnisciently arranging and rearranging their lives within the framework of a 'total institution.'" Rokeach had come to believe he "had no right" to manipulate the lives of the three men.

   [2] For more on this debate, see Kelly (2005), Feldman (2006), Christensen (2007a, 2009), Feldman and Warfield (2010), and Christensen and Lackey (2013).

   [3] Kornblith (1999) is an important discussion of biases of rationalization.

judgments about biases. Our discussion brings two main lessons, which I'll return to in the conclusion (section 5). First, in the face of testimony from those who disagree with us, we may have competence defeaters for our controversial beliefs because we won't be able to debunk dissenting testimony as often as we might like. These defeaters may prompt us to become more doxastically open. Second, we need principled methods for assessing bias in others and in ourselves, and this calls for a dramatic shift in how we make judgments about bias.

Let me underscore why debunking reasoning is a topic worthy of our attention. Debunking plays a crucial practical role while we navigate our information-saturated world. On the one hand, we can't accept everything we hear—on pain of incoherence or the possibility of endless waffling in our views. On the other hand, if we fact-check every last bit of testimony, we'll be hopelessly bogged down in gathering further evidence to make up our minds. Judging that an evidence source is biased lets us swiftly judge its fruits and move on. Reasoning in this way helps us piece together and manage our webs of belief. It is one type of inferential method among others that we use to build our intellectual houses. My own view is that the methods by which we amass and evaluate evidence on controversial topics are often makeshift. Doesn't it occasionally seem that our intellectual houses are poorly constructed, that certain walls or rooms would be rent to chips and splinters if they were truly tested? This will be no surprise if our methods are makeshift, as I say they are. To improve our intellectual houses, we must first scrutinize our building methods.

1. Debunking Reasoning

Debunking reasoning plays a role in debates over the epistemic significance of disagreement. Everyone agrees that learning of disagreement provides or constitutes evidence that may undermine our views. And everyone agrees that reasonably attributing biases to disagreeing thinkers lets us resist a downward push in our confidence in our views. But conciliationists and nonconciliationists have different views about when debunking is appropriate.

For example, David Christensen, a conciliationist, thinks that recognized peer disagreement always provides a reason to reduce confidence in one's own views substantially, unless one has an *independent reason* to downgrade the testimonial evidence one has received. An independent reason must not depend on the original reasoning used to reach one's own view (2007a, 2011). This independence constraint rules out reasoning of the following form: "McCoy disagrees with me about proposition p. But p is true. So McCoy is wrong. And so I don't need to take her disagreement as a reason to doubt my view." On the other hand, an independent reason to think a peer is biased lets us debunk the peer's testimonial evidence, thinks Christensen (2014).

But debunking is not the exclusive practice of conciliationists. Nonconciliationists Michael Bergmann and Richard Fumerton have also suggested that we can downgrade a disagreeing peer's testimony if we have reason to regard her as tending to err. Bergmann's idea is that if a thinker has in hand an explanation for why the peer has made an error—because the peer is biased in this particular case, for instance—then the explanation can preserve reasonable belief in the face of disagreement (2009). And here is what Fumerton says about debunking:

> Do I have reason to suspect that some of my [disagreeing] colleagues are plagued by . . . subtle defects? Perhaps I have some reason to believe, for ex-ample, that they are the victims of various biases that cause them to believe what they want to believe . . . . Indeed, I suspect that I *do* have reason to be-lieve that others are afflicted in such ways. (2010, 102)

By taking others to be biased, Fumerton thinks he may "sometimes discount to some extent the fact that well-known and respected intellectuals disagree with me" (2010, 103).

On all sides, then, philosophers have proposed that we can properly react to disagreement by making bias attributions. But how does the debunking reasoning work? Minimally, it involves two claims:

Bias Premise: Some thinker is biased regarding proposition p.
Debunking Conclusion: We have reason to reduce confidence in that thinker's report about p.

Any instance of debunking reasoning aims to secure the Debunking Conclusion at least partly on the basis of the Bias Premise. There's no one-size-fits-all argument schema to capture every path from premise to conclu-sion. That is because there is no single type of inference pattern here—it may be deductive, inductive, or abductive. Does this mean that we can't begin to understand, in general, when debunking reasoning is successful and when it's not? No. We may safely assume that we can move in appropriate steps from the Bias Premise to the Debunking Conclusion.[4] But spelling out the reasoning in detail will not answer the important question about what counts as a good reason to accept the Bias Premise in the first place. That's where the action is.

2. Debunking Strategies

So what makes it reasonable to accept the Bias Premise? As we move toward an answer, let's consider what the Bias Premise is. It's a claim about a thinker's disposition, in some situation, to form inaccurate or unreasonable attitudes regarding a proposition p. Biases may prevent someone from accurately forming attitudes about p or from being reasonable in responding to evidence regarding p. Being biased does not imply actual inaccuracy or unreasonableness, but it carries a significant risk of error due to a tendency to form attitudes or evaluate evidence in an unreliable way. Being biased, as I'll think of it here, means being unreliable to some degree or other, but the converse does not hold. That is, being unreliable does not mean being biased: the victim of a Cartesian demon's systematic deception is unreliable but not biased, for instance. Thus, affirming the Bias Premise calls for evidence that tells us about a thinker's attitude-forming tendencies.

I examine four potential strategies for securing the Bias Premise. I begin with a strategy that may tempt us. Suppose we disagree with a presumed peer and have reason to think our view is correct. If our view is correct, then our peer's view is mistaken. It follows that we have reason to regard our peer as mistaken. Now, in peer disagreements, we can rule out certain explanations for a peer's mistake—it isn't for lack of relevant evidence or intellectual abilities that a peer is wrong. But abilities are a kind of competence, and even the competent may sometimes blow it. Let's also assume, then, that we can't attribute our peer's mistake to a mere performance error. We can infer

---

[4] For instance, the following offers the makings of a deductively valid route from Bias Premise to Debunking Conclusion: we have evidence for the Bias Premise; evidence that a thinker is biased is evidence that the thinker is unreliable; and evidence that the thinker is unreliable makes it reasonable to reduce confidence in what the thinker reports or believes.

that the peer's mistake is (probably) due to bias. Thus, the Bias Premise is (probably) true.

We can summarize that reasoning as follows:

> *Dogmatic Dismissal Strategy*: We have reasons to accept that (1) the attitude we take toward proposition *p* is correct, (2) if we are correct about *p*, then a disagreeing thinker's attitude regarding *p* is mistaken, (3) the disagreeing thinker's mistake is not due to a lack of relevant evidence or intellectual abilities or to a performance error, and (4) if a thinker's mistake is not explained by a lack of relevant evidence, a lack of intellectual abilities, or a performance error, then it is (probably) due to bias. On the basis of (1) through (4), and what follows from those steps, we can infer that the Bias Premise is (probably) true.

On a first look, the Dogmatic Dismissal Strategy may seem to be a promising route to the Bias Premise. But it's not.

Consider a crucial step in the reasoning: our view is correct, and if we are correct, then our opponent is mistaken, and so our opponent's view is mistaken. If this reasoning is any good, it licenses an extremely dogmatic response to any and all opponents. Whenever others disagree with us—even recognized epistemic *superiors*—this strategy lets us infer that they are mistaken by appealing to our reasons for thinking that we are correct. If we have such reasons in the first place, then we need never change our minds when encountering disagreement. Something has gone wrong.

Here's another strategy. Suppose that we have some evidence—call it *E*—and it is reasonable for us to think that having *E* *rationally compels* some attitude toward a proposition. Now if we know that a thinker has *E* but does not hold the attitude mandated by *E*, then we can conclude that the thinker is in error. To illustrate this, consider an example from Peter van Inwagen:

> There exists an organization called the Flat Earth Society, which is, as one might have guessed, devoted to defending the thesis that the earth is flat. At least some of the members of this society are very clever and are fully aware of the data and arguments—including photographs taken from space—that establish that the earth is spherical. Apparently this is not a joke; they seem to be quite sincere. What can we say about them except that they are intellectually perverse? (2009, 21)

Van Inwagen's idea is that members of the Flat Earth Society are in an evidential situation that rationally compels them to accept that the earth is spherical. It's an established fact that the world is not flat, thinks van Inwagen, because there is compelling, knockdown evidence widely available for that thesis. Since van Inwagen knows these people nevertheless believe the world is flat, he concludes that they are "intellectually perverse." Let's assume that the sort of intellectual perversity at issue here involves bias. All of this suggests a second route to the Bias Premise:

> *Unresponsiveness-to-Compelling-Evidence Strategy*: We have reasons to accept (1) that some body of evidence E rationally compels a particular attitude toward a proposition p, (2) that a disagreeing thinker has E but does not hold the attitude toward p required by E, and (3) that the best explanation for why the disagreeing thinker does not hold the required attitude toward p is bias. On the basis of (1) through (3), we can infer that the Bias Premise is (probably) true.

This strategy moves our disputants aside by the sheer force of our evidence. In the disagreements we are party to, do we plausibly have evidence that rationally compels a particular attitude? If not, this strategy won't help.

As far as I can tell, the Unresponsiveness-to-Compelling-Evidence Strategy is not useful insofar as our disagreements involve *controversial beliefs* in the sense described in Chapter 4—namely, beliefs we reasonably think are rejected by other people who have evidence concerning an issue that's at least approximately as good as ours and who are at least approximately as good at responding to such evidence as we are. Suppose we take ourselves to have evidence that compels our opinion, but we know our opponents hold another view. Then we won't think the issue is genuinely controversial: our opponents will seem to us to be either less well-informed about the issue or less well-disposed to evaluate the evidence than we are.

In general, it's doubtful that we can debunk our peers using the Unresponsiveness-to-Compelling-Evidence Strategy in many cases of controversy. Take philosophical controversies as one example. Are there any philosophical arguments that rationally compel a particular attitude? Philosophers such as van Inwagen (2009, 34, 105) and David Lewis (1983, x) deny that there are conclusive, knockdown philosophical arguments, at least for substantive theses—negative theses, such as Edmund Gettier's thesis that knowledge is not justified true belief, may be supported by such arguments.

But even philosophers who fancy themselves to have discovered rationally-compelling arguments have failed to convince everyone or even a majority of philosophers. The uncertain among us therefore may find it unclear whether or not there are any compelling philosophical arguments.[5]

Even if there are no compelling arguments for controversial philosophical views, it's plausible that many nonphilosophical claims are supported by compelling evidence. Van Inwagen's case of the Flat Earth Society is like that. So is the case of scientists funded by the oil industry who deny certain claims about human-caused climate change. In such cases, the available evidence seems to demand a particular doxastic response. Since certain people have that evidence and yet fail to hold the mandated views, we can plausibly conclude that they are biased. But in most of the disagreements we care about we won't have reason to think our evidence is so potent. Two of the cases I started this chapter with—the ones featuring Putnam and Nozick, and the smart but hotheaded talk show host who attacks her political opponents—do not seem to involve compelling, knockdown evidence for a thesis. At best, the Unresponsiveness-to-Compelling-Evidence Strategy will have limited use. We can set it to the side.

Let's turn now to a potentially more widely applicable strategy for reaching the Bias Premise (again, the claim that some thinker is biased with respect to some proposition) starting with an example given by David Christensen:

> [You are] attending a contest for high-school musicians. After hearing all the performers, and becoming quite convinced that Kirsten's performance was significantly better than Aksel's, [you] hear the man next to [you] express just the opposite opinion. But then [you] find out that he is Aksel's father. (2014, 143)

Christensen thinks you can properly downgrade Aksel's father's testimony. More important, Christensen denies that anything along the lines of the Dogmatic Dismissal Strategy will explain why. According to Christensen, a good reason for reducing confidence in Aksel's father's testimony is *not* that you are sure that Kirsten's performance was significantly better than Aksel's. If that were your reason, of course, you would not have an "independent" reason to debunk the testimony, in the sense noted earlier in section 1.

---

[5] For discussion of whether there are conclusive arguments in philosophy, see Ballantyne (2014), Hanna (2015), Keller (2015), Hu (2017), and Kelly and McGrath (2017).

What would be a better reason? You attribute to Aksel's father a bias with respect to his judgment concerning the relative merits of the musical performances. Why think that Aksel's father is biased? We shouldn't expect that most people will judge their kinfolk impartially on the merits of their musical performances. Family relationships bias our judgments here as elsewhere. Thus, you can reasonably accept the Bias Premise in this case and reach the Debunking Conclusion.

But it's doubtful that all of this captures a sufficient condition for accepting the Bias Premise. Imagine a case just like Christensen's, with one extra detail: you know a further factor holds for Aksel's father, a factor that tends to counteract or neutralize the biasing factor. More specifically, imagine that Aksel's father is a professional judge on the high-school music-contest circuit and he has special training that helps him avoid biased responses toward his own students. Aksel's father may be *enlightened* by his music-contest-judgment expertise, and perhaps this lets him avoid or overcome the biasing influence of fatherhood. In this situation, you would not have reason to infer that Aksel's father is biased, because any bias has been counteracted. Your reason to think that fatherhood biases judgments, and that Aksel's father enjoys paternity, is thus not enough to accept the Bias Premise in this case.

Putting that all together, here is what I call the

Biasing-Factor-Attribution Strategy: We have reasons to accept (1) that a factor F tends to bias judgments about proposition p, (2) that factor F holds for a disagreeing thinker's judgment about p, and (3) that we know of no "enlightening" factor that holds for the thinker's judgment about p (i.e., a factor that tends to counteract or neutralize F's influence). On the basis of (1) through (3), we infer that the Bias Premise is (probably) true.

Here we find an inference that's a kind of statistical syllogism, where we argue inductively from a mostly-true generalization to a specific case. It appears to be available in a wide range of cases given that there are many factors which bias judgments. I examine this strategy in some detail later, but for now I will move on to a fourth strategy. Properly assessing the Biasing-Factor-Attribution Strategy requires us to engage with questions about how people form judgments about biases, the topic of the next section.

As I noted earlier, Richard Fumerton takes himself to have reason to regard disagreeing thinkers as suffering from biases. What is his reason again? He writes:

Do I have reason to suspect that some of my [disagreeing] colleagues are plagued by . . . subtle defects? Perhaps I have some reason to believe, for example, that they are the victims of various biases that cause them to believe what they want to believe . . . . Indeed, I suspect that I do have reason to believe that others are afflicted in such ways . . . . I do, in fact, think that I have got more self-knowledge than a great many other academics I know, and I think that self-knowledge gives me a better and more neutral perspective on a host of philosophical and political issues. I suspect that it is in part the fact that I take this belief of mine to be justified that I do think that I can sometimes discount to some extent the fact that well-known and respected intellectuals disagree with me. (2010, 102–103)

Fumerton doesn't rely on the Biasing-Factor-Attribution Strategy. He doesn't point to some biasing factor that holds for his opponents. So how does Fumerton's reasoning deliver the Bias Premise? Doesn't it presuppose that disagreeing thinkers are biased?

Squinting a bit at what Fumerton says, his reasoning may proceed as follows. Unlike the Biasing-Factor-Attribution Strategy, which involves a kind of statistical syllogism, Fumerton's reasoning relies on an inference to the best explanation. Fumerton takes himself to know things about himself that indicate he is not biased or that at least he is relatively less biased than his opponents on political and philosophical matters. But since these disputes (presumably) concern matters of objective fact, somebody is mistaken. Since Fumerton assumes that he and his opponents share relevant evidence and intellectual abilities, the best way to explain one side's error is to posit a bias. Given that Fumerton purportedly knows he's neutral, it's his opponents who must be biased. Thus, Fumerton has a reason to accept that his opponents are biased.

We may sum up this reasoning as follows:

Self-Exculpating Strategy: We have reasons to accept (1) that we are not biased and (2) that one side of the disagreement has made a mistake due to bias (rather than differences in evidence or intellectual abilities or other factors including a performance error). On the basis of (1) and (2), we can infer that the Bias Premise is (probably) true.

I consider this strategy in some detail later in this chapter, but here's one remark about step (2). Many disagreements can be explained without appealing

to biases: differences in evidence or intellectual abilities as well as mere performance errors are included here. Therefore, reason to accept (2) sensibly
amounts to reason to think alternative, nonbias explanations for why one
side has erred are not as plausible as the explanation that bias offers.[6]

So far, I've noted four types of reasons for accepting the Bias Premise. Since
the Dogmatic Dismissal Strategy does not appear to offer us a good reason,
I will ignore it. Although the Unresponsiveness-to-Compelling-Evidence
Strategy is sometimes effective, I'll set it aside, too, because its use is rather
limited. The two remaining options—the Biasing-Factor-Attribution and the
Self-Exculpating strategies—look more promising. Unfortunately, as I will
argue, in a great many of the cases of disagreement we take to be practically
or theoretically important, these two debunking strategies won't help us out.

The trouble, briefly, is that these strategies carry with them implausible
assumptions about our ability to make good judgments about biases. Once
we understand how people tend to form judgments about biases, we'll be able
to assess critically the Biasing-Factor-Attribution and the Self-Exculpating
strategies. Even if those strategies are sometimes appropriate, we may often
be unable to put them to use properly, in light of what we know about how
judgment of bias works.

And so we come to our third question: How do people tend to make
judgments about biases?

3. The Bias Blind Spot

Psychologists have begun to reveal how we make judgments about biases, and
the lessons are fascinating. A well-established body of work in psychology
observes "a broad and pervasive tendency for people to see the existence and
operation of bias much more in others than in themselves" (Pronin 2007, 37).
This is a kind of *bias bias*—a bias that sways judgment and reasoning *about*
bias—and it has been called the "bias blind spot." It results in the conviction

---

[6] To reasonably accept (2), we must rule out potentially minor asymmetries in relevant epistemic
factors, but this may be difficult. For example, given that "small" differences in evidence may sometimes make "big" differences in how we should think, to accept (2) we'll sometimes need to have a
reason to think there's not even a small evidential difference between us and our opponents. (King
2012 presses this point in connection with evidential symmetry between epistemic peers.) But we
may assume that reasonably accepting (2) is not too hard, since we're supposing that many of us
commonly attribute biases to recognized disagreeing peers. Without that assumption, the range of
disagreements in which we can deploy the Self-Exculpating Strategy will be somewhat limited.

that one's own judgments are less susceptible to bias than the judgments of others. Direct testing confirms that the blind spot is widespread (Pronin, Lin, and Ross 2002). Several cognitive mechanisms have been found to generate the bias blind spot: (*i*) an important evidential asymmetry between judgments of self and others; (*ii*) naïve realism, the tendency to think our perceptions give us an accurate, undistorted view of reality; and (*iii*) the motive of self-enhancement. I'll explain each in turn.

When people make judgments about bias in themselves, they tend to rely on *introspective* evidence; but when they judge bias in others they tend to rely on *behavioral* or *extrospective* evidence. People look into their own minds to judge themselves, whereas they look at outward behavior when judging others, and this evidential asymmetry shapes judgment about bias.

A central idea in psychology is that most biases are not reliably detected by introspection (Nisbett and Wilson 1977; Wilson and Brekke 1994; Kahneman 2003). We typically can't figure out whether we are biased by merely gazing into our minds. Biases normally "leave no trace" in consciousness. As Timothy Wilson and Nancy Brekke quip, "Human judgments—even very bad ones—do not smell" (1994, 121). From the inside, biased attitudes seem just like unbiased ones. We can introspect the particular judgments our cognitive processes produce but not the properties of the processes relevant to the judgments' reliability. In other words, we can't normally introspect the operation of biases on our judgments even when we can detect the outputs of those biases. As the machine chugs along, we can't peek in to see whether it works properly.[7]

Although introspection does not reliably detect the operation of biases, that isn't to say people don't still try. But introspection can lead people astray. People who use it to discover bias may end up with the impression they have acted *in spite of* their own expectations and interests rather than *because of* them. As Joyce Ehrlinger, Thomas Gilovich, and Lee Ross point out, "one's conscious efforts to have avoided bias, in fact to have 'bent over backwards' to do so, are likely to be highly salient" in one's thinking about whether one is biased (2005, 686). The feeling that we've done our level best to be unbiased

---

[7] Can we ever introspect the properties that determine whether a process is biasing? Ehrlinger, Gilovich, and Ross note that "there are some occasions in which introspection does yield evidence of bias, or at least evidence of the motives that prompt bias . . . . A Little League umpire is apt both to realize and recollect how hard it was to utter 'Strike three!' when it was his or her own child in the batter's box" (2005, 686).

will encourage us to think we are unbiased, but that feeling should not be trusted.

Different judgments arise from differences in introspective access—no news there. But it gets worse. It's not just that people actually rely asymmetrically on introspective and behavioral evidence. They also think they *should* place less weight on behavioral evidence in their own case and more weight on their own introspective evidence. In fact, people sometimes show surprising disregard for their own actions even when these actions become salient. Subjects insist their behavior is not relevant to deciding whether they are biased. This is striking. So often in life we are judged by our actions, not our intentions or hopes or feelings. In self-judgment about bias, we overlook our actions and instead cling to how things feel on the inside (Pronin and Kugler 2007). Even when subjects recognize bias *in their judgmental strategies*, they fail to recognize a closely related potential for bias in judgments *based on those strategies* (Hansen et al. 2014). In other words, subjects admit their judgmental strategies are biased while insisting that the judgments they reach through those strategies are objective.

The evidential asymmetry driving the bias blind spot seems to prove the old wisdom: nobody should be a judge in his own case (*nemo iudex in causa sua*). But what if we break down the evidential asymmetry and inform people about others' thoughts and feelings? Will the blind spot vanish? Regrettably not. Even after people are given others' introspective reports, the blind spot tends to persist. In some experiments, psychologists provided observers with a sample of actors' introspections, but observers continued to impute more bias to others than to themselves even when the observers had read and listened to detailed reports from actors and believed that those reports correctly reflected the actors' thoughts (Pronin and Kugler 2007).

A second source of the blind spot is our tendency to presume what psychologists have called *naïve realism*—the idea, noted in Chapter 4, that our experience of the world, others, and ourselves is veridical. We normally assume that our experience gives us a more or less "unmediated" picture of how things really are.

How does naïve realism influence judgment about biases? It turns out that when we discover that others disagree, we often attribute biases to them. In one experiment, American and Canadian undergraduate students who disagreed with the U.S. president's decision to invade Iraq attributed a greater degree of self-interest bias to the president than did students who agreed with him (Reeder et al. 2005). Those in the grips of naïve realism believe that objective thinkers will agree with them. When others disagree with us, we are prompted to ask whether they've missed relevant evidence. If we think they are well-informed, naïve realism leads us to conclude they are biased (Pronin 2007, 39–40). Our tendency to try to resolve cognitive dissonance plausibly explains this sort of effect sometimes. When we find that people disagree with us, we treat this as *prima facie* evidence against our views. Then we resolve the dissonance in favor of our own views, often by way of bias attributions.

Evidential asymmetry and naïve realism are two sources of the bias blind spot—the motive of self-enhancement is a third. Psychological research has established that we see ourselves in an overly positive light. For valuable or desirable traits, we tend to overrate ourselves, even when the evidence tells a different story. In a classic study that should be close to every college teacher's heart, 94 percent of college teachers rated themselves as doing above-average work (Cross 1977). And when people lack a talent or positive trait, they are sometimes oblivious. These sorts of effects stem from powerful "ego-protective" biases. We think well of ourselves, objective evidence be damned, but most people rarely notice this. In fact, psychologists have found that subjects' self-judgments of their desirable behavioral traits tend to be less accurate than others' judgments (Vazire 2010). What accounts for this is that self-assessments are influenced in part by ego-protective processes. In general, self-enhancement bias is thought by some psychologists to be a key element of health (Taylor and Brown 1988).

These psychological findings were anticipated by some observers of human nature. "It is a law of our being," wrote Bertrand Russell, "that, whenever it is in any way possible, we adopt beliefs as will preserve our self-respect" (2004 [1928], 51). As the British essayist William Hazlitt noted, "The narrowness of the heart warps the understanding, and makes us weigh objects in the scales of our self-love, instead of those of truth and justice" (1824, 34). In the *Port-Royal Logic*, Antoine Arnauld and Pierre Nicole picture human beings as radically self-centered, as I noted in Chapter 2: "The human mind is not only naturally enamored of itself, but it is also naturally jealous, envious, and malicious toward others. It allows others to have advantages only with difficulty, because it desires them all for itself" (1996 [1683], 207; III, 20, vi).

But the self-enhancement motive gives us no protective illusions concerning other people—leaving aside the interesting case of family and friends that I'll consider at the end of this chapter. We attribute biases to others with ease. We expect them to make judgments that serve their self-interest and to make overly positive self-assessments. As a result, judgments of bias tend to vary according to who is being judged. The motive to self-enhance thus makes us less likely to find bias in ourselves than in others (Pronin 2007, 37).

To sum up: the bias blind spot stems from an important evidential asymmetry between judgments of self and others, from naïve realism, and from self-enhancement bias. These psychological mechanisms lead to the conviction that our judgments are less susceptible to bias than the judgments of others.

Let me focus in a little more on one important issue. I've noted that to find bias in others we focus on behavioral evidence. But that evidence by itself does not disclose others' inner dispositions. The evidence needs interpretation. We use "abstract theories" of bias to decipher it (Ross, Ehrlinger, and Gilovich 2016). For example, we think people are motivated to seek pleasure and avoid pain. They give heavy weight to their own wants and needs. They are sheltered from reality by psychological defense mechanisms. They view issues through the lens of their ideology and social position. And people are capable of (self-)deception about how nonrational factors influence their own judgments. Such ideas comprise our abstract theories. Our theories tell us when motives, needs, identities, expectations, and context invite bias, allowing us to regard others' behavior as indicating the presence or risk of bias. These theories are rough guidelines, at best. As a matter of fact, they are flawed guides. For instance, experiments show that people sometimes cynically expect others to be more biased than they in fact are (Kruger and Gilovich 1999).

While our abstract theories of bias help us interpret behavioral evidence, that is not to say they are always informed by observations about how biases actually work. They may be constructed from our erroneous ideas about human nature. The sometimes tenuous link between abstract theories and empirical observation can be illustrated with an example.

In 1835, a literary magazine, *Leigh Hunt's London Journal*, noted that "butchers are wisely forbidden to be upon juries; not because they are not as good as other men by nature, and often as truly kind; but because the habit of taking away the lives of sheep and oxen inures them to the sight of blood and violence, and mortal pangs."[8] A few decades earlier, in a treatise defending vegetarianism—*The Cry of Nature; Or, An Appeal to Mercy and to Justice,*

---

[8] *Leigh Hunt's London Journal* No. 60, "Personal Portraits of Eminent Men," Wednesday 20 May 1835, 157.

on Behalf of the Persecuted Animals—we find the following lines: "From the practice of slaughtering an innocent animal, to the murder of man himself, the steps are neither many nor remote. This our forefathers perfectly understood, who ordained that, in a cause of blood, no butcher . . . should be permitted to sit in jury" (Oswald 2000 [1791], 24).

That butchers were excluded from juries in cases of life and death was, according to one English writer in 1798, "a very general opinion," and reports of the exclusion circulated widely, transmitted even by famed authors such as John Dryden, John Locke, and Jonathan Swift.[9] "Every body knows," as Bernard Mandeville noted in 1714, that hard-hearted butchers can't serve on English juries in cases of life and death.[10]

Not everyone distrusted butchers' judgments. William Hazlitt suspected the legal exclusion—the existence of which he apparently didn't doubt— was due to prejudice. Hazlitt said that butchers "look too jolly, rosy . . . to harbor much cruelty in their dispositions" (1824, 38). After reporting the butcher exclusion in 1835, *Leah Hunt's London Journal* backpedaled a month later: "There neither is, nor ever was, it seems" any such exclusion. The journal tried to shirk responsibility for the "involuntary scandal against the butchers," noting the error was passed along by two authorities: John Locke and the seventeenth-century poet, Samuel Butler.[11] But the most spirited and thoroughgoing defense of the butchers is found in *The Experienced Butcher*, a book by James Plumptre and Thomas Lantaffe. The authors report finding no evidence for the jury-exclusion claim in legal books and treatises (1816, 17). They ask, rhetorically, whether there's any reason to believe that shedding animal blood disposes butchers to murderous impulses. Are there disproportionate numbers of murders by butchers listed in public records, such as *The Newgate Calendar* (a notorious bulletin of executions published by London's Newgate Prison)? Further, Plumptre and Lantaffe argue that if butchers should be excluded from juries, then the exclusion must extend to members of other professions:

---

[9] See Thomas Young's 1798 *An Essay on Humanity to Animals*, 5–6; John Dryden, in a prologue for a 1668 play, notes that the law has "excluded Butchers from a Jury"; John Locke repeats the claim in his *Some Thoughts Concerning Education* of 1693 ("Our practice takes notice of this, in the exclusion of butchers from juries of life and death"); Jonathan Swift passes along the report in *Thoughts on Various Subjects, Moral and Diverting* of 1706 ("butchers are not admitted to be jurors upon life and death"). (I learned of the Swift quotation in Stevenson 1954.)

[10] Quoted in Stevenson (1954, 235–236).

[11] *Leigh Hunt's London Journal* No. 64, "The Butcher," Sunday 20 June 1835, 185.

What shall we say of the *fishmonger*, who cuts up some of his animals alive, merely to make them, as it is supposed, taste better? What shall we say of the postboy, the driver of a stage coach, or the gentleman-driver, who make their horses suffer more than a death every day they live? (1816, 22, emphasis in original)

For whatever it's worth, I have never trusted fishmongers or stagecoach drivers.

A group of Scottish butchers took action in 1826. The Incorporation of Fleshers of Edinburgh, a professional butchers' guild, successfully petitioned a court to declare that the Scottish law did not exclude butchers from serving on juries in criminal trials.[12] There is no good evidence to indicate that English law ever excluded butcher jurors either.[13] The story was an urban legend—*avant la lettre*. But how did the story capture the popular mind? Plausibly, people's abstract theories of bias played a role here. People presumed that butchers' intimate, unflinching familiarity with blood and violence biased butchers in cases where common human sympathies were essential for sound judgment. It made good sense to many people that the law would exclude butchers from juries. Just *thinking* about those brutish butchers could make a good gentleperson shudder.

The case of the butcher jurors reveals how abstract theories of bias can be underwritten by errors and prejudice rather than careful observations about human judgment.[14] We should want our abstract theories to be held

---

[12] Incorporation of Fleshers in Edinburgh (1826) Shaw, P. 156 (Scot.) (I am grateful to Alison Shea for tracking down this case for me.)

[13] I contacted some scholars of early modern English and Scottish Law, none of whom knew of any support for the exclusion (email correspondence with the author in June 2017), echoing the judgment of Stevenson (1954), a discussion I discovered later. One researcher, Wilfred Prest, noted that such a specific occupational disqualification would have been "very difficult to contain." Why wouldn't gamekeepers, hangmen, and soldiers also be excluded from juries? Another researcher, Rab Houston, noted that people were passed over for jury service for informal reasons. For instance, people who manifested defects of judgment, due to mental illness or disability, would be deemed unfit for jury service. My thanks to Steven Shapin for pointing me to Plumptre and Lantaffe (1816).

[14] Sydney Penner asked a good question: *do* butchers vary from non-butchers in the moral judgments they make? I don't know of any scholarship addressing that question directly.

But the history of slaughterhouses serves up some atrocious tales about how the Industrial Revolution transformed meat production. Upton Sinclair wrote of the American pork trade in his fictional work, *The Jungle*: "It was porkmaking by machinery, porkmaking by applied mathematics" (2001 [1906], 29, chapter 3). The machines and math turned workers into mere instruments for maximizing capitalists' profits. Sinclair describes meat workers falling into giant rendering vats, their bodies processed along with animal flesh, "till all but the bones of them had gone out to the world as Durham's Pure Leaf Lard!" (2001 [1906], 82, chapter 9). This is fiction, but William Cronon's (1991, chapter 5) historical account of the Union Stockyards in Chicago is not for the faint of heart. Cronon shows how the American meat industry grew up around new railroads, shrewd tricks for utilizing

accountable to our evidence concerning biases, and one crucial body of evidence concerns the bias blind spot. Our abstract theories need to accommodate the fact that we tend to believe that our own judgments are less prone to bias than others' judgments.

Thus concludes my review of research on the blind spot. Let's see how this psychological picture might guide us in the business of debunking.

4. Debunking Strategies and the Psychological Picture

Here is my fourth and final question: How often do we have good reasons to debunk testimony from those who disagree with us?

Recall that debunking reasoning moves from the Bias Premise to the Debunking Conclusion, and we earlier looked at four strategies to get the Bias Premise in hand. The Dogmatic Dismissal Strategy is a nonstarter. The Unresponsiveness-to-Compelling-Evidence Strategy won't apply widely enough to situations where we hope to resist the downward push of testimony from disagreeing thinkers. But the Biasing-Factor-Attribution and the Self-Exculpating strategies show more promise. Let us consider, then, how often we can reasonably follow these two routes to the Bias Premise.

Awareness of the psychological picture brings trouble for anyone who hopes to deploy either the Biasing-Factor-Attribution or the Self-Exculpating strategies in a wide range of important cases. The trouble is that those debunking strategies require particular judgments about biases, but reflection on the psychological picture raises doubts about whether we

creaturely bits and parts, and vast rivers of blood. It's difficult for me to imagine how the people working in such conditions could be unfazed by their experience. Maybe butchers in non-mechanized workplaces, such as the "backyard butcher," would fare better.

At any rate, there's evidence indicating that contemporary butchers, especially ones employed in slaughterhouses, have greater levels of psychological disorders than office workers (Yildiz et al. 2012). One legal scholar catalogues anecdotes of butchers' psychological trauma—on-the-job experiences that many workers can only meet in their nightmares (Dillard 2008). One quantitative study of 581 counties in the United States suggested a positive correlation between slaughterhouse employment levels and crime statistics for violent crime and sexual offenses, compared to other industries (Fitzgerald, Kalof, and Dietz 2009).

But here is a tricky issue. What if butchers' well-being is reduced not because they intentionally kill animals but because their work is stigmatized as "dirty" and has low prestige? Baran, Rogelberg, and Clausen (2016) attempt to tease apart different sources of potential trauma in a large study of Danish employees across many industries. The researchers argue that "the intentional killing of animals likely impacts workers' well-being in deep, psychological ways through their repeated exposure to and involvement in tasks that make them additional victims of the pain they perpetrate" (2016, 357).

reliably make accurate judgments. Accordingly, we should often doubt that it's reasonable for us to deploy these strategies in defense of our controversial views.[15]

Let us begin with the

Self-Exculpating Strategy: We have reasons to accept (1) that we are not biased and (2) that one side of the disagreement has made a mistake due to bias (rather than differences in evidence or intellectual abilities or other factors including a performance error). On the basis of (1) and (2), we can infer that the Bias Premise is (probably) true.

As already noted, (2) requires reason to think that alternative, nonbias explanations for why one side has erred are less plausible than the explanation provided by positing bias. Let's grant for now that (2) can be reasonably accepted. I will argue that our inclination to accept (1) should be curbed by what we know about the bias blind spot.

Richard Fumerton appears to endorse the Self-Exculpating Strategy, as I noted earlier in section 2. Consider what he says about his reasoning: "When I argue this way, I again risk sounding like a bit of a jerk. Do I really suppose that I am justified in thinking that there is an asymmetry between myself and others when it comes to various epistemic defects? Am *I* any less likely to be blinded to what is reasonable to believe by antecedent views or desires? Well, to be honest I suppose that I think I am" (2010, 105). How should we react to this disclosure? You may decide that Fumerton is a poster child for a public service ad campaign by psychologists to raise public awareness of the bias blind spot. ("The Bias Blind Spot: It Makes You Sound like a Jerk.") But perhaps Fumerton's honesty is to be admired. The gist of his reasoning is basically standard operating procedure for us human beings, but people don't normally express this so candidly.

The blind spot neatly explains why Fumerton judges that (1) is true. He doesn't tell us his reasons for (1)—he just says he is justified to think it's true in some disagreements. Plausibly, Fumerton introspects to check for bias in himself and relies on behavioral evidence, guided by abstract theories of bias, to check for bias in others. But, as we have seen, introspective evidence is not a reliable means to recognize subconscious biases in ourselves and may even

---

[15] This leaves open the possibility that people unaware of the psychological picture may commonly reasonably deploy the debunking strategies. Compare to Kelly (2008, 629–630).

leave us feeling we've successfully overcome judgment-distorting influences after "bending over backward" to be neutral.

Even so, we don't know that Fumerton is actually subject to the bias blind spot. What we do know is what the psychological evidence says: humans in general tend to make judgments like his due to the blind spot. An important issue, then, concerns the connection between the psychological evidence and a thinker's reasons to accept (1). Here is my proposal. Evidence about how people judge bias is relevant for assessing the premise that some person is not biased. The psychological evidence is a kind of evidence that tells us about our ability to assess evidence about bias. In Chapter 4, I called this *competence evidence*—evidence about our abilities and dispositions for responding effectively to some first-order evidence. Learning of the psychological evidence tends to undermine reasonable belief in (1): that evidence is what I call a *competence defeater*, a reason to doubt whether we're well-positioned to form a reasonable belief or knowledge on the basis of our first-order evidence. If we ourselves wish to accept (1) in full awareness of the psychological picture, we need to have a reason to think that we are *not* subject to the blind spot. Insofar as we lack reason to think we're not subject to it, we have reason to doubt (1) is true, and accordingly the Self-Exculpating Strategy won't deliver the Bias Premise.

Turning to an analogy will amplify the reasoning I've proposed.[16] Imagine that Earhart is piloting a small aircraft above 10,000 feet. Earhart knows that people in small aircraft flying at high altitudes often suffer from hypoxia— a condition where the brain is oxygen-deprived—and, as a result, their judgments become unreliable. Once hypoxia has taken effect, it will typically seem to the hypoxic person that her reasoning is perfectly good even when it is bad. Hypoxia has an effect on thinking without "leaving a trace" in consciousness. Since Earhart recognizes she may be hypoxic at this high altitude, she has reason to invest much less confidence in her calculations about her remaining fuel. To restore confidence in her calculations, she needs reason to think that she is not hypoxic.[17] If her belief is reasonable, she needs independent means to determine that she's not hypoxic, such as an O_2 detector.

Our situation with respect to bias is not unlike that of the high-flying pilot. Since we know about the bias blind spot, we should reduce confidence in (1),

---

[16] The analogy is based on a case given by Adam Elga (ms).

[17] Suppose Earhart's belief that hypoxia makes her unreliable remains reasonable. If that belief is not reasonable, her confidence in her calculations may be restored—without her having reason to think she is not hypoxic.

the step that says we are not biased, unless we have good reason to think that we are not in fact suffering from the blind spot.

Finding out that we may be hypoxic is similar to finding out that we may be subject to the bias blind spot. As it turns out, the analogy runs deep. Hypoxia is an excellent way to model the blind spot, because hypoxia seems to *induce* the blind spot, or something like it.

In some experiments on hypoxia conducted during the early twentieth century, J. S. Haldane and collaborators, including his son J. B. S. Haldane, set up a steel chamber in a lab and some of them climbed in. A pump removed the chamber's air, and once the pressure equaled pressure at a high altitude, it was held steady using a tap. Test subjects kept notes to record their experience. In low oxygen conditions, their ideas grew strange and irrational, though they didn't know it until later. J. S. Haldane commented on his self-experimentation: "I have always been quite confident in my own sanity, and it was only afterwards that I realized that I could not have been in a sane state of mind" (1922, 126). In one test, two scientists had hoped to remain in the chamber for an hour at the lowest pressure possible "without very serious impairment." Their plan was foiled when onlookers noticed the two subjects were blue, very shaky, and could hardly stand up. At that point, "the emergency tap was therefore opened so as to raise the pressure. There is a corresponding indignant and just legible note 'some bastard has turned tap,' after which the notes become quite legible again as the pressure rose" (Haldane, Kellas, and Kennaway 1919, 185).

The younger J. B. S. Haldane recounted one hypoxia self-experiment. He and a companion were enclosed in a steel chamber and a pump began to remove the air. After a few minutes, the chamber's pressure corresponded to 22,000 feet above sea-level. Haldane recounts what happened next:

[N]ow I have time to observe my own symptoms. I am breathing rapidly and deeply, and my pulse is at 110; but the breathing soon calms down, and I feel much better, though perhaps my writing is a shade wobbly. But why cannot my companion behave himself? He is making silly jokes and trying to sing. His lips are rather purple . . . . I feel quite unaffected; in fact, I have just thought of a very funny story. It is true I can't stand without some support. My companion suggests some oxygen from the cylinder which we have with us. To humour him I take a few breaths. The result is startling. The electric light becomes so much brighter that I fear the fuse may melt. The noise of the pumping engine increases fourfold. My note-book, which should have contained records of my pulse-rate, turns out to be filled with the often repeated but seldom legible statement that I am feeling *much better*, and remarks about my colleague, of which the least libellous is that he is drunk. I put down the oxygen tube and relapse into a not unpleasant state of mental confusion. An hour later, in spite of our indignant protests, the engine is stopped, and we return to normal pressure, no worse off except for a slight and transitory headache. (2002 [1927], 70–71)[18]

In a hypoxic state, Haldane recognizes his companion's debility but fails to fully grasp his own. An asymmetry between self and others, much like the one created by the bias blind spot, is observed in cases of hypoxia.

In general, inebriants of many kinds foster the inability to recognize our poor performance. Here's the great American saxophonist Charlie Parker, commenting on the effect of drugs and alcohol on jazz performance:

Any musician who says he is playing better on tea, the needle or when he is juiced is a plain, straight liar. When I get too much to drink, I can't even finger well, let alone play decent ideas. And in the days when I was on the stuff, I may have thought I was playing better, but listening to some of the records now, I know I wasn't. Some of these smart kids who think you have to be completely knocked out to be a good hornman are just plain crazy. It isn't true. I know, believe me. (Levin and Wilson 1949, 19)

We can imagine a sober Parker, listening to 78s, grimacing at his poor performance in playback. A juiced Parker probably thought the playing was perfectly fine.[19]

These analogies help us understand what counts as a good reason to think we have overcome the bias blind spot. Back in the hypoxia example, for instance, once Earhart suspects she is hypoxic, a reason to regard herself as not hypoxic must arise from a belief-forming method she reasonably thinks is unaffected by high altitude. Likewise, once we suspect we may be blinkered

---

[18] Thanks to Roy Sorensen for telling me about this passage.

[19] Parker was addicted to heroin during parts of his tragically brief life. While on a stint in Los Angeles in 1946, Parker's heroin dealer was arrested and Parker ended up binge drinking to manage heroin withdrawal. Before one recording session, Parker downed a quart of whisky and by the time the tape was rolling the producer had to hold Parker upright at the microphone. One track from this session—Parker's halting, heartrending performance of "Lover Man"—is among the greatest artifacts in the history of jazz. Parker collapsed after the session. He wandered undressed around the hotel where he was staying, lit his bed on fire with a cigarette, and spent the next six months in a psychiatric hospital. When he says, "I know, believe me"—he did and we should.

by the blind spot, any reason to think that we are unbiased must trace back to a method we reasonably think is not biased. That's why introspection alone won't normally dispel doubts about the blind spot—we know introspection is prejudiced in our favor.

If introspection is off-limits, where shall we turn? To avoid biases, thinkers sometimes try to *debias*—to identify and avoid their biases or adjust their judgments to counteract the negative effects of biases (Wilson and Brekke 1994; Wilson, Centerbar, and Brekke 2002; Larrick 2004). Let us say we know of a reliable method to judge our susceptibility to the blind spot. If we reasonably think that our judgment that we aren't afflicted by the blind spot traces back to a reliable debiasing method, we get reason for thinking that we have avoided or overcome that bias. Thus, recognizing we've debiased would permit us to accept step (1), our awareness of research on the blind spot notwithstanding. It's like a pilot having an oxygen mask at her disposal to counteract the effects of hypoxia.

As I'll now argue, reason to think that we've successfully debiased is going to be uncommon. That's because debiasing is extraordinarily hard. As I have already pointed out, we naturally rely on abstract theories of bias to debias, but our theories may lead us astray. For instance, the feeling that we can debias by *carefully thinking things over* is tempting but mistaken (Kenyon 2014, section 2). We need to take our cues from research on debiasing. But even when we do, debiasing in real life demands extensive knowledge of ourselves and the nature of our biases.

To see why, let's consider Wilson and Brekke's prominent account of debiasing (1994; Wilson, Centerbar, and Brekke 2002). In brief, the account proposes that a thinker's inability to debias stems from a number of common sources: (*i*) that thinker's lack of awareness of his or her mental processes (e.g., the extent to which the thinker's positive evaluation was due to a self-enhancement motive); (*ii*) his or her lack of control over mental processes (e.g., the thinker's inability to prevent the fact that his or her status is at issue from influencing self-judgment); (*iii*) inaccurate theories about biasing influences on judgment (e.g., the thinker's failure to appreciate how his or her own status could nonconsciously influence self-judgment); and (*iv*) inadequate motivation to correct for bias (e.g., an insufficient desire to avoid a self-enhancing judgment) (Wilson, Centerbar, and Brekke 2002, 187). Any one of (*i*) through (*iv*) will prevent successful debiasing. In light of how commonly people find themselves in those conditions, Wilson and Brekke are "rather pessimistic" about our ability to debias—and their pessimism even extends to trained psychologists who are familiar with the literature on biases (1994, 120; Wilson, Centerbar, and Brekke 2002, 190–191, 200). This bleak assessment confirms what other psychologists have found: debiasing demands knowledge that individuals often lack (Kahneman 2003).

Psychologists say that our best shot at successful debiasing lies in debiasing techniques. One self-administered technique is to "consider the opposite," to argue against one's own initial judgment.[20] This debiasing advice comes with a warning attached: the technique may backfire. "Ironically, the more people try to consider the opposite," Norbert Schwartz and colleagues observe, "the more they often convince themselves that their initial judgment was right on target" (2007, 128). Psychologists are fond of pointing out the inbuilt fallibility of debiasing techniques. Such techniques may be our best shot to debias, but that doesn't mean they are always a good shot.

Recall that we wanted to know whether debiasing could let us reasonably accept (1), the step that we are not biased, in spite of our awareness of the blind spot. Would-be debiasers face obstacles, as noted. Of course, some of us will still regard ourselves as having successfully debiased. But without instruction in debiasing and practice in implementing the techniques, aren't we just fooling ourselves? Perhaps we have special training to think carefully about arguments in some field, but we are not trained how to debias for the blind spot. Again, rechecking our arguments and finding they still look good to us is not enough. At the very least, we should think it is unclear whether or not we've effectively debiased. The take-home lesson is that good reason for regarding ourselves as having debiased for the blind spot, and thus good reason for (1), is uncommon in the kind of disagreements we care about.

In the end, we might expect a person unknowingly subject to the bias blind spot to use the Self-Exculpating Strategy. But forewarned against the blind spot, we shouldn't deploy that strategy unless, again, we have good reason to think our self-judgment about bias is reliable.

In hopes of finding a better way to debunk our dissenters, let's turn to the

Biasing-Factor-Attribution Strategy: We have reasons to accept (1) that a factor F tends to bias judgments about proposition p, (2) that factor F holds for a disagreeing thinker's judgment about p, and (3) that we know

---

[20] See Lord, Lepper, and Preston (1984), Wilson, Centerbar, and Brekke (2002, 197–198), and Larrick (2004, 323–324). Some debiasing techniques are launched at the social or organizational level: see Heath, Larrick, and Klayman (1998), Larrick (2004), and Kenyon (2014).

of no "enlightening" factor that holds for the thinker's judgment about p (i.e., a factor that tends to counteract or neutralize F's influence). On the basis of (1) through (3), we infer that the Bias Premise is (probably) true.

How does this strategy look against the backdrop of the psychological picture? Here is a general worry to start with. One precondition for successfully using this strategy is that we lack a reason to accept that a biasing factor like F holds *for us*. Otherwise, the strategy will explode in our hands—it will debunk our dissenters and ourselves and fail to preserve our reasonable belief. Recall, though, that we now have reason to doubt that our perspective on ourselves is objective, given our inclination to cling to biased introspective judgments and disregard behavioral evidence concerning ourselves, for instance. Thus, we should sometimes suspect that the biases we attribute to others apply to ourselves as well. But even setting that important point aside, both (1) and (2) are problematic for two other reasons.

First, as we've seen, our abstract theories of bias aren't always well-attuned to reality. We occasionally cynically overestimate bias in others (Kruger and Gilovich 1999). Suppose our theories say some factor F biases certain kinds of judgments. Then we should ask: on reflection, do we have good reason to think that our abstract theories of bias are correct? Suppose we lack such reason. Then it would be strange for us to accept (1): if we are unsure whether our abstract theories are correct, we should also be unsure about whether F really biases. This suggests that, once we reflect, reason to accept (1) amounts to reason to think that our abstract theories are reliable guides to bias; but we may often lack any reason to accept this, especially in light of studies indicating those theories are sometimes problematic.

Second, and shifting to (2), we appeal to behavioral evidence when determining whether some thinker is biased, but our uptake of that evidence may be influenced by unreliable evidence-gathering methods. Psychologists have noted that observers often place heavy weight on others' *characters* to explain their behavior in a particular *situation*, rather than thinking about how their behavior may have been shaped by the situation itself (Jones and Harris 1967; Ross 2018). This has been called the "fundamental attribution error" because it's arguably a central engine of social judgment. We explain how others act primarily by appeal to their characters, not to the situations they are in. When a bicyclist crashes into a parked car, for example, we are apt to judge that he's an unskilled or reckless rider. But that judgment is an error when the crash is explained instead by some part of the rider's situation.

Maybe he's a good rider, but he was late for an appointment and knew he had to ride a bit dangerously around a corner to arrive on time. (Unsurprisingly, we readily regard situational factors as influencing our own behavior.) We should ask: on reflection, are the methods we use for collecting behavioral evidence concerning our disagreeing peers any good? If we lack reason to think those methods are good, it would be strange to accept (2): if we are unsure whether we can competently gather evidence relevant to factor F concerning a disagreeing thinker, we should also be unsure about whether F holds for that thinker's judgment. The idea here is that reason to accept (2) amounts to reason to think that our techniques for gathering behavioral evidence are reliable. But if we take the psychological research seriously, many of us often lack reason to think this.

The psychological picture raises doubts about whether we have good reason to accept (1) and (2), and that sometimes calls into doubt our use of the Biasing-Factor-Attribution Strategy.[21] At the same time, (3) is problematic, too. Recall that (3) is satisfied when we've reason to think that no enlightening factor—one that would counteract a biasing factor—holds for a disagreeing thinker. But this condition is too easy to meet. We could satisfy it, without fail, by remaining oblivious to the presence of potential enlightening factors. As a matter of fact, it's doubtful whether we are normally "on the lookout" for enlightening factors operating in others who disagree with us. Given naïve realism—the presumption that our views are objective—whenever we learn others disagree with us, we tend to be on the lookout for biasing factors. The engine driving this may be confirmation bias. In general, we search for evidence to confirm our hypothesis that we are objective and not for evidence to disconfirm it; it's thus unsurprising that we would search for biasing factors, not for enlightening ones, because we expect that our dissenters are biased. As a result, we may take ourselves to accept (3) reasonably just because we've failed to search adequately for enlightening factors.

This point about (3) suggests a change to the Biasing-Factor-Attribution Strategy. Suppose that we reasonably accept steps (1), (2), and (3). Imagine further, as the psychological picture indicates, we reasonably believe we are not always disposed to search for factors that may enlighten disagreeing thinkers, even when such factors are present. All of this may reveal that the debunking strategy at issue doesn't set down conditions *sufficient* for us to have reason to accept the Bias Premise. If there's a gap, we may fill it with

---

[21] Christensen (2014, 160–161) makes a similar point.

a further step, namely, that we have reason to accept step (4): that we have adequately searched for potential enlightening factors that hold for the disagreeing thinker's judgment about proposition p. Once again, the psychological picture should give us pause. Since it is doubtful that we are in the habit of searching for factors that may enlighten our disputants, we have some reason to doubt whether we would satisfy the extra condition (4).

My suggestion is not that the Self-Exculpating Strategy and the Biasing-Factor-Attribution Strategy can't ever help us debunk testimony from those who disagree with us. The idea is that, in light of psychological findings concerning how we form judgments about bias, including the bias blind spot and the fundamental attribution error, we often have reason to doubt that these strategies help. To make use of them in view of the psychological picture, we must face up to the following questions. What is our reason to think that our self-judgments about biases are reliably formed? Why do we think our abstract theories of bias are any good? Why do we think our methods for collecting behavioral evidence about dissenters are reliable? Why do we think we have adequately searched for factors that may enlighten disagreeing thinkers? To answer well, we must know how to make principled judgments about bias.

To be sure, sometimes we can answer those questions with relative ease and reasonably debunk dissenters. For instance, when we imagine Christensen's high-school music contest, it's natural to assume (1) that you have good reasons to think your abstract theory of bias that implies Aksel's father is biased is in fact correct, (2) that your gathering of behavioral evidence concerning Aksel's father's judgment has been reliable, (3) that you know of no factors that might enlighten him, and (4) that you have reason to believe you've adequately searched for such factors. Thus, you can launch the Biasing-Factor-Attribution Strategy and debunk Aksel's father. The same plausibly goes for the case of the climate scientists sponsored by the oil industry, at least if you have the sort of relevant evidence I have about the matter.[22]

But those are easy cases and we are here concerned with less straightforward ones. In more difficult cases, we will on reflection have reason to doubt that these debunking strategies are appropriate. While we may be tempted to see our intelligent and informed opponents as unable to hear the good sense we're talking, because of their social position or intellectual commitments,

---

[22] I say more about this sort of case in Chapter 9.

we now know that is too convenient. We may be inclined to treat ourselves as the unbiased side in disputes—to see ourselves as judge and jury, prosecution and defense, in our own case. But can we do better? Ordinarily, we do not demand good reasons for our own judgments concerning biases even when we hold other people to tougher standards. The psychological picture encourages us to resist the temptation to intellectual hypocrisy.

5. Step Back

I began this chapter by noting how the debunking reasoning helps us build our intellectual houses. We may now begin to swing our sledgehammer and bust some walls. I said that, to resist the downward push of testimony from those who disagree, we commonly resort to debunking reasoning. Though conciliationists and nonconciliationists disagree over the scope of reasonable disagreement—the range of cases where it's reasonable to keep one's view while recognizing a peer's dissent—both sides agree that sometimes controversial beliefs are reasonable for at least one peer because of debunking. And so both sides should acknowledge a problem: in light of the psychological picture, we often have powerful reasons to doubt that debunking delivers us from epistemological trouble. The upshot is that disagreement should lead us to reduce confidence in our controversial opinions more than we might have previously thought. This conclusion is surprising. It's plausible for us to expect that using debunking strategies will make us less skeptical about our own judgments. Debunking is designed to remove the threat of disagreement. But I have explained how using debunking reasoning with eyes wide open can lead us to become more distrustful of our own judgments.

Let me conclude by highlighting two lessons. The first is that, without the safeguard of debunking reasoning, we should change our minds at least to some extent. If we can't debunk disagreeing peers, then finding out they disagree brings defeaters for our controversial opinions. In Chapter 4, I said we are *doxastically open* insofar as we have some significant doubt about which attitude toward a proposition is reasonable for us to hold given our evidence. Notice that we are often aware of informed and intelligent people who hold each of the available doxastic options on a question. Learning about such conflicts may make us more doxastically open—doubtful to some significant degree about which view is reasonable for us to adopt. After all, if we aren't positioned to debunk any of the contenders in a debate and thus lack a plausible explanation for why one side is more trustworthy than the others, then we should end up confused about what is reasonable for us to think.

A second lesson is that we need better methods to make judgments about biases. We are invested in the practice of making such judgments, but our methods are makeshift, underwritten as they are by assumptions and inferences that have not been scrutinized nearly enough, let alone fully articulated. The case of the butcher jurors suggests how abstract theories of bias may be based on fanciful thoughts. We should wonder about the basis of our own abstract theories. If our theories typically incline us to debunk disagreeing thinkers, and so rarely moderate our confidence in light of their dissent, we might begin to suspect the game is rigged in our favor. When debunking others, we may just be spinning out deluded rationalizations of our own correctness—not entirely unlike the three Christs of Ypsilanti.

Improvement demands that we become more principled in our judgments about bias. Regulative epistemologists can examine the challenges here and hopefully offer guidance. Let me sketch one idea.

Many intellectual problems will not see conclusive resolution in our time. We will fail to reach the bottom. Sometimes issues remain unresolved because of their sheer complexity, a topic I turn to in Chapters 7 and 8. Sometimes they remain unresolved because *we* are the ones trying to resolve them. We get in the way. Here is an image: a photographer is trying to take a photo of himself in the mirror without having the camera appear anywhere in the photo. It can't be done. Similarly, in many disagreements, our judgments about biases in others and ourselves are fraught with difficulty that traces back to the presence of ourselves. Somebody's thinking is either sensitive to evidence and reasons, or it is driven by his or her interests, expectations, or emotions. Who's biased? Me or you? Us or them? In many disagreements, we are not well-positioned to figure this out because our viewpoint is ours.

Perhaps that's just how it goes. In good times and in bad, we are stuck with ourselves. And yet we may hope for impersonal application of our methods—not just methods that we will apply uniformly to everyone, but ones that will bracket out the personal factors that bias application of those methods. Notice how the need for *impersonal* judgment in the shadow of potential bias has been met in the practice of recusal. Judges, managers, and journal editors may recuse themselves from decision-making because of possible bias and thereby preserve justice and fairness. These practices respect an insight: if we can't be trusted to apply methods properly, we should step back and let others do it. We insist on such practices because we want justice both to be done and to appear to be done. Likewise, in intellectual life, as we try to improve our webs of belief, we need a way to step back and to respect the fact that our views are often no less subject to the same biases we readily attribute to others. But we can't always be trusted to decide when to bow out, and so better methods might effectively exclude us at the right times.

How might this work? I am not sure. But let me offer one speculation. Psychologists have noted that people occasionally recognize bias in themselves. Subjects have been observed to accept the idea that they are biased in their judgments "broadly and abstractly construed" while at the same time disavowing bias in any recent judgments they've made (Ehrlinger, Gilovich, and Ross 2005). More important, subjects sometimes go a step further, confessing that some of their specific judgments are biased. For instance, people will admit to being biased in their assessments of their friends and parents will admit they are biased toward their children. Some psychologists have proposed here that "the motivation to be seen as unbiased is not as great—or is balanced by a countervailing motive to be a stand-up friend or a protective parent—so it is easier to admit to the possibility of bias" (Ehrlinger, Gilovich, and Ross 2005, 690).

As someone who often feels unbiased but knows this feeling must be a hard-to-see-through cognitive illusion, I find good news here. The good news is that human motives and impulses may counteract the powerful tendency to see ourselves as unbiased. I take comfort in this and hope one day to see myself more as I really am: biased. What motive could help me? Again, I am unsure. Yet suppose it becomes my central purpose as a thinker to simply consider how things are. Not to judge. Not to conclude. But to abstain from judgment and opinion. To try, as Ralph Waldo Emerson put it, "to keep the balance true."[23] To adopt this motive is to strive for thoroughgoing doxastic openness in some controversies. Could the motive to consider how things are, just like my affection for a friend or a child, help me to more often recognize my biases by counteracting my tendency to resist the thought that I am biased? Possibly so—if the motive is strong enough. But perhaps this too is wishful thinking.

---

[23] "Montaigne; or, the Skeptic" in *Representative Men* (1850).

6

Counterfactual Interlocutors

It is not impossible that in a real dream of sleep, someone may have created an antagonist who beat him in an argument.
—Augustus De Morgan, *Formal Logic*, 1847

The best songs will never get sung
The best life never leaves your lungs
So good you won't ever know
You'll never hear it on the radio
Can't hear it on the radio.
—Wilco, "The Late Greats," *A Ghost Is Born*, 2004

Our intellectual world is a fragile and highly contingent thing. We may feel this acutely when we remember departed interlocutors. We were once instructed and enlightened by their arguments and observations. Now we feel their absence. Were they among us still, how would they respond to our controversial opinions? What would they say about our arguments? They are *counterfactual interlocutors*: conversation partners who could be among us now but are not. We know we don't have all of the objections, arguments, and distinctions they would have brought forward. But it is clear that counterfactual interlocutors, especially the exceptional ones, would have changed our inquiry.

Consider an example of a counterfactual interlocutor. David Foster Wallace studied philosophy at Amherst College and had a brief stint in graduate school at Harvard University on his way to a brilliant but brief literary career, ended by his untimely death in 2008. Wallace wrote his undergraduate philosophy thesis on Richard Taylor's argument for fatalism—the thesis that it's never up to us what we do or become. Taylor's argument appeared in the pages of *The Philosophical Review* in 1962. It generated replies and counter-replies in the pages of professional journals and doctoral dissertations, and by the time Wallace was a college student in the early '80s, the debate still raged on. One of Wallace's teachers, Jay Garfield, remembered first meeting Wallace. The young Wallace wanted to arrange an independent study course with Garfield on Taylor's argument for fatalism and the logical and semantic tools Wallace needed to evaluate it. At the meeting, Wallace expressed his "outrage" that Taylor had claimed to have proven a metaphysical conclusion using merely logical or semantic premises. Wallace, noted Garfield, "was genuinely offended by the failure of professional philosophers to have put things right" (2011, 220). Garfield observed that Wallace's thinking reflected "an unusual combination of philosophical passion and intellectual maturity" (2011, 220). In Garfield's estimation, "had [Wallace] stuck with philosophy, and had he lived, he would have been a major figure in our field" (2011, 221).

Counterfactual interlocutors are legion. Here are two ways to find them. First, we can reflect on actual lives cut short. Wallace is one such example; Mary Wollstonecraft is another. She contributed to late eighteenth-century discussions of morality, education, and human rights. Wollstonecraft's writings articulate a vision of society where men and women pursue greater happiness through the cultivation of virtue. Wollstonecraft died tragically at age thirty-eight in 1797, shortly after the birth of her second daughter, the writer Mary Shelley. What else would Wollstonecraft have written if she had lived? How might her further works have been received? We can also find counterfactual interlocutors in the lives of people prevented from taking up intellectual work and in merely possible lives that never were. If some housewife, farmer, or person never born had been part of our conversation, the foundations of our intellectual world could be surprisingly different.

These observations are patently sensible. Now consider a far less obvious idea. Counterfactual interlocutors need not speak or write in order to teach us. Even though they remain silent, they can help us know our limits. What I call the *Problem of Counterfactual Interlocutors* is the difficulty of having reasonable opinions while recognizing that, if history had turned out differently, our conversation partners very likely would have shared forceful objections to our controversial views. In many situations, we gain competence defeaters (that is, reasons to doubt we are well-positioned to reasonably believe or know on the basis of our first-order evidence) for our controversial beliefs once we appreciate what our counterfactual interlocutors might have done.

Here is my plan for this chapter. First I articulate some ideas we can use to think more clearly about the Problem of Counterfactual Interlocutors (section 1). After I introduce the problem (section 2), I consider a number of objections and replies that help us understand its force (section 3). Then I conclude by assessing the seriousness of the problem (section 4).

1. Epistemic Counterfactuals

I call an *epistemic counterfactual* any proposition stating that if some contrary-to-fact state had obtained, then our evidence or reasons would or might be different. Here are some examples of epistemic counterfactuals:

> If Dieterich had been born with better eyesight, then he would have seen the owl sitting on the fence.
>
> If you had studied for the final exam, you might have known the answer to that question.
>
> If Clara had cannon-balled into the swimming pool, we probably would have had more reason to think she is a good swimmer.

The Problem of Counterfactual Interlocutors focuses on an epistemic counterfactual with a consequent that *we very likely would have a defeater for believing some proposition.*[1] Take an example:

> If the factory manager had told you that the widgets on the assembly line are illuminated by red light, then you very likely would have a defeater for believing that the widgets are red (on the basis of their appearing red).

The consequents of epistemic counterfactuals like that one identify a contrary-to-fact state that, were the antecedent to obtain, very likely would furnish a thinker with a defeater for a particular doxastic attitude. Expressed in the common philosophical parlance, the epistemic counterfactual about the red-appearing widgets can be understood to state that *in the majority of nearby possible worlds* where the antecedent is true, you have a defeater for thinking that the widgets are red. This is consistent with there being nearby

---

[1] As I noted in Chapter 4, defeaters are reasons for giving up some attitude that we hold toward a proposition *p*. *Undermining defeaters* are reasons that attack the connection between your belief in *p* and the reasons that support it, whereas *rebutting defeaters* attack *p* itself. *Full defeaters* for believing *p* make any belief in *p*—no matter the degree of confidence—unreasonable, whereas *partial defeaters* permit some lower degree of confidence in believing *p* to be reasonable.

worlds where the antecedent is true but you do not acquire a defeater. For instance, supposing you had been at the widget factory, talking with the manager, you might not have come to have a defeater for believing the widgets are red. After all, you might have sneezed just when the manager mentioned the red light and so you misheard her words. In general, something might have prevented you from acquiring the defeater for believing the widgets are red even though the factory manager did tell you about the red light. All that matters for the truth of the epistemic counterfactual is this: that the nearby worlds where you do *not* have a defeater are in the *minority* of nearby worlds where the antecedent is true.[2]

The epistemic counterfactuals I will focus on say that *you very likely would have an undermining or rebutting defeater for your doxastic attitude toward proposition p* had some contrary-to-fact state obtained. The idea is that, in the contrary-to-fact state, you'd very likely learn something that gives you reason to give up your attitude concerning *p*—unless and until, in that state, you learn something else that defeats the defeater for your view.

What we have reason to think about the epistemic counterfactuals at issue can be epistemically significant for us. Consider why. Reasonably believing this kind of counterfactual can be a rebutting or an undermining defeater for our actual belief in *p*, where *p* is the proposition embedded in the counterfactual's consequent. That's because we think there very likely would have been a defeater for our belief in *p*. A pair of cases suggests that is so:

First Snow: You are indoors, in a windowless room, and you reasonably believe that it is snowing outside. You have reason to think that your faculties would not suddenly become unreliable if you were to go outside (e.g., because hallucinogenic gas was just sprayed by a low-flying aircraft over your neighborhood). A trustworthy source informs you that if you were standing outside and paying attention, then you very likely would have a defeater for believing it is snowing. You reasonably accept this counterfactual.

---

[2] An anonymous referee reminded me that it's not inconsistent to say "*p* would be the case" alongside "not-*p* might be the case" when we take the might-counterfactual to express an epistemic possibility claim (DeRose 1999). So, in the "widget factory" example, we can properly say: "If the factory manager had told you that the widgets are illuminated by red light, then you would have a defeater for believing the widgets are red" and "You might not have got a defeater for believing the widgets are red (had you sneezed)." As will become clear later in the chapter, this thought helps to underwrite an alternative formulation of the Problem of Counterfactual Interlocutors in terms of an epistemic counterfactual that features a would-counterfactual—not a very-likely-would-counterfactual—in its consequent. See footnote 7 for more.

In this situation, you should no longer believe it is snowing. Reasonably accepting that epistemic counterfactual seems to be enough to rebut your actual belief: you plausibly have reason to believe it is not snowing.[3]

Here is a case where belief is undermined by an epistemic counterfactual:

Second Snow: You are indoors, in a windowless room, and you reasonably believe that it is snowing outside. You have no way to observe the scene outside (e.g., by looking at a video monitor connected to a surveillance camera focused on your house). A trustworthy source informs you that if you were to learn about the reliability of the grounds for your belief that it's snowing, then you very likely would have a defeater for that belief.

Again, you should no longer believe it is snowing, though here that's because your belief is now unsupported. You have an undercutting defeater for that belief.

The defeater you get for your belief in either First Snow or Second Snow is critically distinct from the defeater you very likely would have acquired had the relevant counter-to-fact state obtained. Let me illustrate the point using First Snow and just note that something similar goes for Second Snow. For at least two reasons, in First Snow, the defeater you get for believing it's snowing (call the defeater D_1) is not the same as the defeater you very likely would have gotten had you been standing outside (call it D_2). First, you typically rely on different sources when you acquire these two defeaters. D_2 depends on perception—you would *see* that there's no snow falling. But D_1 depends instead on reasonably accepting the epistemic counterfactual. Second, the contents of D_1 and D_2 are different. The content of the counterfactual defeater D_2 is not the same as the counterfactual content of D_1 delivered by reflecting on the trustworthy source's testimony in First Snow. The content of D_2 is the content of your experience outside ("It is not snowing here") whereas the content of D_1 is the counterfactual you accept ("If I were standing outside . . .").

---

[3] If that is not plausible, add a further detail to First Snow: that you have reason to think you would not gain further evidence that undermines your reasons for believing it's snowing if you went outside. For anyone who's unsure whether that is enough to give you a rebutting defeater, retell the case so that your trustworthy source reports that if you were outside and paying attention, you'd very likely have a rebutting defeater for believing it's snowing. In the end, even if First Snow fails to show an epistemic counterfactual can rebut belief, such a case still shows that belief can be undermined in this way. (Thanks to an anonymous referee and Michael Bergmann for helpful comments here.)

What's most important here is that your reason for thinking *there very likely would be a defeater* in some counter-to-fact state provides an *actual defeater*, even though it is not the same defeater you'd very likely have in that state. This idea is similar to the claim, pithily expressed by Richard Feldman, that "evidence of evidence is evidence"—the claim, roughly, that if we have evidence that there is some evidence for *p*, we have evidence for *p*.[4] I have something closely related in mind. Evidence that there would be a defeater for a belief had something different obtained *can be* a defeater for that belief. More specifically, First Snow shows us that, possibly, evidence that there likely would be a rebutting defeater for a belief had something different obtained is itself a rebutting defeater for that belief; and Second Snow shows us that, possibly, evidence that there likely would be an undermining defeater for a belief had something different obtained is itself an undermining defeater for that belief.

Epistemic counterfactuals can defeat belief. But sometimes they do not, as we find with this case:

> *Rain:* You rationally believe you are not soaking wet. A trustworthy source informs you that if you had been out in a monsoon rain and paying attention, then very likely you would have a defeater for believing that you are not wet.

In Rain and First and Second Snow, you come to reasonably accept an epistemic counterfactual with a consequent according to which you would have a defeater for a particular belief. But only in First and Second Snow, and not Rain, does what you learn defeat your initial, reasonable belief. In Rain, the belief that you are not wet is not threatened in the least.

So what accounts for the epistemological difference between First and Second Snow, on the one hand, and Rain on the other? Why is belief defeated by what is learned in First and Second Snow but not in Rain? To speak about the two kinds of cases, we can say that First and Second Snow feature a *defeating* epistemic counterfactual whereas Rain features a *non-defeating* one. Here are a couple of more examples of non-defeating epistemic counterfactuals:

---

[4] For more discussion, see Feldman (2006, 223 and 2009, 308–309) and Rowley (2012). Compare to Hardwig's "principle of testimony" (1991, 697).

You reasonably believe that Glenn Gould died in 1982. If he were still alive and speaking to you now, then you very likely would have reason to believe he is alive.

You reasonably believe that you have hands. If you had been born without hands, then you very likely would have a defeater for thinking you have hands.

Accepting such counterfactuals clearly won't defeat belief. Even after you learn about those counterfactuals, you should continue believing that Glenn Gould has died and that you have hands.

What ties together the (non-)defeating cases? That's a tricky question. Suppose we answer by giving an account—a set of informative conditions for an epistemic counterfactual's being (non-)defeating with respect to a particular belief. The account proposes what is necessary and sufficient for being defeating or not. Let me record a suspicion. For any account that we produce, we (or our interlocutors) will also produce a counterexample to the account, if we put it to the test. And so, if we want to capture in general the difference between defeating and non-defeating cases, we will remain unsatisfied. Or so I suspect. Others may be more optimistic. Perhaps we will find a defensible account of the difference. This much is inevitable: either we get a defensible account of being a (non-)defeating epistemic counterfactual or we do not. Either way is consistent with my purposes here—to set out the Problem of Counterfactual Interlocutors. That's because, with or without an account, we have a sense for the difference between the two kinds of cases. We can readily tell the difference between them. Although we may wish to develop a general account of the difference, my discussion here does not demand it.

Once we reasonably accept a defeating epistemic counterfactual, we are positioned to appreciate that our belief is defeated. Here's a pattern of reasoning we can follow to figure that out. Let p be the proposition in the consequent of an epistemic counterfactual, belief in which is defeated. (In First and Second Snow, the content of p is *it is snowing*.)

(1) If I reasonably believe a defeating epistemic counterfactual regarding p, then I have a defeater for believing p.
(2) I reasonably believe a defeating epistemic counterfactual regarding p. Therefore,
(3) I have a defeater for believing p.
(4) The defeater for believing p is undefeated.

(5) I recognize that I have an undefeated defeater for believing p.

(6) If I recognize that I have an undefeated defeater for believing p, then either I should suspend judgment regarding p or reduce my confidence that p is true.

Therefore,

(7) I should suspend judgment regarding p or reduce my confidence that p is true.

So far I've explained how we should think about our beliefs once we recognize defeating epistemic counterfactuals.[5] Let me now show how these counterfactuals give rise to the Problem of Counterfactual Interlocutors.

2. The Problem of Counterfactual Interlocutors

As I noted at the outset of this chapter, we know all about counterfactual interlocutors. They would have changed our intellectual world and the state of our debates. Many of them would have offered arguments, objections, and distinctions relevant to controversial views we ourselves now hold.

To see why this is a problem, pick some controversial question or questions and choose for yourself a group of counterfactual interlocutors. Be sure these people are ones whom you regard as committed to a reasonable method of inquiry—one roughly similar to your own methodology, say. The counterfactual interlocutors you have in mind would be inclined to appeal to types of reasons, evidence, and inferences that you yourself would take as legitimate if you were to consider them. These people are *methodologically-friendly* counterfactual interlocutors, we can say. It's hard to deny that some of them very likely would be able to challenge your own best arguments were they around.

In my own case, I like to imagine how my best philosophical arguments would fare if I presented them to Wayne State University's Philosophy Department in the early 1960s, when a talented and tough-minded group of young philosophers plied their trade in Detroit. One member of the department, Robert Sleigh, who had earlier studied under Roderick Chisholm at Brown University, had two mottos: "Write the arguments down" and "Everything fails."[6] In their discussions, the Wayne State philosophers

---

[5] For the sake of simplicity, the pattern of reasoning is framed in terms of believing p. Slightly different reasoning applies to cases where we disbelieve p or suspend judgment concerning it.

[6] Thanks to Keith Lehrer for telling me about Sleigh's methodological mottos.

sought to pin down their arguments on paper and sometimes napkins, and Sleigh thought the dialectical process invariably showed that the arguments brought forward were not airtight. Maybe he wasn't right about that, but if the Wayne State gang had enough time to test out my best arguments, I expect I would learn something new.

Suppose you have written down in a notebook all of your best arguments concerning a view you take toward a controversial question. Now envision your counterfactual interlocutors patiently studying that notebook and then meeting in a seminar room to share their objections with you. By reflecting on this situation, you will have reason to accept epistemic counterfactuals like the following:

> If a group of methodologically-friendly counterfactual interlocutors had scrutinized my best arguments for some proposition p and then shared their thoughts, I very likely would have defeaters for believing p.[7]

We have reason to believe this is a defeating epistemic counterfactual. To appreciate why, recall the earlier cases of defeating and non-defeating epistemic counterfactuals (see section 1). We easily distinguished between the two kinds of cases, and our judgments there seem entirely reasonable. I am inclined to say: we enjoy *prima facie* reason to think First and Second Snow feature defeating epistemic counterfactuals, and *prima facie* reason to think Rain features a non-defeating one, just by meditating on the details of the cases. In step with a commonplace "particularist" methodology in epistemology (Chisholm 1973), we may sensibly distinguish between defeating and non-defeating cases without recourse to a general principle to sort between them. Now return to the epistemic counterfactual concerning the methodologically-friendly interlocutors. Think about it. Quite plausibly, we have *prima facie* reason to accept that it's defeating.

Have I anything for those who are unsure whether the "counterfactual interlocutors" case is defeating? Here's a picture that may help to expose the distinction between First and Second Snow and the "counterfactual

---

[7] I might have stated the Problem of Counterfactual Interlocutors in terms of a *would*-counterfactual, not this very-likely-would-counterfactual. I opted for the latter, though, because I worry that the relevant would-counterfactual looks doubtful in light of the following sort of might-counterfactual: if a group of methodologically-friendly counterfactual interlocutors had scrutinized my best arguments for some proposition and then shared their thoughts, they *might* have had pity on me (and my pitiful arguments) and so not have given me the defeaters they thought up. But see footnote 2 for a strategy to save the would-counterfactual.

interlocutors" case, on the one hand, and Rain and the other non-defeating cases, on the other. In the defeating cases, only the consequent of the epistemic counterfactual features a trouble-making factor, whereas in the non-defeating cases, that factor is in the epistemic counterfactual's antecedent. Let me explain.

I believe that Glenn Gould has died. Then someone tells me: "If Gould were still alive and speaking to you now, you'd very likely have reason to believe he's alive." To evaluate that counterfactual, I consider the nearest possible worlds where he is alive. Those worlds are inconsistent with the truth of my actual belief that Gould died; I can't "get to" those worlds without assuming my actual belief is false. But notice that our defeating cases are different because they've got a different sort of antecedent. Suppose I believe it is snowing outside. Then someone says: "If you were standing outdoors and paying attention, you'd very likely have a reason for believing it is not snowing." Evaluating that counterfactual requires me to consider the nearest worlds where its antecedent is true. Some of those worlds are consistent with my belief that it's snowing, and I can "get to" those worlds without supposing my belief is false. Unlike the non-defeating cases, we find here that the counterfactual makes trouble for my belief. Again, this is just a picture: I do not say any of this captures in general the distinction between defeating and non-defeating cases. But it may reveal there is one.[8]

For counterfactuals like the one about the counterfactual interlocutors, the antecedent could have obtained. The shape of our intellectual world is fragile. It's an accident that a great many counterfactual interlocutors are not here. If only they had an opportunity to study our best arguments. If only they were here among us. If only history had led them to share their insights with us. Then the no-longer counterfactual interlocutors would bring us defeaters we do not now have.

We know all of this. We reasonably accept some epistemic counterfactuals regarding counterfactual interlocutors. We know that had they been around, very likely we'd have defeaters for some beliefs of ours, and we know it is just a quirk of history they are not here. And so we can reason in the pattern outlined earlier in section 1. By following (1)–(7) we'll come to acknowledge that some of our controversial beliefs are at least partially defeated or perhaps fully defeated. We will have reason to either suspend

---

[8] Thanks to Tomás Bogardus and David Matheson for helpful discussion.

judgment regarding some propositions or at least reduce confidence in our opinions.

All of this is an intellectual challenge, because most people apparently regard themselves as having reasonable controversial opinions. How can we hold onto our controversial opinions while we recognize full well that counterfactual interlocutors very likely would offer us reasons to abandon them? One response to the problem, as I just noted, is to admit that we've gained a partial or full defeater for some or other controversial attitude. Suppose we start off believing proposition p (as opposed to disbelieving or suspending judgment about it) and then we acquire a full defeater in light of our reflection on the counterfactual interlocutors. Now we should suspend judgment about p. But imagine we continue to reflect and discover that we have reason to believe that the counterfactual interlocutors very likely would present significant criticism for the new attitude we've adopted; we gain a full defeater for that attitude, too. Thus, we now have significant reason to doubt that *suspending judgment* is a reasonable response to our evidence. We can perhaps run the same exercise, prospectively, with the doxastic option of disbelieving p. The upshot of our deliberation is that we may become more doxastically open than when we started. Reflecting on counterfactual objections will make us unsure, hesitant, or confused about what we should actually believe.

There is more to say about the problem, and I soon turn to some objections in order to clarify it and size up its significance. Before continuing, though, I want to distinguish the problem from two similar issues.

Bertrand Russell, in a pamphlet titled "An Outline of Intellectual Rubbish: A Hilarious Catalogue of Organized and Individual Stupidity," described a cognitive habit that may remind us of the Problem of Counterfactual Interlocutors:

> For those who have enough psychological imagination, it is a good plan to imagine an argument with a person having a different bias. This has one advantage, and only one, as compared with actual conversation with opponents; this one advantage is that the method is not subject to the same limitations of time or space . . . . I have sometimes been led actually to change my mind as a result of this kind of imaginary dialogue, and, short of this, I have frequently found myself growing less dogmatic and cocksure through realizing the possible reasonableness of a hypothetical opponent. (1943, 22–23)

Russell's advice is to imagine conversing with an interlocutor who thinks differently than we do. Russell reports that the imaginative technique helped him change his own mind. I don't doubt it. In the hands of one of the eminent intellectuals of the twentieth century, the technique might accomplish wonders. But dialectical arm-wrestling with imaginary opponents is easier said than done.[9] Part of our trouble, as I noted in Chapters 4 and 5, is that we are naïve realists. Since our controversial beliefs seem obviously correct to us, it isn't easy to envision how anyone could think differently than we do—well, at least anyone who is approximately as informed and intelligent as we take ourselves to be. But the Problem of Counterfactual Interlocutors may challenge our views even if we can't envision what the objections to our beliefs might or would be. We only need to recognize that, under different circumstances, we would very likely come to have good objections—ones unknown to us now.

Second, I should note that the Problem of Counterfactual Interlocutors is not a problem about disagreement. I have not said that epistemic peers or superiors disagree with you. Even if there are no peers or superiors—because you are the only person alive investigating some question—the problem remains for you. And neither have I said that, had the world been different, you would learn that some peers or superiors disagree with you. This is not a problem of merely possible disagreement.[10] Instead, the idea is that, had things turned out differently, some conversation partners very likely would have given you evidence against your opinions, and this evidence is not mere

---

[9] Thielke (2014) argues that we can't actually imagine what would convince us to change our minds, because in doing so we would end up persuaded by those considerations.

[10] That said, it may appear that the Problem of Counterfactual Interlocutors is related to the problem(s) of possible disagreement. And if there's a solution to the problem of possible disagreement, then perhaps that can be used to discharge the present problem. The two problems are crucially different, though, and so what has been said about possible disagreement—mainly, arguments to show that possible disagreements are no reason for doubt in our views—won't apply here. To establish this, I'd need to veer off topic and say considerably more about possible disagreements. Instead, let me note some work on possible disagreements: Kelly (2005a, 181–185), Christensen (2007a, 208–209), Kornblith (2010, 34–39), Carey (2011), Machuca (2011), and Barnett and Li (2016).

But I do not mean to say these problems are entirely unrelated. As it happens, while discussing the difference between actual and possible disagreements, Thomas Kelly brushed past some ideas near the root of the Problem of Counterfactual Interlocutors. Kelly argues that it's evidence that determines what is reasonable for people to think, as opposed to contingent sociological facts concerning what others think, and he makes this observation:

> [T]here might be cases in which we judge that the arguments and evidence that could be brought forth on behalf of a hypothetical dissent are truly formidable, and this might justifiably make us doubt our own beliefs. But in that case, the reasons that we have for skepticism are provided by the state of the evidence itself, and our own judgements about the probative force of that evidence. (2005a, 182)

Our problem begins with cases not unlike the one noted by Kelly.

disagreement. One consequence is that epistemological theories about the significance of disagreement won't resolve the problem I described. Even if you believe that recognized disagreement never requires revision of your views, could-have-been objectors may still bring you doubts.

3. Objections and Replies

The best way to understand the force of the Problem of Counterfactual Interlocutors is to consider how someone may attempt to respond to it. Let me examine a number of objections and replies.

Objection 1:   There are *would*-counterfactuals, *might*-counterfactuals, and *very-likely-would*-counterfactuals. The Problem of Counterfactual Interlocutors is animated by the latter. Clearly, for many of our controversial views, we ought to accept corresponding epistemic might-counterfactuals:

> If a brilliant counterfactual interlocutor had studied my best arguments for believing proposition *p* and shared her thoughts, then I *might* have defeaters for believing *p*.

That is undeniable. But the pertinent epistemic would-counterfactuals are doubtful:

> If a brilliant counterfactual interlocutor had studied my best arguments for believing *p* and shared her thoughts, then I *would* have defeaters for believing *p*.

After all, the counterfactual interlocutor *might not* have had any defeaters to offer us—she might have studied our best arguments and, fully persuaded, found nothing critical to say.

So why accept the relevant very-likely-would-counterfactuals that generate the problem? Notice that the very-likely-would counterfactuals are located somewhere between the corresponding would- and might-counterfactuals. The might-counterfactuals are downstream from the very-likely-would-counterfactuals, and so the former don't imply the latter. The would-counterfactuals are upstream from the very-likely-would-counterfactuals; even though the former give reason to accept the latter, that won't help because the former are doubtful. Given only that we *might* have defeaters, why grant that we *very likely would* have them? Must we accept the relevant counterfactuals?

Reply: This objection is sensible enough. That a brilliant counterfactual interlocutor might object does not *entail* that she very likely would. But at least some counterfactuals concerning what counterfactual interlocutors very likely would do to our arguments should be accepted. We just need to identify ones that we find most plausible. If we find ourselves unsure whether an exceptional possible objector very likely would challenge our controversial views, let's be imaginative.

For a start, the one counterfactual interlocutor need not remain by her lonesome. Imagine instead a large convention of counterfactual interlocutors. They have come together for an extended symposium on your arguments. They intend to study your notebook with the utmost care and intensity. In their critical investigation of your ideas, no rock—indeed, no pebble—remains unturned.[11] Isn't it hard to resist the thought that some members of this group very likely would offer you defeaters for your views? In your most honest moments that should seem pretty much inevitable, given the strength of arguments for controversial views in general and your own modest sense of yourself as a thinker. Now if you consider the nearby worlds where these counterfactual interlocutors scrutinize your arguments and share their thoughts but do *not* give you defeaters, then you should appreciate that something unlikely—something a little strange—has happened in these worlds. Perhaps the symposium members reach a consensus that your arguments are undefeated and successful; or perhaps they have offered defeaters that are properly defeated by your current beliefs, before you even try to respond to the objections and thereby defeat the defeaters. All of this seems considerably less likely than that the counterfactual interlocutors give you defeaters. Importantly, then, you should judge that the nearby worlds where the antecedent is true but you do not get a defeater are a *minority* of nearby worlds where the antecedent holds. But that's just to accept the relevant epistemic very-likely-would-counterfactual.

Objection 2: Granting that if some counterfactual interlocutors were around, they very likely would offer defeaters for some of our controversial

---

[11] We might further imagine that your critics at the symposium have a powerful incentive to refute your arguments: the promise of an all-expenses-paid seven-night Caribbean cruise. Objections to your best arguments may indeed seem elusive. But remember, these critics are highly motivated to reveal your errors. Most of them would exult in sniffing sea air under the vast lapis lazuli dome of the Caribbean sky. (For one important exception to this rule, see the title essay in Wallace 1997.)

beliefs, it doesn't follow that their efforts would give us actual *undefeated* defeaters by our lights. Perhaps we doubt they are trustworthy judges concerning the questions at issue. Perhaps then we have reason to think a counterfactual defeater they might offer doesn't (by the argument schema in section 1) provide an actual defeater for our actual belief, because the actual defeater would be defeated by our current evidence.

Reply: The problem is consistent with this sort of concern. To get the problem going, I suggested that we envision a group of *methodologically-friendly* counterfactual interlocutors: those who would appeal to types of reasons, evidence, and inferences that you would take as legitimate if you were presented with them. If you say that some possible objectors are an unreliable source of evidence concerning the issue at hand, then they can stand outside that group—presumably, you will think they embrace problematic methodologies. I can concede in this context, anyway, that you have reason to doubt that they are a reliable source, given that you reject their methodology. Even so, insofar as you think some different counterfactual interlocutors are reliable sources, you will still face the problem.[12]

Objection 3: If methodologically-friendly counterfactual interlocutors were around, why should we think they very likely would offer defeaters for our controversial beliefs? They have methodological commitments much like our own, after all. So wouldn't they end up *agreeing with us* and thus *not* giving us defeaters?

Reply: That depends on the proposition under consideration. Suppose that methodological commitment M entails some proposition p. If you think your group of counterfactual interlocutors all operate within the bounds of M, as you do yourself, then they probably will not offer defeaters for thinking p (supposing they are coherent). But surely M won't entail every interesting proposition that is up for grabs in typical controversies. M could be something along these lines: sense experience is the source of all concepts and knowledge; the spatio-temporal world is all there is; simplicity is a guide to truth; and so forth. Such commitments (or their negations) fit together with a range of discordant viewpoints about many questions. Two empiricists, for instance, could take different positions on substance dualism, the morality of capital punishment, the legalization of drugs, or the existence of God. So it's doubtful that all methodologically-friendly counterfactual objectors, by

---

[12] If you say that *all* interlocutors who might well produce objections to your arguments are unreliable, I would want to ask: why do you take yourself to be a reliable judge on those matters? What makes you so special?

virtue of their methodological commitments alone, must agree with you about a great many specific propositions.

Objection 4: No doubt there are counterfactual interlocutors who very likely would offer good objections to our views—objections that, were we to have them, would lead us to drop our views unless and until we had a satisfying response. Yet for each objection, doesn't it seem that some counterfactual interlocutor very likely would produce adequate responses to that objection? The idea is that any defeater provided by one counterfactual interlocutor gets defeated by another one. Don't these counterfactual interlocutors therefore *cancel each other out*?

Reply: That is a tempting thought, but it's too quick. I want to suggest that "canceling out" is not helpful here. Notice first that for any satisfying response to an objection to our views, we might expect a counterfactual interlocutor to follow up with an objection to that response. So goes the counterfactual interlocutors' tug-of-war. Reflecting in this way, we'll be inclined to think it is *unclear* how they will leave the matter. Should this comfort us? I doubt it. To begin to understand why, we can think about the following case:

> *Third Snow*: You are indoors, in a windowless room, and you reasonably believe that it is snowing outside after having seen falling snow a few minutes ago. You have no way to observe the present scene outside. A trustworthy source, S_1, informs you that if you were standing outside, very likely you would have a reason for believing it is not snowing. Then another trustworthy source, S_2, informs you that if you were standing outside, very likely you would have a reason for believing that S_1's report is mistaken. You recognize that the trustworthiness of S_1 and S_2 is *roughly equal* and that your initial grounds for believing it is snowing are *not significantly better* than the grounds for accepting the epistemic counterfactuals.

How should you react once you learn about the relevant counterfactuals? You might insist that S_1 and S_2 cancel each other out and just continue believing it is snowing. But that is unreasonable. The proper reaction in Third Snow, once you have learned that S_1 and S_2 conflict, is to be unsure whether or not it's snowing.

According to the objection we're considering, for any criticism a counterfactual interlocutor levels at our argument, another one would likely produce a satisfying response, followed by another objection, another response, and so on. But if that is how we envision things shaking out, our envisioned counterfactual situation is no different than Third Snow in the relevant normative respects.

Here's why. Suppose we believe it is snowing outside. When we learn of two conflicting but trustworthy sources that deliver the relevant epistemic counterfactuals, and we lack reason to think our initial grounds for belief are considerably stronger than our grounds for accepting those counterfactuals, we should suspend judgment about the target proposition rather than stick with believing it. This shows that "canceling out" does not work. On certain assumptions, the objection leads to the conclusion it was designed to avoid. I happen to think those assumptions are rather plausible in many cases where our beliefs are controversial. This objection won't deliver us from the problem.[13]

Objection 5: Some counterfactual interlocutors very likely would offer evidence against our arguments, but what if the majority of them would agree with us and by their agreement furnish support for our arguments? Suppose that we have reason to think the following. If the counterfactual interlocutors scrutinized our arguments, then (*i*) we very likely would gain defeaters for our arguments but (*ii*) many of those interlocutors very likely would support our arguments with their agreement. Won't the counterfactual "agreement" evidence and the counterfactual defeaters "cancel out," thereby preventing us from getting actual defeaters?

Reply: This objection adds a twist to Objection 4. Note that our reason to accept (*i*) is typically stronger than our reason to accept (*ii*). That's due to our weak grasp of the relevant counterfactual facts related to (*ii*). What proportion of the relevant counterfactual interlocutors would affirm that our argument is sound? That is difficult to say.[14] But going on only what we know

---

[13] In fact, the reply to Objection 4 suggests that we face the problem not only when we reasonably believe a defeating epistemic counterfactual is true but also when we reasonably suspend judgment or become doxastically open toward one. Let's consider the former type of situation. For instance, if you properly suspend judgment whether *if you were standing outside, very likely you would have a reason for believing it is not snowing*, then you get a defeater for your belief that it's snowing—which is precisely what happens in Third Snow. I focused on cases where we properly *believe* the "counterfactual interlocutors" epistemic counterfactual, because I think we have good reason to believe it and this poses the clearest challenge to our controversial beliefs; but the problem looks menacing even if we suspend judgment about the counterfactual at issue. (Thanks to Andrew Moon for helpful discussion.)

[14] A related question about (*ii*): what are the relevant "antecedent" conditions we should have in mind? If we pick out worlds where all of the counterfactual interlocutors have learned about the defeaters that have very likely been thought up, then (*ii*) looks somewhat doubtful. What would the majority think if they had a chance to mull over our argument *and* the counterfactual defeaters? Again, it is hard to know, given our ignorance concerning the relevant facts.

about the shortage of actual agreement on controversial matters, (*ii*) appears doubtful.

Let us grant, though, that we have equally good reason to accept (*i*) and (*ii*). That's not enough for the "agreement" evidence and defeaters to "cancel out." Plausibly, *if* we have reason to think that the counterfactual interlocutors who would accept our arguments would have special insights that the ones who would offer defeaters would miss; or *if* we have reason to think the agreement evidence would defeat the very-likely-to-be provided counterfactual defeaters; *then* the counterfactual defeaters won't give us actual defeaters. What would finding ourselves with such reasons be like? Consider an analogy. It's like we reasonably believe that if counterfactual interlocutors gave us defeaters, then an angel hovering over our shoulder would whisper supporting evidence in our ear, defeating the defeaters. But when we imagine what would probably happen if those counterfactual interlocutors scrutinized our arguments and shared their thoughts, do we have reason to expect anything at all like that? Surely not. No angel will save us. We lack reason to think that the counterfactual interlocutors who would support our arguments enjoy insights the others who would offer defeaters have missed, or that the agreement evidence defeats the very-likely-to-be provided defeaters, or anything else that implies the counterfactual defeaters don't give us actual defeaters.

So this objection leaves us stuck in the same spot as Objection 4. Trustworthy sources deliver (*i*) and (*ii*). That makes for a conflict in the evidence we would likely get if the counterfactual interlocutors did their thing. Upon learning of this conflict, however, it's unreasonable to continue believing *p*. Thus, the objection moves us to the conclusion it was meant to avoid.

Objection 6: Suppose that our best arguments have been tried and tested by actual objectors and have returned to us unscathed. Could that give us reason to think that our best arguments have been scrutinized by a *representative sample* of methodologically-friendly *actual* interlocutors?

If so, perhaps we can reason as follows. (*a*) Our belief in some proposition is undefeated after our best supporting argument has been scrutinized by a representative sample of methodologically-friendly *actual* interlocutors. (*b*) The actual methodologically-friendly objectors are a representative sample of all methodologically-friendly objectors (counterfactual ones included). (*c*) Then, on the basis of (*a*) and (*b*), we have reason to think it is unlikely that some member of the class of methodologically-friendly counterfactual interlocutors very likely would provide us with an undefeated defeater. It follows from (*c*) that we don't face the Problem of Counterfactual Interlocutors, because we can reject the relevant epistemic counterfactual.[15]

Reply: By appealing to a representative sample of methodologically-friendly actual interlocutors, you may develop a sense for what methodologically-friendly counterfactual ones very likely would do with your arguments. I can grant that, sometimes, the reasoning captured by (*a*)–(*c*) allows us to resist the relevant epistemic counterfactuals. Often enough, though, it will be easy to conjure up sensible doubts concerning (*a*) and (*b*), and so the objection won't help.

Let's suppose that the argument supporting some belief of yours is written down in your notebook. At the moment, you don't believe you have any defeaters for your argument provided by any actual methodologically-friendly interlocutors. We might worry about your ability to reliably recognize good objections to your views, given your biases and other cognitive limitations, but ignore that issue. Here is another problem: why think your argument has been scrutinized by a *representative sample* of actual methodologically-friendly interlocutors? Maybe you are of the academic persuasion and you've published your article in a professional journal. It's doubtful that the handful of journal referees, or the colleagues who commented on your article, are a representative sample of actual interlocutors. Certainly, it's doubtful that your friends and colleagues are included among the most insightful thinkers around today. (Just don't mention it to them.) And the overworked referees who may have dashed off reports on your manuscript do not necessarily represent the most careful or critical kind of reader. So the people who've tested your argument do not stand the best chance of catching its subtle errors. Thus, sensibly accepting (*a*) is often not possible.

But let us grant you have reason to accept (*a*): that your argument is undefeated and it has been scrutinized by a representative sample of actual methodologically-friendly interlocutors. Even here, (*b*) often looks doubtful. Intellectual tastes and pedagogical practices vary across time and between cultures. So thinking you have a representative sample of *all* methodologically-friendly interlocutors' responses to your argument on the basis of a representative sample of actual methodologically-friendly interlocutors who've lived within your lifetime seems like a stretch. Aside

---

[15] Daniel Howard-Snyder suggested this objection.

from the fact that they would come bearing objections, could you even guess what sort of things the most perceptive minds of medieval Europe or early modern China—or remarkably gifted and creative counterfactual interlocutors much closer to your own situation, ones who died in adolescence or had no access to education or faced overwhelming discrimination and never made their mark—could you guess what *they* would have to say about your argument had they scrutinized it? If some of them happen to be methodologically-friendly interlocutors on some topics, don't you expect they'd have surprisingly different reactions than what you got from your friends and colleagues, in virtue of the alternative sets of insights and inclinations they would bring to the evaluation of your argument? Or is your intellectual fishpond really no different than all of the many others?

As far as I can tell, whatever you know about actual interlocutors doesn't indicate that you would also be able to defeat the potential defeaters offered by counterfactual interlocutors, especially ones from different times and places.

Objection 7: It's no stretch to suppose that we have reason to think our best arguments are sound. And methodologically-friendly interlocutors would, like us, recognize that those arguments are sound. But then we've reason to regard as methodologically unfriendly any philosopher, actual or counterfactual, who does not accept our arguments. All of this together gives us reason to deny the epistemic counterfactual. If methodologically-friendly counterfactual interlocutors were to scrutinize our best arguments and then share their thoughts, they would accept our arguments.

Reply: There are two problems with this objection. First, the objection's notion of methodological "friendship" is too narrow. Methodologically-friendly interlocutors need not regard all of the same arguments as sound. An example will suggest why. Recall past cases when we ourselves were convinced of an argument's soundness and then, after more reflection, decided that we got it wrong. Our methodology need not have changed in order for this to happen. Different selves (past/present or yourself/myself) can be methodological friends even when they split over whether an argument is sound. A second problem is that the objection licenses a dubious kind of dogmatism.[16] Suppose that we have reason now to think our best arguments are sound. Later on, if we come across evidence indicating the arguments

---

[16] Objection 7 is reminiscent of the Dogmatic Dismissal Strategy I discussed in Chapter 5 as well as the reasoning in one version of Saul Kripke's "dogmatism paradox." For more on the dogmatism paradox, see Harman (1973, 148–149), Sorensen (1988), and Kelly (2008, 613–617).

may not be sound, believing they are sound may no longer be reasonable for us. That seems to be precisely what happens when we reflect on what the counterfactual interlocutors would likely do to our arguments. Reflection furnishes new evidence concerning our arguments. But the objection, if correct, allows us to continue with unchanged confidence in our arguments even after confronted by counterevidence.

Objection 8: Why can't we deny that counterfactual interlocutors very likely would deliver defeaters for our opinions *given the strength of our arguments*? If we take ourselves to have conclusive, knockdown arguments—ones to which there can be no reasonable objection—then there is no problem for us.

Reply: At least some people believe that there are conclusive arguments in support of their controversial views. Witness, as an example, the undiluted confidence expressed by Ludwig Wittgenstein in the preface to his *Tractatus*. "[T]he *truth* of the thoughts that are communicated here," he wrote of what was to come, "seems to me unassailable and definitive. I am, therefore, of the opinion that the problems have in essentials been finally solved" (2003 [1922], 5). Something not unlike the young Wittgenstein's self-assurance underlies the objection. For those who suspect that such confidence is typically misplaced in discussions of controversial questions, the objection is a bust. Yet someone may have an unassailable, knockdown argument for each of her opinions. The question is: how could she reasonably think that about her arguments, given the presence of people who are approximately as informed and intelligent as she is who do not accept her views? Importantly, merely believing that some arguments are unassailable isn't enough to avoid the problem. For in order to reject the claim that counterfactual interlocutors very likely would offer defeaters, we seem to need good reason to believe our arguments knock down all objections, even ones we have not been given. So this objection calls for serious argumentative backup.

4. O Defeater, Where Art Thou?

The Problem of Counterfactual Interlocutors threatens our controversial convictions by pointing to what seems simple and obvious. Curiously, our discussion could have proceeded without bringing up counterfactual objectors at all. They are a "delivery method," as it were, for an insight. It is this: *we have very likely overlooked or missed defeaters for our controversial opinions.*

That is the trouble that the problem leads us to contemplate. This problem reveals how we may come to have competence defeaters—reasons to doubt whether we are well-positioned to adopt a reasonable view on the basis of all the things we know through actual inquiry, including contact with actual interlocutors. I said the counterfactual interlocutors would have changed the state of our discussion. They very likely would have given us defeaters for our beliefs. Surprisingly perhaps, the counterfactual interlocutors can still offer us defeaters in a sense even though they cannot speak to us.

I am inclined to measure the seriousness of the problem with the help of an analogy. We hold some controversial view on the basis of our best argument, but we realize that if we had been spending time in the company of geniuses and luminaries, or peers who tend to be critical of the sorts of views we hold, then we'd very likely have reason to doubt that our argument is much good. Now imagine that we are stranded on a deserted island after a three-hour tour gone horribly wrong. We can't talk with those formidable interlocutors. We are alone. Geographical isolation won't make our controversial opinion reasonable *given that we accept that our argument would very likely be seriously challenged had we been in the company of those interlocutors.* Something not unlike that analogy captures our native condition as inquirers. Our reflection on counterfactual interlocutors helps us recognize as much and then adjust our thinking accordingly. We are separated from counterfactual interlocutors and we know that they very likely would take the wind out of our best arguments. We know that if we were not separated from them, and if those interlocutors spoke to us face to face, then very likely we would have defeaters for many of our controversial beliefs. That is enough to see that there are in fact defeaters for many of our opinions.

By thinking about the ways our intellectual communities might have been, we can come to better know our limits. In the next chapter, I return to our actual situation. The world contains a great deal of evidence that concerns our controversial opinions, but we only possess a small fraction of it.

7

Unpossessed Evidence

You want to explain everything by the facts that are known to you. But the facts that are not known to you? What do they say?
  —Joseph Joubert (1754–1824), *Pensées*, published posthumously

At our first sally into the intellectual world, we all march together along one straight and open road; but as we proceed further, and wider prospects open to our view, every eye fixes upon a different scene; we divide into various paths, and, as we move forward, are still at a greater distance from each other. As a question becomes more complicated and involved, and extends to a greater number of relations, disagreement of opinion will always be multiplied; not because we are irrational, but because we are finite beings, furnished with different kinds of knowledge, exerting different degrees of attention, one discovering consequences which escape another, none taking in the whole concatenation of causes and effects, and most comprehending but a very small part, each comparing what he observes with a different criterion, and each referring it to a different purpose.
  —Samuel Johnson, *The Adventurer*, No. 107, 13 November 1753

The universe of print we live in now, on page and screen, is an infinitely capacious memory and an inexhaustible reservoir of new thought. That its best potentialities are not often realized, that its best moments often pass unobserved or unvalued, only certifies its profound humanity.
  —Marilynne Robinson, *The Givenness of Things*, 2015

Our opinions are based on just part of the relevant evidence. There is evidence we do not have. For many topics, evidence we do not have comprises most of the evidence there is, and it is easy to learn that there is much relevant unpossessed evidence for nearly anything we care to think about. All of this is obvious. But what is the epistemological significance of these facts? Could our awareness of them ever lead us to think differently about our controversial beliefs?

Here are two examples to bring those questions into focus. Imagine you are wandering among rows of bookshelves at the library. These books concern questions about which you hold opinions. But you have read only a few of them. Let's imagine you think that free will and determinism are compatible, having studied a dozen journal articles and a couple of books some years ago. Scanning the shelves, you see that there are several dozen titles relevant to whether compatibilism about free will is true. Some books contain arguments against your view. You hadn't considered these books until now and you haven't yet looked at them.

Take a second example. Five or ten years ago, you thought carefully about economic ideas and arguments. Then life changed. With a family or busy job, or both, you have not kept pace with recent discussions in economics. You now wonder what has happened in the intervening years, so you search a database using some keywords ("government spending + economic growth"). Your searches return thousands of results. As you quickly recognize, there are hundreds of articles and books, all potentially relevant to figuring out what to think about this one economic issue about which you once had carefully considered views. You knew the arguments, replies, and counter-replies, and you had a good rationale for your favored positions in the debate. It's evident to you that some of the recent discussion challenges your thinking. You have not studied any of it, however. Rehearsing your earlier rationale, it still seems perfectly right to you, but you know of new evidence you do not have.

Examples like these may leave us feeling that reasonable belief—in compatibilism or the economic thesis that government spending stimulates economic growth—is threatened by learning about unpossessed evidence. If we further imagine ourselves with unflinching confidence in our opinions, we may sense that we've made a mistake.

Is reasonable belief and knowledge sometimes incompatible with recognizing we have only part of the relevant evidence? If so, why and when? What is the tension between reasonable belief and knowledge, on the one hand, and finding out our evidence is limited, on the other? Those questions offer our first look at what I call the *Problem of Unpossessed Evidence*.

This problem challenges many of our controversial beliefs about politics, philosophy, ethics, history, and religion, among other topics. Given the rising tide of available research and commentary and the narrowing of disciplinary expertise, one person can usually scoop up only a small share of the relevant evidence for a single topic. No surprise there. We have access to mind-bogglingly vast stockpiles of information stored in libraries and archives. We can discover an overabundance of facts and figures and arguments and commentaries, waiting on computer servers connected to the internet, summoned at once to tiny screens people carry around in their pockets. Any one of us can easily learn that we have only a small part of the relevant evidence for many controversial questions. And yet, normally, many of us confidently answer such questions, and believe that our answers are entirely reasonable, despite knowing that our evidence is partial.

In this chapter, I propose means to help us recognize the significance of these observations. I begin with the fact that there is evidence against our views that we know about but do not have. I argue that reflection on such evidence poses a challenge to our controversial beliefs. That is, thinking about unpossessed evidence often delivers defeaters. Unless these defeaters are challenged by further reasons, we'll find ourselves in the end with reasons to change our views and possibly to doubt that particular views are an appropriate response to our evidence. So these defeaters can bring us greater doxastic openness. But even when we are able to defeat the *prima facie* defeaters, the Problem of Unpossessed Evidence helps us understand what it takes to sustain reasonable beliefs in an information-glutted world. Maintaining reasonable beliefs while knowing our evidence is partial is no easy matter, and sometimes our best response to the problem will be to doubt our views.

To that end, I explore two types of principles that let us view the two opening examples from different angles. The principles are motivated by the following thought. When we envision ourselves in the two opening cases—which I will call *Library* and *WWW*—we focus on propositions about the relevant evidence. When we are in the library, we see those shelves of previously unknown books on free will. Looking at internet search results, we are confronted with hundreds of contributions to an economic debate over government spending and economic growth that has advanced since we surveyed the field. Our reflection here naturally leads to questions about evidence. *Do I have evidence that there is counterevidence for my view? Is my evidence a fair sample of the total relevant evidence?* As I argue, our answers to such questions may give us defeaters. That is, our reflection on those questions can bring to light evidence to doubt our competence to form reasonable, well-grounded views.

Here is my plan. First, I briefly ask why the Problem of Unpossessed Evidence has not been more widely appreciated as a challenge to our controversial beliefs (section 1). Then I articulate and defend two different types of principles to reason about unpossessed evidence (sections 2 and 3). To highlight the force of the problem, I offer two analogies (section 4) before concluding with some speculations concerning how we might deal with the problem (section 5).

1. That Horrible Mass of Books

Curiously, the Problem of Unpossessed Evidence has not been widely appreciated. Of course, the psychological and practical significance of massive amounts of information is often noted. The phrase "information overload" is emblematic of the present age. It's not entirely new, though. "Of making many books there is no end," we learn in *Ecclesiastes*, and in the early modern period, scholars struggled to keep up with rapidly burgeoning literatures and libraries. Gottfried Leibniz lamented "that horrible mass of books that keeps on growing" and feared that the glut of books could lead people to be "disgusted with the sciences, and that a fatal despair may cause them to fall back into barbarism" (1951 [1680], 29). Jean-Jacques Rousseau may have been gripped by that "fatal despair" when, in his *First Discourse*, he envisioned Socrates "reborn among us." Rousseau said that the ancient Athenian philosopher "would continue to despise our vain Sciences" and "would not help swell the mass of books that flood in on us from all sides" (1997 [1750], 13; Part I, 30). A deluge of books doesn't mean most of those books have any readership, though. William Hazlitt remarked on "the countless volumes that lie unopened, unregarded, unread, and unthought-of" and noted "[w]e can no more read all the new books that appear, than we can read all the old ones that have disappeared" (1998 [1827], 141, 143). Sustained anxiety among writers and readers about vast quantities of printed materials eventually led to the specialized field of library and information science.[1]

---

[1] The articles in Rosenberg (2003) discuss early modern "information overload."

In recent decades, epistemologists have been concerned with know-ledge based on testimony, a topic I address in Chapter 9, and they have been aware of vast quantities of information we don't possess. For instance, John Hardwig writes: "Scientific propositions often must be accepted on the basis of evidence that only others have. Consequently, much scientific knowledge rests on the moral and epistemic characters of scientists . . . . [T]he relevant data and arguments are too extensive and too difficult to be had by any means other than testimony" (1991, 706). But I have noticed few discussions of epis-temological doubts or worries arising from awareness of our condition.

I know of a few exceptions. Francisco Sanches, in his late sixteenth-century work *That Nothing Is Known* (*Quod nihil scitur*), says that books are "so numerous that if one lived a hundred times a hundred thousand years one would not have years enough to read them all" (1988, 93). (In case you were wondering, that's 10 million years.) Sanches uses that claim in support of the skeptical conclusion of his book's title. The vastness of worlds made by printed words is one thing; the natural world itself is something else entirely. In his *Penseés*, Pascal recognizes the relevance of unpossessed evidence about nature for our theories of nature (2004 [1662], 58–64; S230/L199). In the lengthy "disproportion of man" section, Pascal helps his readers envision the immense depths of the physical world and the miniscule recesses of its tiniest parts. "What is man in nature?" asks Pascal. "A nothing compared to the in-finite, an everything compared to the nothing, a midpoint between nothing and everything, infinitely removed from understanding the extremes" (2004 [1662], 59; S230/L199). Pascal's guided tour of reality in this intriguing and beautiful passage is designed to correct overconfident thinkers who presume to know nature, "a presumption as infinite as their object" (2004 [1662], 60; S230/L199). Pascal's skeptical reasoning is underpinned by his observations about the relevance of our recognizing that there are many facts we do not and cannot know.[2]

Unpossessed evidence has been noted in more recent epistemological discussions. David Christensen, for instance, notes that one reason we live in "epistemic imperfection" is that "the evidence on which we base our beliefs is limited" (2007a, 187), but he doesn't say more about the theme. Richard Feldman (2003b), discussing work by Alvin Plantinga, presses a problem for "exclusivism"—according to which some religious doctrine is true and

---

[2] I am grateful to Joseph Milburn for sharing his draft paper on Pascal's skeptical reasoning in the "disproportion of man" section of *Penseés*.

incompatible ones are false—and Feldman highlights the presence of un-possessed evidence. Feldman suggests that if the exclusivist grants she has reasons to believe proposition p while knowing of others who have "equally good reasons" for believing not-p—reasons the exclusivist herself lacks—she's sometimes not justified in believing p. Although discussions of exclusivism in the philosophy of religion from the 1980s and '90s helped to fuel subsequent discussions of the epistemology of peer disagreement, Feldman's case did not get taken up. Finally, and most significantly, John Schellenberg (2007, chapter 1 and 2014) has posed a challenge for defenders of theism that capitalizes on human ignorance of the total evidence.[3]

Why hasn't the Problem of Unpossessed Evidence been explored in more detail? I have a pet theory. The problem is historically emergent. It wouldn't have been a problem for, say, ancient Greek philosophers in the same way it is today. Aristotle had around 400 books in his library, and that was a large collection for his time. If your library is that size, maybe you can't study everything with great care, but you can know your way around the books. It is no accident that Francisco Sanches blasted his skeptical note soon after Gutenberg's printing press transformed the world. Sanches was troubled by many thousands of books.[4] Today, the mass of literature has reached hard-to-fathom proportions. The material conditions underwriting the plausibility or intuitiveness of our problem have grown through the ages. The problem raises a special difficulty for inhabitants of this age of information overload.

What have philosophers made of the fact that there is considerable unpossessed evidence? Not much and not enough. True, some philosophers have undertaken information-organizing projects—encyclopedias, indexes, databases—because they have been acutely aware of that fact. It seems, though, to have received less theorizing than we might have expected. But I'll briefly note two points of contact between the present chapter and recent epistemological themes.

---

[3] E.J. Coffman brought Feldman's article to my attention, and Michael Bergmann told me about Schellenberg's argument.

[4] Wiesner-Hanks (2005, 58) comments on the scale of the post-Gutenberg deluge of books:

> Historians estimate that somewhere between 8 million and 20 million books were printed in Europe in the 50 years between Gutenberg's invention and 1500. These numbers may seem small compared to today, when the fifth volume in the Harry Potter series sold nearly 7 million copies in one day (making it the fastest-selling book ever), but it was much more than the total number of books produced in all Western history up to that point.

First, some philosophers have argued that unpossessed counterevidence we are oblivious to undermines our knowledge.[5] These arguments prompt us to observe, from a third-person perspective, that misleading evidence not possessed by a thinker can prevent that thinker's justified true belief from graduating to knowledge. The Problem of Unpossessed Evidence is related but different. It presses us to recognize that *awareness* of unpossessed evidence undermines reasonable belief. Second, my discussion is also related to recent debates concerning the possibility of reasonable disagreement between epistemic peers, a topic I considered in Chapter 5. Peers are equally familiar with evidence and arguments that bear on a question. But peer disagreement is, arguably, a relatively idealized and uncommon sort of disagreement.[6] In many disputes, we do not face epistemic peers because we have important evidential differences with our dissenters. When we learn a peer disagrees with us, we do not learn that we are missing some relevant evidence. Even so, reflecting on unpossessed evidence promises us a better understanding of the epistemological standing of many controversial beliefs. Often enough, when we disagree with others, there is evidence we don't have (which they do have) and there is evidence they don't have (which we do have). Those cases apparently fall outside discussions of peer disagreement, but I take them up here.

2. Evidence of Unpossessed Evidence

Let us begin with a plain thought about how a belief could be defeated by recognizing that our evidence is partial. Roughly, when we learn that there is evidence we don't have, we often learn that part of the unpossessed evidence would defeat a particular belief of ours. But evidence that there is an unpossessed defeater for a belief is a *prima facie* defeater for that belief, and we have no defeater-defeater in situations like Library and WWW.

To develop this idea, we can distinguish between different situations where our evidence tells us about some unpossessed evidence. Our evidence can vary in richness: it may or may not tell us what the unpossessed evidence supports, how strong that evidence is, and whether it is misleading, among other things. Our evidence may tell us the unpossessed evidence supports

---

[5] For discussion, see Harman (1973, chapter 9), Goldberg (2016), and Benton (2016).
[6] Frances (2010), Lackey (2010), and King (2012) discuss this theme.

a particular proposition, or it may leave it open what that other evidence supports. Let's zero in on cases, like the opening two examples, where our evidence indicates that at least some of the unpossessed evidence supports some particular proposition.

Suppose that we believe proposition *p*. There are different ways our evidence may, just by telling us about the unpossessed evidence, challenge our belief. For one, our evidence may indicate that the evidence we don't have supports not-*p*—in other words, we have evidence of a rebutting defeater for believing *p*. For another, our evidence may indicate that the unpossessed evidence tells against the support we have for believing *p*—it is evidence of an undermining defeater.

Keep that distinction in mind. Now, sometimes our evidence indicates there's unpossessed evidence that is a defeater *relative to our own evidence*. This is what happens when we learn there is some evidence we don't have such that if we got it in hand, then we would have a defeater. These cases are straightforward: our evidence of the evidence delivers us a defeater. But it isn't obvious whether, or how much, such cases overlap with Library and WWW. Given only the details of the opening examples, do we have evidence that the unpossessed evidence *would* bring us defeaters? It is less than clear. After all, maybe we would easily defeat challenges posed by the unpossessed evidence were we to have it—perhaps all of the books we haven't read just contain feather-weight arguments we can easily dismiss. Leaving that matter sidelined for now, let's instead focus on cases where our evidence indicates there is unpossessed evidence that is a defeater *relative to some body of evidence we don't have*.

Here comes the problem. Suppose our belief in *p* is reasonable and we gain evidence indicating that there is unpossessed evidence which contains either a rebutting or undermining defeater for belief in *p* relative to that unpossessed evidence. Imagine we are in the library, for example, and spot a few titles—*An Essay on Free Will* and *Living Without Free Will*, among others. We realize these books contain arguments against compatibilism. Plausibly, the set of evidence comprised by several books that defend incompatibilism (the thesis that free will and determinism are not compatible) features defeaters for belief in compatibilism. Whoever has that set of evidence has defeaters for believing compatibilism. Perhaps the relevant set of incompatibilist evidence is too narrow and lacks some important evidence. Perhaps that set contains misleading evidence. But how can we deny *that relative to that set* there are defeaters for believing in compatibilism? If our only evidence were what is contained in some pro-incompatibilism book, presumably our belief in compatibilism would be at least partially defeated. Now we can reason as follows:

M_1 Evidence of the existence of a defeater for believing p relative to some body of evidence is a *prima facie* defeater for believing p relative to any body of evidence.

M_2 I have evidence of the existence of a defeater for believing proposition p relative to some body of unpossessed evidence.

M_3 I have no defeater for that *prima facie* defeater for believing p.
Therefore,

M_C I have an undefeated defeater for believing p.

I call this the *Meta-defeater Argument*. M_1 is related to an epistemic principle noted in Chapter 6: "evidence of evidence is evidence" (Feldman 2006, 223).[7] M_1 says, roughly: that evidence of a defeater for believing p is a *prima facie* defeater for believing p. M_1 seems a little more modest than Feldman's slogan, though. M_1 is consistent with the possibility that evidence of a defeater for believing p relative to some body of evidence is not an *ultima facie* defeater for believing p relative to some other body of evidence. M_1 looks rather plausible, but I won't defend it in full here.

M_2 is given by the details of Library and WWW. In those examples, we can easily imagine learning about an unpossessed defeater—that is, a defeater relative to evidence we don't have. Importantly, we may believe M_2 without having the unpossessed defeater in hand. Imagine hearing from a friend that the authors of some books we haven't read happen to endorse incompatibilism. Or imagine reading the dust jacket blurbs for those books and learning that they contain arguments for incompatibilism. Then we would have reason to think that there is a defeater for compatibilism relative to some unpossessed evidence, but we would not have the defeater itself.

What about M_3? Do we have a defeater for the defeater in our examples? Plausibly not. Here is why many realistic examples will be consistent with our having reason to believe M_3. By design, the opening examples leave some background details to the reader's imagination. However, I meant the following details to make good sense: (*i*) we lack reason to think that all of those

---

[7] For more discussion, see Feldman (2009, 308–309) and Rowley (2012). Compare to Hardwig's "principle of testimony" (1991, 697).

library books and digital documents are unreliable sources of information; and (*ii*) we lack reason to think our original evidence for our beliefs is representative of the total evidence, in the sense that we would be unlikely to gain a new defeater if we were to read those books and articles. More generally, I was envisioning ourselves in Library and WWW having no reason to think our original evidence is *better than* the unpossessed evidence.

Let me say some more. In the examples, we have just one subset of the total evidence regarding some proposition. Our evidence may or may not contain as much accurate, non-misleading evidence as other subsets. It may or may not be as representative of the total evidence as other subsets. Following our evidence may or may not be as good a guide to the truth as following other subsets of evidence. Suppose we pit our evidence head-to-head against other subsets of the total evidence. Which dog wins? We won't always know how our evidence finishes the race. The trouble is that we normally can't tell whether our evidence is *more likely to indicate what's true* than the subsets containing evidence we don't have. We should not presume our evidence is superior. That is what I expected readers to naturally "fill in" when reflecting on Library and WWW. This is a natural interpretation of the examples: we lack reason to believe that our original evidence is better than the unpossessed evidence, in the sense noted. Thus, we won't have a defeater-defeater but will have reason to affirm M_3.

The Meta-defeater Argument is one way to see why there is a defeater in the opening cases. Of course, we may be able to defeat the defeaters, and explaining how that might work will illuminate what is needed to overcome the Problem of Unpossessed Evidence. As I'll argue, however, we only have defeater-defeaters for this argument when our evidential situation is unusually strong.

We can begin here:

D_1 The evidence I don't have that apparently defeats belief in proposition p has been produced by an unreliable source—that is, a source not likely to produce mostly truths regarding p.

Let's say we believe that smoking is unhealthy. Then we learn that Big Smoke, a cigarette manufacturer and proud sponsor of a BASE jumping team, has funded scientists to investigate the long-term health effects of smoking. Contrary to received expert opinion, Big Smoke's research team concludes that smoking is not a health hazard. We have not cracked the seven-hundred-page doorstopper of a report and so don't have the alleged defeater for our belief that smoking is unhealthy. Yet we have learned *about* the report, and so, by the Meta-defeater Argument, we have a defeater for believing that smoking is unhealthy.

But even before we turn a single page of the report, we get a defeater-defeater. That's because we have reason to believe something like D_1—that the source of the unpossessed defeater is unreliable. The smoking-friendly researchers were bankrolled by Big Smoke and we know that such partnerships don't reliably produce good evidence, due to problematic incentives and biases.

D_1 can defeat the defeater, but in cases like Library and WWW, what reason do we have to believe D_1? The reasons built into the example involving Big Smoke's report are a lot different than what's assumed in the opening examples; in fact, there is plausibly good reason in the latter to reject D_1. To see why, be mindful of our evidence source for our opinions. In Library, for instance, we've read some works on free will and reflected on the arguments. Our evidence source is apparently the *same type* of source that produced the incompatibilist arguments in those books we have not read. Not unlike us, the authors of those books studied works of philosophy and reflected on arguments. Note the parity between our source of evidence and the sources of unpossessed evidence. If we have reason to think the sources of the unpossessed evidence are unreliable, and thereby have reason to believe D_1, then we would presumably also have reason to think our own source is unreliable. So, unless we are content to regard our source as unreliable, we should not believe D_1 in Library or WWW.[8]

Try out another potential defeater-defeater:

D_2 If an undefeated defeater for believing *p* were included in the evidence I don't have, then I (probably) would have heard of it by now. But I have not heard of it and the "silence" gives me reason to think that the unpossessed defeater is probably defeated.[9]

Suppose we know of a brand-new book we haven't studied that apparently contains a defeater for something we believe. Our friends have read the book

---

[8] I am assuming here that if we reasonably believe our source of evidence is unreliable, we have a defeater for beliefs based on that evidence.

[9] Thanks to Tim Kenyon for proposing something along the lines of D_2. This defeater-defeater relies on a principle defended by Sanford Goldberg (2009a): "If it were the case that *p*, then you would have found out about that *p*."

and we have reason to think that if they had found a new undefeated defeater for our belief, they would probably break the news. But nobody has said a peep. Plausibly, what we know is sometimes good reason for thinking the unpossessed defeater is probably defeated. That's how D_2 works.

For cases like Library and WWW, though, D_2 appears to be implausible. Consider an assumption needed to believe it reasonably in those cases: we are in touch with other people who would share the news of a new defeater if there were one. It should be clear we can't sensibly accept D_2, given the details of our two examples. Are we in league with people who've waded through the continuous flood of information, who are ready to tell us when they have found defeaters for our beliefs? Probably not. This draws near the source of our problem. For one, we sometimes tend to "sort" ourselves into groups along demographic and ideological lines, avoiding people inclined to reject or challenge our views. For another, on many important issues, knowing our way around a significant part of the relevant evidence takes tremendous ability and effort. Even when we are able, life is too short and too busy. For many controversial topics, there's too much evidence for any one person to know.

There is further reason to doubt that D_2 helps. Often there is not the "silence" required by D_2. In a case such as Library, for instance, we know that some people *do* think those books we haven't read successfully defeat belief in compatibilism: the authors themselves and perhaps their friends, students, and devotees. We know that if we had a way to listen in on them, we would get the news: there is a defeater for our belief. Though D_2 helps sometimes, it demands reasons we do not find in our examples.

Let us move to another defeater-defeater:

D_3 The evidence I don't have contains defeaters for believing p and also defeaters for the defeaters for believing p—for every defeater for believing p, there is a defeater for that defeater.

Imagine you have excellent reason to believe this claim: each and every theory of knowledge you know of fails, because someone has published a good counterexample for it. Say you reach this opinion after studying many dozens of articles on the Gettier Problem. That debate looks like a demolition derby to you—no theory has come out unscathed. And thus you believe, for each and every theory put forward, someone has given a good defeater for it. You have this all mapped out on a big chart, hanging on your bedroom wall. For every positive theory of knowledge you have seen, you have found a counterexample for it.

Today, in the library, you realize that there are some theories of knowledge contained in books and articles you have not read. (Your chart stands incomplete!) By the Meta-defeater Argument, your belief in the total failure of theories of knowledge would be defeated by learning of an exception-less theory out there. A defeater for your belief in total theoretical failure is evidence of an exception-less theory. So, M_1 is satisfied. By M_2, you receive a *prima facie* defeater for your belief. Now suppose something more: you have excellent reason to think that all of the unpossessed defeaters (for example, exception-less theories) for your belief in total theoretical failure are themselves defeated—in articles that you haven't read yet. Then you defeat the defeater for your belief by learning about those unread books. Armed with D_3, you can reject M_3.

This extravagant example suggests that reasonably believing D_3 calls for considerable evidential backup. Perhaps it's true that all of the unpossessed defeaters are "canceled out" by unpossessed defeater-defeaters. But we will probably have no clue about this and so will lack reason to believe D_3. Nothing about Library or WWW appears to us to be like the extravagant example and so this defeater-defeater won't prove useful.

In sum, I've argued that we have reason to believe D_1–D_3 only if we are in a rather strong evidential position, and we enjoy such a position only in unusual circumstances. Thus, often enough, in cases like Library and WWW, we will not have those defeater-defeaters, and the Meta-defeater Argument tells us why sticking with our opinions is not (fully) reasonable. I will identify more potential defeater-defeaters for this argument soon enough, but let me turn to a different argument first.

3. Doubtful Fairness

We have just part of the total evidence, but that part reaches us by a particular route. For example, a *fair sample* of evidence of a particular size is drawn from a body of evidence by a process that makes it equally probable that each possible sample of evidence of that size will be selected. Confrontation with unpossessed evidence can lead to reasonable doubt about our sample's fairness and, in turn, to reasonable doubt about any belief based on our sample. Here we find another angle on our problem.

Start with a simple illustration. Imagine the contents of an opaque jar exhaust our (first-order) evidence regarding some question: what kind of marbles are in the jar? The marbles near the top of the jar are blue and the ones at the bottom are cat's eyes, but we don't know that. Then we sample (without replacement) fifty marbles by drawing from the top. Our sample is all we know about the marbles. Notice that the process we use to select the fifty marbles didn't make it equally probable that we would get each possible sample of fifty. Our sample is not fair. It was much more likely that we'd end up with fifty blue marbles than some mix of fifty blue marbles and cat's eyes. But imagine we are oblivious to the sampling problem. We reasonably think the marbles had been thoroughly mixed up in the jar before we removed any. In that case, our sample gives us a reasonable belief that the jar's marbles are blue. Our belief is based on a large enough sample and we can reasonably regard the sample as fair. No matter that we are mistaken about the marbles as well as the sample's fairness. Reasonable beliefs may be wrong, and I assume reasonable beliefs can be based on an unfair sample.

But will our reasonable belief remain untouched once we discover that the sample on which it's based is unfair? It seems not. If we have sufficient reason to believe that our sample is unfair, what we learn should reduce our confidence in our belief. Will reasonable belief here survive suspending judgment whether the sample is fair? Again, it seems not. Reasonably suspending judgment whether the sample is fair likewise gives us reason to diminish our confidence. I'm proposing that doubts about the sample's fairness give us reasons to reduce our confidence in any belief based on the sample.

Here are two observations about this proposal. First, if it's not obvious why doubts about a sample's fairness will defeat belief based on it, then note the close relationship between the thought *that our evidence for proposition p is not a fair sample* and the thought *that our evidence is a reliable source of information about p*. Coming to think that, or suspend judgment whether, our evidence is an unfair sample often commits us to disbelieving that, or suspending judgment whether, our evidence is a reliable source. But holding those attitudes toward the proposition *that our evidence is a reliable source about p* is widely thought to lead to defeaters for believing p on that evidence. Second, suppose that our basis for believing a proposition is a statistical syllogism. Let the proposition be *that some randomly selected marble is blue*. For our inference, the major premise is our sample of evidence from the jar (that our sizable sample features only blues), and the minor premise is that some particular marble is from the jar. We conclude that (probably) some randomly selected marble is blue. But doubts about the fairness of our sample can make that inference unreasonable. We should hope our sample of evidence is fair or "unbiased" whenever we believe on its basis.

I'll state my main proposal as follows:

> F_1 If I believe proposition p on the basis of some evidence E and I have either (*i*) (*prima facie*) reason to disbelieve that E is a fair sample or (*ii*) (*prima facie*) reason to suspend judgment whether E is a fair sample, then I have a (*prima facie*) undermining defeater for believing p.

F_1 is plausible given our discussion so far. That is not to say we couldn't make it more informative. The degree to which belief in p is defeated apparently depends on what we've got reason to think about various factors: how large our sample is, how "far" from fair we have reason to think the sample is, and the evidence or support for our initial belief. These details can be left aside for now. F_1 is a modest starting point. What we reasonably think about the fairness of our sample of evidence is a kind of competence evidence—again, evidence concerning our abilities and dispositions for responding well to the relevant evidence—that may change what is reasonable for us to believe.

We need only add some other premises to F_1 to get the *Doubtful Fairness Argument*:

> F_2 I believe p on the basis of some evidence E and I have either (*i*) reason to disbelieve that E is a fair sample or (*ii*) reason to suspend judgment whether E is a fair sample.
>
> F_3 I have no defeater for the undermining defeater for believing p.
> Therefore,
>
> F_C I have an undefeated undermining defeater for believing p.

This argument applies to the opening examples as follows. We learn of extensive bodies of unpossessed evidence, and so it's natural to wonder whether our sample of evidence is fair. We can simplify the matter by assuming each distinct argument for and against compatibilism, or for and against the economic thesis that government spending stimulates economic growth, is like a single marble in a jar filled with many marbles. Those arguments comprise the relevant total evidence. Our beliefs in the two examples are based wholly on our evaluation of the arguments we've encountered, both for and against. But we know our evidence is partial.

In WWW, the difficulty in thinking our sample is fair to any degree seems acute. A great deal of new evidence has been added to the total evidence. Thus, our evidence fifteen years ago couldn't have been gathered by a process that made it roughly equally probable that any sample of the same size would have been selected *from the present-day total evidence*. To say our sample is fair here appears analogous to the following case. We sample some marbles from a jar and conclude that all the marbles are one color. Then we realize a bunch of new marbles— ones that, for all we know, are different colors—have been added to the jar after we sampled. Knowing what we know, we keep our original level of confidence in our belief about the marbles. That's patently dubious and the same lesson holds for WWW. At best, we should suspend judgment whether our sample is fair.

Fairness is likewise doubtful in Library. Notice that the process we've used to select our evidence is probably haphazard. Perhaps we looked at a couple of books and some articles that were recommended to us, or ones with titles that caught our eye. We didn't sift through the literature systematically, in a way that would give us reason to think our sample of the available evidence was fair. The evidence we have is a matter of the accidents of our personal history.[10] These observations may pull in one of two directions, depending on how we fill in the details. We might reasonably disbelieve our sample is fair because our history just so happened to expose us to much more (or better) evidence favoring our belief than against it. Or we might reasonably suspend judgment on whether our sample is fair because it's unclear to us whether our exposure to the evidence was unbiased. I submit that, in both Library and WWW, we should doubt whether our sample is fair and so should affirm F_2. But then, by F_1, we've got defeaters.

Are the defeaters undefeated? Our discussion has so far noted three potential defeaters, D_1–D_3, some of which could apply here. But in section 2 I argued that, plausibly, situations like Library and WWW do not let us believe reasonably each of D_1–D_3, and so I say nothing more about them in connection with the Doubtful Fairness Argument. Are there other defeater-defeaters? Here is one possibility:

[10] Peter van Inwagen says that his philosophical opinions depend "on what university I selected for graduate study in philosophy, who my departmental colleagues have been, the books and essays I have read and haven't read, the conversations I have had at APA divisional meetings as a result of turning right rather than left when I was wandering aimlessly about at a reception" (2004, 342). See Garber (2009), White (2010), Ballantyne (2012), Bogardus (2013), Schoenfield (2013), Vavova (2018), and Elga (ms) for discussion of the skeptical potency of such reflections.

D_4 My sample of evidence regarding p is representative of the total evidence.

D_4 works as follows. You could have reason to think your evidence is representative even while doubting its fairness. Suppose you know other reasonable thinkers have drawn fair samples of evidence and they believe p on their fair samples. You doubt your sample is fair, but you concur with them on p. Then you may sensibly think your doubtfully-fair sample is probably representative and continue to believe p on its basis.

This defeater-defeater is worth a closer look. A sample of evidence is *representative* of a body of evidence if the sample (roughly) accurately reflects that body of evidence. More fully, a sample of evidence is representative insofar as it exhibits a particular property in the same measure (relative to its size) as the body of evidence from which the sample is drawn. Suppose that a jar holds one hundred marbles, and half are red and half are cat's eyes. A maximally representative subset of ten marbles from the set is five reds and five cat's eyes. (Subsets can be more or less representative, but leave that aside.) The specific property we are interested in here is whatever makes belief in some proposition reasonable. So we can say, to a first approximation, that a sample of evidence represents a body of evidence with respect to a proposition p only if the sample captures *enough* of the body's evidential features, so that the sample makes reasonable the same type of attitude to p that the total available evidence makes reasonable. A sample is not representative if the attitude to p that it makes reasonable is an entirely different type of attitude than the one made reasonable by the total evidence.

In general, having reason to doubt our sample is fair need not require us to lower our confidence in our belief. All we need is D_4. Recall that a fair sampling process draws from the total evidence so that each possible sample of some size is equally probable to be selected. Now since most possible large samples from some body of evidence are representative, a fair sampling process gives us a relatively high probability that a particular fair sample is representative. An unfair sample is problematic because it's probably not representative. But since an unfair or doubtfully-fair sample can be representative, and we can sometimes sensibly believe that our sample is representative, D_4 is a defeater-defeater for the Doubtful Fairness Argument.

Might we believe D_4 in cases like Library and WWW? It seems not. The crucial question is whether our sample makes reasonable the same attitude as the total evidence makes reasonable. But we face darkness here. We don't know enough about the total evidence to know which attitude *it* makes reasonable, so we have no grounds to say our sample is representative. Usually, we get reason to think a sample is representative by selecting it in particular ways—using fair sampling processes, say. But we haven't done that in our two cases. From our perspective, the total evidence may make reasonable the same attitude our sample does, or it may not.

The Doubtful Fairness Argument provides an undefeated defeater in our two examples, and so it clarifies why our awareness of unpossessed evidence can bring us reasons for doubt about our controversial views.

4. Jigsaw Puzzles and Tsunamis

The Problem of Unpossessed Evidence is the difficulty of squaring reasonable belief with the recognition that our evidence is partial. The two arguments I have set out explain why it's a problem to retain the same level of confidence in our original beliefs in Library and WWW. In these examples, we plausibly find reason to think the following: there are defeaters for beliefs we hold relative to some body of unpossessed evidence, and it is doubtful our sample of evidence is fair. All of this naturally gives us *prima facie* defeaters for our beliefs. Though the opening examples shaped our discussion, I suggest they are just like situations we commonly meet, and so the arguments apply to many of our actual beliefs about controversial matters. None of these arguments necessarily knock down our beliefs. We can sometimes resist and I pointed to some possible defeater-defeaters. The price of reasonable confidence is finding reasons to accept those defeater-defeaters, but the price is often high.

The Problem of Unpossessed Evidence helps expose our intellectual impoverishment. The Meta-defeater and Doubtful Fairness arguments give us guidance for making sense of our condition. But what's the guidance, exactly? As we deliberate on our controversial opinions, two analogies can clarify the significance of the arguments.

C. A. J. Coady compares our "search for truth" to a person trying to complete an "indefinitely large" jigsaw puzzle. The puzzle-builder is seated at a table with many pieces set out, but more pieces frequently pop out of a tube in the wall. Coady writes:

He puts together a lot of the pieces in a way that shows a picture, and he is constantly under the impression that now he has, or soon will have, the whole picture, but it is of course only a small segment of the whole huge picture. Every now and then, as new pieces are fitted, the player realises that his or her interpretation of the picture is seriously at fault. It is not that the pieces have been fitted together wrongly; their fit is fine, "correspondence with reality" has been achieved. But the correspondence is not quite what it seemed; a wider perspective requires a difference of interpretation. The dog is indeed chasing the child who has dropped the stolen apple while his companion can be seen viewing things with fear from high in the apple tree, [but] this scene is a painting within the larger reality of the puzzle and this is revealed by the correct assemblage of more pieces. (2002, 369)

If assembling a jigsaw puzzle is not exciting enough for some readers, let me try a second analogy. Richard Saul Wurman, an American architect and graphic designer, says there is "a tsunami of data that is crashing on to the beaches of the civilized world" (1997, 15). The tidal wave hits us, but we lack means to make sense of the "unorganized, uncontrolled, incoherent cacophony of foam" (1997, 15). And yet, strangely, many of us on shore do not feel overwhelmed by the tsunami:

As it washes up on our beaches, we see people in suits and ties skipping along the shoreline, men and women in fine shirts and blouses dressed for business. We see academics, designers and government officials, all getting their shoes wet and slowly submerging in the dense trough of stuff . . . . The tsunami is a wall of data—data produced at greater and greater speed, greater and greater amounts to store in memory . . . . On tape, on disks, on paper, sent by streams of light. Faster, more and more and more. (1997, 15)

Wurman describes how most people react to the tidal wave of information:

[T]hey "uh-huh, uh-huh, uh-huh" making believe they understand a reference to a name, a reference to a fact, the references to knowledge that supposedly make the world coherent. They "uh-huh" some friend, some teacher, a boss, a peer when a book or movie or magazine article, or a piece of machinery, or software, or hardware is discussed. They "uh-huh" everybody because they were taught when they were young that it is not good to look stupid, that it is not good to say "I don't know," it is not good to ask questions, not good to focus on failure. Instead, the rewards come from acknowledging or answering everything with "I know." (1997, 15)

Uh-huh.

Expecting reasonable belief and knowledge on a range of controversial matters is like constructing a complex jigsaw puzzle when more pieces are added to the puzzle continually and feeling confident we've figured out what the whole puzzle depicts.[11] Or it's like trying to make sense of the jetsam and flotsam brought to shore by a tsunami—understanding one single issue requires us to sift through so much stuff, most of which is irrelevant. As far as I am concerned, I am kidding myself if I believe it's possible for me to make sense of all of this.

Insofar as we find ourselves in commonplace situations like Library and WWW, we should reduce our confidence in our controversial opinions. By how much exactly? It's hard to say in general. I have argued that the Meta-defeater and Doubtful Fairness arguments often deliver (at least) partial undefeated defeaters for our beliefs in situations like Library and WWW, because we probably won't be able to accept defeater-defeaters. If we find ourselves with multiple, independent partial undefeated defeaters, those defeaters may collectively dilute our confidence to a fairly considerable degree. Partial defeaters can add up to full defeat or something near enough, as I noted in Chapter 4. And if we already think high confidence on controversial matters is misplaced, even one partial defeater might be enough to eliminate whatever positive epistemic status we have for some attitude. I suspect some significant reduction of confidence is often called for—at least for people who have evidence that's largely like my own. Nothing about this conclusion necessarily means we should stop trying to discern the truth, a claim I defend in Chapter 11. It means living with reasonable doubt about many of the issues that interest us most. And it may mean we should be more doxastically open about many controversial questions.

---

[11] As Jason Baehr mentioned to me, Coady's analogy highlights the significance of awareness of unpossessed evidence that will or may exist *in the future*—a topic connected to the arguments in this chapter, but one I haven't touched on here.

5. Solutions?

The Problem of Unpossessed Evidence draws our attention to significant challenges for effective inquiry in a world awash with evidence. Let me conclude with some impressionistic thoughts about how specialization, trust in experts, and new research tools may help to solve, or at least mitigate, our problem.

When faced with large bodies of unpossessed evidence, intellectuals and scholars may aspire to be masters and possessors of a manageable body of evidence. They will try to divide and conquer. Imagine that you swear off opinion on free will in general and instead look into more slender topics—say, the status of Peter van Inwagen's "Consequence Argument" for incompatibilism and responses in the literature between 1990 and 2020. (That could be a dissertation title.) You might be confident that no evidence in this corner of the free will literature has slipped your notice. Specialization dissolves our problem.

But even for those of us with the luxury and the inclination, specialization is only feasible on a handful of topics; the problem remains for our opinions on much else. Moreover, the views we do hold may seem to suit the hyperspecialist—someone who knows much about little. But many important conversations, even ones relevant to specialized fields of inquiry, are expansive and unwieldy. So, it's crucial to ask: When is specialization wise?

Obviously, the limits of our lives call for balancing the rigors of narrow specialization with everything else. Perhaps we should sometimes explore bigger, more significant topics where hyperspecialization would leave us with barely the glimmer of an insight. Maybe we should sometimes strive to become the sort of inquirers who can roam widely in a field or between fields. Our goal may not always be to get reasonable belief and knowledge by any means necessary, but rather to sort out tough issues as best we can, all the while suspecting that the end of inquiry will come only after long collective efforts, if ever. This sort of inquiry has its difficulties and I discuss some of them in Chapters 8 and 11.

Specialization is not a surefire solution because even seemingly narrow issues can "explode," as it were, and heave up more issues. For example, specialists on van Inwagen's Consequence Argument will find questions about the laws of nature and causation—and thus they will need to possess and master still more specialist literature to avoid the problem. In many fields, mastery of narrow subfields is impossible. This should be no surprise given the stunning proliferation of professional journals. In 2009, one researcher (Jinha 2010) estimated that no fewer than 50 million journal articles had appeared since the inception of the first modern journals in 1665: *Le Journal des Sçavans*, a French periodical, and *Philosophical Transactions*, published by the Royal Society of London. Even if we find a way to zoom in on minutia, we will quickly find ourselves overrun with details. Consider an illustration of academic information overload from professional philosophy.[12] Scott Soames in 2003 published his two-volume *Philosophical Analysis in the Twentieth Century*. The work's title notwithstanding, Soames's story ends in 1972. Soames explained:

> The number of philosophers has exploded, the volume of publication has swelled, and the subfields of serious philosophical investigation have multiplied. Not only is the broad field of philosophy today far too vast to be embraced by one mind, something similar is true even of many highly specialized subfields. (2003, 463)

The lesson for would-be philosophical hyperspecialists is that the Problem of Unpossessed Evidence has a head start. Good luck catching up.

Turn to a second non-skeptical response. If we can't gain reasonable beliefs or knowledge on a good range of topics after reflecting on the unpossessed evidence, why not trust what experts tell us? Reliance on experts is often reasonable and essential, but it's of small help here. For one, how can we novices identify the experts? Plato poses this question in his dialogue *Charmides* where Socrates wonders how to distinguish real doctors from quacks. Maybe we sometimes know how to recognize experts. Still, the experts on a topic such as free will disagree. Expert disagreement, at least to some extent, is the norm for many controversial questions. How will novices reasonably trust experts when there is conflict? I turn to these questions in Chapter 9. For now, let me say that there are daunting obstacles for novices facing rival experts. Those obstacles may be overcome—perhaps by becoming a specialist.

The problem I have considered in this chapter challenges individual inquirers because one thinker alone can't get hold of enough of the relevant evidence. Perhaps many inquirers can. This suggests a third non-skeptical response. Collaboration is standard practice in the sciences, and computers

---

[12] Gawande (2009) describes the increasing complexities of surgery, constructing skyscrapers, and flying airliners.

and the internet have given us powerful opportunities for working together. This idea raises interesting issues, but it is unclear how our collective energies can be harnessed to resolve our problem. The idea may be that groups can build research tools—bibliographies, encyclopedias, indexes, search engines, and more. We may hope for a list of the "must reads" on a topic, or a no-evidence-left-behind literature review article. Such resources could tell us where to find the evidence we don't have, flag dead ends to ignore, and tell us what we need to move forward. Though highly desirable, those tools are of limited value to resolve the present problem. Part of our predicament is that we lack the expertise and the time to grasp a great deal of the relevant information, even when we know what to read. We can't be experts about much. Notice, too, that creating a one-stop, authoritative research tool is not simple, because experts sometimes disagree on what the relevant evidence is, how the evidence should be presented, and the like.[13] And, critically, research tools can become hard to use as they tremble under their own weight. As they grow to accommodate new bodies of evidence, research tools add to the evidence we don't have.

Our discussion has not come to its end. Befitting our topic, there is considerably more to say.

---

[13] Csiszar (2010) describes the challenges of organizing scientific literature during the nineteenth century, and the articles in Rosenberg (2003) discuss early modern "information overload."

8

Epistemic Trespassing

All that men really understand is confined to a very small compass; to their daily affairs and experience; to what they have an opportunity to know and motives to study or practise. The rest is affectation and imposture.

—William Hazlitt, "On the Ignorance of the Learned," 1822

But I am far from criticizing men on that account; they are not really at fault; rather it is the knotty situation they find themselves in and they don't know how to guide themselves in it. . . . Man is born to a limited position; he is able to understand simple, near, determined purposes, and he gets used to using the means that are immediately at hand to him. But as soon as he comes to a wider field, he knows neither what he wants to do, nor what he should do.

—Johann Wolfgang von Goethe, *Wilhelm Meister's Apprenticeship*, 1795–96

If you want to avoid being a charlatan, you must flee podiums, for if you get on them, you are forced to be a charlatan or else the audience will stone you.

—Nicolas Chamfort, *Maximes et Pensées*, 1795

Epistemic trespassers are thinkers who have competence or expertise to make good judgments in one field, but move to another field where they lack competence—and pass judgment nevertheless. We should doubt that trespassers are reliable judges in fields where they are outsiders.

A few examples will guide our discussion. Linus Pauling, the brilliant chemist and energetic proponent of peace, won two Nobel Prizes: one for his work in chemistry, another for his activism against atomic weapons. Later on, Pauling asserted that megadoses of vitamin C could effectively treat diseases such as cancer and cure ailments like the common cold. Pauling was roundly dismissed as a crackpot by the medical establishment after researchers ran studies and concluded that high-dose vitamin C therapies did not have the touted health effects. Pauling accused the establishment of fraud and careless science. This trespasser did not want to be moved aside by the legitimate experts.

Scientists sometimes encroach on one another's fields. But philosophers are especially wary of intruders on their turf. To take one example, Neil deGrasse Tyson, an astrophysicist and media personality, has offered his opinions about philosophy. Tyson has said that philosophy is "useless" and that majoring in philosophy "can really mess you up." But if we look closely at what Tyson apparently thinks philosophy is, we will see the astrophysicist would benefit from taking a philosophy course or two. Tyson is an intelligent scientist, but we may think he should stick to topics about which he can rightfully claim to know something. "It has often been said," Albert Einstein quipped, "and certainly not without justification, that the man of science is a poor philosopher."[1]

Trespassers occasionally annoy philosophers, but that doesn't mean philosophers always stay inside their own intellectual boundaries. For instance, reviewers panned Colin McGinn's book *The Meaning of Disgust* (2011), asserting that McGinn had written a "tragically flawed" book (Kelly 2012) and completely bypassed "the received wisdom amongst empirically-minded scholars of disgust" (Strohminger 2014). According to critics, McGinn had theorized about disgust while in a state of ignorance concerning past research on the topic. Of course, the question of whether or not someone has trespassed is often up for grabs, and indicted trespassers may plead not guilty, offering justifications for their cross-field judgments.[2]

Trespassing is a significant problem in an age of expertise and punditry, but it's not new. In Plato's *Apology*, Socrates tells us he tracked down citizens in Athens who had reputations for being skilled. He met politicians, poets, and craftsmen and tested their mettle. As Socrates says, he "found those who had the highest reputation were nearly the most deficient" (1997, 21; 22a). Socrates diagnosed the problem: because these men had been so successful in their particular crafts, each one "thought himself very wise in most

---

[1] Quoted in Shapin (2010, 38).

[2] In a response to critics, McGinn (2015) claimed that ignoring the empirical literature on disgust was appropriate because he "wanted to elucidate [disgust's] broad psychological significance to us as reflective beings." According to him, his book's main question is the exclusive domain of philosophy.

important pursuits, and this error of theirs overshadowed the wisdom they had" (1997, 22; 22d–e). Puffed up by their achievements in one domain, the successful Athenians trespassed on matters about which they were ignorant.[3]

Epistemic trespassing is a topic that cries out for investigation.[4] Here is my plan for this chapter. I first say more about what trespassing is (section 1) and how common it is (section 2), and I articulate why it is an epistemological problem (section 3). Then I defend two theses: reflecting on trespassing leads us to doubt our controversial opinions (section 4) and helps us recognize the importance of cross-field dialogue and collaboration (section 5).

1. What Is Epistemic Trespassing?

Epistemic trespassing of the sort I've noted is easy to recognize. Experts drift over a highly-visible boundary line and into a domain where they lack either the relevant evidence or the skills to interpret the evidence well. But they keep talking nonetheless. Experts on a public stage are cast in the role of the Public Intellectual or Celebrity Academic. They may find trespassing all but impossible to resist. Microphones are switched on, TV cameras zoom in, and sound bites come forth, coaxed out of the commentators by journalists. (So what do you have to say about philosophy, Neil deGrasse Tyson?) I don't think trespassing is exclusively a problem for intellectuals in the limelight, however, and one of my goals here is to explain why ordinary inquirers often risk trespassing, too.

---

[3] Did Socrates have to trespass in order to judge that the elite Athenians were overreaching? Not necessarily. One of Socrates' dialectical techniques was to tease out contradictions in his interlocutors' thinking. Recognizing that someone is committed to an inconsistent set of statements may not require any trespassing. For more on Socrates and expertise, see LaBarge (1997) and Hardy (2010).

[4] I should add that scholars in science studies, the history of science, and philosophy of science have examined how boundaries between fields are created and crossed (see, for example, Gieryn 1999 and McKaughan 2012). Patricia Kitcher (1992, chapters 6 and 7) describes how Sigmund Freud's attempt to build an interdisciplinary science of the mind fizzled out when psychoanalytic theory "lost contact with the rest of science." Freud committed himself to a policy of trespassing when new scientific findings didn't fit with his initial expectations. (Thanks to Hilary Kornblith for pointing out Kitcher's book.) Bryan Frances (2010) discusses "reflective epistemic renegades"—philosophers who knowingly disagree with recognized philosophical superiors—and argues that renegades are sometimes blameworthy. Tom Nichols (2017, chapter 6) discusses "cross-expertise poaching," which is what I call trespassing, and uses Linus Pauling as an example of a poacher. (Thanks to Lucy Randall and Coran Stewart for telling me about Nichols's book.) Mikkel Gerken kindly shared with me an article on the phenomenon he had developed independently of my own work on trespassing: see Gerken (2018).

Its deeper causes aside, trespassing brings many kinds of epistemic costs, both personal and social. Trespassers pay some costs themselves when they hold beliefs or make assertions that do not satisfy the standards for reasonable belief or knowledge. If trespassers do happen to arrive at the truth, that's thanks to a stroke of good luck, not because they have reliably or responsibly responded to the available evidence. I say more later about the epistemic status of the opinions held by reflective trespassers, but for now notice two points. First, the intellectual characters of trespassers often look unsavory. Out of their league but highly confident nonetheless, trespassers appear to be immodest, dogmatic, or arrogant. Trespassers easily fail to manifest the trait of intellectual humility and demonstrate one or another epistemic vice (Cassam 2016; Whitcomb et al. 2017). Second, it's useful to distinguish between people *holding confident opinions* and those *investigating questions in another field*. I assume it can be epistemically appropriate for people to look into questions beyond their competence, even when it would be inappropriate for them to hold confident opinions. I want to examine cases where people do hold confident views about topics beyond their intellectual grasp. One lesson will be that it's often preferable, from an epistemic point of view, to investigate questions in another field than to adopt opinions about those questions. We can learn and observe without judging confidently.

Trespassing can also harm other people. Bystanders may be led into error when they trust the word of trespassers. The genuine experts may expend precious resources refuting the trespassers' mistakes or managing public relations campaigns to correct dangerous misinformation. Recall Linus Pauling's advocacy of megavitamin therapies. Pauling threw his heavyweight reputation as a double Nobel laureate into a bogus medical cause. From an epistemological perspective, it's unclear how the world could be better off because of Pauling's trespassing. Even so, manufacturers of vitamin C tablets were pleased. They bankrolled Pauling in his public war against conventional medicine and amassed fortunes in the sale of vitamin supplements.

Let us now sharpen our focus on the idea of epistemic trespassing. I invoke two terms of art: *fields* and *experts*. Let's say that a field is fixed by a set of questions or topics. For example, the questions of biochemistry (the study of chemical substances and processes inside living things) make up a field. That is not to say there are always sharp cut-offs between biochemistry and other fields. The line between biochemistry and molecular biology (the study of the molecular basis for activities inside a living cell) is blurry. Biochemists and molecular biologists examine some of the same questions, though they bring different perspectives and resources to inquiry. We can keep that point about blurry divisions between fields and shared questions in mind for later. A field, in my sense, can be fixed by an extremely narrow set of questions, so what I call a field may not be coextensive with the ordinary boundaries of any academic or scientific discipline.

Expertise is a status of thinkers and it is relative to a field at a particular time. Let's say thinkers count as experts in a field only if they possess two things at one time: first, enough relevant evidence to answer reliably their field's questions, and, second, enough relevant skills to evaluate or interpret the field's evidence well. While novices or laypersons can sometimes reliably accept answers to a field's questions by trusting expert testimony, the experts themselves answer on the basis of their evidence and skills.

Whatever else it is, expertise is built out of evidence and skills. Notice that expertise does not entail that one can give firm answers to all of a field's questions; there can be "open questions" in a field. Experts are well-positioned to survey their fields and recognize what is known and unknown. Furthermore, expertise does not eliminate differences between thinkers who have enough evidence and skills to evaluate the evidence well. Some experts may have a "deeper" understanding of the evidence, or better skills for evaluating it, than other experts do. Two experts in a field may also reach different conclusions. But they both must meet some threshold for having enough evidence and skills.

I am concerned with epistemic or intellectual expertise. Other types of expertise are fixed by the credentials and social markers needed for someone to pronounce authoritatively on a field and its questions. Epistemic expertise is more closely tied to the ability to acquire reasonable beliefs, true beliefs, or knowledge.[5] Normally, when we call people "experts" concerning vast professional or academic disciplines, we use the term to ascribe a social standing, not genuine epistemic expertise. Expertise in my sense is an intellectual competence that is consistent with fallibility. Someone can be an expert about a field where the relevant evidence is incomplete or misleading, or where the tools for evaluating the evidence are unreliable, so that even a flawless expert performance won't track the truth. Isaac Newton is one example. Even though many of Newton's judgments were ultimately mistaken, he was

---

[5] For some discussions of epistemic expertise, see Goldman (2001, 2018), Goldberg (2009b), Scholz (2009), Pigliucci (2010, chapter 12), Coady (2012, chapter 2), and Stewart (forthcoming).

an epistemic expert about the physics of his day, because he had enough evidence and skills to evaluate the relevant evidence well.

2. How Commonplace Is Trespassing?

I began with cases where Pauling, Tyson, and McGinn apparently stepped over an epistemological line. Trespassing happens. But does it happen often? Pauling and company are easy-to-recognize, public examples of trespassing; but subtle, harder-to-detect sorts of trespassing could be commonplace—and sometimes more dangerous because they are unobvious.

To recognize more subtle forms of trespassing, we need to find connections forged between different fields. We need to see how these connections cause experts unwittingly to overstep their limits. This easily happens when experts investigate what I call *hybridized questions*—ones addressed and answered by combining evidence and techniques from two or more fields.

Fields are fixed by a set of questions, and expertise is fixed by bodies of evidence and skills needed to answer a field's questions. But note that sometimes fields overlap or converge and come to share a question. This may happen in one of three ways: (*i*) the evidence required to answer a question reliably comes from two or more fields, (*ii*) the skills required to evaluate the evidence well come from two or more fields, or (*iii*) both the relevant evidence and the relevant skills required to answer a question reliably come from two or more fields. In such situations, the experts in one field will not all satisfy the same evidence or skill conditions as the experts in another field. Since the experts are in different fields, the evidence and skills that constitute their expertise differ. A hybridized question, then, is one that experts in distinct fields could try to answer using their own resources. Take the question, "What caused the Cretaceous-Paleogene extinction event?" It is addressed by experts in paleontology, geology, climatology, and oceanography, among other fields. The question is thoroughly hybridized and answering it calls for a host of evidence and skills. A question can be hybridized even if it is addressed by experts from only one field. But once investigators recognize that a question is hybridized, they should think that answering it reliably calls for cross-field resources.

These days, hybridized questions abound. Let's consider one case from philosophy in some detail before noting others more briefly. From the 1950s through the 1980s, philosophers approached questions about human freedom using the tools of conceptual analysis and counterexample. Principles meant to articulate the nature of freedom were tested using "thought experiments." Questions about free will were treated as metaphysical or conceptual questions. Recent decades have seen an explosion of interest in free will from beyond metaphysics. Normative ethicists, for instance, investigate the nature of moral responsibility and blame, connected with the conditions for freedom. Neuroscientists and psychologists have also joined the conversation. Scientists who study conscious will and intention have alleged that there are "unconscious precursors" for what appear to be our free choices. Experimental philosophers have examined "free will" thought experiments, seeking to discover what influences philosophical judgment. The evidence that bears on the question "Are we free?" is presently much more diverse than it was in earlier decades. The question has been hybridized.

Examples of hybridized questions are common and entire interdisciplinary fields have been created to address some of them. Much of philosophy is ripe for hybridization. Questions in philosophy may become hybridized when bodies of empirical fact, experimental evidence, and empirically-driven theories are recognized to be relevant to answering those questions. As a matter of fact, the era of narrowly analysis-driven philosophy represents an anomaly within the history of philosophy. In many periods, philosophers have sought to blend together ideas from different quarters of their intellectual worlds and engage with broad social and cultural debates. Certainly, compared to the golden era of analysis, a more multidisciplinary approach toward many philosophical questions can be witnessed in the present.

Take some examples. The question "Are we rational?" now invites contributions from psychology and the cognitive sciences (Stein 1996; Samuels and Stich 2004; Mercier and Sperber 2011). The question "What is knowledge?" has been opened to intrusions from empirical fields (Craig 1990; Kornblith 2002). A range of scientific ideas have hybridized the question "Is there a God?" such as the "fine-tuning" of the universe (Davies 2007) and scientific models purporting to explain theistic beliefs (Wilson 2003; Atran 2004). Furthermore, many questions from philosophical ethics have been linked to empirical fields. Philosophers have used ideas from evolutionary biology to challenge moral realism (Joyce 2006; Street 2006). Some moral psychologists claim that evidence from neuroscience challenges Kantian deontological theories and may support consequentialism (Greene 2008). Philosophers have argued that the situationist paradigm in social psychology undermines, or calls for reinterpretation of, classical virtue theories (Harman 1999; Doris 2002; Miller 2014).

So traditional philosophical questions are now front and center in many interdisciplinary debates. Here are two issues to consider. First, what does hybridization have to do with trespassing? The answer is that investigators who address hybridized questions will often lack expertise in one or more of the relevant fields. Second, how common is trespassing? Judging from what I know about my own field, my answer is: quite. Growing numbers of philosophers have become aware of research from empirical disciplines— either because that research grew more prominent in general, or because intellectual entrepreneurs carried insights from the sciences into areas traditionally studied by philosophers. Let me also hypothesize that academic deans and grant agencies often incentivize trespassing by funding interdisciplinary research. From the perspective of academic philosophy in the English-speaking world, if the middle to late decades of the twentieth century were a period of fracturing and splintering of philosophical subfields into increasingly smaller bits and pieces, practitioners are beginning to feel forces pulling together many kinds of researchers into shared conversations about philosophical matters. This strikes me as a potentially good development, though it brings risks. When experts in one field try to answer hybridized questions, they need evidence and skills located outside of their home field. Otherwise, they appear to be treading on someone else's turf.[6]

3. What Makes Trespassing a Problem?

In the opening examples starring Pauling and company, we find experts who issue judgments about questions beyond their training and competence. But consider experts who knowingly take a stand on hybridized

---

[6] Here are two points about the scope of my discussion in this chapter. First, I focus on trespassing scholars and researchers, but the problem of trespassing also arises in everyday life. People who have no special expertise in any technical field hold views about scientific, social, and political questions that can be addressed using specialized evidence and skills. People lacking the relevant competence oftentimes knowingly reject experts' positions. For now, I set to the side questions about the normative evaluation of such trespassers. Second, I also mean to restrict my focus to questions where the answers are not reasonably believed in a "properly basic" way on the basis of widely shared experiences or intuitions due to nature or nurture. One upshot is that people who hold ordinary perceptual or memory beliefs don't count as trespassing on radically skeptical philosophers, who reject such beliefs on the basis of specialized evidence and skills. This restriction fits with my suggestion in Chapter 4, footnote 9, that commonsense beliefs rejected by radical skeptics needn't be treated as controversial. (Thanks to Michael Bergmann and Tomás Bogardus for discussion.)

questions—specifically, questions that call for more than their field-specific expertise alone. How should these experts react to learning there is more relevant evidence and skills than just what they have brought to the table?

One response is to obtain further expertise. If you know you have trespassed, then decide to stop and figure out what you're missing. That is what philosopher of action Alfred Mele did when he heard tantalizing claims defended by neuroscientists, physiologists, and psychologists. Scientists had claimed to have discovered that free will is an illusion. Mele learned enough of the science to understand its bearing on debates about free will (Mele 2008 and 2009). His response is far from ordinary, however. Most scientists studying human freedom have apparently not followed in Mele's footsteps by developing cross-field expertise themselves; most philosophers interested in free will have not either.[7]

Here is a different response. Experts can retreat to the relative safety and security of their disciplinary trenches. The idea is that experts will refrain from confidently accepting answers to hybridized questions once they recognize they are not cross-field experts. Instead, these modest thinkers might only confidently accept answers to "narrower," non-hybridized subquestions. For example, metaphysicians who think about human freedom could quit confidently judging whether humans are free and instead only judge the narrower matter of whether freedom is compatible with causal determinism. Metaphysicians could insist that the compatibility of freedom and determinism is neither neuroscience nor psychology. It is metaphysics—straight, no chaser.

Does the fallback maneuver work? That depends on whether metaphysicians reasonably think some hybridized question "decomposes" into non-hybridized questions, or at least ones that are properly investigated only by the field or fields in which they have expertise. In the case at hand, notice that the question about the compatibility of freedom and determinism is connected to evidence uncovered by experimental philosophers who investigate intuitions prompted by "free will" thought experiments. Furthermore, compatibilism raises questions from the philosophy of science about the laws of nature. These points suggest that even the subquestion

---

[7] Increasingly, in a number of philosophical subfields, graduate education aims to equip students with cross-disciplinary competence. For example, doctoral students in the philosophy of physics must complete a standard sequence of graduate courses in physics.

about compatibilism has become hybridized by the mixing and mingling of philosophical subfields.[8]

Thus far, I have noted two reactions to learning that we are trespassers: become cross-field experts or stick to confidently answering only non-hybridized questions. But hard work and modesty are both uncomfortable. What other options do we have? I will argue that, a great deal of the time, the other alternatives are unattractive. For many cases of trespassing on hybridized questions, the most reasonable option will be one of the two just surveyed: either stop trespassing by gaining cross-field expertise or stop holding confident answers to hybridized questions. For many cases, there is no reasonable middle ground. My strategy will be to scrutinize some *defenses of trespassing*. Defenses explain how trespassing thinkers' confident answers to hybridized questions are reasonable. I contend that each attempt to justify trespassing will not help trespassers a great part of the time.

But first we must understand what the epistemological problem with trespassing is. There is not only one problem. Consider three types of problematic trespassing cases where two different fields share a particular question: (*i*) experts in one field lack another field's evidence and skills, (*ii*) experts in one field lack evidence from another field but have its skills, or (*iii*) experts in one field have evidence from another field but lack its skills.

One kind of epistemic trouble with trespassing stems from recognizing we are in one of those three cases. I call the *Problem of Epistemic Trespassing* the difficulty of explaining how our confident beliefs fit together with the observation we have trespassed.[9] Passing judgment on a question we know is hybridized looks dubious. Why do we confidently hold a view when we lack relevant evidence, skills, or both? Learning we're in one of the three situations should trigger a sort of intellectual perimeter alarm in our thinking. Here we are trespassing on somebody else's property, after climbing over a barbed wire fence. Let's split before any guard dogs show up.

That is an impressionistic look at why trespassing is problematic, but I will say more. If we recognize we are trespassing, we may thereby discover a reason to reduce our confidence or give up our belief—a defeater. The reason

---

[8] Trespassing experts may "conditionalize" their assertions by arguing in this way: if some other field shows that p is true, then q follows. Experts wary of trespassing could hedge like that while denying they have knowledge or reasonable belief that the antecedent is true. For present purposes, I treat conditionalized claims as being properly part of an expert's own field. Conditionalizing lets experts stick to answering non-hybridized questions.

[9] I don't mean to suggest that trespassing doesn't bring other kinds of trouble. Here I focus on one particular problem that arises because we become reflective about our situation.

to change our mind is the fact that we have trespassed. Taking stock of that fact will show us we have violated an epistemic norm and that our judgment is properly subject to criticism.

As I've noted, trespassing cases come in three varieties: we are experts in one field, but we lack evidence from another field, or its skills, or both. The reflective trespasser, learning she is in such a case, could reason as follows:

> I believe that proposition p is the correct answer to a question hybridized by two different fields. I know the other field where I lack expertise contains relevant evidence or skills, but I reasonably believe I do not satisfy the evidence or skill threshold for expertise there. At best, I am a novice with respect to the other field's evidence or skills. Thus, I have formed a belief without some relevant evidence or skills. But that is not a reliable way to form a belief about the question. To arrive at a reliably-formed view about p, I would need to satisfy the evidence and skill threshold for expertise in both fields. Thus, I seem to have violated an epistemic norm in reaching my view and so I have reason to reduce confidence in my judgment.

This soliloquy illuminates why our opinions are epistemically dubious when we knowingly trespass on another field. Recognizing we have trespassed is a kind of higher-order evidence. It tells us about our competence to judge well in particular circumstances. Specifically, it tells us about the manner in which we have reached our belief in p. It is not evidence bearing directly on p's truth value, but it tells us about the reasonableness of holding particular attitudes toward p.

Let me set to the side a tempting, but incorrect, alternative account of what the reflective trespasser could be thinking.[10] We might assume the reflective trespasser takes her own field's resources to be alone sufficient for reliable belief-formation. Assuming she does not know what the other field's resources are, when she realizes she has not accounted for them in forming her view, she apparently gains reason to think she has made a mistake. In particular, she recognizes she has neglected evidence and skills from another field that might lead her away from her belief. But that need not bother her in the least. If the trespasser reasonably thinks her own resources are sufficient for reliable belief-formation, then consciously neglecting another field's resources may be appropriate for her, and her belief may be beyond criticism.

---

[10] I am grateful to David Christensen for discussion here.

Take an analogy to suggest why such a trespasser may be beyond criticism. Suppose you are a mechanic and you know of two reliable tests for diagnosing a particular engine problem. One test takes five minutes, whereas the other requires several hours of work. Each test is fairly reliable but not perfect. If you run the quick test, and it indicates the engine doesn't have the problem, then you can sensibly ignore the other test. You can reasonably judge the engine doesn't have the problem while you are fully cognizant of the fact you don't know what the other test would indicate. After all, you know the test you used is fairly reliable.[11]

The analogy suggests a lesson for the reflective trespasser. If she reasonably thinks her field's resources are sufficient for reliable belief-formation, her answer to the hybridized question need not display any epistemic defect. But this alternative account of the reflective trespasser's reasoning is not accurate. The trespasser does not believe her field's evidence and skills are sufficient to properly answer the hybridized question. The trespasser knows the question she answers has been hybridized; she thereby has reason to doubt the sufficiency of her single-field resources to answer the question properly.

Trespassers are a crafty bunch, of course, and they may resist reasoning in the way I've described. They may grant they are in one of the three reflective cases but insist they have not thereby flouted any epistemic norm and don't have an undefeated defeater. How could that work? For any particular trespassing case, the presumption that there is some epistemic trouble can be defeated by good reason to think there's no epistemic trouble in the case. I call reasons that defeat the presumption of epistemic trouble *defenses*. Defenses are reasons indicating no epistemic norm has been violated—in other words, they are defeater-defeaters.

Let me illustrate the basic idea of a defense. Suppose you are an expert on the metaphysics of free will, but you lack evidence and skills from neuroscience and psychology that are relevant to "free will" debates. Realizing that, you reason as follows:

I answer the hybridized question "Are we free?" by judging we lack free will. I know scientists have evidence and skills that are relevant to the question I have answered. I lack the scientific evidence and skills. At best, I am a novice with respect to the science of free will. But I have reason

---

[11] Your practical circumstances may sometimes require you to run the other test before judging that the engine doesn't have the problem at issue. I assume that is due to practical, not epistemic, norms.

to think that the evidence contributed by science could only *support* my belief. In other words, the scientific evidence could only pose a challenge to thinkers who reject my view. So, if scientists make an evidential contribution to the question, it will be consistent with my belief. Thus, I have trespassed without violating any epistemic norm.

The defense is the trespasser's reasonable belief that the cross-field evidence would only support the trespasser's answer to the question. I say more about defenses shortly.

To sum up, recognizing we are trespassing gives us a defeater for our belief, unless we have reason to think we have not violated an epistemic norm—that is, unless we have reason to accept what I've called a "defense." We can capture these key ideas with a principle, which supplies a schema for reasoning about cases of trespassing:

> If we are experts in one field and believe proposition p, and we recognize that (*i*) we lack another field's evidence concerning p or (*ii*) we lack another field's skills to evaluate the p-relevant evidence, then we have a defeater for our belief that p, unless we have reason to accept some defense (that is, we have reason to accept there are facts indicating we do not violate any epistemic norm by accepting p).

4. What Makes Trespassing Permissible?

If some defenses are readily available in trespassing situations, then my claim that reflective trespassers often have defeaters for their views will be undercut. Trespassers armed with defenses need not dial down their confidence in their answers to hybridized questions. But what defenses are out there?

I will examine three strategies to justify acts of trespassing and thereby preserve rational confidence in trespassers' answers to hybridized questions. Again, we are assuming that some trespassers are experts in one field but encroach on another field.

> *No-Relevant-Evidence Defense*: I am trespassing on another field, but that field does not feature any relevant evidence or skills that bear on my view about p.

Conclusive-Evidence Defense: I am trespassing on another field, but my own field's evidence conclusively establishes my view about *p*.

Transfer Defense: I am trespassing on another field, but my own field's skills successfully "transfer" to the other field.

These defenses are designed to allow reflective trespassers to conclude that their views about *p* are reasonable. I will argue that trespassers—at least ones with total sets of evidence roughly similar to my own in important respects— are rarely positioned to reasonably accept any of the three defenses. Typically, reflective trespassers should be doubtful whether any of the defenses are available to them. I will discuss the No-Relevant-Evidence and Conclusive-Evidence defenses briefly before looking at the Transfer Defense in greater detail.

The No-Relevant-Evidence Defense says that the trespassed-upon field does not feature any relevant evidence or skills that bear on the trespasser's view. I already noted this basic idea when illustrating a defense. If a metaphysician knows that the scientific evidence in the "free will" debate could only support her judgment, then learning she lacks that evidence is no epistemological problem for her; reasonably believing this defense justifies her trespassing. Similarly, if trespassers learn that investigation in another field is ruled by degenerate or pseudoscientific research programs, or that the field assumes a known scientific law is false, they can reasonably accept the No-Relevant-Evidence Defense. For example, trespassers may know that some cross-field researchers compete for resources and acclaim by defending the novel and the bizarre. Problematic social conditions in the field have spoiled its evidence. Members of the field are merely *perceived* as experts. If trespassers are aware of a field's shortcomings, they can be justified in holding their views while disregarding the other field's resources. One example is provided by the field of astrology. I believe the substantive claims of astrologers are false—"occultism is the metaphysic of the dopes," as Theodor Adorno once noted. But I admit that astrologers have evidence and skills I lack. My considered view, however, is that astrologers' evidence and skills do not constitute a reliable method to establish their claims, and so my dismissal of those claims is reasonable.

Here are three observations about the No-Relevant-Evidence Defense. First, when experts begin in relative ignorance about another field's resources, they need good reason to accept this defense. To come to reasonably believe it, a single-field expert may rely on testimony from cross-field experts, or she may need to gain cross-field expertise herself. In the latter event, reasonably accepting the defense will not excuse the trespasser—she will have stopped trespassing. Second, we could get the defense in hand by noticing that the cross-field resources could only bolster our view. But bodies of evidence in interdisciplinary discussions usually have a "mixed" character, with different pieces supporting different hypotheses, and so that sort of response will be uncommon. Finally, trespassers hoping to reasonably accept the No-Relevant-Evidence Defense will often need to explain why the other field's resources would not help them reliably or responsibly hold a view. Researchers can be unduly dismissive about research programs they do not contribute to and don't have well-formed views about.[12] It's easy for us to opine that some field is degenerate, lacking helpful resources for addressing a question. It is far harder for us to reliably recognize degeneracy. Suppose we think we know why some field's evidence or skills are a sham and why its practitioners are cranks. Let's see what the apparent experts think. They may school us on the actual nature of their field's practices and reveal our ignorance. That outcome wouldn't be so surprising given that we are non-experts. Plausibly, reasonably accepting the defense at issue will typically require considerable effort.

A second potential defense is the Conclusive-Evidence Defense: the idea that a trespasser's own single-field evidence conclusively establishes the truth of his or her view. While there could be conclusive evidence to settle a hybridized question, it's hard to sustain the idea that such powerful evidence is often available concerning ongoing, often contentious hybridized debates. Why would interdisciplinary discussion continue apace if the questions were in fact known by someone to be settled? If you think you have reason to accept this defense but have not dropped your bombshell, you might wonder: Is my evidence really as powerful as I believe? To accept the Conclusive-Evidence Defense reasonably, you need an account for why the discussion grinds on—as it shouldn't, on the assumption that this defense is reasonable for the relevant disputants. Normally, our evidence for answering interesting, hybridized questions falls well short of conclusive, knockdown arguments, or at least it will be reasonable for us to think that it does. But then this defense will not often justify trespassing.

---

[12] Unfortunately, I have lost count of how many professional philosophers, ones working far outside of epistemology, have said in my presence that the Gettier Problem was "a complete waste of time."

I expect something like the Transfer Defense will be among the most common justifications given by trespassers. A scientist like Neil deGrasse Tyson may believe, for example, that his scientific training has taught him critical thinking—the only skill needed to answer philosophical questions. In general, if the trespasser's expertise successfully transfers from one field to another, then the trespasser does not violate any norms related to lacking the other field's skills.

How does transfer work? If an expert's skills transfer to a different field, the expert will satisfy the relevant skill threshold for expertise in that field. In other words, although she is at best an evidential novice in the other field, she must still meet the skill conditions for expertise there. This reveals one limitation of the Transfer Defense. Even if someone can reasonably accept that defense, there is still the matter of her lacking the other field's evidence. For the Transfer Defense to justify a trespasser, a reason to accept it must be joined by a reason to believe she satisfies the relevant evidence threshold for cross-field expertise.

This defense will help trespassers only if they can reasonably accept it. So the crucial question is: Under what conditions do we have reason to think skills successfully transfer from an expert's field to another field? Answering from the comfort of the armchair is not feasible, as the mechanics of a successful transfer are not obvious to us by introspection or casual observation. What I will do instead is describe some psychological research that suggests general constraints on reasonably accepting the Transfer Defense. First, I consider research on what psychologists and cognitive scientists call "knowledge transfer" and "transfer of learning." The upshot of this empirical research is that attempts to transfer skills between different fields will run into obstacles. Second, I point out research on metacognition that explains why many trespassers who fail to transfer skills will mistakenly believe they have successfully done so.

Transfer has been studied extensively in the cognitive and social sciences since the early twentieth century. The starting point is the observation that we often do not treat new problems as new problems. We leverage old knowledge to gain new knowledge. We "find the old in the new." The literature on transfer is vast, bridging many subdisciplines. I will briefly describe one classic experiment first performed in 1908 and replicated in 1941 (Judd 1908; Hendrickson and Schroeder 1941).

In the replication, boys at an elementary school in Cincinnati, Ohio had to complete a practical task: fire a BB gun and hit a small target submerged in water. The boys were randomly assigned to an experimental group and a control. The control group was told to try to hit the underwater target. By contrast, the experimental group was first given an explanation of how light refracts as it passes between one medium and another. This group learned about how objects in water are not located where they *appear to observers to be* located. Because of refraction, the light changes direction at the surface of the water and the light waves are bent. The apparent displacement of the target was fairly considerable from where the boys were positioned. The depth of the target and the degree of refraction made it certain that shooters in either group who aimed the BB gun at where the target appeared to them to be would miss. Then the experimenters changed the depth of the target for both groups. The goal was to determine how the groups adjusted to the new task of hitting the target at a different depth.

Leaving aside the happy fact that no schoolboy shot his eye out, here is what the researchers found. The boys who had been given the principle of refraction were able effectively to adjust their shots in the new task. They took fewer shots to hit the underwater target at its new depth than boys in the control group. The boys who had knowledge of refraction transferred their knowledge to a new target-shooting situation.

Transfer has been studied in a plethora of contexts. In an important article, Susan Barnett and Stephen Ceci (2002) offer a useful taxonomy for thinking about transfer. Barnett and Ceci identify two categories of factors that influence any transfer: content and context. For any instance of transfer or attempted transfer, there are three main questions: What is transferred? Where is it transferred? And when is it transferred? The content answers the "What?" question. It is what gets transferred to the new situation: a principle, a heuristic, a representation of a fact, or the like. The context answers the "Where?" and "When?" questions. Context tells us about the type of subject matter involved, the physical situation, the temporal situation, the functional situation, and the like. Take some examples of each contextual element. The subject matter of a transfer could be astrophysics to philosophy, or the metaphysics of free will to the neuroscience of free will. The physical situation could be anywhere from a classroom to a supermarket checkout line. The temporal situation could be within a one-hour period, or across a span of several years. The functional situation could be two academic exams, or an academic exam and supermarket checkout line.

One standard idea in the transfer literature is that transfers come in degrees. Some transfers are relatively "near," whereas others are relatively "far." The analogical "distance" here concerns the similarity between the context of "old learning" and the context of "new learning." Near transfer involves greater similarity along dimensions of context than far transfer. The studies involving shooting underwater targets involved relatively near transfer, for instance. A short time had elapsed between contexts, and the specific task had changed, but the physical, functional, and motivational contexts were identical. A transfer of skills between a context involving, say, questions about astrophysics and questions about the philosophy of mind would be considerably further. This point is widely appreciated by instructors and trainers in many domains, from athletics to the military. They often try to mimic the target context as closely as possible so that training occurs in a situation that is highly similar to where the skills will be used.

Researchers often express pessimism about far transfer.[13] But there is some evidence of successful transfer. Here is one example. An educational psychologist, Samuel Wineburg, recruited high school seniors and professional historians to determine how they would explain historical events on the basis of some fragmentary and inconsistent source documents (1991). The participants had to explain some events in the first military conflict of the American Revolution, the Battle of Lexington. Some of the historians were not trained in American history but others were Americanists. Each historian approached the documents by scrutinizing the perspectives and intentions of the witnesses so as to assess the relative credibility of each source document. The high school students evaluated each document in light of their own experiences. But both the historians and the students used their prior knowledge in efforts to understand the new texts. As commentators on Wineburg's study observed: "From the vantage of most schooling practices, the [high school] students demonstrated appropriate transfer. They tried to make sense of the facts in the texts by connecting them to prior knowledge" (Schwartz, Chase, and Bransford 2012, 210). The historians and high school students all transferred knowledge, but, unsurprisingly, the historians proved more effective at the task; their prior knowledge and practices were better suited to good historical judgment and reasoning.

Importantly, many researchers have suggested that when we know something, that item of knowledge is less helpful for learning new things the "further away" we move from the context where it was acquired. For example,

---

[13] See Barnett and Ceci (2002) for more. Researchers do not all agree about the best way to properly conceptualize transfer. Lobato (2006) provides an introduction.

in Wineburg's study, the experts in American history performed better than historians trained in other fields, but the historians as a group outperformed the high school students. When a transfer involves moving into a rather dissimilar context—dissimilar along the various contextual dimensions noted earlier—we should be more doubtful that the transfer was successful than when the context is rather similar to the context of initial learning.

Consider some examples of transfer failure. One study of impoverished children in Brazil showed they could perform mathematical calculations while selling corn-on-the-cob and peanuts out in the street; but they could not solve similar problems using pencil and paper in a traditional school context (Carraher, Carraher, and Schliemann 1985). The researchers noted that "[i]n many cases attempts to follow school-prescribed routines seemed in fact to interfere with problem solving" (1985, 28). Some research has focused on transfer of skills in solving brain-teasing problems. One experiment modified the subject matter of a brain-teaser—changing Duncker's "radiation problem" from being about medicine to being about warfare instead. Participants who solved the one problem failed to solve the other. They didn't see that the two problems had the same "deep" structure (Gick and Holyoak 1980). Our skills in one context do not always follow us to new ones.

A different kind of transfer failure involves what has been called "overzealous" transfer: our skills from one context successfully move to a new context, but the skills are inappropriate (Schwartz, Chase, and Bransford 2012). There is an old saying: if all you have is a hammer, everything looks like a nail. One example is the high school students in Wineburg's study who interpreted Battle of Lexington source documents in light of their personal experiences and were led into error. In another study, experimenters asked middle school students the following question, slipped in among ordinary mathematics problems: *There are 26 sheep and 10 goats on a ship. How old is the captain?* Roughly three-quarters of the students gave a numerical answer. One fifth-grade student, when asked why he had given 36 as his answer, remarked, "Because that's the kind of thing you do in problems like this. This was an easy one, I only had to add" (Schwartz, Chase, and Bransford 2012, 206). Overzealous transfer can occur when thinkers mistakenly assume a new context is just like a previous one.

Transfer failures are unsurprising in view of disheartening findings from contemporary educational research. The development of critical thinking skills is a central goal of modern education, but researchers say critical thinking does not easily generalize across domains. Psychologist Deanna

Kuhn remarks that "the most pressing practical issue" in teaching critical thinking is that the gains students make "most often do not generalize beyond the immediate instructional context" (1999, 16). Linus Pauling, Neil deGrasse Tyson, and company are poster children for the perils of trespassing. They are cautionary tales for how critical thinking in one field does not generalize to others.

In view of research on transfer, I offer a modest proposal about transfer to help us evaluate the Transfer Defense. Recall that our question about that defense is: Under what conditions do we have reason to think that an expert's skills successfully transfer to another field? Reasonably accepting this defense requires us to know when an expert's skills are likely to transfer from her home field to another one. But research on transfer of knowledge strongly suggests that it's difficult to have reason to accept the defense. Here are two reasons why.

First, the defense should be doubtful to trespassers because they lack a track record of good judgment in the other field. A track record in that field could suggest they have successfully transferred their skills in forming the judgment at issue. But, ordinarily, thinkers do not know whether they are performing well in some domain without checking their track records. Trespassers might assert that their good track record in their home field indicates they *would have* a similarly good record elsewhere. But that optimistic idea ignores the fact that, in experiments, slight changes between the contexts—different subject matter, or physical situations, or temporal situations, or functional situations—can derail transfer. The absence of a track record in the other field suggests that trespassers should be unsure about the Transfer Defense. Here's an analogy. If a classically trained pianist claims he can play bebop jazz piano in the style of Oscar Peterson without ever having studied jazz piano, we should think the pianist's claim needs to be backed up by a satisfactory jazz performance. Start playing—we're listening. Something similar goes for trespassers who appeal to this defense.

Second, background knowledge is crucial for the successful application of skills in any domain (Barnett and Ceci 2002, 616), but trespassers often lack such knowledge. The kind of skills that trespassers hope to transfer include strategies for thinking about thinking, including metacognitive heuristics such as "consider both sides of an issue" or "generate alternative explanations for the evidence." Deploying those sorts of metacognitive tools is a nonstarter in contexts where we lack rich background evidence: we can't easily consider both sides or generate alternative explanations without an expert's perspective. As psychologist Daniel Willingham notes, "metacognitive strategies can only take you so far. Although they suggest what you ought to do, they don't provide the knowledge necessary to implement the strategy" (2007, 13).

These points strongly suggest that reasonably accepting the Transfer Defense will be a stretch for trespassers already out of their element. Of course, skill transfer is possible. If experts know at the outset that the same "deep" structure obtains in another field, then they can take this as a good omen for successful transfer. But if they have no reason to believe the fields share deep structure, modesty about their ability to transfer their skills should prevail. For example, if the school boys in the BB gun task learn about refraction and know that a new shooting task involves water, they have reason to think their skills will transfer. But if they know a new shooting task involves a liquid with different properties, all bets are off.

I have examined three justifications for trespassing and have found them of limited value to trespassers. I argued that trespassers will rarely have reason to accept these defenses. As a result, in many cases of judgment on hybridized questions, trespassers can't avoid the reasoning I proposed earlier, unless they find defenses that apply more widely than the No-Relevant-Evidence, Conclusive-Evidence, and Transfer defenses. My recommendation, therefore, is that trespassers should recognize that they have violated some epistemic norm and reduce their confidence in their judgment on hybridized questions. There are further questions about how much reduction is required in any particular case, but those must be sidelined for now. I think that, quite often, the upshot is that trespassers have powerful reasons either to seek cross-field expertise or to hold confident answers only to non-hybridized questions.

I am aware that many trespassers will be unconvinced. Before concluding, I'll explain briefly why many trespassers will remain confident about their judgment on hybridized questions.

I claim that trespassers typically lack good, reliably-formed judgment once they cross a disciplinary boundary or answer a hybridized question. One hallmark of trespassing, however, is a lack of awareness of the failure to render good judgments. Trespassers are not timid or self-doubting. Pauling and company appeared not to know they were in over their heads. But that is precisely what a well-confirmed idea from psychology predicts.

The Dunning-Kruger effect says that thinkers who are ignorant in a domain tend to be ignorant of their ignorance (Kruger and Dunning 1999).

This is a bias influencing metaknowledge. People who lack first-order knowledge often lack second-order knowledge about their lack of knowledge. Psychologists have described this as a kind of intellectual "double curse" (Dunning et al. 2003). As Justin Kruger and David Dunning note, "the same knowledge that underlies the ability to produce correct judgment is also the knowledge that underlies the ability to recognize correct judgment. To lack the former is to be deficient in the latter" (1999, 1121–1122). Trespassers' lack of competence leads their self-assessments to be systematically off-track, and so I predict that many trespassers will be oblivious to their lack of good judgment. For trespassers, their incompetence is for them an "unknown unknown," as former U.S. Secretary of Defense Donald Rumsfeld might put it. Self-ignorance about trespassing is dangerous. Sometimes trespassers will have enough knowledge to give them false confidence that they are not trespassers but not enough knowledge to avoid trespassing.

5. No Trespassing

My main proposal in this chapter is that trespassing is ubiquitous in contemporary research on hybridized questions and that reflective trespassers violate norms of good judgment. Recognizing that we are in situations where we may trespass should lead us to reconsider our views and perhaps change our minds. I will consider briefly some implications and further issues.

In 1944, the physicist Erwin Schrödinger published a book on biology.[14] He opened the preface with these words: "A scientist is supposed to have a complete and thorough knowledge, at firsthand, of *some* subjects and, therefore, is usually expected not to write on any topic of which he is not a master. This is to be regarded as a matter of *noblesse oblige*" (1967, 1). Schrödinger then tried to explain why he had deviated from the ordinary ground rules for good scientific practice by writing about biology. But exactly what did he mean by his "*noblesse oblige*" remark? *Noblesse oblige* is the idea that privileged people should act kindly and generously toward others who are less privileged. Schrödinger seems to say that scientists are honor-bound to remain inside their field of expertise as a matter of kindness, presumably kindness toward novices as well as experts in other fields. Schrödinger had a good point, but he didn't go far enough. Trespassing is not exclusively a problem

---

[14] Thanks to Benjamin Wilson for telling me about Schrödinger's book.

for novices led astray by overreaching experts, or for miffed experts who are trespassed upon by overconfident intellectual outsiders. Trespassing is also a problem for the trespassing experts. Trespassers are unkind to themselves. Their confident views are epistemically problematic. Ordinarily, the most reasonable response to finding out we have overstepped our limits is, as I have argued, to gain cross-field expertise or stick to holding confident opinions only on non-hybridized questions.

One general reaction to the problem of experts trespassing on other experts is to redesign our research communities. Perhaps we could minimize problematic trespassing by encouraging researchers in cognate fields to rub shoulders more than they ordinarily do now. In the 1930s and '40s, some members of the Vienna Circle promoted what they called the "unity of science." This was an attempt to collect together and interpret the findings of disparate scientific fields, advanced through congresses held in Europe and the United States as well as an encyclopedia project. Proponents of the unity of science wanted to resist fragmentation and disconnection in scientific knowledge so that science could play a greater role in planning social and political life (Reisch 2005). Some historians of social science have described how pockets of interdisciplinary research flourished in the middle decades of the twentieth century in the United States, supported by Cold War–era grants and patronage, incubated in interdisciplinary institutional spaces created during the prewar period (Isaac 2012). For example, in Harvard University's peculiar Department of Social Relations, which existed from 1946 to the early 1970s, anthropologists, psychologists, and sociologists worked together on problems of theory and policy. These researchers wanted to devise a comprehensive theory of human behavior, an unachievable task from inside one academic discipline.

I suspect we *must* trespass to answer most important questions. Perhaps this means we should never trespass alone. Instead, we must rely on the expertise of others. What we need, to extend the trespassing metaphor, is an "easement" or "right of way" for travel beyond our fields' boundaries. The right of safe passage could be secured by our collaboration with cross-field experts. Imagine your colleague is a representative source of evidence, skills, and potential criticism from another field, and also that you can recognize your colleague's expertise. Even if you don't have direct knowledge of that field, if your colleague tests out your answer to a hybridized question and tells you it sounds right to her, then your view is apparently more reasonable than it would have been otherwise. Trespassers may gain reasonable beliefs by engaging in certain kinds of discussion with cross-field colleagues.[15]

Even if we can acquire an "easement" or "right of way" by collaboration, a question remains: how can we enter into productive cross-field partnerships? Here we could draw on insights from researchers who study interdisciplinary and multidisciplinary research (National Academies et al. 2005; Hirsch Hadorn et al. 2008; Bammer 2013). The unorganized knowledge that's relevant to answering hybridized questions is sometimes like an unassembled jigsaw puzzle. Researchers from different fields pull up their chairs to the table and try to arrange the pieces into a coherent whole. But these people have different technical backgrounds and vocabularies, different goals for research practice, and different perceptions of the problem. Presumably, the group could benefit from some guidance, lest their collaboration devolve into grabbing pieces and bickering over whose perspective is best. The field of integration and implementation science (Bammer 2013) seeks to understand the challenges of synthesizing disciplinary knowledge, communicating across boundaries, and understanding the objectives of interdisciplinary research. Lessons from this field could help us develop effective collaboration practices as we tackle hybridized questions.[16]

In this chapter, I defended the idea that recognizing the risks of trespassing should often encourage doubts about our views and our capacities to hold reasonable controversial views. Researchers on interdisciplinary collaboration have also affirmed that sort of recommendation. For example, some researchers note that the "first step" for cross-field collaborators "is to acknowledge, respect, and explore the diversity of perspectives" (Hirsch Hadorn, Pohl, and Bammer 2010, 437). When researchers tackle together so-called wicked problems—from epidemics to poverty to nuclear arms control—they should presume they don't have in hand what is required to hold confident answers to the questions, or even to know what those questions are. Their ignorance is what prompts the collaboration, and so

---

[15] The possibility of an "easement" or "right of way" for trespassing raises questions I won't address here. (Shane Wilkins suggested the "easement" label.) How can trespassers know their collaborators are a representative source of evidence, given that the trespassers do not have an expert-level understanding of the other field's evidence? How can trespassers deal with the possibility that their collaborators disagree with other well-qualified experts? These questions raise an old epistemological problem concerning non-expert perception of expertise, a subject I turn to in the next chapter.

[16] The broad research project I promote in this book—regulative epistemology—calls for this sort of collaboration. The fact that I wrote this book without cross-field coauthors is one of its shortcomings; but it was the best I could do in the circumstances, and I tried to acquire easements where it was possible.

they should begin the conversation knowing there are significant unknowns. My proposal is that many questions not ordinarily viewed as interdisciplinary call for a similarly modest response. We should be more sensitive to the inherent difficulties of confidently answering hybridized questions. At the same time, we may be encouraged by the possibility that cross-field efforts will enhance our understanding of important questions.

One issue I have left mostly unmentioned until now, though it came up briefly at the end of Chapter 7, concerns the limits on developing expertise. There is an idea captured by aphorisms and sayings from every human culture. Where I live, people sometimes say: *jack of all trades, master of none.* In the Czech Republic they say, *nine crafts, the tenth is misery.* In Mexico they say, *you aim for everything, but you hit nothing.* We can't become experts on each and every hybridized question about which we may want to hold confident beliefs. It is apparently easier for us to become less sure of our views and perhaps more doxastically open, than to expand our expertise. The strict limits for gaining expertise make social and institutional responses to the Problem of Epistemic Trespassing indispensable. Trespassing is a problem for individual thinkers, but it points toward solutions that make use of our capacity for working together.

All of us are trespassers at heart. Don't we sometimes find inside of ourselves the overreaching inclinations of Linus Pauling, Neil deGrasse Tyson, and their kin? If we hold trespassers in contempt, do we condemn ourselves as well? For my own part, whenever I consider the fabric of our intellectual practices—the clever, intriguing, and embarrassing things we do as we inquire and pass judgment—my feelings are decidedly mixed. Being so limited and acting as though we know it all is no reason for joy. But I find some hope that careful reflection on our practices can make all of us a little wiser. If we become a bit more doubtful about our own ideas, we may be more willing to listen to the people who really know.

9

Novices and Expert Disagreement

I always follow orders when they make sense.
—Colonel John Paul Stapp (1910–1999), U.S. Air Force medical
doctor, biophysicist, and rocket sled test driver

"If you came awake tomorrow in the Middle Ages and there was an
epidemic raging, what could you do to stop it, knowing what you
know about the progress of medicines and diseases? Here it is practically the twenty-first century and you've read hundreds of books and
magazines and seen a hundred TV shows about science and medicine. Could you tell those people one little crucial thing that might
save a million and a half lives?"
" 'Boil your water,' I'd tell them."
"Sure. What about 'Wash behind your ears.' That's about as good."
—A conversation between Heinrich Gladney and Jack Gladney in
Don DeLillo, *White Noise*, 1985

When a true genius appears in the world you may know him by this
sign; that the dunces are all in confederacy against him.
—Jonathan Swift, *Thoughts on Various Subjects, Moral and
Diverting*, 1706

We know little about the world without trusting experts. Experts themselves
are in a similar predicament, because the proliferation and growth of expert knowledge requires experts to trust other experts. But when we defer to
experts, we sometimes encounter a serious challenge: expert disagreement.
We novices need to determine which experts to trust. That challenge is the
focus of this chapter. Here are three examples to focus the discussion.
  One recent meta-study of climate science research shows that 97 percent
of climate scientists accept that climate change is caused by human activity.

There is a consensus about anthropogenic global warming (Cook et al. 2013; Cook et al. 2016). Although I have watched my fair share of documentaries and have read scores of popular-science articles on climate change, I am mostly ignorant about the empirical facts and theoretical models behind the consensus. I am neither a climate scientist nor a student of climate science. And yet I hold a view about the matter by deferring to the majority of the experts. A bit more specifically, I defer to the majority on the basis of my understanding of how science works, the distribution of expert opinion, and the financial and political pressures that have encouraged some scientists to dissent from the consensus.

As a second example, here's a story about an unnamed friend of mine. After the general election in the United States in November 2016, my friend started reading about foreign policy and international relations. He told me he wanted to understand the potential implications of an American withdrawal from the North Atlantic Treaty Organization and other pertinent questions concerning the threat of nuclear war. Touched a little by obsession, he devoured articles and analyses, finding sharp disagreements among experts. Insofar as it was possible, he checked the credentials and forecasting track-records of the rival experts. But he said he couldn't really gauge the credibility of most experts in order to sift out the most trustworthy ones. A few weeks after the presidential inauguration in January 2017, I asked him what he thought now. He said he wasn't sure what to make of the complex issues, but he told me he was ready to quit his foreign policy reading and get on with the task of constructing a fallout shelter in his backyard.

A third example is a slight twist on a case I brought up in Chapter 8. In the 1970s and '80s, Linus Pauling, the Nobel Prize–winning chemist, asserted that megadoses of vitamin C could effectively treat cancer. Pauling was dismissed by the medical community: high-dose vitamin C therapies didn't work. But many cancer patients and their families knew about Pauling's view and urged doctors to prescribe megadoses of vitamin C. One oncologist remembered how, during Pauling's heyday as supplement guru, families would pressure doctors to prescribe megavitamins. "We struggled with that," the oncologist recalled. "They would say, 'Doctor, do you have a Nobel Prize?'"[1] Patients and families knew that doctors and scientists didn't agree and so they deferred to the celebrated Pauling.

---

[1] Offit (2013, 55) quotes a pediatric oncologist, Dr. John M. Maris, Chief of Oncology and Director of the Center for Childhood Cancer Research at the Children's Hospital of Philadelphia.

Those examples are three among many, but they illustrate our main problem. It is easy to find disagreement among experts on many important issues. All of us are novices about the vast majority of questions, and so the problem is ours. How should novices react to finding out that experts disagree? And when is it reasonable for novices to defer to one side? This is what I call the *Problem of Conflicting Expert Testimony*. Given that many of our controversial opinions rely in some way on testimony from experts, we can only evaluate our views by grappling with this problem.

A few notes on terminology are in order. I will stipulate, as I did in the previous chapter, that an *epistemic expert* about a question has sufficient evidence and skills needed to answer that question reliably. Although experts have some relatively high degree of epistemic competence, they need not be infallible. Let's say that a *novice* about a question lacks the relevant sufficient evidence and skills to answer the question reliably on his or her own. Even though novices lack expertise, they can still have reliably-formed views, so long as they can defer to experts who have reliably-formed views. *Deference* is simply a matter of believing a putative expert's testimony. The idea of putative expertise is important, because novices can defer to others who are also novices but present themselves as experts. Deference may be reasonable or unreasonable. If a novice has sufficient reason to believe that a putative expert is a trustworthy source of information on a question and also takes the expert at her word, then the novice defers *reasonably*. On the other hand, if a novice lacks reason to trust a putative expert but still believes the expert's testimony, the novice defers *unreasonably*. Unreasonable deference involves an epistemic shortcoming.

The Problem of Conflicting Expert Testimony is perennial. Plato discussed it in his dialogues.[2] Augustine of Hippo, in his discourse *On the Usefulness of Believing*, touched upon one crucial aspect of the problem when he asked: "[H]ow will we fools be able to find a wise man?" (1947 [391/392], 429; 13, 28). Augustine noted that most people will recognize that fools are better off obeying the precepts of the wise than living according to their own judgments (1947 [391/392], 428; 12, 27). But, from the fool's perspective, the right advisors don't leap out. Augustine suggests the fool will be unable to pick out the wise person from among all the fakers and the frauds, because the fool doesn't himself know wisdom and, thus, can't recognize it in others (1947 [391/392], 429; 13, 28).

---

[2] See LaBarge (1997) and Hardy (2010).

When faced with the Problem of Conflicting Expert Testimony, what a novice needs to know is this: In situations where I confront expert disagreement, what must I do to respond reasonably, in general, and to defer reasonably, in particular? That issue has only been obliquely addressed in discussions. Epistemologists have, in the main, investigated whether it's possible, in principle, for a novice to defer reasonably to one expert. They have considered different kinds of empirical evidence a novice could use to assess putative expertise. But proving in the abstract that reasonable deference is possible is not too helpful when we need to know whether deference is reasonable in our own case. To shift our perspective on the problem, I propose that we think of it as a regulative matter. The novice needs guidance to manage conflicting expert testimony more effectively in order to figure out when, and to whom, deference is reasonable. To develop that guidance, we need to combine descriptive, normative, and practical perspectives.

Here I make a start on developing some guidance by addressing a pair of questions. First, what is reasonable deference? Or, in other words, what is required for a novice to defer reasonably to one side in a conflict between experts? Second, is reasonable deference easy or hard? That is, how difficult is it for novices to satisfy the conditions for reasonable deference? As I proceed, I offer an account of reasonable deference that will help novices know how to respond to learning about expert disagreement (section 1). Presumably, if novices know the conditions for reasonable deference and also know when those conditions are satisfied in ordinary situations, they will be well-positioned to regulate their deference (section 2). Then I explain why reasonable deference is so difficult by considering the psychology of perceiving expertise as well as the social conditions that produce misinformation about experts (sections 3–5). The cognitive mechanisms and social world that influence novices' judgments about experts are highly relevant to the Problem of Conflicting Expert Testimony, but this fact has been neglected in ongoing discussions. I conclude with a few observations about the implications of the account for both novices (section 6) and experts (section 7).

Before I start, I want to underline how the problem raises weighty questions about our social and political commitments. In a liberal democracy, for example, novices are expected to be judges of facts and values. Novices vote, serve on juries, and hold political office. They are confronted by expert disagreement. They decide to defer to one side or the other, or perhaps go it alone. But when we embrace the ambitions of liberal democracy, we will want to promote the possibility of reasonable deference in important cases. We want novices to use their own autonomous judgments, constrained by some normative conditions, as their basis for deference to experts. We don't want the manipulations of corporations, the media, or authoritarian rule turning voters, juries, and elected officials into marionettes. And many people don't want the experts to decide on behalf of the novices while at the same time hoping novices will actually defer to the right experts. Reasonable deference promises to help novices balance the competing values of autonomy and trust. But threats to reasonable deference are threats to the ideals of liberal democracy.

Institutions of higher education in a liberal democracy are sometimes presumed to help novices learn the art of reasonable deference. At Oxford University, just a few years before the First World War, a philosophy lecturer, John Alexander Smith, made a promise to his students:

> All of you, gentlemen, will have different careers—some of you will be lawyers, some of you will be soldiers, some will be doctors or engineers, some will be government servants, some will be landowners or politicians. Let me tell you at once that nothing I say during these lecturers will be of the slightest use to you in any of the fields in which you will attempt to exercise your skills. But one thing I can promise you: if you continue with this course of lectures to the end, you will always be able to know when men are talking rot.[3]

About a hundred years later, Andrew Delbanco, an American Studies professor at Columbia University, wrote: "[T]he best chance we have to maintain a functioning democracy is a citizenry that can tell the difference between demagoguery and responsible arguments . . . . [T]he most important thing one can acquire in college is a well-functioning bullshit meter. It's a technology that will never become obsolete" (2012, 29). Academics, administrators, and benefactors lap this sort of stuff up. And maybe claims like these are even true. But our highest social and educational ideals may be undermined by epistemological reflection. What if reasonable deference is rarely feasible for the great majority of novices? What if novices' BS meters do not always work as well as we might wish they did? And what if a college

---

[3] The source of this quotation is indirect and thus uncertain. Before the First World War, Smith gave a lecture at Oxford, and Harold Macmillan was in the audience. Macmillan (who later served as the British Prime Minister) reported Smith's words to Isaiah Berlin, who in turn reported them to an interviewer. See Berlin and Jahanbegloo (1992, 29).

or university education—even a really expensive one—can't provide a reliable BS meter?[4]

The Problem of Conflicting Expert Testimony forces us to consider uncomfortable possibilities. Here are just two. First, if reasonable deference is a vain hope for many novices, their controversial beliefs face a significant threat. Arguably, novices won't be able to regard their beliefs as reasonable unless they can defer reasonably. Second, insofar as reasonable deference is rare, some observers may rethink their social, political, and educational ideals.

Speaking for myself, more widespread reasonable deference is worth aspiring to as a goal in our communities and in our own intellectual lives. Even if it is a lofty goal, we should not give up on it. So let's begin by asking: What is it?

1. What Is Reasonable Deference?

The idea of reasonable deference is an important, but curiously neglected, element of the Problem of Conflicting Expert Testimony. To a first approximation, novices can defer reasonably when they have sufficient reason to believe one expert over another. But that's only a first pass. To get a better grip on the idea, I will explore an example in which critical background details are stipulated, letting me simplify what is often complex about a novice's deference to an expert and then isolate the essential features of reasonable deference.

You are flying a small aircraft through stormy skies at night. You are navigating exclusively by radio. Your destination is an airstrip on a small island, far from the mainland. To ensure you are on the right course, you need some information. Running low on fuel, you know you must correct course soon if the winds have swayed you even one degree from your original flight plan. But tonight your navigational instruments are not working. So you dispatch

---

[4] If a college education fails to equip students with a well-functioning BS meter (see Arum and Roksa 2011), what other options are there? Students may try the School of Hard Knocks. The late chef and writer Anthony Bourdain remarked in an interview:

> I was a long-time drug addict, and one of the things drug addiction did, especially when you have to score cocaine or heroin every day on the streets of New York—you learn a lot of skills that are useful when dealing with Hollywood or the business world. In a world full of bullshit, when you need something as badly as drugs, your bullshit detector gets pretty acute. Can I trust this guy with money? Is this guy's package going to be all he says it was? It makes it a lot easier to navigate your way through Hollywood when you find yourself at a table and everybody says, 'We're all big fans of your work'.... You don't fall victim to amateur bullshit when you've put up with professional bullshit. (Woods 2014)

a radio call to air traffic controllers in the region, requesting further guidance. In response, you receive advice from two air traffic controllers. Their advice conflicts. After you curse under your breath and get over your initial sense of disbelief, you begin to wonder: Which expert should you trust, if either one? What explains the conflict here?[5]

Let's assume that you have sufficient reason to eliminate one kind of explanation for the apparent conflict: that the two controllers do not actually disagree. They might only apparently disagree because one uses nautical miles and the other uses land miles, or because you misheard the radio communications and mistakenly think the advice conflicts. But you've triple-checked and you have excellent reason to believe the conflict is genuine, in the sense that the experts give incompatible answers to the same navigational query.

One plausible idea is that if the two experts are, from your perspective, equally likely to answer the question correctly, you can't defer reasonably to either one. Maybe you can flip a coin, randomly choosing to defer to one air traffic controller. Doubtless, in view of your perilous circumstances, deference to one side would be prudential: you want to land the aircraft safely, and staying on your current flight path is not recommended by either expert. But a coin flip wouldn't permit you to believe that one expert is more likely than the other to be correct.

On the other hand, you may be positioned to defer reasonably to one expert if you break the symmetry between the two experts by having grounds to think they are *not* equally likely to get the right answer. That is what I call *asymmetry evidence*. Asymmetry evidence is an indicator, or grounds for believing, that one expert is more likely than the other to correctly answer a question. To illustrate, I will add a further detail to the original example. After you realize the air traffic controllers disagree, you remember that one control tower is around 50 miles closer to your present location. The remembered difference is asymmetry evidence. It suggests the nearest controller should be trusted, given your background knowledge that radar systems

---

[5] Thanks to Noah Hahn for informing me that, for logistical and legal reasons, two air traffic controllers are typically never assigned to guide one aircraft. But on rare occasion pilots may encounter "rogue" radio transmissions, sent by hoaxers with VHF radios dialed to official frequencies. These radio pirates sometimes imitate genuine controllers' messages, endangering pilots and panicking the real controllers. For example, during several weeks in 1993, an unemployed custodian in Roanoke, Virginia regularly drove around the local airport in his Buick, dispatching misleading messages on his transmitter. He told pilots their runway was closed; that they weren't cleared to land; that they needed to switch radio frequencies. He sang a line from the horror movie *Child's Play 3*. The radio hoaxer was dubbed the "Roanoke Phantom." One of his messages, if a pilot had heeded it, would have led the aircraft to crash into nearby mountains.

become increasingly less reliable when detecting aircraft further away. Now you can explain the conflict, and perhaps what you know makes deference to one of them reasonable for you.[6]

Importantly, having asymmetry evidence is only part of what you need. Asymmetry evidence is an indicator that one expert is more likely correct than the other. But any piece of asymmetry evidence may be neutralized by other pieces of evidence. So it must be the case that your first-order evidence, taken in its entirety, supports the view that one expert is more likely correct than the other.

To see why, recall your situation. You believe one air traffic controller is using a radar system located closer to you than the other controller, and so the one nearby is more likely to give accurate navigational advice than the distant one. You have "location" asymmetry evidence. Let's assume you are correct about all of that—your evidence is accurate or non-misleading. But now imagine you realize that, for all you know, there could be an important asymmetry between the two controllers: the nearby controller is based in a small town, but the distant controller is based at an airport in a large city, where there's potentially a much more powerful radar system. You recognize that if the one radar system is in fact more powerful, then the distant expert may be more likely to provide accurate advice than the one nearby, or the two are equally likely to impart accurate advice. You have some "radar power" asymmetry evidence, which raises doubts in your mind about the significance of the "location" asymmetry evidence.

Here's what this means for you. Using the "location" asymmetry evidence as a basis for deference now depends on your being able to distinguish between two distinct states of affairs: (*i*) being nearby makes the nearby expert relatively more accurate than the distant expert and (*ii*) the relative location of the experts does not ultimately change their relative accuracy. You are trying to get the most reliable navigational advice and you rely on a proxy: evidence about the locations of the two air traffic controllers. At this point, your question is simple: Is the proxy I've chosen signal or noise? If you can't tell, then your initial asymmetry evidence does not settle the matter of which controller to trust.

---

[6] I should add that asymmetry evidence won't always explain the expert conflict. Suppose a trustworthy advisor tells you one expert is more likely to be correct than another expert. You are given no explanation for why that is so, but your asymmetry evidence could make deference reasonable for you. Even so, having some sort of explanation for the expert conflict is the customary type of asymmetry evidence and so I focus on it here.

You may be able to gather more evidence, of course. Perhaps you radio the two controllers again and learn they are using identical radar systems. In that event, if you can trust the controllers' reports about their respective radar systems, your "radar power" asymmetry evidence is eliminated and you have no reason to doubt that the "location" asymmetry evidence is accurate and non-misleading. Consider an account that expresses the idea that you can now defer reasonably:

> *Simple Account*: When you consult two conflicting experts, E1 and E2, concerning a question, you can defer reasonably to E1 if and only if (1) your asymmetry evidence positions you to believe E1 is more likely than E2 to answer the question correctly.

The Simple Account is not correct. Even if condition (1) is necessary for reasonable deference, it is not sufficient.

To see this, recall the condition of hypoxia, which I described in Chapter 5 when discussing bias perception and the bias blind spot. Pilots in small aircraft flying at high altitudes may suffer from hypoxia when they become oxygen-deprived.[7] Hypoxia debilitates our reasoning without "leaving a trace" in our consciousness. Hypoxic pilots normally think they're perfectly sharp even when they are making grave errors. Let's assume you now have evidence to defer to the nearby air traffic controller and that your evidence is non-misleading. But then you suddenly recognize you may be hypoxic—one of the air traffic controllers mentions the possibility you are flying a little too high. You realize your assessment of the relative expertise of the controllers may be off-track. As a result, you come to have reason to think that hypoxia may have hampered your evaluation of your asymmetry evidence.

If you can't eliminate the credible doubt that you are hypoxic, you can't defer reasonably to one expert. That is true even though, as we are assuming, you are in fact correct to believe the nearby expert is the more likely one to deliver accurate navigational advice. Now let's imagine you activate an O_2 detector on board and learn that, thankfully, you aren't in low oxygen conditions. What you've learned eliminates your doubt about your ability to evaluate your evidence properly.

Let's recap your situation. Initially, your reliability as a judge of your evidence was called into doubt, because you believed hypoxia could be

---

[7] Elga (ms) introduced an example along these lines.

influencing your thinking. You addressed the doubt by gaining evidence to believe you are not hypoxic. This information allowed you to rely on your judgment concerning facts about how the experts' locations influenced their relative accuracy. You know you are good at making such judgments, we can assume, in virtue of your flying experience and training. So apparently you can now defer to the one expert over the other.

Two details should be underlined. First, you had a credible doubt about being hypoxic. But then you checked your O_2 detector and thereby gained reason to accept that you reliably judge whether the asymmetry evidence is accurate or non-misleading. So your "location" asymmetry evidence helped you defer reasonably to one controller. Second, there is a kind of normative "trigger" that, when squeezed, demands higher-order evidence to affirm your reliability as a judge of the asymmetry evidence. Your doubt about hypoxia required you to get evidence of your judgmental reliability. You need not always seek out higher-order evidence of your judgmental reliability, because your reliability is not always credibly called into doubt.[8]

At this point, we may expect you can finally defer reasonably to one controller. Here is a modified account of reasonable deference:

Reliability Account: When you consult two conflicting experts, E1 and E2, concerning a question, you can defer reasonably to E1 if and only if (1) your asymmetry evidence positions you to believe E1 is more likely than E2 to answer the question correctly and (2) you have reason to believe you are a reliable judge of your asymmetry evidence if your reliability is credibly called into doubt.

But even if conditions (1) and (2) are individually necessary for reasonable deference, they are still not jointly sufficient. Consider one problem for the Reliability Account.

Suppose you find out the storm has produced atmospheric circumstances that degrade the accuracy of radar systems. For example, if you learn that 99 percent of radar systems are massively unreliable in this weather, you can't defer reasonably to one expert. That's true even if you know one expert is more likely than the other to deliver accurate information in normal

---

[8] I say that credible doubts call for higher-order evidence in favor of your reliability as a judge of the asymmetry evidence. An alternative requirement is that we must always gain higher-order evidence of reliability. That requirement threatens to induce widespread skepticism. For more on the issue, see David Christensen's helpful discussion of two types of belief-revision principles (2011, section 6).

weather. Perhaps the nearby expert is your best bet of the two, but if you defer to that one, your deference is still unreasonable—you should think that expert is likely unreliable in this weather.[9] Condition (1) requires that a novice believes one expert is *relatively more likely to be correct* than the other. We need a further condition stating that the expert you defer to does not, so far as you know, fall below some *absolute threshold for being likely to be correct*.

Here's a modified account of reasonable deference:

> *Threshold Account*: When you consult two conflicting experts, E1 and E2, concerning a question, you can defer reasonably to E1 if and only if (1) your asymmetry evidence positions you to believe E1 is more likely than E2 to answer the question correctly, (2) you have reason to believe you are a reliable judge of your asymmetry evidence if your reliability is credibly called into doubt, and (3) you do not have reason to believe that E1 is unlikely to answer the question correctly.

Doubtless, we could continue to refine this account of reasonable deference.[10] Questions about the account remain. For one, it treats reasonable deference as a categorical, all-or-nothing affair, but reasonable deference obviously admits of degrees. How should we think about that? How should we assign a particular level of confidence to our deference? For now, I say nothing more about the account. It's a serviceable conception of reasonable deference and

---

[9] Let me emphasize that we care about epistemological evaluation here, and that believing an expert's testimony can be subject to many types of evaluation. You may be morally, prudentially, or professionally permitted or required to believe something that is epistemically problematic.

[10] Let the chisholming continue in this footnote. Consider a case that requires an extra condition for the Threshold Account. Suppose you are confronted by the conflict between the air traffic controllers, and again you have "location" asymmetry evidence: one radar system is closer to your present location than the other. On reflection, you have no reason to accept you are a reliable judge of the accuracy of your asymmetry evidence, but you have no credible doubts about your competence. Furthermore, you have no reason to think the nearby controller is unlikely to be correct.

So far, conditions (1)–(3) of the Threshold Account are met. But they seem to be insufficient for reasonable deference. Suppose you know you are oblivious to credible doubts about your own judgmental reliability. You recognize that even though open-minded, informed observers would have credible doubts about your reliability in this situation, you don't and can't. We can even imagine that you wouldn't come to doubt yourself even if such observers told you about their doubts. Your obliviousness is total. This means condition (2) is satisfied—not because you have reason to think you are reliable but because, as you know, you are insensitive or impervious to credible self-doubt. Plausibly, once you have reflected on your obliviousness to self-doubt, it won't be reasonable for you to defer to one expert on the basis of the asymmetry evidence. Instead, you should be unsure whether your asymmetry evidence is accurate or non-misleading, or whether it's misleading but you just fail to recognize that.

I suggest accommodating this case by appending to the Threshold Account an extra necessary condition: you do not have reason to believe that you are insensitive to credible doubts concerning whether you are a reliable judge of your asymmetry evidence.

it will help us understand why the Problem of Conflicting Expert Testimony is so daunting.

2. Is Reasonable Deference Easy or Hard?

The "easy or hard" question concerns novices' ability to defer reasonably on the basis of their total evidence. The question is whether novices' actual evidence positions them to satisfy all the conditions for reasonable deference in situations where they would be confronted by expert conflicts. If novices' actual evidence would position them to defer reasonably to one or other of the rival experts a great deal of the time, reasonable deference is relatively "easy" for them. Alternatively, if they would often need to seek out more evidence and knowledge in order to defer reasonably, then doing so is relatively "hard." If reasonable deference is hard for some novices, different responses to expert disagreement will often be appropriate for them. (I discuss three alternatives in section 6.)

My basic answer to the "easy or hard" question goes as follows. For novices who are informed and reflective, reasonable deference will still be hard in a great many situations. Reasonable deference demands work. Novices will need to expand their sets of evidence, adding evidence to believe they reliably judge the accuracy of their asymmetry evidence. The reason is that all novices are often at risk of falling into a situation where reasonable deference demands additional evidence of judgmental reliability; and informed, reflective novices often will—in virtue of what they know—find themselves in such a situation. Here's the upshot for all of us—decent candidates for being informed, reflective novices about some topics if there ever were. We will often need to get additional reliability evidence in order to defer reasonably.

To develop my case for that contention, I focus on condition (2) from the Threshold Account—namely, you have reason to believe you are a reliable judge of your asymmetry evidence if your reliability is credibly called into doubt. I call this the *Reliability Condition*. Why pick on this particular condition rather than the others? It's plausibly the most evidentially strenuous condition to meet, once its antecedent is satisfied. Comparatively, condition (1) will be easy to satisfy: novices can generate asymmetry evidence on the fly. I also set to the side condition (3). If reasonable deference is like a chain, the Reliability Condition is the weak link.

Past work on the Problem of Conflicting Expert Testimony has focused almost exclusively on condition (1): that your asymmetry evidence positions you to believe one expert is more likely right than another. I call that the *Asymmetry Evidence Condition*. In an article titled "Experts: Which Ones Should You Trust?" (2001), Alvin Goldman identifies five categories of empirical evidence that may sometimes position a novice to justifiably discriminate between rival experts. Goldman's five types of evidence include (*i*) arguments presented to a novice by experts to support the experts' own opinions; (*ii*) the agreement from additional putative experts on one side of the question; (*iii*) the evaluations of "meta-experts" concerning the experts' expertise, including experts' formal credentials; (*iv*) evidence of the experts' interests and biases concerning the question; and (*v*) evidence of the experts' track records.

How does this sort of evidence help a novice defer? To illustrate, return to the opening example involving anthropogenic climate warming. I described myself as having evidence of a scientific consensus. I also know about research by social scientists and historians, such as Naomi Oreskes and Erik Conway (2010), on the influence of oil-industry funding for scientists who deny the consensus view. The oil industry has made doubt its product, shaping public perceptions of a "controversy" over climate warming by bankrolling the advocacy work of pundit scientists, demagogues, and empty suits. True, I am a climate-science novice. But I have empirical evidence about the experts and this lets me defer reasonably to one side, assuming the other conditions for reasonable deference hold.[11]

Goldman's five types of empirical evidence can be thought of as rough-and-ready norms or principles, equipped with "other things being equal" clauses. One norm says that if you learn that two experts disagree and only one has financial incentives to accept a particular view, then, other things being equal, you have reason to think the other expert is more likely to be correct. Another norm says that if two experts disagree, and one has been correct about these matters much more often in the past than the other, then, other things being equal, you have reason to think the one with the better track record is more likely to be correct. And so forth. I mention norms for evaluating relative expertise only to observe that, in order to generate asymmetry evidence, the novice will ordinarily use such norms to draw inferences,

---

[11] Elizabeth Anderson (2011) defends a set of criteria for lay assessment of scientific testimony and uses the case of anthropogenic climate change as her main example.

implicitly or explicitly, from pieces of empirical evidence. Merely getting such evidence in hand will let the novice satisfy the Asymmetry Evidence Condition.

In complex situations, a novice's total evidence concerning disputing experts will be settled by a subtle balancing act. One norm tilts toward this expert, another norm tilts toward that expert, and the novice's resting place in judgment depends on assessing the mixed body of evidence. There are difficult questions about whether our naïve norms deliver accurate judgments, and about how good we are at assessing complex bodies of evidence, concerning putative expertise. Our norms are sometimes skewed. That's unsurprising because some norms make use of imperfect cognitive tools for perceiving bias, a matter I considered in Chapter 5. I'll say nothing more about the matter here, though the topic deserves attention.

Novices can display remarkable facility at generating putative asymmetry evidence, especially when they prefer one expert's viewpoint. Experts have noses of wax—novices tweak those noses as they wish.[12] In one of the opening examples, I described cancer patients and families who appealed to oncologists to prescribe megadoses of vitamin C. These desperate people wanted to trust Linus Pauling instead of the medical establishment and they invoked Pauling's impressive Nobel Prize. Who are you to disagree with a Nobel Laureate?[13] But Pauling misled the novices and, plausibly, the novices easily could have known better. The Reliability Condition sets the bar for reasonable deference much higher than merely generating asymmetry evidence.

The Reliability Condition includes a kind of "trigger," as I noted. If novices' reliability as judges of their asymmetry evidence is called into doubt, then they need higher-order evidence to affirm their judgmental reliability. I use the term *reliability evidence* to refer to that higher-order evidence of competence. Once a novice's judgmental reliability has been credibly called into doubt, the novice can defer reasonably to one expert on the basis of the asymmetry evidence only if the novice gains sufficient reliability evidence to believe the following proposition:

[12] As Alan of Lille, the twelfth-century French theologian, wrote in his *A Defense of the Catholic Faith Against Heretics* of 1185–1200: "Now since authority has a nose made of wax—one that can be twisted in any direction—it needs to be strengthened with reasons." (Thanks to Peter King for the translation from the Latin.)

[13] Some scientists were overly deferential to Pauling. As J. D. Watson remarked, Pauling's fame made others "afraid to disagree with him. The only person he could freely talk to was his wife, who reinforced his ego, which isn't what you need in this life" (1993, 1813).

R   You are a reliable judge of the accuracy or non-misleadingness of the asymmetry evidence.

If the novice should disbelieve *R*, suspend judgment on *R*, or remain doxastically open toward *R*, the Reliability Condition is not satisfied.

There is the bad news for novices. They are often at risk of falling into a situation where they should doubt whether *R* is true. That's because it is fairly easy for them to gain evidence that challenges *R*, making doubts concerning *R* credible. But whenever they have credible doubts, they must gain reliability evidence in order to defer reasonably.

In the next three sections, I describe three types of evidence for doubting *R*: (*i*) facts about the tendency for novice assessments of expertise in a domain to be biased by novices' lack of knowledge, (*ii*) facts about the tendency for novice assessments of expertise to be biased by novices' values, and (*iii*) facts about the risk in some social circumstances for people to intentionally manipulate novices' norms and evidence in order to "manufacture deference."

3. Ignorant Novices

Work on the Dunning-Kruger effect, a bias I noted in Chapter 8, provides evidence for doubting whether *R* is true. The Dunning-Kruger effect describes how ignorance delivers a "double curse": our first-order ignorance tends to encourage second-order ignorance of our ignorance (Kruger and Dunning 1999; Dunning et al. 2003). Across a surprisingly wide range of situations, people who perform poorly in a domain of knowledge tend to lack knowledge of their status as poor performers. The classic lesson from the Dunning-Kruger literature is that self-judgment is biased. In further work, David Dunning (2015; Dunning and Cone ms) has investigated how subjects' own knowledge influences judgment of other people's knowledge. If lacking knowledge leads to poor self-evaluation, how does it affect the evaluation of others?

Dunning and Cone discovered that subjects have "lopsided accuracy" in social judgment of expertise. Subjects more accurately evaluate the competence of people they outperform than people who outperform them. Knowing who knows less is easier than knowing who knows more. In Dunning and Cone's studies, average-performing subjects on knowledge-based tasks were better at correctly recognizing poor performers than top performers. Here's why. Subjects rely on their own knowledge[14] in order to evaluate the knowledge of other people. They tend to treat any deviation or departure from their own thinking as evidence of other people's incompetence. For example, when average subjects are assessing low performers, they interpret deviations from their own views as incompetence in the low performers; and since average subjects are assessing low performers, these judgments are basically right on track. But when average subjects instead judge top performers, the average subjects still treat deviations as evidence of incompetence. That turns out to be a mistake: the fact that top performers deviate from average thinking tends to be a sign of special insight, not ineptitude. Consequently, low and average performers in some knowledge domains can't effectively distinguish top performers from the rest and often incorrectly rate average performers higher than top ones. As Dunning and Cone note, "genius, in our data at least, hid in plain sight . . . . For experts, it took one to know one" (ms, 17). There's empirical support for Jonathan Swift's quip, used as an epigraph for this chapter, that a true genius can be recognized by the confederacy of dunces who oppose her.

To give you some sense of the evidence supporting these claims, I'll describe one study. Dunning and Cone examined chess players' assessments of other chess players. The participants, recruited from college chess clubs or online, had U.S. Chess Federation rankings of at least 700—a typical ranking for "scholastic" players or advanced beginners. They were first administered a multiple-choice test, asking them to "choose a move" in a chess game situation, either near the middle or end of a game. Participants had to choose which of four alternatives was the best move. After completing their own test, participants then graded five tests, putatively filled out by other participants, and had to indicate whether the target player was right or wrong in choosing each particular move. After grading each test, the participants had to indicate the likelihood, out of 100 percent, that they would win a game against the target, lose against the target player, or draw. What the experimenters discovered was that top chess performers were more severely misjudged than were the worst performers. As participant expertise increased, accurate assessment of the target increased. Perfect-score participants thought they had a 49 percent chance of defeating the top scoring target, whereas participants scoring zero judged their chances of beating the top target around 72 percent.

---

[14] I use the term "knowledge" here to include mistaken and unreasonable beliefs.

Only high scoring participants had the expertise necessary to correctly assess the challenge posed by the top target.

So far, I have noted empirical evidence that bears on novice perception of expertise. How does it create doubts concerning R, the proposition that you are a reliable judge of the accuracy of your asymmetry evidence? When novices form views about some experts' relative credibility, they may examine statements and arguments given by the experts. In fact, Goldman and others have suggested that novices can sometimes justifiably judge the "dialectical superiority" of one expert over the other. As Goldman notes, the dialectically-superior expert may appear to novices to dish out more apparent rebuttals to the other expert's apparent counterarguments and to give quicker responses to the other expert's counterarguments (2001, 95). Goldman says that novices who witness the experts' argumentative performances can infer that one expert has greater expertise.[15]

To see how Dunning and Cone's research bears on questions about reasonable deference, imagine the following situation. You are a novice sizing up rival experts. You come to believe one expert is more likely to be correct, because it seems to you her dialectical superiority over her opponent was revealed in a debate you watched. If you were to learn of psychological research showing how expertise can "hide in plain sight," then you would have some reason to doubt that your asymmetry evidence is non-misleading. Your reason for doubt is that novice-level knowledge often leads novices to inaccurate judgments of relative expertise. Learning the psychological research would give you some reason to disbelieve R, suspend judgment concerning it, or otherwise become more doxastically open toward it. After all, you are deciding to whom to defer, and you are relying on a proxy: facts about apparent dialectical superiority. In light of what you know about novice perception of expertise, why believe the proxy you have chosen is signal rather than noise?

4. Partisan Novices

I've argued that novices' lack of knowledge can bias their evaluation of expertise. Their values can do the same. Evidence that values bias the evaluation of

---

[15] For discussion of some norms guiding judgments of dialectical superiority, see Matheson (2005).

expertise comes from cultural cognition researchers. Cultural cognition is the tendency for people's values to influence their perceptions of policy, risk, and related empirical facts. Dan Kahan, a psychologist and legal scholar, has investigated with colleagues the *cultural cognition thesis*: the idea that people are disposed to believe that behavior they find respectable and honorable is socially beneficial, and behavior they find disrespectable and base is socially detrimental (Kahan and Braman 2006). Cultural cognition researchers try to explain highly polarized social debates. On one hand, it's plausible that many partisans in such debates typically form beliefs about policy and risk due to the operation of the same basic psychological mechanisms—biased assimilation, the affect heuristic, the availability heuristic, and so on. On the other hand, partisans have diametrically opposed and highly polarized perceptions of good policy and risk. How could that be? What explains sharp conflict between partisans, given that they tend to be outfitted with the same set of basic psychological mechanisms? According to the cultural cognition thesis, it's the interaction of values with psychological mechanisms that produces polarized opinions. Cultural cognition researchers explain conflict over topics such as gun control, capital punishment, and vaccinations by appealing to the ways that people's moral and political values function in processing policy-relevant information.

One interesting line of research in this paradigm focuses on politically motivated reasoning. How we process information is not isolated from our values, and our values move our opinions in predictable patterns. Sometimes, our views about policy-relevant issues become a badge of group membership, a way of signaling that we belong. As a result, people end up being selective in how they credit information in patterns that are consistent with their groups' views. That is just *motivated reasoning*: the tendency to assess factual claims in view of some goal that's independent of their correctness (Kunda 1990; Ditto and Lopez 1992). Politically motivated reasoning involves a goal that researchers call *identity protection*: "the formation of beliefs that maintain a person's status in [an] affinity group united by shared values" (Kahan 2016, 3). Briefly put, politically motivated reasoning involves a person's crediting or discrediting new information in accord with the impact it will have on fitting her beliefs with the beliefs of people in an identity-defining group, not some truth-related norms.

Politically motivated reasoning can influence novice evaluations of expertise. People tend to trust experts whom they believe share their values and worldview, distrusting experts they perceive to hold different commitments.

These patterns of trust and distrust can be explained by the mechanisms of politically motivated reasoning if people selectively credit or dismiss expert testimony in patterns that fit the values of their identity-defining group. And that's precisely what Kahan and his collaborators have observed (Kahan, Jenkins-Smith, and Braman 2011). In one study, subjects were presented with statements putatively from highly credentialed scientists. Subjects were asked to indicate how strongly they agreed or disagreed with the claim that each scientist was an expert on a risk or policy issue. The experimenters manipulated the positions the scientists held on cultural and political values. Subjects treated the experts as credible or not depending on whether the experts supported or contradicted conclusions that were favorable to the subjects' own values. In other words, subjects sorted the experts as trustworthy or untrustworthy by taking cues from their group's values. Novices are highly attuned to information about experts' characters, but the information they pick up on does not necessarily track experts' reliability.

Here is a story about how values can influence novices' evaluations of experts. Physicist Hans Bethe was a pioneer in nuclear physics, a leader in the Manhattan Project, and a Nobel Prize winner. The celebrated physicist occasionally felt flummoxed when he tried to explain the benefits of nuclear power to opponents, many of whom were not trained in science. Bethe remarked that convincing them was like "carving a cubic foot out of a lake" (Walker 2006, 21). Bethe argued that every energy system has risks; but the risks of nuclear power were manageable, and nuclear power could actually deliver more energy with less environmental risk than the alternatives. One historian recounts a story Bethe told about speaking to an audience in Berkeley, California: "After [Bethe] had presented his position on the need for nuclear power, a woman in the audience stood up, turned her back on him, and shouted, 'Save the Earth!' The crowd reacted, he said, with 'thunderous applause'" (Walker 2006, 21). Let's hear it for the antinuclear novices! Their values prevented them from seriously considering Bethe's claims. Intoxicated with solidarity and righteousness, they spurned the physicist.[16]

Evidence of how values influence novice assessment of expertise should lead novices to doubt R. If you learn that novices tend to evaluate conflicting experts in line with how well their positions fit with the values of their identity-defining group, you should think: *How convenient!* To generate asymmetry evidence, novices often attribute biases to one expert, but

[16] Thanks to Benjamin Wilson for sharing this story.

this sort of dialectical maneuver may just be politically motivated reasoning. That's not a reliable method for judging expertise—unless there happens to be some correlation between clusters of values and expert reliability. There are important questions here about how we could learn that values are in fact correlated with expert reliability, and how values might themselves be a source of evidence, but for now my contention is simple. Learning about this psychological evidence should prompt novices to wonder whether they reliably judge the accuracy of their asymmetry evidence.[17]

5. Toxic Epistemic Environments

I have argued that facts about novices—both about their lack of knowledge and about their values—can be evidence that leads us to doubt whether R (the proposition that we are reliable judges of the accuracy of some asymmetry evidence) is true. Facts about our social environments can also compromise our ability to evaluate expertise. We sometimes learn that people seek to "manufacture deference" or sow doubts in our minds, with the goal of nudging us toward one side of an expert debate.

Naïve norms for evaluating expertise are typically public. Since the norms can be recognized by observers, non-experts can sometimes learn to perform and self-present in conformity with the norms. Non-experts can appear to be trustworthy when they are far from it. Examples of "BS artists" abound. In the United States, there are a number of partisan political organizations devoted to training pundits in the art of appearing credible on television. At Pundit School you learn to smile and interrupt your interlocutors effectively, to wear the right clothes or hip glasses, to dodge tricky questions (Parker 2008). Pseudoscientists receive advanced degrees from unaccredited universities. Crank researchers publish bogus articles in predatory and vanity journals where there are virtually no editorial checks on quality.[18]

---

[17] For more discussion of the epistemological implications of cultural cognition research, see Greco (forthcoming).

[18] John Bohannon (2013) describes his "sting operation" to try to publish bogus articles in open-access journals. The articles all had fatal errors that any competent peer reviewer would spot easily. One article was putatively authored by a researcher named Ocorrafoo Cobange, a biologist at the Wassee Institute of Medicine in Asmara, Eritrea. Cobange's paper described the anticancer properties of a chemical extracted from lichen. Both Cobange and the Wassee Institute of Medicine were totally fictitious. Worse, the paper itself was a meaningless pastiche of technical jargon, "a scientific version of Mad Libs" (2013, 62). None of this stopped the *Journal of Natural Pharmaceuticals* from accepting Cobange's article. Bohannon's sting was wildly successful, placing many sham articles in journals hosted by publishing conglomerates such as Elsevier and SAGE Publications.

Scientists get hired by industry to shill for pro-industry positions in media interviews and congressional hearings (Conway and Oreskes 2010). Nothing is new under the sun. As I already noted, the Problem of Conflicting Expert Testimony goes back at least to Plato, who had encountered those teachers of rhetorical persuasion, the Sophists. In ancient Athens, the Sophists helped paying fools appear wise. Athenian novices faced obstacles in choosing between rival experts.

If non-experts masquerading as experts is not depressing enough, novices can also find themselves in situations where people fashion and distribute misleading evidence about genuine experts. One well-known example has been dubbed "Climategate." In 2009, an email server at the University of East Anglia in England was hacked. Emails belonging to climate scientists were leaked by climate warming denialists. At first, many media outlets reported the emails had revealed, or at least suggested, that anthropogenic climate warming is a vast scientific conspiracy. But according to eight official investigations in the United Kingdom and the United States, there was no scientific misconduct or wrongdoing. Even so, many novices came to doubt the credibility of the scientific consensus about climate warming. Denialists had perpetrated a cunning smear campaign.

When I was wrapping up work on this book, "fake news" became a topic of public and academic discussion (Lazer et al. 2018). Prominent examples of fake news are written texts designed to spread misinformation, but some fabricated stories are circulated online merely in order to generate webpage traffic and advertising revenue. Fake news has also made the leap from text to video. Video editing technologies allow purveyors of fake news to create videos of interviews that appear legitimate. A team of computer scientists developed a system that records video of someone talking and, in real time, modifies that person's facial expressions (Thies et al. 2016). Other new technologies can modify speech and audio in no less startling ways.

It doesn't take too much imagination to anticipate what is likely in store.[19] Climate warming denialists may create videos of climate scientists appearing to confess some "conspiracy" of science, and they'll then spread the videos on social media platforms. Climate warming advocates may get even by making videos of denialists appearing to admit, cynically, they are just in it for the

---

[19] That is what I wrote in late 2016 when working on the first draft of this chapter. As I send the book to the press a little more than two years later, I doubt any imagination is required. We have entered the era of "deepfakes" (a portmanteau of "deep learning" and "fake")—videos altered using artificial-intelligence-based techniques that appear to show things that didn't happen.

money. As the quality of counterfeit video improves, novices and experts alike will have trouble telling the difference between real and fake footage. The power of images to influence our perceptions of experts' credibility should not be underestimated.

We should not believe everything we see. Indeed, if novices have reason to believe they are in toxic epistemic environments where some people seek to manufacture deference, or to spread doubt about particular experts' credibility, novices may have reason to doubt whether R is true. For instance, if novices come to think their evaluations of some experts may easily depend on misleading evidence, they should doubt whether their asymmetry evidence is accurate. Once this happens, novices need reliability evidence in order to defer reasonably.[20]

I've now described three types of evidence that novices can easily acquire and which, once acquired, should cause them to doubt whether R is true. Informed, reflective novices will find themselves in the following predicament. For a great many recognized conflicts between experts, if we can defer reasonably to one side, we will need reliability evidence that offers grounds to believe we are reliable judges of our favored asymmetry evidence. For us, reasonable deference will often be hard.

6. Lessons for Novices

For those of us trying to become more informed and reflective about some topic, what reliability evidence is there and how can we get our hands on it? There is no general, one-size-fits-all advice. That's because evidence for doubting R can only be countered, eliminated, or ruled out by learning about

---

[20] Let me briefly compare what I have said about toxic epistemic environments to an example given by Gilbert Harman, who argued that someone's knowledge can be eliminated by the mere presence of misleading counterevidence in her social environment. In his "assassination" example (1973, 143–144), Harman stipulates you know that a politician has been assassinated on the basis of reading an early-edition newspaper that correctly reports the event. Later in the day, the early-edition papers are pulled from the shelves and the state-controlled media begins reporting—falsely—that the politician is alive. All of this happens unbeknownst to you. According to Harman, your toxic epistemic environment eliminates your initial knowledge. You don't learn anything new, but since you could very easily hear the false reports, you now lack knowledge that the politician was assassinated. You lose your knowledge, Harman says, even if you don't even read a misleading newspaper or hear the false reports from a neighbor.

The idea I've deployed here is similar but even more plausible: if we are *aware* that we may easily be in a situation where misleading evidence concerning disagreeing experts circulates around us, then we have reason to doubt that our favored asymmetry evidence is accurate.

the specifics of an expert dispute. Return to the aircraft example. Your "location" asymmetry evidence indicated that the nearby air traffic controller was more likely to impart accurate advice than the distant one. Then you had a doubt whether you were well-positioned to evaluate your evidence. You realized you could be hypoxic. Using your O_2 detector, you cast aside your doubt that you were in low oxygen conditions. This was enough to shore up your judgmental reliability, ensuring you could defer reasonably to one expert on the basis of your asymmetry evidence.

One general lesson is that informed, reflective novices who satisfy the Reliability Condition will have done their homework. To get reliability evidence, novices need to learn about experts' disputes, their methods, and their enterprise of making knowledge. That work can take considerable time and energy. And so a second general lesson is that, when life is too short and too busy for us to meet the Reliability Condition for at least some of the issues we care about, we should adopt alternative responses to expert disagreement.

Realistically, reasonable deference is practically impossible for the vast majority of controversial issues. What are the alternatives? I can think of three main options.

First, we can *defer unreasonably* to one expert, lacking any epistemic reason to favor that one over the other. This response amounts to some kind of "blind trust," an attitude that some philosophers say we must sometimes hold toward testifiers.[21] Second, we can use a method to *aggregate the experts' conflicting judgments*—at least if such a method is available to us—and reach a view that's distinct from expert judgment on both sides. Third, we can *abstain from holding a view*, refusing to take sides in the experts' conflict, choosing instead to mind our own intellectual business. There are different ways to abstain. If one expert believes a proposition and the other disbelieves it, we may suspend judgment about it. In more complicated disagreements, where different experts hold each of the three doxastic attitudes, we may become doxastically open and refrain from belief, disbelief, and suspension of judgment.

As I have argued, the conditions for reasonable deference won't be met in many situations. An upshot is that we novices will often have to reconcile ourselves to one of these three alternatives, at least until we gain reliability evidence. The alternatives may not be as satisfying to us as reasonable deference

---

[21] See, for example, Baker (1987) and Hardwig (1991). (Thanks to Johnny Brennan for telling me about Baker's article.)

would be. But they are often the best we can manage as we try to be informed and reflective novices.

In addressing the "easy or hard" question, I ignored uninformed, unreflective novices. But doesn't the account I defended have implications for them? One possibility is that it makes their reasonable deference too easy. Suppose a novice meets the conditions for reasonable deference set down by the Threshold Account and then systematically avoids new evidence, burying his head in the sand. Surely this novice is not reasonable. But doesn't my account imply that his deference is entirely reasonable?

Here are three observations about the objection. First, someone's inquiry can be properly or legitimately "closed" when he has reached the goal at which inquiry aims.[22] Suppose the head-in-sand novice has properly closed inquiry. On that assumption, we should not insist that the novice's opinion is unreasonable. Instead, the novice seems to be entirely within his epistemic rights to defer to one expert. If that's how we understand the case, though, it does not appear to threaten the account of reasonable deference. Second, we can grant that the novice's ostrich-esque policy gives him reasonable deference—so long as he doesn't recognize that he is evading new evidence. If he becomes aware of what he's doing, he should begin to doubt that he is well-positioned to evaluate his asymmetry evidence. If he knows what he's doing, he will be unreasonable to do it. Third, and most crucially, the head-in-sand policy is fundamentally defective. It is implausible that anyone should aim to defer reasonably *by any means necessary*. We should not always value reasonable deference more than gaining new information about expert disputes, or reflecting on our asymmetry evidence, or the like. Good epistemic policies will include being an informed and reflective thinker, being open to new evidence, trying to defer reasonably, and so on. A balance must be struck. Even if we grant that the head-in-sand novice has some positive epistemic status for his deferential belief, we can still epistemically evaluate him harshly.

7. A Problem for Experts

The Problem of Conflicting Expert Testimony challenges our social and intellectual commitments. It calls us to reflect on the manifold ways in which

---

[22] For discussion of what is required to properly close inquiry, see Kvanvig (2011) and Kelp (2014).

novices and experts relate to each other. As I have argued, novices who are informed and reflective must seek out evidence of their own reliability. That recommendation concerns what novices should do. But progress in addressing the problem should also consider what experts should do. I conclude this chapter by turning the spotlight from novices to experts, noting how they figure into solutions to the problem.

Some researchers study how novices react to experts' testimony. How can experts share their findings so that non-experts don't miss the message? Why is misinformation so resistant to correction? This increasingly important field of research goes under the banner of "science communication," but it encompasses questions about how experts in any truth-aiming field can communicate with outsiders effectively (Lewandowsky et al. 2012; Schwarz, Newman, and Leach 2016; Jamieson, Kahan, and Scheufele 2017). Research on science communication sometimes examines questions about how novices reach accurate or inaccurate opinions on the basis of expert testimony. The basic model is that experts are attempting to insert accurate opinions into novices' heads—maybe gently, or maybe out of frustration for the tenth time. How can experts get novices to accept correct views?

If reasonable deference is essential for the functioning of liberal institutions, it isn't enough for experts to always "insert" accurate opinions into novices' heads. Good reasons must somehow get in there, too. And so we should not overlook a slightly different question: How can experts help position novices to defer reasonably? Researchers could examine the matter. Novices who defer reasonably must navigate their way through a thicket of evidence, guided by their norms. But which norms are good ones? How can novices learn to use those norms effectively? How should experts testify to limited and ignorant novices who are nevertheless trying their best to defer reasonably?

Science communication researchers need not sort out these questions all alone. Epistemologists could join in, too. Scientists could describe the psychological and social factors that create and sustain the problem of conflicting expert testimony. Epistemologists could describe good intellectual conduct for novices and testifying experts. They could together devise ideas to guide novices and experts, with the hoped-for outcome that novices receive guidance that helps them defer reasonably more often than they do now. Effective testimonial practices need novices and experts to play their roles well. They must collaborate in order to achieve the outcome of reasonable deference. I am suggesting that understanding how testimonial practices can be effective also calls for collaboration. This is one part of the hard but vital work that lies ahead for regulative epistemologists.

10

Self-Defeat?

It is painful to give an account of one's faults; one wants to have them
excused, and pass the burden on to someone else.
—Jean de la Bruyère, *Characters*, 1688

The sentence must also contain its own apology for being spoken.
—Ralph Waldo Emerson, "Spiritual Laws," 1841

The previous six chapters described a regulative method designed to help
us see the difference between reasonable and unreasonable controversial
beliefs. This method can help us meet a series of intellectual challenges: the
problems of Peer Disagreement, Counterfactual Interlocutors, Unpossessed
Evidence, Epistemic Trespassing, and Conflicting Expert Testimony. When
we are guided by the method, our doxastic deliberation can reveal to us when
we should doubt our controversial views.

In the final two chapters, I examine objections to the method. One objection asserts that the method is self-defeating. If we are guided by the method,
shouldn't we doubt the method, given that its correctness is controversial?
Another objection claims that the method undermines our motivation to
inquire into controversial questions. If we can't expect to gain reasonable
beliefs or knowledge about the right answers to those questions, why bother
trying? These two objections threaten the method's viability. We should not
be satisfied with a method for managing our controversial beliefs that's unreasonable to believe or at odds with our pursuit of the goals of inquiry.

In this chapter, I consider the Self-Defeat Objection. First, I summarize the
method set out in Chapters 4 through 9 (section 1). Then I set out the objection (section 2), along with a number of potential replies (section 3) and the
reply I endorse (section 4). Finally, I consider one criticism of my reply (section 5) and explain what I think about the method's correctness (section 6).

1. Looking Back

The method consists in a set of principles and observations intended to guide inquiry concerning controversial questions. The principles describe contingent conditions in which we have *prima facie* defeaters for controversial beliefs. Sometimes, it isn't immediately clear to us when we're in those contingent conditions: the observations are meant to illuminate the matter. The defeaters—which I call *competence defeaters*—concern our ability to form reasonable beliefs about controversial matters on the basis of our evidence. When we have competence defeaters for some beliefs, we have reason to doubt that those beliefs are a reasonable response to our evidence. If the defeaters are undefeated, we should change our minds, at least to some extent.

The method is an abstract set of considerations and so it may seem ill-suited for improving inquiry. How exactly can words printed on paper or displayed on a screen guide us in the hustle and bustle of our intellectual lives? As I argued in Chapter 3, to follow the method effectively we need the right intellectual character. We can't just passively receive the method by learning about it. We need to engage in activities to set it in our minds and carry it into our daily lives. These activities create in ourselves dispositions that will let us bring the method to bear on our inquiry and doxastic deliberation. How that process could actually work raises questions I must leave for scientists to answer, as I explained in Chapter 3. But I suspect the method (or something like it) can in fact be taught and learned, because people often do follow abstract principles and normative ideals. Figuring out how to implement a method is part of the broad project of regulative epistemology.

The method offers us metacognitive insights into our controversial opinions. We are naïve realists and think of ourselves as unbiased observers, presuming that our controversial opinions are the sober truth. But controversial opinions are, as I defined them in Chapter 4, beliefs concerning the answers to questions over which we recognize intelligent, informed people do not agree. Awareness of controversy can easily, and often should, prompt us to wonder whether we are right. Why do others reject our views? What if we have made a mistake? Are our controversial beliefs unreasonable? By asking ourselves such questions, we have an opportunity for doxastic deliberation and self-improvement. The method promises to aid us. It leads us to reflect in distinctive ways on our place in the intellectual world.

What can the method show us? Its principles and observations highlight ways in which we may easily lack the competence needed to hold reasonable answers to controversial questions based on our evidence. But how can we fail to be competent, exactly? Let me briefly present snapshots of the arguments from Chapter 5 through 9.

When we learn that informed, intelligent people reject our views, we may thereby gain reasons to change our minds. One common response to our opponents is to attribute biases to them, as I explained in Chapter 5. But debunking our opponents in that way sometimes looks dubious because we tend to believe that our own judgments are less prone to bias than other people's judgments, even when that is probably not correct. We should be less inclined to treat others as more biased than we are ourselves; and, as a result, we must face the fact that their disagreement can't be so easily dismissed.

In Chapter 6, I suggested that the potential of criticism from merely possible interlocutors challenges our controversial views. If the intellectual world were different, we would very likely face powerful objections. Realizing that counterfactual interlocutors could devise objections to our strongest arguments can help us keep our confidence in check. Counterfactual interlocutors show us that we could have easily overlooked defeaters, an insight into our evidential situation that may defeat our views.

Then in Chapter 7, I returned to the actual world and considered the fact that, for the vast majority of controversial topics, there's far more evidence than we could ourselves possess. When we learn of unpossessed evidence, we gain two types of reasons that may indicate we have made an error. First, evidence of unpossessed evidence against our views can be evidence itself; and, second, evidence of unpossessed evidence may prompt doubts that we have formed our controversial views on the basis of a fair or representative sample of the total evidence.

One natural response to learning about vast bodies of unpossessed evidence is to retreat to one corner of our intellectual world and then learn a great deal about some narrow question. But in Chapter 8, I noted how many controversial questions are properly explored using tools from multiple fields of inquiry. We risk epistemic trespassing when we hold controversial views on the basis of evidence and skills that aren't drawn from all of the relevant fields. Once we learn we have trespassed, we should often lower our level of confidence in our opinions. We can't go it alone; we must trust experts in other fields.

But trusting experts is no simple matter when the experts don't agree, a topic I turned to in Chapter 9. To defer reasonably to one expert over another, we need to identify an epistemological asymmetry between them, but we are often not well-poised to distinguish between rival experts, given what we know about ourselves and our intellectual world.

The principles and observations on offer are metacognitive tools for recognizing whether we have competence defeaters for holding controversial views. If we have *prima facie* competence defeaters for some beliefs, we should give up those beliefs, or at least reduce our confidence in them, unless the defeaters are defeated. For many controversial views, the method can reveal multiple, independent competence defeaters. Even if the individual defeaters only induce partial defeat of some view, several defeaters working together can defeat it fully.

Does following the method lead us to suspend judgment on all controversial questions? As I explained in Chapter 4, the method is not a thesis about the scope of reasonable belief. The method's implications for us hang on our total evidence. The method highlights *prima facie* competence defeaters. Some part of our evidence may allow us to defeat the defeaters, thereby restoring the positive epistemic status of the targeted opinions. If we lack defeater-defeaters, what then? We may end up suspending judgment on many controversial topics. But suspending judgment is not an inevitable outcome of using the method, for we can even have competence defeaters for *suspending judgment*. That attitude can be controversial, too, no less than belief or disbelief. Sometimes we can't see our way through to reasonably adopting any one of the three doxastic attitudes. We are *doxastically open* when we have significant doubt about which of the three attitudes is reasonable to adopt on the basis of our evidence. In essence, doxastic openness is a way to describe or model our confusion, hesitation, indecision, or uncertainty about what to believe. I suggested the method may well induce greater doxastic openness in us. If we become more doxastically open, we can honor the fact that controversial issues are often perplexing.

I remain silent on where the method will take anyone else, as I noted in Chapter 4, since I don't know what anyone else's total evidence is. But I should probably comment briefly on my own predicament, in case the reader is curious and hasn't already figured it out.

I encounter disorder and chaos in most quarters of my intellectual world. Oftentimes, the best response I can muster is to confess that I don't know what on earth is going on out there. I look on as an outsider, a dabbler, a know-nothing. Whenever I think I have some point to which I can cling and fasten myself, it shakes free and leaves me behind. Nothing stays still for me. What is the use of pretending to have powers I don't? What do I know?[1] On many controversial matters, I have reasons to doubt my ability to arrive at confident and settled views on my evidence, even though on many uncontroversial topics I readily take myself to know a lot. Bertrand Russell once wrote that, after thinking philosophically, "we shall find doubt more frequently justified than we supposed" and we will "substitute articulate hesitation for inarticulate certainty" (1995 [1950], 11).[2] I know doubt and hesitation. I see I should only be confident about what lies close to hand. Let me seek, learn, and try to see, not make-believe I know more than I do.

Where does this stance leave me? Some objections to the method focus on possible implications of doubts. Potentially, the method leads us to suspend judgment or become more doxastically open about controversial questions. But given that the method is controversial, won't it undermine belief in itself? Let me turn to that question now.[3]

2. The Self-Defeat Objection

Self-defeat is like a firecracker. Watching something blow up can be fun, but you don't want it in your hands when it explodes. There are many forms of self-defeat. Clever children sometimes point out that saying "Never say 'never'" is inconsistent. An author suffering from writer's block sits

---

[1] The last four sentences echo lines from works by Pascal, Emerson, and Montaigne.

[2] Thanks to Leopold Stubenberg for telling me about Russell's remarks.

[3] I can't address all of the objections to the method I know of. One kind of objection asserts that if the method is widely adopted, it could induce alarming social and political consequences. If some people follow the method but others don't, for example, there may be a dangerous imbalance in society between the doubtful and the dogmatic. W. B. Yeats' celebrated poem "The Second Coming" voices a disconcerting sentiment: "The best lack all conviction, while the worst / Are full of passionate intensity." Yeats wrote his poem in the aftermath of the First World War. Just a little over a decade later, Bertrand Russell was vexed about the rise of the "Hitlerites" in Germany and he confidently declared: "The fundamental cause of the trouble is that in the modern world the stupid are cocksure while the intelligent are full of doubt" (1998 [1933], 28). Russell then floated the possibility that "scepticism and intellectual individualism are luxuries which in our tragic age must be forgone, and if intelligence is to be effective, it will have to be combined with a moral fervour which it usually possessed in the past but now usually lacks" (1998 [1933], 28).

Objections along those lines seek to highlight moral and political reasons to reject the method or perhaps to restrict its use. Here is all I will say about such objections for now: the method concerns epistemic evaluation or normativity, and the question of whether doubt is morally or politically appropriate in particular circumstances is distinct from the question of whether doubt is epistemically appropriate. (Thanks to Roy Sorensen and Shane Wilkins for discussion.)

down at his desk and jots down the first and only thought that comes to mind: "I can't write a single sentence." The writer expresses a proposition whose content falsifies that proposition. In the 1942 movie *Casablanca* (which I have never managed to watch in its entirety), Rick Blaine, played by Humphrey Bogart, operates a nightclub and gambling den, Rick's Café Américain, and in one scene a policeman, Captain Louis Renault, shuts down the establishment:

Renault: Everybody is to leave here immediately! This café is closed until further notice. Clear the room, at once!
Blaine: How can you close me up? On what grounds?
Renault: I am shocked—*shocked*—to find that gambling is going on in here!
Croupier: [hands Renault a fistful of money] Your winnings, sir.
Renault: Oh, thank you very much. Everybody out at once!

Self-defeat is commonplace. Sometimes claims demand their own rejection or undermine our reasons for holding them, to some greater or lesser degree.

On first blush, one special type of self-defeat afflicts the regulative method I offer in this book. I call it *epistemic self-defeat*. Some methods, principles, and rules describe conditions in which people lack knowledge or reasonable belief. But a method like that can be applied to someone's belief *that the method is correct*. The method can defeat belief in itself by indicating that belief in the method is not known or reasonable. In general, a method is epistemically self-defeating when following it commits one to thinking one cannot know or reasonably believe the method is correct.

The method may discourage us from having confident opinions about controversial questions. But the method appears to be controversial in the sense described in Chapter 4, where I stipulated that a belief is controversial when it's rejected by thinkers who have evidence that's at least roughly as good as ours and who are at least approximately as good at responding to that evidence as we are. So shouldn't we doubt the method's correctness? Here the worry is that the method gets caught in its own snare—and that anybody following the method will be "hoist by his own petard," as Alvin Plantinga (1995, 200) put it in a Shakespearean turn of phrase.[4]

---

[4] A petard is a type of bomb, invented in the sixteenth century, for blowing a hole in a door or a wall. A bomb-maker blown up by his own bomb is an ironic character, as we find in *Hamlet*, Act 3, Scene 4.

Let's spell out the reasoning behind the Self-Defeat Objection a bit more. Suppose we believe the method is correct, but then we learn it's controversial. Then we should evaluate our belief in the method using the method. Now suppose—as self-defeat objectors will temporarily concede—the method gives us *prima facie* competence defeaters for believing the method is correct. And suppose further—again, as self-defeat objectors will grant—the *prima facie* defeaters for believing the method are full defeaters. If those defeaters are undefeated, we should give up belief in the method altogether. Suppose they are undefeated. Then we should not believe the method is correct. If being guided by a method means holding it or taking it for granted (as I suggested in Chapter 3), and on reflection we should not hold or take for granted whatever we should not believe is correct, then on reflection we should not be guided by the method. In essence, that is the Self-Defeat Objection.

The objection alleges that if some contingent conditions hold, then the method is not reasonable for us to believe. One necessary condition is that the method is controversial for us because we recognize it is rejected by informed and intelligent people. Is that our lot?

Speaking for myself, I am unsure. The method is a set of fairly natural ideas. It helps us identify *prima facie* competence defeaters that bear on our controversial beliefs. The theory or "logic" of defeat built into the method is not a highly contentious part of philosophy. Epistemologists have a good grasp of how defeat works across a wide range of situations, and I've made assumptions about defeat that are widely embraced. The method applies insights about defeat to our deliberations about controversial opinions. Many of the considerations I've used to construct the method—the arguments in Chapters 5 through 9—will appeal to philosophers who defend conflicting theories about knowledge, justification, warrant, and the like. As far as I can tell, the method is far from the most controversial kind of philosophical claim. It isn't as controversial as the claim that capital punishment is always wrong, nor the claim that humans are wholly material things, nor the claim that freedom and determinism are compatible.[5]

---

[5] As I noted in Chapter 4, footnote 14, some epistemologists accept "anti-defeater" views, denying that (undefeated) defeaters always undermine knowledge or justification. Those views are compatible with the basic normative recommendations of the method. But it is clear that some questions about the method are highly controversial. Take the claim that if we are guided by the method, then we should suspend judgment on all or most controversial questions. That claim is certainly controversial, though I don't embrace it, as I explained in Chapter 4, section 6. A related claim seems considerably less controversial: for many people, the method is a better long-term strategy for them to avoid false and unreasonable beliefs than merely trying to follow their first-order evidence.

But if the method implies skepticism or anything like skepticism, those implications will be highly controversial. Most people will happily reject skepticism about their controversial opinions. But skepticism is not part of the method. To repeat: the method is not a thesis about the scope of reasonable opinion concerning controversial questions. It's a way for us to determine when opinions are unreasonable for us to hold. In principle, some people could adopt the method and still reasonably hold all of their controversial opinions if their total evidence positions them to defeat the *prima facie* competence defeaters. In that event, the method helps confident believers count the costs of their confidence. When they deliberate about controversial matters, they will better recognize that they're committed to particular views about the strength of their evidence and their own abilities as inquirers. On reflection, if confident believers find those views doubtful or implausible, they may be prompted to open their minds more.

Of course, self-defeat objectors will surely think the method, independently of its results, will be controversial among those who can understand and evaluate it. Although I'm not convinced that is correct, let me grant that assumption.

Recall that the Self-Defeat Objection claims we shouldn't believe or follow the method since by its own standards, we shouldn't believe it. The reason we can't reasonably believe the method is correct is that it's controversial; and, further, we have an undefeated full (as opposed to partial) competence defeater for believing it. The objection succeeds only if four assumptions are reasonable for us to believe: (*i*) that the method's correctness is controversial, (*ii*) that the method induces a full defeater for believing the method, (*iii*) that the full defeater is undefeated, and (*iv*) that we must believe the method is a good one in order to be guided by it.

What shall I say about the Self-Defeat Objection? I am unsure what to make of it. Among philosophers, self-defeat objections are sometimes controversial, not least because such objections may carry with them an air of paradox. To speak for myself, when the method takes aim at my belief in the method, I feel perplexed and uncertain about what to think. The objection leaves me feeling I've possibly witnessed a philosophical sleight of hand. By contrast, when the method apparently reveals I have competence defeaters for some other controversial opinion of mine, I feel I have gained an insight—my competence doesn't position me to have a reasonable opinion.

3. Six Replies

I doubt the Self-Defeat Objection is successful in part because I know about potential replies. Before I describe those replies, consider a closely related epistemological matter.

The objection I focus on is similar to ones leveled at conciliationist views concerning peer disagreement. Conciliationists, as I noted in Chapter 5, say that if we recognize we disagree with an epistemic peer, we always have a reason to reduce confidence in our disputed belief. One stock objection to conciliationism notes that such principles are rejected by apparently informed, intelligent peers.[6] David Christensen, a conciliationist, admits that he respects epistemologists who reject his theory. "Insofar as I practice what I preach," Christensen writes, "it seems that [conciliationism] requires me to become much less confident in [conciliationism]" (2013, 78). When conciliationists learn of recognized peer disagreement about their view, they apparently have reason to doubt it is correct. But Christensen and others deny that rejecting conciliationism is in fact the correct response to self-defeat objections.

Importantly, according to the regulative method, *prima facie* defeaters come from more than merely recognized disagreement. But the replies given by conciliationists can illuminate how we might address the Self-Defeat Objection for the regulative method. Let me set out six replies.

The first begins by noting that the method may deliver full or partial defeaters for controversial views. As I argued in Chapter 4, a defeater is full or partial relative to some body of evidence. Depending on our total evidence, the method may only generate partial defeaters for believing the method. If so, we can maintain a reasonable belief by lowering our confidence. I call this the *Partial-Defeat Reply*. This reply is consonant with the spirit of the method, for it may turn out that we should hold particular controversial opinions with a low degree of confidence rather than give them up altogether. But a low degree of reasonable confidence in the method is consistent with realizing we have a partial competence defeater for believing the method. If the first-order evidence supporting our belief in the method is strong, then the competence defeaters may push down our confidence only a little. The

---

[6] For discussions of self-defeat objections for various conciliationist principles, see Plantinga (1995), Elga (2010), Frances (2010), Christensen (2013), Weatherson (2013), Decker (2014), Matheson (2015), Pittard (2015), and Machuca (2017).

method may call for some doubt about itself, but not enough doubt to properly eliminate our belief in it.

A second reply claims the Self-Defeat Objection fails because, in general, methods can be exempted from self-application. Adam Elga (2010, 179–182) has defended this idea using an analogy. Imagine that *Consumer Reports* is a magazine that reviews consumer appliances, but then it also begins reviewing magazines that review consumer appliances. One day we want to buy a new toaster. *Consumer Reports* instructs us to only buy toaster X whereas *Smart Shopper* magazine instructs us to only buy toaster Y; but *Consumer Reports* also states that *Smart Shopper* is the ratings magazine to follow. *Consumer Reports* imparts incoherent advice. It tells its readers to only buy toaster X and only buy toaster Y. We apparently can't follow that advice. According to Elga, the analogy can help us understand what to do when a method implies its own rejection. Since we can't follow the advice of such a method, Elga says we should stipulate that our methods can't recommend their own rejection.

That is what I call the *Self-Exemption Reply*. If it works, the Self-Defeat Objection fails because our belief in the method can't be defeated by the method. The reply is consistent with the method, which gives immunity to some types of beliefs from defeat by the method. I have suggested, for example, that many claims about commonsense, science, and history are not controversial in the way that triggers our deliberation using the method—or, if we do deliberate on beliefs in such claims, they will survive (relatively) unscathed, given the evidential conditions most of us find ourselves in. In effect, the Self-Exemption Reply moves belief in the method into a protected class of beliefs. And insofar as the method is the elucidation of widely-shared, commonsensical intuitions about cases, this strategy seems promising. But isn't it arbitrary and ad hoc to self-exempt a method from defeat at its own hands? Elga denies the charge. If we don't exempt our methods from self-application, they can't be coherent—they will give inconsistent recommendations in possible cases. As Elga puts it, "in order to be consistent, a fundamental policy, rule, or method must be dogmatic with respect to its own correctness" (2010, 185).[7]

A third reply to the Self-Defeat Objection employs a distinction due to John Pittard (2015). Being committed to a method is different from being committed to a belief arrived at by that method. As we've seen, the objection involves a situation where we follow the method and then get an undefeated

---

[7] Matheson (2015) and Pittard (2015) critically discuss Elga's argument.

full competence defeater for believing the method. The objection apparently shows we can't be committed to both the method *and* a particular belief arrived at through the method, namely, the belief that constitutes the undefeated full competence defeater for believing the method. So what happens now? Advocates of the Self-Defeat Objection will tell us to stay committed to the belief—call it *the defeater*—we have reached through the method. But notice what follows if we remain committed to the defeater. We affirm a reason for giving up our belief in the method that presupposes the method's correctness. Being committed to the defeater means being committed to the method. In other words, we can't escape commitment to the method here. As Pittard says about such situations, "modesty" or complete doubt about our method "would simply not be an option. And where modesty is impossible, immodesty is not objectionable" (2015, 460). Being committed to the regulative method is, at some level, defensible. Faced with the Self-Defeat Objection, we need to be committed either to the method or to the belief we arrived at using the method. But, crucially, our commitment to the defeater presupposes the method is correct. I call this the *Inevitable-Commitment Reply*.[8]

A fourth reply explains why the Self-Defeat Objection is so perplexing and tries to smooth over that fact. David Christensen (2013) spells out how two general types of epistemological ideals can conflict. On one hand, "modesty" ideals say we should respect evidence that we've made errors. For instance, if we learn our initial level of confidence in an opinion is too high, we should moderate our confidence. On the other hand, "level-connection" ideals dictate that our confidence in a proposition should be constrained by our higher-order thinking about the amount of confidence our evidence allows. Reasonable thinkers will seek to live by such ideals, but Christensen observes that modesty and level-connection ideals can clash—and not just in situations where we're thinking about self-defeat objections (2013, 92). Take cases where a thinker correctly recognizes that her first-order evidence (say, a deductively valid argument) supports believing proposition p, but then she gains higher-order evidence for believing her evaluation of the first-order evidence is mistaken. Insofar as this thinker respects her higher-order evidence by moderating confidence in her belief that p, her level of confidence

---

[8] This reply is inspired by Pittard's (2015) defense of "resolute conciliationism," but I do not mean to attribute it to him. Pittard offers a thoroughgoing argument for the thesis that "the conciliationist who remains firm in a dispute over conciliationism is being no less deferential to her disputant than one who decreases her confidence in conciliationism" (2015, 443).

will deviate from what her first-order evidence indicates her confidence should be. Thus, by living up to one ideal—roughly, respecting higher-order evidence of error—her thinking will fall short of another rational ideal—roughly, respecting deductive logic. Christensen says that sometimes "one will end up violating some ideal or other, no matter what one ends up believing" (2013, 91). The fact that the method can lead to a dilemma in a case of self-application does not mean it should be rejected.

According to what I'll call the *Conflicting-Ideals Reply*, the Self-Defeat Objection prevents us from honoring all of the epistemological ideals endorsed by the regulative method. That's because the method identifies competence defeaters and we should respect those defeaters; but when the defeaters target our belief in the method itself, we find ourselves in an awkward situation where we feel pressure to doubt our means for identifying defeaters. Being uncomfortable is just what we get for trying to live up to our ideals. Who can blame us for that? In the end, the Self-Defeat Objection doesn't provide a reason to doubt that the conflicting ideals in the method are correct or worth striving to follow inasmuch as we can.[9]

A fifth reply notes that our beliefs sometimes bring about good outcomes. In a famous case mentioned by William James (1896, 347), an alpine climber is in danger and must leap over an icy crevasse in order to survive.[10] The climber knows he will make the leap only if he believes he can do it. We can suppose the climber's total evidence should make him unsure whether he can make the leap. His reason to believe he can do it is instrumental—holding the belief at issue conduces to his survival. Similarly, our belief in the method could be supported by instrumental epistemic reasons. I call this the *Instrumental-Benefits Reply*.[11]

The basic idea is simple. We are supposing that the method gives us an undefeated full competence defeater for believing the method. But imagine we know or reasonably believe the following: if we are guided by the method, we will acquire some epistemological benefits in the future. Suppose that if we are guided by the method, our inquiry will be more likely to succeed. In particular, let's say the method helps us respond to disagreement and evidential complexity in ways that increase our chances of successful inquiry, and we

---

[9] For development of this somewhat "tragic" view about the lives of rational thinkers, see Christensen (2007b, 2010, and 2013).

[10] The example is often attributed to William James, but James's famous lecture introduces it in a quotation from James Fitzjames Stephen, a nineteenth-century British lawyer and judge.

[11] I am grateful to Samuel Kampa for helpful conversation here.

know that. Here we have an instrumental reason to be guided by the method even if we have epistemic reason to give up belief in the method.[12] The basic idea has some independent motivation, as many epistemologists embrace one or another form of epistemic consequentialism: the idea that what is epistemically "right" should be understood in terms of what conduces to the epistemically "good." Insofar as the method conduces to what's good, being guided by it is right.[13]

The Instrumental-Benefits Reply says that, faced with the Self-Defeat Objection, we won't think that believing the method is epistemically reasonable for us, but at the same time it's plausible that the method provides epistemic benefits if we're guided by it. Moreover, those benefits instrumentally justify our being guided by it.

But what is it to be guided by the method? The question arose briefly in Chapter 3, where I said that being guided by an epistemic principle means, to a first approximation, that we do what the principle advises because we hold or take for granted the principle, not because of accidental or irrelevant influences. But what is it to "hold or take for granted" a principle? I left the matter unsettled in part because there are many cognitive states that allow people to be guided by a principle, as the discussion of "intuitive expertise" and "epistemic pictures" underlined in Chapter 3. For present purposes, what matters is how we reach the instrumental benefits. Possibly, we get the benefits when or only when we believe the method is correct—in the same way the alpine climber will survive only if he believes he can make the leap. If so, the reply requires that we must believe the method is correct, meaning we'll recognize our belief is epistemically unreasonable and practically reasonable at the same time. That idea seems dubious. Some philosophers have argued that we can't believe in opposition to what we take our evidence to support and that we can't believe for reasons we recognize are merely instrumental.[14]

---

[12] In Chapter 11, I describe some epistemological benefits that inquirers following the method can gain. For now, I assume without argument that we reasonably believe or know that if we are guided by the method, then epistemological benefits are in the offing. Let me add that the Instrumental-Benefits Reply can be made to work only if we are not positioned to reasonably believe or know that we would secure *greater* epistemic benefits by accepting the Self-Defeat Objection and thereby rejecting the method.

[13] For discussion of epistemic consequentialism, see Berker (2013), Ahlstrom-Vij and Dunn (2014), and Singer (2018).

[14] For some discussion, see Williams (1970), Winters (1979), and Archer (2017). To begin to see what the problems with believing against our evidence might be, suppose I promise you a pot of gold if you believe leprechauns exist. You would like a pot of gold. But can you bring yourself to believe leprechauns exist if you possess the evidence that informed, intelligent people have concerning leprechauns? Sorry—I'm keeping the gold.

Alternatively, to gain the instrumental benefits, we may only need to "hold or take for granted" the method in some non-doxastic sense—for example, by taking the method as a premise in our theoretical and practical reasoning and not believing it at all. Either way, the Instrumental-Benefits Reply treats the method as a tool, not just for evaluating our controversial beliefs, but also for improving our prospects for successful inquiry. Being guided by the method is justified by its good epistemic consequences.[15]

A sixth and final reply begins with the observation that self-defeat threatens any sensible method or principle that's designed to manage competence defeaters or other sources of self-doubt. David Christensen notes a principle which he calls "Minimal Humility":

> If I have thought casually about [proposition] P for 10 minutes, and have decided it is correct, and then find out that many people, most of them smarter and more familiar with the relevant evidence and arguments than I, have thought long and hard about P, and have independently but unanimously decided that P is false, I should become less confident in P. (2009, 763)

Christensen notes that Minimal Humility will self-defeat in certain situations. Just imagine you accept that principle and then learn that most of the experts and authorities reject it. Of course, Minimal Humility is exceedingly plausible—if any principle is true, how could this one not be? Christensen rightly urges caution before we assume self-defeat is a good reason to reject a principle (2009, 763). On reflection, we'll find that any method which advises us to sometimes doubt our views in light of competence defeaters can recommend its own rejection (unless the method happens to exempt itself from self-defeat). But if self-defeat is, in principle, a problem for all of those methods, it becomes less clear why the objection poses a powerful challenge for the method in this book. I call that the *Partners-in-Guilt Reply*.

So far, I have described six potential replies to the Self-Defeat Objection: Partial-Defeat, Self-Exemption, Inevitable-Commitment, Conflicting-Ideals, Instrumental-Benefits, and Partners-in-Guilt. I have

---

[15] In footnote 3 earlier in this chapter, I sketched one objection that focuses on (alleged) bad social and political consequences of the method. Such objections may seem to be more forceful if we accept the Instrumental-Benefits Reply. But it's possible to distinguish between instrumental benefits that are epistemic and others that are social or political. If we accept the Instrumental-Benefits Reply, that distinction may be dialectically useful for fending off "bad consequences" objections.

nothing more to say about these replies, but I think each one is at least defensible in the sense that some informed, intelligent people will be inclined to judge it's a helpful reply. Each one is a contender and might take some of the bite out of the objection. But I won't here defend any of them. My strategy is different.

4. A Moorean Reply

In light of the Self-Defeat Objection and the six replies, we face a choice. Either a disjunction of six replies to the objection is correct or the objection itself is correct.[16] I contend that we can reasonably prefer the first option over the second, allowing us to set aside the Self-Defeat Objection.

This reply takes its cues from an anti-skeptical strategy articulated in the first half of the twentieth century by the British philosopher G. E. Moore. Here is how William Lycan (2001) reconstructs Moore's basic gambit.[17] Some of Moore's colleagues defended radical skeptical claims. They argued, for instance, that *time is unreal* using premises such as "temporal modes such as pastness and futurity are monadic properties of events" (2001, 38–40). Moore wasn't having it. He set out to defend a commonsensical picture of our knowledge of the world and ourselves. His anti-skeptical insight was to contrast his colleagues' premises with the ordinary, commonsense claims their arguments were alleged to undermine. Take Moore's claim (*i*) that he had breakfast before lunch on a particular day alongside the claim (*ii*) that "temporal modes are monadic properties of events." Comparisons like the one between (*i*) and (*ii*) are, as Lycan puts it, "nobrainers" (2001, 40). Moore insists he has knowledge of various claims—most famously, *that he has hands*—and these knowledge-claims are more plausible than the premises of skeptical arguments designed to threaten them.

One of Moore's key anti-skeptical ideas is that we should resolve conflicts among our beliefs by favoring the more plausible over the less plausible.[18]

---

[16] I don't mean to say there is a dilemma here. Perhaps neither option is correct, in which case the Self-Defeat Objection fails. That possibility can be ignored for now, as I am considering the idea that the objection, if correct, puts pressure on us to abandon the regulative method.

[17] John Greco (2002) offers a complementary reading of Moore and shows how Moore's anti-skeptical strategy follows in the footsteps of Thomas Reid, the great eighteenth-century Scottish commonsense philosopher. Moore was not always so commonsensical in his outlook. As Patrick Rysiew told me, a twenty-something G. E. Moore defended some skeptical, non-commonsense ideas about time: see Bosanquet, Hodgson, and Moore (1897).

[18] Kelly (2005b) critically examines a variety of norms involved in Moorean anti-skeptical reasoning.

That seems basically right to me. I have taken it for granted in this book that some of our beliefs are more plausible than others and that we can sometimes recognize as much.

Return to the Self-Defeat Objection. The objection succeeds only if it is more plausible for us to accept than the regulative method. Is it? In Moorean fashion, let me contrast (*i*) a disjunction of the six replies and (*ii*) the Self-Defeat Objection. If just one of the replies is successful, then the objection does not offer a good reason to reject the method. By my lights, (*i*) is more plausible than (*ii*). Here are three ways for us to see that.

First, we may believe that one reply is successful: the Partial-Defeat, Self-Exemption, Inevitable-Commitment, Conflicting-Ideals, Instrumental-Benefits, or Partners-in-Guilt Reply. Take your pick. If one disjunct is true, the whole disjunction is true. Second, even if we are unsure which reply to the Self-Defeat Objection succeeds, we may think one (or more) of the replies can be made to work in the sense that it looks more plausible than the objection. In other words, it may seem to us that the disjunction of replies has a better shot at success than the objection. Third, we can compare, side by side, the objection to the kind of reasoning I used to defend the method. The claims used to bolster the method are, in my view, intuitively resonant. I used simple cases to elicit judgments on the basis of which I fashioned principles to identify *prima facie* defeaters. If we were in agreement with each step, we have some sense of the method's overall plausibility. Even after we learn about the Self-Defeat Objection, that sense of plausibility may remain strong. But our sense of the objection's plausibility may pale in contrast, especially if the objection leaves us with the sense that something tricky is going on. Put in the balance, our assessment of the plausibility of the method and the objection may suggest to us that (*i*) has greater plausibility than (*ii*), even if we can't put our finger on a specific reply we think is right. That's because at least one of those replies could well be correct if the method is highly plausible and the objection is a dialectical conjuring trick.

The Self-Defeat Objection fails to convince me to give up the method. But I know the success or failure of this objection hangs on what's in our total evidence. You may think differently about the objection than I do, given that your background evidence and your judgments of plausibility may differ from mine. That is fine. But I've at least begun to suggest why the objection does not incline me to reject the method.[19]

---

[19] One further worry is that the replies to the Self-Defeat Objection may be controversial themselves. If we are guided by the method, shouldn't we reduce our confidence that the replies are good

5. Hypocrite!

I have suggested that some people may see things the other way around. Unlike me, they will judge that (*i*) the disjunction of six replies is less plausible than (*ii*) the Self-Defeat Objection.[20] What do I have to say to them?

Consider what could explain someone's judgment that (*i*) is less plausible than (*ii*). She may make that comparative judgment simply because her evidence supports it. Alternatively, she may fail to evaluate correctly the relative plausibility of (*i*) and (*ii*) given her evidence, because she overestimates the force of the Self-Defeat Objection (or underestimates the force of the disjunction of replies). I want to explore the second possibility. Insofar as someone has reason to doubt she correctly evaluates her evidence for judging the relative plausibility of (*i*) and (*ii*), she has reason to doubt her judgment that (*i*) is less plausible than (*ii*). And that reason will make her less confident in wielding the Self-Defeat Objection. As far as I can tell, there's a decent case to be made for doubt.

But let me first recount how I came to wonder about explanations for the self-defeat objector's thinking. While working on this book, I delivered academic talks of draft versions of Chapters 5 through 9. In Q&A sessions, audience members occasionally expressed worries about self-defeat for the principles I had put forward. Some questioners presented the Self-Defeat Objection as a "Gotcha!" Their words and behavior suggested their feelings. They felt their objection was a devastating takedown from which there

---

ones? If so, the Self-Defeat Objection appears to resurface at a new place in the dialectic, undermining the viability of the Moorean Reply.

Here's a brief reaction to this sensible worry. Insofar as we think the replies are controversial, we should apply the method to them. I doubt most of them are as controversial as prototypical controversial matters—capital punishment, materialism about human persons, the existence of free will, and the like. Leaving that aside, in the worst outcome, the method *fully* defeats belief in the replies. That would tank the Moorean Reply, for (*i*) the disjunction of replies would not be more plausible than (*ii*) the Self-Defeat Objection. But supposing the method only *partially* defeats belief in the replies, the Moorean Reply may still succeed. That's because the partial defeat of our belief in (*i*) is compatible with (*i*) having more plausibility for us than (*ii*).

There is more to say about these matters—including questions about whether the replies should all be regarded as controversial—but I leave them aside for now. (Thanks to Patrick Rysiew and Peter Seipel for discussion.)

[20] Alternatively, people may be unsure whether (*i*) is more plausible than (*ii*), and so they suspend judgment or remain doxastically open about the relative merits of (*i*) and (*ii*). If that is how things shake out, what follows? The objection, in order to succeed, must be more plausible than the method. If we judge there's a stalemate, it isn't entirely clear what follows. I suspect that being unsure whether (*i*) is more plausible than (*ii*) may nonetheless induce skeptical problems for inquirers wanting to be guided by the method, but I say nothing more about the issue here.

could be no feasible reply, no hope of recovery. Why didn't I see they had demolished my position?

The "Gotcha!" reaction is an expression of the alleged potency of the objection, but it's distinct from the content of the objection itself. Although I think I grasped the objection that audience members presented, I didn't feel the way they apparently did. While the objection puzzled and perplexed me (and still does), I never felt the method had been shown to be completely wrongheaded. And I came to suspect the "Gotcha!" implicitly expressed a judgment toward me. My objectors thought I was not abiding by my own method, that I was an epistemic hypocrite—or at least that I would be one if I didn't renounce the principles I had just defended.

So far, nobody has been candid enough to call me a hypocritical epistemologist to my face. Even so, I believe that's what some audience members were thinking. But how do I know? Here are two reasons.

First, on occasion I judge certain other philosophers and their imperfect efforts to abide by their principles. My own judgment gives me a hint about what they think of me and my efforts. Surely, some of them have repaid me the compliment.

Second, and more seriously, one influential idea from psychology is that human beings are on the lookout for cheaters. Psychologists have argued that people have a "cheater detection module" (Cosmides and Tooby 1992). This module is an ability or skill to search for information that's relevant for determining whether a certain person doesn't play by the rules, taking benefits from others without providing benefits in return. There is experimental evidence for the cheater detection module. In the classic study, participants were asked to solve reasoning problems. When the problems were framed as social exchanges and participants needed to determine whether someone else has cheated, the rates of success were greater than when participants were given identical problems not framed as social exchanges (Cosmides and Tooby 1992). The cheater detection module operates effortlessly as part of what psychologists call System 1, independently of our general cognitive resources (Van Lier, Revlin, and De Neys 2013). In other words, our cheater detection module generates fast, automatic "intuitive" judgments about whether someone has cheated, without our having to reflect consciously on our evidence.[21]

---

[21] For more on dual systems psychology, see Chapter 3, section 2.

The charge of cheating or hypocrisy is socially potent. When the charge is credible, it damages reputations and leads to ostracism. Our judgments about cheaters and hypocrites are complex and have been studied by psychologists and philosophers.[22] In one study, psychologists Jillian Jordan, Roseanna Sommers, Paul Bloom, and David Rand (2017) note a puzzle about moral hypocrisy. Condemning bad behavior is typically a good thing, given that a condemnation can sometimes discourage bad behavior. People who fail to condemn bad behavior thus neglect to do something good. But hypocrites condemn bad behavior while also doing it. Why are hypocrites judged more harshly than other people who act identically but do not condemn what they do? What's going on here? Jordan and her collaborators suggest that people disapprove of hypocrites more because hypocrites use their condemnation as a "false signal" about their own activity. "[H]ypocrites inspire moral outrage," say Jordan and coauthors, "because they dishonestly signal their moral goodness—that is, their condemnation of immoral behavior signals that they are morally upright, but they fail to act in accordance with these signals" (2017, 357). Like its moral cousin, epistemological hypocrisy may also be harshly condemned because it falsely signals intellectual uprightness and seriousness. The epistemic hypocrite talks the talk about an intellectual ideal but doesn't walk the walk.[23]

My suggestion is that our judgments about the Self-Defeat Objection could be influenced by processes that lead us to judgments about hypocrites and cheaters. The cheater detection module, or similar judgmental abilities, could drive someone's response to the objection. I am not saying that is actually the case. But it is possible, and here's why that matters. Suppose I adopt some epistemological method and tell you about it. You come to think I fail to follow my method consistently because I don't apply it to my belief in the method itself. You take yourself to perceive a kind of hypocritical misalignment between what I have said I should believe and what I actually believe. I haven't played by the rules I've endorsed, because I don't use my method to scrutinize all of my controversial beliefs, even though I present the method as a tool others should use to scrutinize their own beliefs. Furthermore, let's imagine you think I am worthy of criticism for my inconsistency. Your

---

[22] See, for example, McKinnon (1991), Aikin (2008), Alicke, Gordon, and Rose (2013), and Effron et al. (2018).

[23] The reader can now better explain why, in Chapter 3, I gave Descartes a bit of a ribbing for his epistemic hypocrisy. The Frenchman was falsely signaling his commitment to at least one of his method's rules: the ideal of reviewing everything carefully and completely so he could "be sure of leaving nothing out" (1985 [1637], 120; ii, 19).

thoughts about me could lead you to judge that the Self-Defeat Objection is more plausible than the disjunction of six replies to the objection noted earlier.

For all I've said, you may be completely right. But should you trust yourself? One explanation for your judgment about the objection is that it's based in part on an intuition produced by your cheater detection module. Your judgment may persist, even when you are confronted by counterevidence, because of the salience of your "cheater" intuition, which comes to you effortlessly and automatically. That intuition grabs your attention for reasons that have nothing to do with its correctness. Even if your total evidence actually indicates that the disjunction of six replies is more plausible than the Self-Defeat Objection, you may fail to correctly evaluate your evidence because the "cheater" intuition has its hooks in you. Think about it like this. We all know how it feels when we catch a cheater or hypocrite in the act. Sometimes, it feels pretty good, doesn't it? We feel confident in ourselves, in our rightness, and in the wrongness of the offender.[24] My point is that if you are inclined to judge that the objection succeeds, maybe that's because your cheater detection module has been triggered.

Gotcha! The story I have told is completely speculative, though the studies I've drawn upon are not. I don't know why anyone thinks the way they do about the Self-Defeat Objection. But the psychology of judging inconsistency in others may reveal something interesting about how people evaluate self-defeat objections. Philosophers discussing self-defeat objections typically focus on logical and evidential questions concerning abstract formulations of such objections. But the cognitive dynamics of thinking about self-defeat objections should not be overlooked. In the present case, that is especially important because we evaluate the Self-Defeat Objection by assessing the relative plausibility of competing claims, and our sense of plausibility depends on the operation of our minds. Learning how our minds work is, as I have argued in this book, a kind of evidence that should be accommodated as we deliberate.

There is more to say about self-defeat, cheater detection, and epistemic hypocrites. For now, I only mean to offer two recommendations for

---

[24] As Coran Stewart suggested to me, contemporary philosophical training and professional culture may encourage some practitioners to feel deeply moved by self-defeat objections. A philosopher on the warpath salivates at the chance to annihilate another philosopher's argument. Imagine demolishing your opponent's entire intellectual project just by uttering four little words: "Apply it to itself!" (How could that takedown not be followed by a battle cry and a spirited double fist-pump?)

self-defeat objectors. First, if they are confident their objection is more plausible than the disjunction of replies, they could sensibly ask themselves: Am I moved too much by the objection because I take myself to have caught a cheater or hypocrite? Maybe that is not implausible. Self-defeat objectors can decide for themselves. But notice that if one of the replies to the objection succeeds, the method doesn't lead to any intellectually troubling cheating or hypocrisy. Second, in an important sense, I am inviting proponents of the objection to use the regulative method themselves. They presumably think the method should be rejected, but my point here is that they shouldn't be so sure of their decision to reject it.

6. Conceding Defeat

As far as I can tell, the Self-Defeat Objection does not knock down the regulative method. The reason is that the disjunction of replies to the objection is more plausible than the objection. Not everyone will share my judgment about the relative plausibility of these claims, to be sure, and so I've tried to undermine the intuitive allure of the reverse judgment: that the objection is more plausible than the disjunction of replies. Everything here could change as debates about the objection and replies evolve. For the time being, I am not persuaded by the objection.

If the Self-Defeat Objection fails, what then? Do I think it's reasonable for me to believe the method is correct? For better or worse, not really.

Writing about the Self-Defeat Objection felt uncomfortably autobiographical. I took a step back from the details set out in earlier chapters and reflected on the method's correctness. I brooded over the imperfections of this thing and its author for a while. I prepared myself to fly the white flag. Please, don't shoot. I can't declare, as Wittgenstein wrote in his *Tractatus,* that "the problems have in essentials been finally solved" (2003 [1922], 5). But if I haven't solved the problems, what do I take myself to have accomplished?

The method in these pages is a first draft. It could be clarified and corrected, elaborated and emended. Even as I send to the press the final page proofs, some part of me wants to keep rethinking and rewriting. But in finishing this book, don't I tacitly endorse and stand behind it? That assumption would be hasty. In 1830, the great English writer William Hazlitt lay dying and wrote these words:

I do not recollect having ever repented giving a letter to the postman, or wishing to retrieve it after he had once deposited it in his bag. What I have once set my hand to, I take the consequences of, and have been always pretty much of the same humour in this respect. (1998 [1831], 205)

Unlike Hazlitt, I freely repent. The next draft would have been better.

I have tried to contribute something to a conversation about epistemological questions in hopes that continuing the discussion is worthwhile and may bear fruit one day. I know I have failed to conclusively answer my questions, and I'm not sure what I've offered up is correct. Such is the work of a doubtful epistemologist. But I hope others can succeed where I came up short—and I would like to hope I've added something small to ongoing conversation and debate. In the next chapter, I say more about these hopes and how a community of inquirers might investigate big, stubborn questions. For now, let me point out one source of my doubt about the method's correctness.

Boiled down to basics, the method is a hypothesis to explain data. But I can't seriously entertain the idea that my hypothesis is the best hypothesis out there, or even that I have gathered together all of the relevant data such a hypothesis should explain. The data I considered concerns inquiry into controversial questions, evidence about our abilities to inquire well, and so forth. The hypothesis on offer strikes me as better than alternatives. Take, for instance, the hypothesis that when we learn about undefeated competence defeaters, we should always, if possible, boost our confidence in our controversial views. Or consider the hypothesis that we should always ignore competence defeaters and never heed evidence indicating we are unfit to pass judgment about controversial matters. Those alternative hypotheses can't be correct. Instead, and roughly put, I have argued that *prima facie* competence defeaters can be defeated in certain conditions, but those conditions are met only when people have considerable intellectual skill and evidence for answering controversial questions. The method is the best hypothesis I have hit on so far, but it may be the best of a bad lot. After all, there is evidence I don't have. Counterfactual interlocutors could offer me objections I haven't thought of. I risk overextending my limited competence when evaluating some of the empirical ideas I used to inform the method. If better hypotheses are out there, I wouldn't in the least be surprised.

Unmistakably, that kind of doubt-inducing reasoning is part and parcel of the method. Do I have doubts about the reasoning? Not really. I distinguish between data and hypothesis. The data includes judgments about cases and observations about intellectual life. The hypothesis is my attempt to eluci-date and regiment the data. But some of the data are manifest commonsense. These are claims that everyone who is intelligent and informed should ac-cept. Even though I am doubtful about the hypothesis itself, I am confident about some of the data. And I can see how those bits of commonsense curb my confidence in my hypothesis. This is not "self-defeat." It is the recogni-tion that reasonable confidence about something like an epistemological theory is hard won—an insight built right into the method. For now, the best hypothesis I know of—a hypothesis I know is not correct in all of its details—will be my guide.

11
The End of Inquiry

But the effect of her being on those around her was incalculably dif-
fusive: for the growing good of the world is partly dependent on un-
historic acts; and that things are not so ill with you and me as they
might have been is half owing to the number who lived faithfully a
hidden life, and rest in unvisited tombs.
　　　　　　　　　　　　—George Eliot, *Middlemarch*, 1871–72

So that when asked to what end does my work proceed I can do no
more than answer in the most tentative and hesitant fashion imag-
inable, thus: Perhaps it is in the maintenance of some sort of single
plank in some sort of bridge.
　　　　　—David Jones, a Welsh artist and poet, in a statement from 1959

The teachers are everywhere. What is wanted is a learner.
　　　　　　　　　　—Wendell Berry, *What Are People For?*, 1990

Philosophers who promote skeptical, open-minded ideals routinely struggle
to persuade their audience. Human beings are believers by nature, not
skeptics. Convictions appeal to people more than nagging doubts; we prefer
confident affirmation to perplexity. As Ralph Waldo Emerson wrote, "We are
born believing. A man bears beliefs as a tree bears apples."[1] Perhaps people
following the regulative method described in this book will cut and trim their
controversial opinions down to size and become more doxastically open. But
the method is bound to seem unnatural to those who need it most.

Many people will feel the regulative method is unwelcome if it tells them
to quit having confident opinions about controversial matters. Who wants
such advice? Bertrand Russell said that "people hate skeptics far more than

---

[1] "Worship" in *The Conduct of Life* (1860).

they hate passionate advocates of opinions hostile to their own" (2004 [1928], 3). Confident beliefs can give us meaning and comfort. When our beliefs are challenged, we may feel anxious and insecure. Confident believers on opposing sides of controversial questions will often dislike one another, but whoever insists that nobody really knows what they're talking about is perhaps more upsetting still. Imagine that some philosophers barge uninvited into a party. The partygoers had been enjoying themselves in passionate debates about politics and religion, trading repartees, dismissing anybody who disagrees. The party-pooping philosophers announce that everyone should give up many of their cherished convictions. The partygoers are scandalized by the crashers. *Who do they think they are? How dare they spoil our fun!*

Let's suppose we are guided by the method and the upshot is that we stop reveling in our controversial opinions, adopting greater doxastic openness instead. What comes next? The method is revisionary. In order to bring our inquiry into step with the method, some of our important beliefs, our belief-forming habits, and our attitudes toward inquiry must change. But changing these things may be destabilizing. Recall the old Cartesian image that compares our beliefs to a building in need of repair. The metaphor allows for the possibility of unintended catastrophe—where everything in our intellectual life falls down, including walls and rooms we had meant to keep. Given the prospect of catastrophe, we may have reason to maintain stability and thus not follow the method. That is a possibility I examine in this final chapter.

Here is the basic issue. On the assumption that the method guides us to greater doxastic openness, what could make our inquiry successful and worth the effort? Prior to adopting the method, we likely assumed our investigation could give us reasonable belief and knowledge about controversial matters. But that assumption may appear implausible now. If we don't think we can get to the bottom of controversial questions, we may become intellectually lazy or downcast, unmotivated to bother trying. In what sense can our inquiry succeed if we can't know the right answers to controversial questions? What else could motivate our inquiry? What is the end of inquiry?

Exploring these questions will help us understand the practical challenges of implementing regulative theories, a topic broached in Chapter 3. In order to create epistemological theories that can guide inquirers, we must address questions that stretch beyond the normal boundaries of epistemology. We need to turn to issues about human motivation, behavior, and the social world. I am sensitive to the risks of trespassing on fields of inquiry that aren't my own, a problem explored in Chapter 8, and I will proceed as cautiously as I can.

I start off our discussion by distinguishing between two worries about the compatibility of the regulative method and inquiry (section 1). Then I address the worries by explaining, first, how an inquirer can think about his or her contribution to a successful inquiry (sections 2–3) and, second, how inquiry may be motivated by a special kind of mindset (sections 4–8). Finally, I conclude by revisiting some questions posed at the beginning of the book about the significance of epistemological inquiry (section 9).

1. Why Bother?

Inquiry is supposed to help us make up our minds. We want a clearer view and knowledge concerning the right answers to our questions. That is why we ask and try to answer controversial questions in the first place. Our efforts may be thwarted by our intellectual imperfections, however, and the regulative method promises to make us wiser inquirers. As I explained in Chapter 4, following the method can help us acquire a disposition or virtue of being sensitive or attentive to the marks of unreasonable beliefs, allowing us to draw a line between reasonable and unreasonable controversial beliefs.

But someone might think it's not just our imperfections that hamper inquiry—paradoxically, the method itself may threaten successful inquiry. Here's the idea, to a first approximation. Suppose our desire to gain reasonable beliefs or knowledge about the answers to controversial questions motivates our inquiry. Then the method draws our attention to *prima facie* competence defeaters: reasons to doubt we are well-equipped to gain reasonable views about these controversial questions. If the defeaters remain undefeated, we may become more doxastically open; that is, we may come to have significant doubts about what's reasonable for us to believe given our evidence. Our thinking may become more unsettled, neutral, or perhaps divided. Insofar as the method opens our minds, our inquiry won't settle our thinking. We will reach neither a reasonable belief nor knowledge of the right answers to our questions. Inquiry and the method appear to clash. One reaches for what the other takes away.

That initial pass at the problem is too simple. Following the method doesn't necessarily prevent us from gaining reasonable beliefs and knowledge. Even if we have undefeated defeaters for our controversial beliefs at one time, further inquiry may give us evidence that defeats the defeaters. In fact, the undefeated defeaters may prompt us to discover such evidence. In other words, the method can help us acquire reasonable views.

But undoubtedly, the method will sometimes lead us to pessimism about the value of further inquiry. To see why, suppose we have undefeated defeaters for many controversial beliefs. We should be doxastically open to some extent. The method helps us appreciate our inability to gain reasonable beliefs using our evidence. It also points us toward improvement, since defeating the competence defeaters is typically a matter of gaining new evidence and skills to evaluate evidence. Here is the catch: our time, energy, and intelligence are limited. Even if we set aside one month, one year, or a full decade, there's only so much we can figure out, only so many defeaters we can defeat. Many controversial beliefs remain unreasonable and off-limits for us.

Let's focus on the "worst case" scenario: we know or reasonably believe that we won't defeat the competence defeaters no matter how much we try. Consider two ways that might go. First, we may know that even if we study some controversial question in economics, history, or metaphysics for forty hours each week for the next five or ten years, we will still have the competence defeaters. In a less disappointing scenario, we know we won't defeat the competence defeaters in light of what we will actually do. Maybe we know that, possibly, if we exerted considerable effort for five or ten years, using our weekends and evenings to study up, we might defeat the defeaters. But let's say we know we will not burn the midnight oil.[2] We will be stuck with the defeaters.

In dispiriting scenarios like those, we reasonably anticipate that *even after further inquiry* we will remain doxastically open. Let's assume the disappointing scenarios are a fairly common condition when we're guided by the method, given our self-knowledge about our track record in defeating competence defeaters. For many controversial questions, we expect more inquiry won't defeat the defeaters that prevent us from holding reasonable opinions.

An apparent conflict between our inquiry and the method has come to the surface. We aim to obtain reasonable beliefs or knowledge about controversial questions, but the method frustrates our aims. We should ask

---

[2] Thus, we heed the warning of the nineteenth-century Scottish scholar and poet, John Stuart Blackie: "Blinking eyes, and bad digestion, / Sleepless nights and brain-congestion, / That's the fruit of midnight oil!"

ourselves: What is the point of more inquiry on these controversial questions? Will we venture something only to gain nothing? In short, why bother?

The apparent conflict between the method and inquiry involves two distinct worries. To draw each one out, I distinguish between two ways to evaluate or assess an inquiry. Let's call inquiry into a question *successful* if someone gets evidence that enables her to reasonably believe or know the answer.[3] Perhaps you want to know whether your copy of the Oscar Peterson Trio's classic 1963 album *Night Train* is on your shelf. You look at the shelf carefully and spot the album. Your inquiry is successful because your perceptual evidence positions you to know that the album is on the shelf. But your inquiry could have been unsuccessful: if you had hurriedly scanned a short section of the shelf but failed to learn one way or the other whether *Night Train* is there, you wouldn't be in a position to reasonably believe or know the answer to your question.

A second way to evaluate an inquiry focuses on our motivations or reasons for pursuing it. Let's call inquiry into a question *well-motivated* when someone has appropriate reasons to use evidence to answer it. I use "reasons" here in an inclusive sense to include a desire to know the answer, curiosity, and other motives that incentivize figuring out the answer. You are motivated to find your *Night Train* album, for example, because you want to hear the soulful sounds of Oscar Peterson on piano, Ray Brown on bass, and Ed Thigpen at the drums. Anyone reading this book is probably motivated, by a plethora of reasons, to investigate questions about morality, politics, religion, science, technology, history, and so forth.

Of course, not every question is worth our time and effort. Did Cleopatra bite her fingernails? Was the first human being to walk across the Bering land bridge between Siberia and Alaska right-handed? Can you eat twenty hotdogs in under an hour? Between 1984 and 2004, how many pixelated ducks were shot by players of the video game *Duck Hunt* for the Nintendo Entertainment System? Is the number of words printed in this book even?

I assume that all of us lack reason to investigate many questions (though perhaps the questions just noted piqued your interest). Here are three general explanations for why trying to answer some questions is not worthwhile. Knowing the answer to a question may be insignificant to us. Or sometimes

---

[3] If reasonable belief and knowledge come in degrees, there are degrees of successful inquiry. I ignore that issue here.

knowing its answer is harmful to us.[4] Other times we can't know the answer, or at least knowing it would require a greater investment than we are willing to make. For some questions, we will judge that coming to know the answers will be pointless, harmful, or impossible for all intents and purposes. That means, in general, our inquiry into a question can be unmotivated, poorly motivated, or well-motivated. The latter two kinds of assessment are normative and admit of degrees.

Notice why the difference between successful and well-motivated inquiry is important for understanding the worry about the regulative method. When we deliberate over controversial questions and also recognize that our competence defeaters won't be defeated by further inquiry, an uncomfortable question arises: *Why bother?* In light of the difference between successful and well-motivated inquiry, the question poses a pair of challenges. The first involves explaining how our inquiry could possibly be successful, given our expectation that we won't gain reasonable beliefs or knowledge concerning the right answers. The second challenge involves explaining how our inquiry could be well-motivated, in cases where we reasonably expect that inquiry won't deliver reasonable beliefs or knowledge.[5]

The method will be less attractive if it undermines successful and well-motivated inquiry in a wide range of situations. But does it? Let me consider each objection in turn.

2. Superpersonal Inquiry

The first "Why bother?" objection says that the regulative method prevents us from gaining reasonable beliefs and knowledge. Let me acknowledge what's right about the objection. If we cannot hope to succeed in a task, we should give it up. "Where there is no hope," Samuel Johnson wrote, "there can be no endeavour."[6] But we need not abandon all hope when it comes to inquiry into controversial questions.

---

[4] Recall the question about whether you can eat twenty hotdogs in under an hour. Suppose that knowing the answer requires you to step up to the plate and give it your best attempt, consuming vast quantities of emulsified meat, mechanically separated poultry, sodium phosphates, maltodextrin, and more. Then I presume you'll be harmed by knowing the answer.

[5] These two challenges may be related. For example, if we know an inquiry must be unsuccessful, that knowledge can make our inquiry unmotivated.

[6] *The Rambler*, No. 110, 6 April 1751. In the same vein, C. S. Peirce noted: "We are in the condition of a man in a life and death struggle; if he have not sufficient strength, it is wholly indifferent to him

Consider an example to illustrate what I have in mind. In 1921, Dr. Montrose T. Burrows, a pathologist and surgeon, addressed a meeting of the American Association for Cancer Research in Cleveland, Ohio. Burrows told his colleagues: "What is known about cancer today, aside from clinical considerations, is little more than was known many years ago. This is appalling but true" (1921, 132). The scandal of ignorance was the springboard for Burrows's lecture. He proceeded to identify several poorly understood questions about cells, their structures and properties, and noted that one question about tumors "the future alone can answer" (1921, 138). Burrows and his colleagues may have thought they wouldn't find the correct answers to their questions. They may have believed their questions weren't necessarily the *right* questions—the ones that would lead to theoretical insights as well as effective therapies.[7] At the same time, the researchers may also have been confident that their striving to understand cancer was worthwhile.

Can we reconcile these thoughts? The cancer researchers could have expected that their own inquiry wouldn't give them reasonable beliefs or knowledge about answers to their central questions and, simultaneously, they could have believed that investigating those questions was valuable. But if they anticipated their own failure, why would they keep trying?

One commonplace answer is that inquirers can also believe they contribute to what I call a *superpersonal inquiry*. Even when they can't hope to attain reasonable beliefs or knowledge for themselves, they can hope that others will reach the mark. Superpersonal inquiry involves a group of people who are separated from each other in time, all making contributions that help answer some question using evidence. Their contributions accumulate over time. At the end of the process, some inquirers may be positioned to gain reasonable beliefs or knowledge.

The idea of superpersonal inquiry is a bit intangible, but we can picture it in different ways. The members of a bucket brigade try to extinguish a fire. They pass buckets of water down the line, until finally the water reaches the blaze and, hopefully, puts it out. Or here's another analogy, first expressed by the twelfth-century philosopher and statesman John of Salisbury (1115/20–1180) in his *Metalogicon*:

how he acts, so that the only assumption upon which he can act rationally is the hope of success" (1934, 222; 5.357).

[7] Burrows and his contemporaries used histology—the study of cells using a microscope—to understand cancer. More recent researchers have thought about cancer in terms of histology and genomics—how DNA and genes operate inside a cell.

[O]ur age enjoys the benefit of the age preceding, and often knows more than it, not indeed because our intelligence outstrips theirs, but because we depend on the strength of others and on the abundant learning of our ancestors. Bernard of Chartes [a twelfth-century French philosopher] used to compare us to (puny) dwarfs perched on the shoulders of giants. He pointed out that we see more and farther than our predecessors, not because we have keener vision or greater height, but because we are lifted up and borne aloft on their gigantic stature. (1958 [1159], 167; Book III, Chapter 4)

Superpersonal inquiry may be like a dutiful bucket brigade or a crew of dwarfs in matching uniforms climbing up on giants' shoulders to scope things out. Either way, such an inquiry involves the cumulative effort of multiple inquirers. It aims to generate reasonable belief or knowledge about the answer to a question. It can be successful, too, though possibly only some inquirers will see the rewards.

My basic proposal is this. Even if we expect that we won't ourselves gain reasonable beliefs or knowledge about controversial questions, we can *reasonably hope* for successful inquiry when we have reason to believe we contribute to a superpersonal inquiry that could succeed eventually. Emboldened by our hope, we can strive to investigate controversial questions. We can try to identify the best extant arguments and the strongest objections to those arguments; to understand what would be a good test of a hypothesis; to discuss controversial questions in open debate and dialogue; to diagnose sources of disagreement and agreement among investigators; to create research tools that organize relevant evidence; to understand how the contributions of past inquirers have brought us to this point; and so on. Even if we can safely bet against our personally coming to know the answers, we can sometimes act, and reasonably so, on the assumption that our inquiry may be successful in the end.

3. Risky Business

We can hope for successful inquiry when we have reason to believe we are contributing to a superpersonal inquiry with some good enough chance of success. But what is it to contribute to a superpersonal inquiry? And what reasons do we have to believe it could succeed? I venture into these issues by recounting a story.

In late 1943, the Allied forces launched an offensive against the German army in Italy after a successful campaign against the Nazis in northern Africa. The surge of Allied forces required materiel and supplies, and a crucial seaport for their campaign was at Bari, a port city on the Adriatic. In December, Bari harbor was bustling. Allied cargo arrived by ship and was unloaded around the clock. Jetties were stacked with supplies awaiting transport to the advancing British Eighth Army. One American vessel, the S.S. *John Harvey*, arrived at Bari carrying a secret cargo that would soon play a role in one of the greatest naval catastrophes of the war.

On the night of December 2, the harbor was aglow with lights as dockworkers unloaded supplies. Overhead, more than 100 German bombers descended. Falling bombs hit ships loaded with ammunition; massive explosions shattered windows up to seven miles away. One bomb struck a petrol pipeline on the docks and a large quantity of fuel gushed out into the water. Before long, the harbor was blanketed with burning fuel, causing ships unscathed by German bombs to catch fire. Explosions sprayed shrapnel and lifted boats out of the water. Giant mushrooms of smoke and fireballs lit up the night. One witness compared the large colored explosions to a "huge Roman candle, surpassingly brilliant and beautiful" (Southern 2002, 55). The harbor was a fiery pandemonium. Historians have estimated that one thousand military personnel and at least as many civilians died in the attack on Bari—nearly the number of deaths in the Japanese attack on Pearl Harbor two years earlier. Twenty-eight ships and 31,000 tons of cargo were lost. One of the ill-fated ships was the S.S. *John Harvey*.

The *John Harvey* was loaded with 2,000 mustard gas bombs.[8] Although the Geneva Protocol of 1925 had banned the "first use" of chemical weapons, the Americans had shipped the mustard bombs to strike back if the Germans attacked with chemicals. As the *John Harvey* exploded and sunk, some conventional weapons aboard detonated and disseminated the mustard gas, which then mixed with oil and petrol in the water, providing a solvent for the gas. Hundreds of sailors jumped from their ships into this poisonous water. Survivors, screaming for help, clung to life-rafts and flotsam until they were

---

[8] The term "mustard gas" is doubly misleading. Mustard gas bears no relation to mustard, either the plant or the condiment. Mustard gas is not even a vaporized gas. It is more dense than air and, at normal temperatures, remains a viscous liquid. In war, mustard gas is typically distributed in an aerosol and so a mustard bomb contains a mist of liquid droplets.

plucked from the harbor by rescuers. Survivors were covered in what one witness described as "a thick, greasy liquid which was black as pitch [tar] and gave off a foul stench" (Southern 2002, 50).

All aboard the *John Harvey* perished, and the few people in Bari who knew of the deadly cargo didn't remember it. At first, doctors and nurses in military hospitals didn't realize that some survivors had been exposed to the gas. They focused medical attention on patients who apparently had the most critical injuries, such as severe blast wounds and burns from fire. Other survivors were served hot tea, wrapped in blankets, and left for up to twenty-four hours wearing their sulfur-soaked clothing. One medical commentator later called this "a sure recipe" for systemic mustard intoxication (Hirsch 2006, 1519). Soon, survivors began to present painful blisters, burns, and conjunctivitis. Some had trouble breathing and later developed pneumonia; some went temporarily blind. One nurse reported how her patients began tearing off their clothes and bandages; their blisters were "as big as balloons and heavy with fluid" (Southern 2002, 52). Now the medical staff suspected there had been a chemical attack, but they were unable to help the victims. One nurse recounted her patients in grave distress: "Their eyes asked us questions we could not answer" (Southern 2002, 53).

An American chemical-warfare expert and medical doctor, Lieutenant Colonel Stewart F. Alexander, was flown in to investigate, and he found telltale signs of a mustard agent. Alexander observed in his report about the incident that three or four days after the attack, survivors' white blood cell counts began to drop precipitously (1947, 9). He recognized the mustard gas interfered with the body's production of white blood cells. Pathologists in Bari collected tissue samples during autopsies and sent them to England for analysis; the samples showed low levels of lymphocytes, a type of white blood cell in the immune system that resists infections.

In effect, the victims at Bari had received a horrifying dose of what we now call chemotherapy. At first, Alexander didn't realize what had happened exactly, but he wrote his report and soon it circulated among cancer researchers in the United States. One researcher, Dr. Cornelius P. Rhoads, the scientific director of Memorial Hospital and Sloan–Kettering Cancer Center in New York City, came across an unpublished version of the report. In a lecture delivered in 1946, Rhoads noted the importance of the Bari tragedy for cancer research and remarked that Alexander had written a "classic report" (1946, 300). Up to that time, surgery and radiation therapy had been the customary cancer treatments. Rhoads said that Alexander's clinical observations at Bari "illustrate as adequately as any example can, the effects of the mustard compounds on blood formation" (1946, 306). The Bari disaster was of great consequence because it pointed cancer researchers toward potential treatments for lymphomas (blood cancers that develop from a type of white blood cell) and leukemias (cancers that originate in the bone marrow and produce high numbers of abnormal white blood cells).

Rhoads and his colleagues were inspired by Alexander's report, as well as newly declassified research on mustard agents secretly conducted at the Yale School of Medicine during the war years. The researchers searched for substances that could attack cancer and one discovery was mustine, a nitrogen-based mustard and the first anticancer chemotherapy drug. In his lecture, Rhoads expressed his hope that "[t]he lives and suffering saved from the knowledge developed through chemical warfare may be significant" (1946, 309).[9]

Let me make a long story short. A naval tragedy that involved mustard gas created evidence that helped medical researchers discover a new type of cancer treatment. Their question was: "How can we treat cancer?" Their answer was mustine and, subsequently, a new class of anticancer chemotherapy drugs. The horrendous experiment in Bari helped researchers fit the puzzle pieces together and find new ones. Superpersonal inquiry can be grisly.

Recall that I characterized superpersonal inquiry as involving a group of people who are separated from each other in time, who make contributions to answer some question using evidence. Who contributed in the case at hand? Most obviously, we must mention Lieutenant Colonel Stewart Alexander and the cancer researchers, such as Cornelius Rhoads, who capitalized on Alexander's observations. But perhaps other contributors should be recognized, too. Consider the American military planners who chose to send mustard bombs to Italy on the *John Harvey*. Then there are the Luftwaffe commanders who ordered the attack and the air crews who carried their payloads to Bari. Should they be included? And what about the sailors and merchant marines who were afflicted by the mustard agent, becoming unwitting guinea pigs in a nightmarish medical experiment? And might we also mention the chemists who originally synthesized mustard gas and

---

[9] The brief account of the Bari harbor tragedy and its implications for medical research is based on details from Rhoads (1946), Alexander (1947), Saunders (1967), Infield (1971), Southern (2002), Hirsch (2006), and Freemantle (2015, chapter 14).

discovered how to produce it in mass quantities for warfare? Arguably, all of these contributions were part of what led researchers to mustine.

In a superpersonal inquiry, the lines of influence can get messy. One lesson may be that contributions to a superpersonal inquiry come in degrees— perhaps Alexander and Rhoads added more than (or less than) the chemists who synthesized mustard gas. We could argue about who played a greater role here. Another lesson may be that we should exclude some particular causal factors as genuine contributions. Perhaps the American military planners who shipped mustard gas and the German air crews who dropped bombs weren't contributing to inquiry in any meaningful sense. But I can't see why not. While it's obviously true that none of these people *believed* they were involved in the discovery of mustine, why does that matter? Alexander apparently did not believe he was involved in a superpersonal inquiry about cancer treatment when he noted the drop in survivors' white blood cells. Can't some people who add to a superpersonal inquiry neither know what they do nor intend to do it?

The Bari tragedy suggests how a wide range of actors can add to super-personal inquiry. I don't know of a fully general account of superpersonal inquiry that will help us think about the nature of such inquiry.[10] For pre-sent purposes, I just mean to stipulate that whoever contributes to someone's knowing or reasonably believing the answer to a question contributes to a superpersonal inquiry. On that assumption, the bomber crews, the factory workers, and the chemists who discovered mustard gas contributed to cancer research. But isn't that bizarre? Not really. Most contributors could never have sensibly expected they were adding in some way to knowledge about cancer treatment, and that point fits with the following observation: some actions we perform *might* contribute to a superpersonal inquiry, even though there is never any reason for us to believe that they will. But for a certain class of actions—including the activities that advance research, debate, and education—it can sometimes be reasonable for us to hope we will contribute. Cancer researchers may, for example, reasonably hope to push their field a little closer to effective treatments.[11]

---

[10] Thanks to Marcello Fiocco and Daniel Greco for discussion here.

[11] I won't give an account of when an inquirer's hope to contribute to a superpersonal inquiry is reasonable, but let me be clear about what I am not saying here. I don't claim we can justify our opinions about a controversial question when we can reasonably hope that a superpersonal inquiry to which we contribute will succeed. Nor do I say that reasonably hoping for such success is a good reason to remain steadfast in the face of controversy. If we reasonably hope to contribute, we can chip away at a controversial question, but that does not necessarily mean it is (epistemically) reasonable

Let me record one further observation about superpersonal inquiry. If we could know the full story of many complex superpersonal inquiries, we'd be flabbergasted. When we think about investigation and discovery, we like unambiguous stories about Great Thinkers who roll up their sleeves, reach their colossal arms up to the heavens, and pull down profound truths from the thundering clouds. But that is a cartoon. How things get figured out is almost always more mundane—and sometimes much weirder. Along the way to successful inquiry there are accidents, surprises, and apparent failures. These twists and turns are sometimes a genuine part of the inquiry. That's how I view the attack on Bari, at any rate.[12]

Here is a further issue. The more we restrict the scope of who contributes to superpersonal inquiry, the less likely we will get to take part. If we think adding meaningfully to some superpersonal effort is hard, it will be difficult to see ourselves as doing something useful. And yet we may believe that it isn't too hard to contribute something. Even researchers who don't stand on the "right side of history" can add to a superpersonal inquiry. The fact is, some sincere and diligent inquirers will only contribute evidence that is misleading or irrelevant; their arguments will be shown to be fallacious; the viewpoints they defend will be shown to be meaningless, neither true nor false. But their work and energy may nonetheless animate a community of inquiry, making progress a possibility down the line. That is perhaps our main role in investigations of controversial questions—not to devise bright ideas that clear everything up, but to keep inquiry alive until others come along and make the real breakthroughs.[13]

for us to believe anything at all about the answer to the question. In fact, if we are guided by the regulative method, confident opinion may be off-limits for us.

[12] Consider another example where an accident figures into a superpersonal inquiry. After the Second World War, Boris Vannikov worked as head of the First Main Directorate of the Council of People's Commissars of the USSR. Vannikov worked under Stalin's secret police chief, overseeing research on the Soviets' atomic bomb. Vannikov inadvertently helped Soviet scientists develop a convincing criticality test for their bomb (basically, a test to determine when the nuclear chain reaction is self-sustaining). The historian Richard Rhodes writes: "To test a core for criticality, physicists build a shell around it with material that reflects neutrons, measuring the increasing neutron multiplication from fission as they go. Any light-element material will do for a reflector—cubes of beryllium, blocks of paraffin, even body fat" (1995, 352). One physicist recalled observing Vannikov on a day when the core was set up in a lab: "[Vannikov] came close and began to read the gauges. He was a large man, very fat. He went back and forth and read the gauges. . . . So during this episode we understood: the bomb would definitely work" (1995, 352). This is a superpersonal inquiry and Vannikov was involved. The question was "Is this bomb critical?", and Vannikov's body provided the answer by reflecting neutrons at the right moments. (Thanks to Alex Wellerstein for clarifying some of the details of this example.)

[13] Sometimes inquirers are less than sincere in their efforts. There are frauds, pettifoggers, and obstructionists. Some scientists, for instance, have sought to undermine the consensus concerning the link between smoking and cancer, often at the behest of cigarette manufacturers (Diethelm and

Intellectual ventures tend to be risky. Out of the happenstance and confusion of our own inquiry into difficult questions, we hope something good
will come. But it isn't always easy to hold out hope for success. Are we part
of superpersonal inquiries that will succeed? Or are we involved in projects
that will become yesteryear's fashions and fads? If we consider the history of
some fields—philosophy being a prime example—we see how styles change
over time, and so perhaps we can safely predict that current lines of inquiry
will fade away. On this score, the British philosopher Mary Midgley offers a
caution. She says philosophers engaged in "winning arguments"

> build up a set of games out of simple oppositions and elaborate them until,
> in the end, nobody else can see what they are talking about. All this can go
> on until somebody from outside the circle finally explodes it by moving the
> conversation on to a quite different topic, after which the games are for-
> gotten. Hobbes did this in the 1640s. Moore and Russell did it in the 1890s.
> (2013)[14]

If we expect future inquirers will burn their bridges to the past, ignoring the
discussions we have invested in, we can have no reason to hope for success.

But even if we expect future inquirers will keep going, we may doubt
whether success is in store for them. Will anyone ever be in a better position
than we are right now? It can be hard to tell. And then our uncomfortable
question comes up again: *Why bother?* If we doubt whether future inquirers
will ever be in a position to gain reasonable beliefs or knowledge *because of
our small contribution*, this can spoil our hope for success. We may sense the
inevitability of failure—either our failure to contribute anything useful or future inquirers' failure to finish the job well. If we come to significantly doubt
the possibility of successful superpersonal inquiry, the idea of passing along
buckets of water may look unattractive to us.

McKenn 2009; Oreskes and Conway 2010). These people are mistaken, but could they possibly "contribute" to some inquiry? Yes—if their activities pave the way for deeper and more secure knowledge.
That said, by merely contributing in the particular way they do, they may not necessarily deserve
credit or praise for what they have done. Moreover, whatever good they add to inquiry may not always outweigh the bad effects their efforts may have. (Thanks to Shane Wilkins for discussion.)

[14] David Zeaman, a twentieth-century psychologist, noted: "One of the differences between the
natural and the social sciences is that in the natural sciences, each succeeding generation stands on
the shoulders of those that have gone before, while in the social sciences, each generation steps in the
faces of its predecessors" (1959, 167). For a defense of the idea that there's progress in philosophy, see
Stoljar (2017).

Supposing we can reasonably hope for a successful superpersonal inquiry, here is a further concern: What is in it for us? Imagine we are part of a bucket brigade, passing along buckets of water to put out a house fire. But it isn't our house burning down—nothing bad happens to us if we use our time and energy for other projects. *So why bother?* Well, I don't think that adding to a superpersonal inquiry will only be attractive for self-sacrificing intellectual do-gooders. The realistic view is that we have benefited richly from the efforts of past inquirers. Many questions that were once controversial are now settled, or are on their way to being settled, because earlier inquirers stood their ground. To drop our buckets now means gaining from the past while neglecting the future. Speaking for myself, I don't want to be a freeloader.[15]

That said, I am aware that the worry about self-interest may still appeal to some people. I will address it now. Investigating controversial questions can give us valuable things, even if it doesn't give us reasonable beliefs or knowledge.

4. Motivating Open Inquiry

Recall that the "Why bother?" question raises two objections. The first asks how our inquiry could be successful when we expect we won't figure out the answers to controversial questions. In reply, I argued that we can hope for successful inquiry at least sometimes when we have reason to believe we contribute to a superpersonal inquiry that could succeed. The reply shifts our attention toward reasons to hope that future inquirers will succeed in our stead. But we may be left wondering: What do *we* get out of our inquiry? That worry is closely related to the second objection, which asks how our inquiry could be well-motivated given that we expect we ourselves will not figure out the answers to controversial questions. Doesn't the method make us intellectually lazy, downcast, or otherwise not inclined to keep trying?

This is an important type of challenge. It isn't obvious to me how we can evaluate it without looking carefully at human psychology and behavior. How is being guided by the method and being doxastically open connected to our actual motives to investigate? Answering requires empirical investigation I can't undertake. That isn't to say I will ignore the objection, however. To begin to explore these issues, I will consider one ambitious version of the

---

[15] I am grateful to Andrew Rotondo for helpful discussion of these issues.

objection: that an *inevitable outcome* of following the method and becoming doxastically open is intellectual laziness or despondency. More modest versions of the objection say that intellectual laziness is a *likely outcome* given certain other conditions, such as facts about an inquirer's personality. But I think articulating those modest challenges, and showing they are plausible, will require concerted engagement with the relevant empirical facts, whatever they turn out to be. We don't know how the method and doxastic openness influence motives to inquire. My purpose here is only to argue that the method does not fail because it *necessarily* "demotivates" inquiry.[16]

My strategy will be to argue that the following claims are consistent: (*i*) we can be guided by the regulative method; (*ii*) we can expect we won't attain reasonable beliefs or knowledge about the answers to some controversial questions; and (*iii*) we can still engage in well-motivated inquiry about those questions. In other words, our being guided by the method and becoming doxastically open is compatible with our sincerely investigating controversial questions. Some inquirers manifest doggedness to figure things out as well as pessimism that they will ever do so. They are exemplars of what I call *open inquiry*: the kind of inquiry pursued by people who expect to remain unsettled about what to think about the issues they investigate. Their lives suggest that the second objection is not correct as a general claim about how the method influences human motivation. I'll try to describe one type of open inquirer.

Envision someone who is deliberating about a controversial question. She is unable to see her way through to reasonably adopting one view over another, but she inquires still. Her persistence is partly explained by the fact that she has a particular mindset. She can tolerate significant intellectual conflict. In order to learn more, she puts herself intentionally in situations where she's confronted with her ignorance about her question. She can deliberate independently, without being swayed by other people's opinions unduly. She sometimes feels a sense of wonder about her question. Her mindset is a collection of intellectual skills and cognitive dispositions that help explain why she's motivated to keep searching. I elaborate these elements of this open inquirer's mindset in the following four sections.[17]

If you don't see yourself in the quick sketch of the mindset, you are not alone. A lot of the time, we don't tolerate intellectual conflict too well. We

---

[16] Thanks to Klaas Kraay for discussion.

[17] I don't deny there are other factors that can motivate open inquiry, including social ones. For example, being a part of a community that encourages open inquiry among its members can be a powerful motivation. Here I focus on the qualities of individuals, not groups.

are unwilling to confront our deep ignorance. We uncritically follow along with the opinions of others. And since we think we've figured things out already, we lack any sense of wonder about controversial questions. But suppose the mindset of the inquirer I just described strikes us as valuable. If we had it, we could see ourselves more clearly and know our own limits better. Suppose, furthermore, being guided by the method could be a *means* to grow in that mindset. In other words, the mindset could be one outcome of using the method to wrestle with controversial questions. Then it's possible we can attain something valuable—this mindset—by following the method. The prospect of gaining the mindset could then motivate our inquiry into controversial questions.

I want to describe the mindset by offering some snapshots of people who have it, as well as some ideas that reveal the mindset in greater relief. All of this will help me address the second "Why bother?" objection, which asserted that if we expect we won't figure out controversial questions, we won't be well-motivated to keep trying. The method might help us become the sort of inquirers who will indeed bother.[18]

5. Tolerating Conflict

Some objects can tolerate physical stress and others can't. Try to bend a stick of chalk and it crumbles in your fingers. But if you bend a maple tree sapling, it flexes and then whips back into shape. Likewise, our minds can manifest different degrees of tolerance for intellectual conflict. For example, when there's discord in our own thinking, perhaps we suppress our doubts and second thoughts. Or when we are confronted by social conflicts, we may listen carefully to all sides and try to develop a synoptic perspective on issues.

"[T]he test of a first-rate intelligence," wrote F. Scott Fitzgerald, "is the ability to hold two opposed ideas in the mind at the same time, and still retain the ability to function" (1936, 41). I call this *tolerance for self-conflict*. People can allow two (or more) conflicting elements into their thinking. These elements could be incongruent pieces of evidence, opposing hypotheses to

---

[18] I won't claim any of this is actually correct. I argue that it is possible the open inquirer's mindset motivates her inquiry and that following the method can produce the mindset in us. To more fully understand the psychological and practical implications of using the method, we need a concerted multidisciplinary effort. That is part of the broad project of regulative epistemology described in Chapter 1.

explain the evidence, or divergent attitudes. To be tolerant of self-conflict means living with dissonance.

Here's how this could work. Somebody asks herself whether there are good arguments for the morality of capital punishment or for God's existence or for some other controversial matter. She may be simultaneously pulled toward arguments from different sides. She may be unable to weigh the competing arguments; she may have significant doubts about her competence to evaluate her total evidence. But if she can tolerate self-conflict to a great enough degree, she can investigate her question while being mindful of the rival arguments.

Unfortunately, strong psychological forces work against this kind of tolerance. People seek to resolve their mental dissonance into a more comfortable state. Psychologists study what they call "need for closure," a trait related to our motivations for judgment and information processing (Webster and Kruglanski 1994). A person who has a powerful need for closure on some subject will display decisiveness, closed-mindedness, and discomfort with ambiguity. This person will have low tolerance for intellectual self-conflict.

Tolerance for self-conflict has a social analogue: our ability to tolerate beliefs and arguments that are at odds with our own. I call this *tolerance for social conflict*. People manifesting it attend carefully to other people's ideas and arguments. They listen conscientiously to all sides of an issue, rather than automatically tune out particular voices. They will approach foreign ideas and arguments with respect and seriousness. Andrew Abbott, a sociologist, describes this sort of tolerance in action:

> An eclectic is always losing arguments. One lacks the closed-mindedness necessary to treat others' positions with the contempt they so easily display for one's own. Of course in interaction I fake this contempt as well as the next academic. But I usually rush off to bone up on what I have just been denying. And I have never managed that happy disregard of whole areas of intellectual life—mathematics, say, or history—that so simplifies the lives of some of my colleagues. (2001, x)

Is the ability to tolerate intellectual conflict, either with ourselves or others, valuable? I think so. Insofar as we care about leading a good intellectual life, we have reason to favor tolerance over intolerance. Imagine you are offered a pill to make yourself more tolerant of intellectual conflict. Whatever reasons you have for refusing the pill seem motivated exclusively by your desire for convenience or personal comfort. Maybe you feel the "happy disregard" of ignoring complexities and complications. Or maybe you enjoy the feeling of shutting down people who disagree with you. Surely those motivations to refuse the pill don't reveal that tolerance for conflict is not a valuable way to promote good inquiry.

Moreover, each kind of tolerance can be valuable for securing other benefits. Here are two. First, tolerance for social conflict can contribute to intercultural competence: the ability to display sensitivity to cultural differences. Tolerance for social conflict can help us move a little beyond our cultural presuppositions, letting us better discern how differences and similarities between ourselves and others are either deep or superficial. This kind of tolerance can also keep us mindful of the fact that other people see issues quite differently than we do.[19]

Second, both kinds of tolerance can bring in their wake epistemological benefits. One is that tolerating conflict will tend to sharpen our sensitivity to the available evidence. That's because people who can tolerate conflict tend to pay attention to a wider array of evidence than those who can't tolerate it, all other things being equal. Another benefit is that people tolerating conflict will be more inclined to detect the shortcomings of existing hypotheses to explain the available evidence than those who don't, all other things being equal. Suppose you tolerate self-conflict about a question and you bear in mind a piece of recalcitrant evidence that's not explained by popular hypotheses. You are open to more of the relevant evidence, and so you will more readily recognize that a better explanation of the evidence is called for than if you don't tolerate self-conflict. As a matter of fact, inquirers often develop better viewpoints because they devise new hypotheses to make sense of recalcitrant evidence. By living with dissonance, we can move closer to new insights. Tolerating intellectual conflict may be a valuable tool for inquiry.[20]

---

[19] Michel de Montaigne connected tolerance for social conflict with intercultural competence:

> I do not at all hate opinions contrary to mine. I am so far from being vexed to see discord between my judgments and others', and from making myself incompatible with the society of men because they are of a different sentiment and party from mine, that on the contrary, since variety is the most general fashion that nature has followed, and more in minds than bodies. . . . I find it much rarer to see our humors and plans agree. And there were never in the world two opinions alike, any more than two hairs or two grains. Their most universal quality is diversity. (1957 [1579–80], 597–598; "Of the Resemblance of Children to Fathers")

[20] Compare to Jennifer Whiting's (2003, 227) discussion of the value of philosophical "ambivalence."

Here is my suggestion. If we want to grow in tolerance for conflict, then following the method may help us. That's because the method makes us more attuned to the shortcomings of our own evidence by drawing our attention to competence defeaters. If we are guided by the method, we'll be better able to tolerate conflict than if the method doesn't guide us, all other things being equal.

6. Confronting Ignorance

Some people can face up to their own ignorance more easily than others. In Plato's *Apology*, Socrates professes a kind of self-aware ignorance. Socrates says he's "very conscious that I am not wise at all" (1997, 21; 21b) and "conscious of knowing practically nothing" (1997, 22; 22d). Ignoring the air of paradox—how can Socrates be conscious of knowing nothing if he doesn't know anything?—and the possibility that Socrates didn't really mean what he said, this much is clear: sometimes people know they are ignorant about a topic or question. But it's not always easy to own up to ignorance. As I have already pointed out, psychologists observe that ignorance begets itself: people who lack knowledge about a topic tend to lack meta-knowledge of that fact (Kruger and Dunning 1999; Dunning et al. 2003). For another, notice how accusations of ignorance sting. Take this early modern put-down, aimed at the poet John Dryden by a critic: "You do live in as much ignorance and darkness as you did in the womb."[21] Dryden couldn't have been pleased by the sentiment—and perhaps the prenatal Dryden, floating serenely in amniotic fluid, would not have approved either. When people call us ignorant, we may feel defensive and rebuff the charge. But if the charge is true, it's epistemically better for us to not remain perfectly oblivious of our obliviousness. We should hope for Socratic ignorance. A pinhole of light is better than pitch darkness.

Importantly, if we want to investigate difficult and controversial questions, we must confront our ignorance. As the physicist Erwin Schrödinger noted, "In an honest search for knowledge you quite often have to abide by ignorance for an indefinite period. Instead of filling a gap by guesswork, genuine science prefers to put up with it" (1996 [1954], 8). But what exactly does it mean to confront our ignorance? Consider some examples.

---

[21] The jab was delivered by Martin Clifford, quoted in Samuel Johnson's *Life of John Dryden* (1779).

Alfredo Gaitán went on a sailing trip in the Norfolk Broads, a network of navigable rivers and lakes in England. Gaitán, a psychology lecturer, had no sailing experience. "Having grown up in the Colombian Andes," he wrote, "water sports had not been a part of my upbringing. I'd rather be on a horse than on a boat" (2017, 46). But for one week, he found himself a crewmember of a 28-foot, gaff-rigged mahogany sloop. He had to learn about jibing, tacking, and how to handle the main sheet and tiller. He learned to follow spur-of-the-moment orders from the boat's skipper in order to avoid collisions with motorboats operated by "inexperienced holidaymakers" (2017, 48). Whenever the winds on canals died down, Gaitán had to quant (stick a long pole into the mud to keep the boat moving). Although he had read about quanting in a sailing handbook, the instructions were useless in practice; while quanting, he feared falling overboard and nearly did several times. As sailors go, Gaitán was a total novice. But he persistently confronted his practical and intellectual ignorance about sailing. That is how he improved his skills.

Some novice sailors would rather swim for shore than deal with their ignorance. Confronting our ignorance can be unpleasant, distressing, and demoralizing. An American biologist named Martin Schwartz recounted a conversation with a friend from graduate school who had decided to leave the field:

> After a couple of years of feeling stupid every day, she was ready to do something else. I had thought of her as one of the brightest people I knew and her subsequent career supports that view. What she said bothered me. I kept thinking about it; sometime the next day, it hit me. Science makes me feel stupid too. It's just that I've gotten used to it. (2008, 1771)

Schwartz says he actively seeks out new opportunities to feel stupid—"I wouldn't know what to do without that feeling" (2008, 1771). He does not seek "relative stupidity," where he has less knowledge about a topic than his peers, but "absolute stupidity," where he ventures into the unknown. This sort of stupidity, Schwartz says, is an "existential fact, inherent in our efforts to push our way into the unknown." In uncharted territory, "[w]e just don't know what we're doing. We can't be sure whether we're asking the right question or doing the right experiment until we get the answer or the result" (2008, 1771).[22]

---

[22] Schwartz's praise for stupidity may involve a bit of self-styling. Researchers and intellectuals commonly overemphasize how they reject the safety of land and sail on open waters. Understood

Gaitán and Schwartz both recognize that confronting ignorance has implications for education. Gaitán's sailing experience led him to think more carefully about why capable graduate students often feel incompetent and insecure when faced with an unfamiliar world of ideas and how mentors can help them stick with it. Schwartz proposed that if PhD students in the sciences can be taught to practice "productive stupidity," they'll be better able to transition from learning about others' discoveries to making their own.

Confronting our ignorance is an intellectual skill that involves more basic abilities and motives. We first need the ability and willingness to grasp where our ignorance lies. Next we need the ability and willingness to encounter situations—to put ourselves in situations—where the existence and scope of our ignorance is revealed to us. The "willingness to be surprised" is a trait praised by Tracy Kidder, a nonfiction writer, and his longtime editor, Richard Todd, who note:

> [The willingness to be surprised] isn't very hard to cultivate, once you discover—a constant in reporting—that your preconceptions were wrong. Finding this out can be bracing. It can feel as if you're making real discoveries when you first, or once again, discover that the world is too complex to be imagined fully, that it needs to be watched. (2013, 98)

We face our ignorance not merely by knowing we are ignorant about a topic, but also by intentionally coming to recognize how or why we fall short. For example, we can learn about the type of experience, skill, and evidence that would make us less ignorant. Of course, even when we shine light on some of our ignorance concerning a topic, we may remain in the dark about many other parts. Indeed, some of our ignorance is *unknowable*, in some sense, because we lack, either contingently or necessarily, the conceptual resources to even grasp at what we don't know.[23]

The ability to confront ignorance is valuable. It allows us to recognize where we may need to invest effort in order to expand our knowledge.

---

rightly, Schwartz's proposal is not that we should take blind leaps into the unknown, like incautious BASE jumpers risking life and limb. Pushing into the unknown requires a great deal of expertise. We must know a lot in order to undertake fruitful new inquiries in domains where we lack knowledge. (Thanks to Benjamin Wilson for discussion here.)

[23] Wu and Dunning (2017) explore hypocognition (the lack of cognitive or linguistic grasp of concepts).

Confronting our ignorance won't dispel our ignorance all on its own, but it can provide a basis for learning more.

Here is my proposal. The regulative method may help us confront our ignorance. It offers us a way to recognize which controversial questions we're ignorant about. It helps us reflect on why and how we have failed to recognize the appropriate doxastic attitude to hold on the basis of our evidence: we lack competence. If we are guided by the method, we will be better positioned to confront our ignorance than if the method doesn't guide us, all other things being equal.

7. Seeking Independence

Thus far, I have noted two elements of an open inquirer's mindset: tolerance for intellectual conflict and the ability to confront ignorance. A third element is the ability to resist conformity while we inquire.

Social scientists have devised many concepts for thinking about conformity. The "bandwagon effect" is the tendency for people to accept something because many others accept it. "Groupthink" refers to the phenomenon of seeking consensus on an issue, where group cohesiveness thwarts critical thinking (Janis 1972; Turner and Pratkanis 1998). Communication and media researchers study "echo chambers," environments where an opinion or idea is repeated inside a defined system, amplifying the message as a result. People inside echo chambers feel that their views are more commonplace and convincing than they may be in fact (Sunstein 2017). Networked computers have apparently exacerbated the problem: "filter bubbles" encourage online environs where users consume information that's friendly to their existing viewpoints. Social media technology, as Microsoft founder Bill Gates has said, "lets you go off with like-minded people, so you're not mixing and sharing and understanding other points of view . . . . It's turned out to be more of a problem than I, or many others, would have expected" (Delaney 2017). And, as I pointed out in Chapter 9, social and cognitive scientists who study "cultural cognition" argue that our beliefs about controversial matters of fact are influenced by the values that define our social identities (Kahan and Braman 2006; Kahan 2016). What this means is that our opinions signal our group memberships. Beliefs serve as badges of belonging. Our beliefs tend to gravitate toward the attitudes of kith and kin.

"It is essential to remain outside," wrote Virginia Woolf in her diary, "& realise my own beliefs: or rather not to accept theirs. A line to think out" (1984 [18 November 1940], 340). The possibility of making up one's own mind without the interference of others' beliefs captures the imagination. This is part of the origin story of modern philosophy. There is Immanuel Kant's slogan of intellectual enlightenment: *Sapere aude!* (Dare to think for yourself!) Ralph Waldo Emerson implored each person to be guided by the inner spirit alone, cautioning his audience not to be "the parrot of other men's thinking."[24] In recent days, the enlightenment tradition has found able exponents. Intellectual autonomy has been celebrated by punk rock bands. Propagandhi, a Canadian punk ensemble, proclaims in one song: "You boycott your brain. You answer with fists. But my questions still persist. You can rearrange my face, but you can't rearrange my mind. You can beat this shell about me, but you can't touch what's inside."[25]

Maybe part of the allure of thinking for ourselves is that, deep down, we doubt that other people are as good at thinking as we are. Of course, intellectual autonomy isn't valuable merely because it lets us turn from the crowd. As a matter of fact, each of us must trust other people, especially experts and authorities, in the process of building and repairing our intellectual houses—lest we become what C. A. J. Coady calls an "autonomous ignoramus" (2002, 358). A sensible ideal of intellectual autonomy says that we should not give *undue* influence to the opinions of others. Testimony and consensus have their rightful place but should be set in the balance alongside our own efforts to assess, evaluate, and understand the matter at hand—insofar as we reasonably believe we are capable of doing those things well. Conformity with others' opinions is a problem when we give those opinions too much weight in our scales or disengage from the work of private deliberation.

The social world presses in on us and extracts our allegiance. Resisting the crowd is often enormously difficult, as Marilynne Robinson notes:

> To step back and appraise any question around which consensus has formed is a very difficult thing to do because consensus by definition is assumed on all sides to be true and right, and this makes it difficult for skepticism to find

---

[24] "The American Scholar" (1837).

[25] Propagandhi, "Who Will Help Me Bake This Bread?", Track 11 on *How to Clean Everything*, 1993, Sputnikmusic, Compact Disk. (Thanks to John Keller for mentioning this song to me.) If Emerson and Kant ever found themselves at a punk show, I have the sneaking suspicion that Emerson would enjoy crowd surfing but Kant wouldn't.

a purchase even in the minds of people who pride themselves on their read-
iness to act as critics. (2010, 14)

The crowd beckons. We can remain outsiders if we manifest an intellectual
skill I call *independence*.[26] This is the ability for inquirers to reasonably balance two things: their personal evaluation of the evidence concerning a question and the weight they assign to others' opinions. The skill allows them
to keep fixed in mind what they have figured out and not to be compelled
without good reason by the force of others' opinions. The independent inquirer is sensitive to good reasons to follow the crowd. But she will remain a
party of one if she should.

Independence has an intrapersonal analogue. We are independent from
ourselves when we have appropriate separation from our own past beliefs.
Our past beliefs can be relevant to our present thinking, but we should not
overvalue them.[27] We find a sort of *self-independence* in the practice of second
guessing. When people make a first judgment and then later qualify or clarify
it, or even contradict it, they may be exercising the skill of self-independence.
They are trying to resist the undue influence of their past selves.

By declaring self-independence, we may become uncertain and conflicted, but this may make us better attuned to reality. Our best theories
may fail to capture some part of what is, and a second-guessing inquirer can
help us understand what our theories have left out. We may be prompted to
second-guess because we suspect the truth is not fully reflected in our initial judgment. So we try again. A writer who illustrated this kind of self-
independence is the late David Foster Wallace. One literary commentator
finds in Wallace the quality "of being inwardly divided" (Sullivan 2011).
Wallace would frequently hedge, clarify, and qualify his clarifications. The
"essential Wallace," said the commentator, is "forever wincing, reconsidering,
wishing he hadn't said whatever he just said" (Sullivan 2011). Videotaped
interviews of Wallace literally show the author grimacing as he tries to articulate his thinking. He was somehow trying to subdue ideas and expressions
that he found imperfect. So he tried again. The effect of Wallace's literary style

[26] Why haven't I called this intellectual autonomy instead? Briefly, intellectual autonomy is arguably a complex trait that involves something along the lines of what I call independence, but also
abilities that enable self-creation and integrity. Coady (2002) examines these aspects of intellectual
autonomy. Pritchard (2016) discusses the distinctive value of intellectual autonomy.

[27] For more on trusting our past opinions, see Foley (2001, chapter 5).

is a synoptic, obsessive, and erudite depiction of his subject matter and his own self-conscious attempts to sort things out.

If we are guided by the method, we are better positioned to be independent than if the method doesn't guide us, all other things being equal. Here are two reasons why. First, if we are sensitive to competence defeaters concerning controversial beliefs, we have a ready supply of "second thoughts"—namely, doubts concerning our competence to settle upon one view over another on the basis of our evidence. (Just call to mind counterfactual interlocutors, unpossessed evidence, or the bias blind spot.) Second, if the method makes us more doxastically open concerning controversial questions, we will be less inclined to follow others' opinions out of kinship or loyalty. That's because we won't have the customary doxastic "badges" of group membership. Confident opinions bind people together. But if there is no social group we can join in virtue of being unsettled, hesitant, and confused, so much the better for our remaining independent. The inquirer who is doxastically open will more easily stand alone in a world of self-assured partisans.

8. Wonder

As I've suggested, the method may produce in us skills and traits for tolerating intellectual conflict, confronting our ignorance, and judging independently. In addition, the method can help us experience emotions that may motivate further inquiry. Chief among those emotions is wonder.

In early modern natural philosophy, wonder was a key to understanding the world. As Lorraine Daston and Katherine Park (1998) have argued, wonder was often thought of as an inquiry-inspiring emotion. Descartes, for example, said that wonder is "a sudden surprise of the soul which makes it tend to consider attentively those objects which seem to it rare and extraordinary."[28] Wonders (objects, not feelings) were collected by natural philosophers and stored inside a cabinet of wonders (*Wunderkammer*): the lodestone, unicorn horns, and artifacts from monstrous births. Observers watched comets and *aurora borealis* in the night's sky. Wonders marked the outer limits of what human beings knew. Eventually, some of these curiosities were explained, or explained away, and the role of wonder in inquiry and its phenomenology were transformed. At present, wonder may seem a bit

---

[28] Quoted in Daston and Park (1998, 13).

quaint, embarrassingly sincere, or even childish. As Daston notes, "modern wonder has become infantilized, the stuff of children's entertainment, whether in the form of cartoon fairy tales or science museum exhibitions" (2014). I intend to take wonder more seriously than that, so let me proceed carefully.

The idea of wonder may conjure up pastoral scenes of nature:

> There was a time when meadow, grove, and stream,
> The earth, and every common sight,
>> To me did seem
>> Apparelled in celestial light,
> The glory and the freshness of a dream. (Wordsworth 1807)

Cynics may read these lines with an eye-roll. But William Wordsworth was not poetry's Thomas Kinkade, the infamous American "painter of light," cranking out kitschy stanzas to make a fortune.[29] Wordsworth's style stemmed from a high-minded intellectual and artistic perspective. His friend Samuel Taylor Coleridge wrote that Wordsworth tried "to give the charm of novelty to things of every day." The poet intended, wrote Coleridge,

> to excite a feeling analogous to the supernatural, by awakening the mind's attention from the lethargy of custom, and directing it to the loveliness and the wonders of the world before us; an inexhaustible treasure, but for which in consequence of the film of familiarity and selfish solicitude we have eyes, yet see not, ears that hear not, and hearts that neither feel nor understand. (1817, 2–3)

Some people may feel this is dubious. Can reading Romantic poetry really peel from our eyes the "film of familiarity"? How could poetry possibly reveal to us a pristine world of meadow, grove, and stream? What poem could create in our minds a luminous playground for cuddly creatures, and a double rainbow across the sky?

I want to ignore cynicism for a moment. In a passage from *The Problems of Philosophy*, Bertrand Russell says that philosophy fails to give us knowledge

---

[29] The comparison between Wordsworth and Kinkade is not exactly right, but it's close enough. In *Spirit of the Age* (1825), William Hazlitt commented on Wordsworth: "To one class of readers he appears sublime, to another (and we fear the largest) ridiculous." (Thanks to David Christensen and Sydney Penner for sharing with me vigorous defenses of Kinkade's painting.)

of the answers to its questions but "it keeps alive our sense of wonder by showing familiar things in an unfamiliar aspect" (1997 [1912], 157).[30] Russell added that philosophy can also "enlarge our thoughts and free them from the tyranny of custom" and remove "somewhat arrogant dogmatism" (1997 [1912], 157). In a slightly different mood, Russell might well have written that philosophy could remove what Coleridge called the "film of familiarity," rousing us from the "lethargy of custom." At bottom, Russell's idea that philosophy keeps wonder alive may not be so different from Wordsworth's idea about poetry. Philosopher and poet alike try to readjust how people view the world. They devise ways of seeing what is ordinarily imperceptible. One gift of these new perceptions is a sense of wonder.

Intellectual practices that show us reality afresh often help us appreciate our ignorance, inattention, and dogmatic presumptions. I want to propose that where the regulative method reveals to us our lack of reasonable beliefs and knowledge, it can open up space for wonder.

Wonder visits us in many kinds of experience and induces many effects. Sometimes wonder makes us feel admiration and elevation. Sometimes wonder shows us some overpowering immensity not so easily crammed inside our skull-sized conceptions of things. Wonderstruck, we feel small, humbled, and disoriented. Apparently, Russell thought that philosophy could induce wonder because it takes away our dogmatism, our feeling that we have knowledge of the correct answers to philosophy's questions. Russell's idea fits with some basic observations about wonder. In some situations, wonder comes when we can't explain what we encounter. But when we think we know something and feel we can make sense of it, we don't feel wonder. Francis Bacon noted that people feel no wonder about a puppet show once they peek behind the curtain. We are dumbfounded by a magician's trick—until she shows us the sleight of hand. Johann Wolfgang von Goethe described little children "who, after peeping into a mirror, turn it round directly to see what is on the other side." Once the children figure out the mirror's optical properties, their wonderment is gone. The presence of explanations for a phenomenon can undermine our wonder about it.[31]

Wonder has valuable upshots. In its grip, we tend to be less intellectually self-centered. We recognize that our own ideas are just one potential way to make sense of things. If we feel wonder about some questions, we are more

[30] I noted this passage from Russell in Chapter 4.
[31] R. W. Hepburn (1980) makes this point and discusses the examples from Bacon and Goethe I've noted here.

inclined to seek to understand them. And wonder sometimes mingles with other states of mind that aid inquiry: curiosity, awe, and a sense of the mysteriousness of reality. If we feel we are in the dark, we are more inclined to try to flip on the lights.

The method might help us experience wonder. For one, the method enjoins patterns of reflection that can reveal the vertiginous complexity of our intellectual world and our insignificant place in the whole. For another, the method promises to make us more doxastically open about controversial questions. That openness can remove our wonder-obstructing certainties. If we are guided by the method and become doxastically open, we stand a better chance to feel wonder about controversial matters than if we're not guided by the method, all other things being equal.

9. The End of Inquiry into Inquiry?

Let me sum up my reply to the second "Why bother?" objection. The objection alleges that if we expect we won't figure out controversial questions, our inquiry will not be well-motivated, leaving us intellectually lazy or downcast. But there's possibly a mindset available to the open inquirer that can underwrite serious investigation in the face of doubts. This mindset can help us tolerate conflict, confront our ignorance, exercise independent judgment, and feel a sense of wonder. We may grow in the mindset by being guided by the method, because using the method to wrestle with controversial questions can help us develop the habits and traits that constitute the mindset.[32]

As I come to the end of this book, I return to some unanswered questions I noted at the beginning. Epistemologists reflect on inquiry carefully. Why? Which parts of inquiry matter to them? What is the purpose of epistemology? I admitted that these questions are disquieting to me.

I remember a hallway conversation from years ago when I was in graduate school. Perhaps betraying my doubts about my chosen field, I asked one professor, Tom Christiano, why he thought philosophical research was

---

[32] The "Why bother?" objection may easily reemerge in a new guise. Even if following the method may bring various goods, we may ask whether they are *sufficient* to motivate our investigation. We may be unsure whether they could actually move our feet in inquiry into controversial matters. *So why bother?* Addressing this variant of the objection calls for empirically informed study of human motivation and behavior. For now, I am satisfied to have tried to defend this claim: it is possible the method does not immobilize the open inquirer. But I recognize these issues are not simple. (See footnote 18.)

worthwhile. After his first couple of answers didn't persuade me, Tom told a story. During the Enlightenment, he said, philosophers wrote on social and political ideas—big ideas like toleration, liberty, and equality. These ideas were powerfully articulated in original philosophical works and gradually transformed Western culture. Of course, it wasn't as though scholars sat in their studies, envisioned the future of social and political progress, and then watched as it materialized at barricades, in legislatures, in voting booths. The changes were complex and gradual, Tom explained, and required many years and many lives. But philosophers helped to hasten the progress. Philosophers' work can make the world more just and humane. Tom writes on contemporary political philosophy, and I didn't begrudge him his answer. But what was a PhD candidate working on epistemology to say about the value of his theorizing?

Not having an answer didn't stop me from graduating and entering the hectic world of full-time teaching. Eventually I found my answer. It turned out to be similar to Tom Christiano's. I recall reading Antoine Arnauld and Pierre Nicole's *Port-Royal Logic* for the first time in the months of sleepless nights after my daughter was born. Arnauld and Nicole say their *Logic* is meant for "educating our judgment and making it as precise as possible" (1996 [1683], 5). They say their project is important because so many "faulty minds" are unmoved by good reasons, and that greater reliability in our judgments will prevent many errors not just in science but also in everyday life—"unjust quarrels, ill-founded lawsuits, hasty opinions, and badly organized enterprises" (1996 [1683], 6). In studying historical works of epistemology and natural philosophy, I reached the view that careful reflection on inquiry could have a significant role to play in human affairs. It had once before, anyway. I figured: Why not again one day? But I was slow to understand the implications of my newfound regulative ambition.

Earlier in the book, I confessed to one false start I made while writing it. Here is another. At first, I had planned to begin the book with a chapter titled "What Is Epistemology Good For?" and I even wrote a first draft. That draft chapter was my attempt to promote regulative epistemology by arguing that regulative theorizing promises greater benefits to humankind than merely "descriptive," non-regulative theorizing. I was aware that saying that could have annoyed epistemologists who work on descriptive epistemology exclusively. I was willing to risk hurt feelings. At some level, I agreed with regulative epistemologists such as Michael Bishop, J. D. Trout, Robert Roberts, and W. Jay Wood, whose ideas I discussed in Chapter 1. I agreed with them that professional epistemology needed to make a U-turn toward regulative questions, though I didn't share their contempt for the field's standard methods.

But then I realized my error. I came to see that I am a member of a community of inquiry. I saw that I was invested in a superpersonal inquiry where my small efforts as a researcher could only potentially be meaningful as one input into a vast collective effort spread out across time. Epistemologists have been, are, and will be motivated by a host of reasons. Some practitioners desire to regulate imperfect inquiry. Others seek to understand the central concepts of inquiry, or to articulate powerful skeptical challenges to human knowledge, or to refute those challenges and vindicate a commonsense picture of the world. So what kind of inquiry into inquiry is most worthwhile? Which contributions to this community have the greatest value? The draft chapter offered an answer: the regulative parts promise greater value than the non-regulative parts. That was a false start.

Here's some of the trouble. Always seeking "application" for epistemological research may hinder progress. If practitioners steer away from "basic," non-applied questions that are relevant for application in ways not yet apparent, the field will lose out on insights. Always seeking application for research may be self-defeating. Moreover, regulative ideas depend on non-regulative ideas. Notice how I've developed regulative proposals that use the idea of the defeater, one invention of descriptive epistemological theorizing in the twentieth century. In general, efforts in non-regulative epistemology can be a tremendous impetus for regulative theorizing. From our present viewpoint, it's exceedingly hard to say what type of projects will turn out to be useful, if any will be. In order to create something useful, epistemology needs both regulative and non-regulative projects—to say nothing of good luck.

It will come as no surprise to the reader that I believe reflection on inquiry is valuable when it contributes something to mitigating the problems of imperfect inquiry. As I see it, professional epistemology has become fractured by the forces of specialization and isolated from cognate fields, and the prospect of seeking to develop guidance for inquiry offers practitioners a unifying mission.[33] Regulative epistemology is a broad approach to theorizing

---

[33] Let me be the last person to deride my own professional discipline: but contemporary epistemology—not unlike other areas of academic philosophy—has a public relations problem, not just with the non-academic world, but with other fields of inquiry. By encouraging new regulative projects, the discipline may be able to rediscover and reassert the significance of epistemological inquiry.

that's consistent with different methodologies. It requires stitching together our knowledge about how human inquiry works, how it should work, and how it can work better. It calls us to pay more attention to the fabric of real-world inquiry and to reflect on questions about cognition, society, and education. It calls for collaboration. My conviction is that regulative themes and questions are fascinating, under-explored, and worth the effort.

Researchers who care about understanding and improving inquiry might work together and make some headway. But the idea of a superpersonal inquiry into epistemological questions may seem a little curious. Cancer research is a collective effort. But is epistemology? Epistemologists work mostly in solitude, not entirely unlike Descartes inside his stove-heated room. But no professional epistemologist is self-made. They are members of a guild. They reflect on inquiry in the ways they do because mentors and teachers passed along questions, methods, and habits of mind. Epistemologists owe their careers to search committee members who fought to hire an epistemologist over candidates who wrote dissertations on bioethics or political philosophy. They depend on persistent journal editors who hunt down referees for overdue reports on manuscripts.

I sometimes feel gratitude toward long-gone epistemologists—people I never met. In the 1950s, Roderick Chisholm helped to forge a new, distinctive style of epistemology, after imbibing the rationalism of Bertrand Russell and Gottfried Leibniz as well as the commonsense philosophy of G. E. Moore and Thomas Reid. In his day, Chisholm was an exemplar of philosophical clarity, seriousness, and honesty; his work was a model for researchers in the burgeoning subfield of analytic epistemology. If Chisholm hadn't done his work, and if I hadn't read works by Chisholm's students and acolytes at an impressionable moment, my education would have been a lot different. Probably, I would not have gone to graduate school to study epistemology. It is interesting to me that the Chisholmian tradition has focused almost exclusively on describing epistemic principles, states, and statuses. Beneath the steady waves of analytical precision, I feel the ripple of regulative concern. This is all part of an effort to understand good intellectual conduct.

What do I owe the various epistemological traditions that have influenced my thinking? As a professional philosopher, many of my inclinations aim at self-preservation and self-advancement. In my better moments, though, I see that I am only a caretaker. It is my role to help keep some or other epistemological conversation going—to teach, collaborate, and write in such a way that a few important questions and ideas will live and breathe in another generation. Here is the sober truth. I am an extra in the unfolding drama of inquiry into inquiry. That metaphor is no ego boost, I know, but it is the truth about the vast majority of intellectuals in any field. We don't play even a bit part in a whole career. We blend in with the background. We set the scene alongside props and spotlights. When the curtain falls and the scene changes, we are at once forgotten.

Being an extra can be a satisfying role to play when you care so much about the story. We are glad to be of use. The long tradition of inquiry into inquiry has wrought some genuine good for human beings striving to make sense of reality and for cultures in the slow struggle to become more humane. The marks of good epistemological ideas upon this world have been profound.

What will become of epistemology? Will its practitioners continue to craft ways and means for bettering inquiry?

I hope for the best. We all have faulty minds. We are caught up in unjust quarrels, ill-founded lawsuits, hasty opinions, and badly organized enterprises. Public opinion is swayed by campaigns of misinformation and propaganda. Technological systems beyond anyone's control distort our most basic perceptions. What will we do with all of this? At the heart of our personal mishaps and collective tragedies, we find questions about knowledge and method, character and authority, opinion and ignorance. For all I know, a community of researchers may help bring order to inquiry and to life. But in a time of crisis, they must live in the world a little more. Do I have *reason* to hope for success? It's honestly difficult for me to say. Tremendous gains in specialized knowledge and techniques for studying human inquiry suggest the time is opportune. But humanity's challenges have become more complex than ever before. The future of civilization may already have slipped from the grasp of those with the audacity to try to save it. Of course, optimism and pessimism have perennial appeal. I try to keep an open mind.

Bibliography

Abbott, Andrew. 2001. *Chaos of Disciplines*. Chicago: University of Chicago Press.

Ahlstrom-Vij, Kristoffer, and Jeffrey Dunn. 2014. "A Defence of Epistemic Consequentialism." *The Philosophical Quarterly* 64 (257): 541–551.

Aikin, Scott. 2008. "*Tu Quoque* Arguments and the Significance of Hypocrisy." *Informal Logic* 28 (2): 155–169.

Alexander, Colonel Stewart F. 1947. "Medical Report of the Bari Harbor Mustard Casualties." *The Military Surgeon* 101 (1): 1–17.

Alicke, Mark, Ellen Gordan, and David Rose. 2013. "Hypocrisy: What Counts?" *Philosophical Psychology* 26 (5): 673–701.

Alston, William. 1993. "Epistemic Desiderata." *Philosophy and Phenomenological Research* 53 (3): 527–551.

Alston, William. 2005. *Beyond "Justification": Dimensions of Epistemic Evaluation*. Ithaca, NY: Cornell University Press.

Anderson, Elizabeth. 2011. "Democracy, Public Policy, and Lay Assessments of Scientific Testimony." *Episteme* 8 (2): 144–164.

Annas, Julia, and Jonathan Barnes. 1985. *The Modes of Scepticism: Ancient Texts and Modern Interpretations*. Cambridge: Cambridge University Press.

Archer, Sophie. 2017. "Defending Exclusivity." *Philosophy and Phenomenological Research* 94 (2): 326–341.

Arnauld, Antoine, and Pierre Nicole. 1996 [1683]. *Logic or the Art of Thinking*. Translated and edited by Jill Vance Buroker. Cambridge: Cambridge University Press.

Arum, Richard, and Josipa Roksa. 2011. *Academically Adrift: Limited Learning on College Campuses*. Chicago: University of Chicago Press.

Atran, Scott. 2004. *In Gods We Trust: The Evolutionary Landscape of Religion*. Oxford: Oxford University Press.

Augustine of Hippo. 1947 [391/392]. "The Advantage of Believing." Translated by Luanne Meagher. In *Writings of Saint Augustine*. Vol. 2. Edited by Ludwig Schopp. New York: CIMA.

Bacon, Francis. 1996. *Francis Bacon: The Major Works*. Edited by Brian Vickers. Oxford: Oxford University Press.

Bacon, Francis. 2000 [1620]. *The New Organon*. Edited and translated by Lisa Jardine and Michael Silverthorne. Cambridge: Cambridge University Press.

Baehr, Jason. 2011. *The Inquiring Mind: On Intellectual Virtues and Virtue Epistemology*. Oxford: Oxford University Press.

Baehr, Jason. 2013. *Intellectual Virtues and Education: Essays in Applied Virtue Epistemology*. New York: Routledge.

Baird, Davis, and Mark S. Cohen. 1999. "Why Trade?" *Perspectives on Science* 7 (2): 231–254.

Baker, Judith. 1987. "Trust and Rationality." *Pacific Philosophical Quarterly* 68 (1): 1–13.

Baker-Hytch, Max, and Matthew Benton. 2015. "Defeatism Defeated." *Philosophical Perspectives* 29 (1): 40–66.

Ballantyne, Nathan. 2012. "The Problem of Historical Variability." In *Disagreement and Skepticism*. Edited by Diego Machuca, 239–259. New York: Routledge.

Ballantyne, Nathan. 2014. "Knockdown Arguments." *Erkenntnis* 79 (Supplement 3): 525–543.

Bammer, Gabriele. 2013. *Disciplining Interdisciplinarity: Integration and Implementation Sciences for Researching Complex Real-World Problems*. Canberra: Australian National University Press. doi: 10.22459/DI.01.2013.

Baran, Benjamin E., Steven G. Rogelberg, and Thomas Clausen. 2016. "Routinized Killing of Animals: Going Beyond Dirty Work and Prestige to Understand the Well-Being of Slaughterhouse Workers." *Organization* 23 (3): 351–369.

Barnes, Jonathan. 1990. *The Toils of Scepticism*. Cambridge: Cambridge University Press.

Barnett, Susan, and Stephen Ceci. 2002. "When and Where Do We Apply What We Learn?: A Taxonomy for Far Transfer." *Psychological Bulletin* 128 (4): 612–637.

Barnett, Zach, and Han Li. 2016. "Conciliationism and Merely Possible Disagreement." *Synthese* 193 (9): 2973–2298.

Battaly, Heather. 2008. "Virtue Epistemology." *Philosophy Compass* 3(4): 639–663.

Battaly, Heather. 2009. "Review of Robert C. Roberts and W. Jay Wood's *Intellectual Virtues*." *International Philosophical Quarterly* 49 (1): 136–139.

Beddor, Bob. 2015. "Process Reliabilism's Troubles with Defeat." *The Philosophical Quarterly* 65 (259): 145–159.

Bender, Thomas, and Carl E. Schorske, eds. 1997. "American Academic Culture in Transformation: Fifty Years, Four Disciplines." *Daedalus: Journal of the American Academy of Arts and Sciences* 126 (Winter).

Benton, Matthew A. 2016. "Knowledge and Evidence You Should Have Had." *Episteme* 13 (4): 471–479.

Bergmann, Michael. 1997. "Internalism, Externalism, and the No-Defeater Condition." *Synthese* 110 (3): 399–417.

Bergmann, Michael. 2005. "Defeaters and Higher-Level Requirements." *The Philosophical Quarterly* 55 (220): 419–436.

Bergmann, Michael. 2006. *Justification Without Awareness: A Defense of Epistemic Externalism*. Oxford: Oxford University Press.

Bergmann, Michael. 2009. "Rational Disagreement after Full Disclosure." *Episteme* 6 (3): 336–353.

Bergmann, Michael. 2015. "Religious Disagreement and Rational Demotion." In *Oxford Studies in Philosophy of Religion*. Vol. 6. Edited by Jonathan Kvanvig, 21–57. Oxford: Oxford University Press.

Berker, Selim. 2013. "The Rejection of Epistemic Consequentialism." *Philosophical Issues* 23 (1): 363–387.

Berlin, Isaiah, and Ramin Jahanbegloo. 1992. *Conversations with Isaiah Berlin*. London: Phoenix Press.

Bishop, Michael, and J. D. Trout. 2005. *Epistemology and the Psychology of Human Judgment*. Oxford: Oxford University Press.

Bogardus, Tomás. 2013. "The Problem of Contingency for Religious Belief." *Faith and Philosophy* 30 (4): 371–392.

Boghossian, Paul. 2006. *Fear of Knowledge*. Oxford: Oxford University Press.

Bohannon, John. 2013. "Who's Afraid of Peer Review?" *Science* 342 (6154): 60–65.

BonJour, Laurence. 1985. *The Structure of Empirical Knowledge*. Cambridge, MA: Harvard University Press.

Bosanquet, Bernard, Shadworth H. Hodgson, and G. E. Moore. 1897. "In What Sense, If Any, Do Past and Future Time Exist?" *Mind* 6 (22): 228–240.

Broughton, Janet. 2003. *Descartes' Method of Doubt*. Princeton, NJ: Princeton University Press.

Brown, Jessica. 2018. *Fallibilism: Evidence and Knowledge*. Oxford: Oxford University Press.

Burnyeat, Myles. 1980. "Aristotle on Learning to Be Good." In *Essays on Aristotle's Ethics*. Edited by Amélie Oksenberg Rorty, 69–92. Berkeley: University of California Press.

Burrows, Montrose T. 1921. "Problems in Cancer Research." *Cancer Research* 6 (2): 131–138.

Carey, Brandon. 2011. "Possible Disagreements and Defeat." *Philosophical Studies* 155 (3): 371–381.

Carraher, Terezinha, David Carraher, and Analucia Schliemann. 1985. "Mathematics in the Streets and in Schools." *British Journal of Developmental Psychology* 3 (1): 21–29.

Cassam, Quassim. 2016. "Vice Epistemology." *The Monist* 99 (2): 159–180.

Chinn, Clark A., Luke Buckland, and Ala Samarapungavan. 2011. "Expanding the Dimensions of Epistemic Cognition: Arguments from Philosophy and Psychology." *Educational Psychologist* 46 (3): 141–167.

Chisholm, Roderick M. 1973. *The Problem of the Criterion*. Milwaukee, WI: Marquette University Press.

Chisholm, Roderick. 1979. "Critical Review: Castañeda's *Thinking and Doing*." *Noûs* 13 (3): 385–396.

Chisholm, Roderick. 1989. *Theory of Knowledge*. 3rd edition. Englewood Cliffs, NJ: Prentice Hall.

Chisholm, Roderick, H. G. Alexander, Lewis Hahn, Paul C. Hayner, and Charles W. Hendel. 1958–1959. "Graduate Education in Philosophy." *Proceedings and Addresses of the American Philosophical Association* 32: 145–156.

Christensen, David. 2007a. "Epistemology of Disagreement: The Good News." *The Philosophical Review* 116 (2): 187–217.

Christensen, David. 2007b. "Does Murphy's Law Apply in Epistemology? Self-Doubt and Rational Ideals." *Oxford Studies in Epistemology* 2: 3–31.

Christensen, David. 2009. "Disagreement as Evidence: The Epistemology of Controversy." *Philosophy Compass* 4 (5): 756–767.

Christensen, David. 2010. "Higher-Order Evidence." *Philosophy and Phenomenological Research* 81 (1): 185–215.

Christensen, David. 2011. "Disagreement, Question-Begging and Epistemic Self-Criticism." *Philosophers' Imprint* 11 (6): 1–22.

Christensen, David. 2013. "Epistemic Modesty Defended." In *The Epistemology of Disagreement: New Essays*. Edited by David Christensen and Jennifer Lackey, 77–97. Oxford: Oxford University Press.

Christensen, David. 2014. "Disagreement and Public Controversy." In *Essays in Collective Epistemology*. Edited by Jennifer Lackey, 143–163. Oxford: Oxford University Press.

Christensen, David, and Jennifer Lackey, eds. 2013. *The Epistemology of Disagreement: New Essays*. Oxford: Oxford University Press.

Churchland, Paul. 1996. "The Neutral Representation of the Social World." In *Mind and Morals: Essays on Cognitive Science and Ethics*. Edited by Larry May, Marilyn Friedman, and Andy Clark, 91–127. Cambridge, MA: MIT Press.

Clark, William. 2006. *Academic Charisma and the Origins of the Research University.* Chicago: University of Chicago Press.

Clarke, Desmond. 2006. *Descartes: A Biography.* Cambridge: Cambridge University Press.

Coady, C. A. J. 2002. "Testimony and Intellectual Autonomy." *Studies in the History and Philosophy of Science* 33 (2): 355–372.

Coady, David. 2012. *What to Believe Now: Applying Epistemology to Contemporary Issues.* Malden, MA: Wiley-Blackwell.

Coffman, E.J. 2017. "Gettiered Belief." In *Explaining Knowledge: New Essays on the Gettier Problem.* Edited by Rodrigo Borges, Claudio de Almeida, and Peter Klein, 15–34. Oxford: Oxford University Press.

Cohen, Stewart. 1995. "Is There an Issue about Justified Belief?" *Philosophical Topics* 23 (1): 113–127.

Cohen, Stewart. 2016. "Theorizing about the Epistemic." *Inquiry* 59 (7–8): 839–857.

Coleridge, Samuel Taylor. 1817. *Biographia Literaria; or Biographical Sketches of My Literary Life and Opinions.* Vol. II. London: Rest Fenner.

Conee, Earl. 2008. "Critical Notice: *Epistemology and the Psychology of Human Judgment.*" *Philosophy and Phenomenological Research* 77 (3): 837–840.

Conley, John J. 2009. *Adoration and Annihilation: The Convent Philosophy of Port-Royal.* South Bend, IN: University of Notre Dame Press.

Cook, John, Dana Nuccitelli, Sarah A. Green, Mark Richardson, Bärbel Winkler, Rob Painting, Robert Way, Peter Jacobs, and Andrew Skuce. 2013. "Quantifying the Consensus on Anthropogenic Global Warming in the Scientific Literature." *Environmental Research Letters* 8 (2): 024024.

Cook, John, Naomi Oreskes, Peter T. Doran, William R. L. Anderegg, Bart Verheggen, Ed W. Maibach, J. Stuart Carlton, Stephan Lewandowsky, Andrew G. Skuce, and Sarah A. Green. 2016. "Consensus on Consensus: A Synthesis of Consensus Estimates on Human-Caused Global Warming." *Environmental Research Letters* 11 (4): 048002.

Cooper, J. M., ed., and D. S. Hutchinson, associate ed. 1997. *Plato: Complete Works.* Indianapolis, IN: Hackett.

Cooper, John. 2012. *Pursuits of Wisdom: Six Ways of Life in Ancient Philosophy from Socrates to Plotinus.* Princeton, NJ: Princeton University Press.

Corneanu, Sorana. 2011. *Regimens of the Mind: Boyle, Locke, and the Early Modern Cultura Animi Tradition.* Chicago: University of Chicago Press.

Cosmides, Leda, and John Tooby. 1992. "Cognitive Adaptations for Social Exchange." In *The Adapted Mind: Evolutionary Psychology and the Generation of Culture.* Edited by Jerome Barklow, Leda Cosmides, and John Tooby, 163–228. New York: Oxford University Press.

Craig, Edward. 1990. *Knowledge and the State of Nature: An Essay in Conceptual Synthesis.* Oxford: Oxford University Press.

Cronon, William. 1991. *Nature's Metropolis: Chicago and the Great West.* New York: W. W. Norton.

Cross, K. Patricia. 1977. "Not Can, But Will College Teaching Be Improved?" *New Directions for Higher Education* 17: 1–15.

Csiszar, Alex. 2010. "Seriality and the Search for Order: Scientific Print and Its Problems during the Late Nineteenth Century." *History of Science* 48 (3–4): 399–434.

Daston, Lorraine. 2014. "Wonder and the Ends of Inquiry." *The Point.* https://thepointmag.com/2014/examined-life/wonder-ends-inquiry.

Daston, Lorraine, and Peter Galison. 2007. *Objectivity.* Brooklyn, NY: Zone Books.

Daston, Lorraine, and Katherine Park. 1998. *Wonders and the Order of Nature, 1150–1750*. Cambridge, MA: MIT Press.

Davies, Paul. 2007. *The Goldilocks Enigma: Why Is the Universe Just Right for Life?* New York: Houghton Mifflin.

Dear, Peter. 2009. *Revolutionizing the Sciences: European Knowledge and Its Ambitions, 1500–1700*. 2nd edition. Princeton, NJ: Princeton University Press.

Decker, Jason. 2014. "Conciliation and Self-Incrimination." *Erkenntnis* 79 (5): 1099–1134.

Delaney, Kevin J. 2017. "Filter Bubbles Are a Serious Problem with News, says Bill Gates." *Quartz* (February 21). https://qz.com/913114.

Delbanco, Andrew. 2012. *College: What It Was, Is, and Should Be*. Princeton, NJ: Princeton University Press.

DeRose, Keith. 1999. "Can It Be That It Would Have Been Even Though It Might Not Have Been?" *Philosophical Perspectives* 13: 385–413.

Descartes, René. 1984 [1641]. "Meditations on First Philosophy." In *The Philosophical Writings of Descartes*. Vol. 2. Translated by John Cottingham, Robert Stoothoff, and Dugald Murdoch, 1–62. Cambridge: Cambridge University Press.

Descartes, René. 1984 [1642]. "Seventh Set of Objections with the Author's Replies." In *The Philosophical Writings of Descartes*. Vol. 2. Translated by John Cottingham, Robert Stoothoff, and Dugald Murdoch, 302–383. Cambridge: Cambridge University Press.

Descartes, René. 1985 [1637]. "Discourse on the Method." In *The Philosophical Writings of Descartes*. Vol. 1. Translated by John Cottingham, Robert Stoothoff, and Dugald Murdoch, 111–176. Cambridge: Cambridge University Press.

Descartes, René. 2000 [1641]. "Meditations on First Philosophy." In *Philosophical Essays and Correspondence*. Edited by Roger Ariew. Indianapolis: Hackett.

Diethelm, Pascal, and Martin McKee. 2009. "Denialism: What Is It and How Should Scientists Respond?" *European Journal of Public Health* 19 (1): 2–4.

Dillard, Jennifer. 2008. "A Slaughterhouse Nightmare: Psychological Harm Suffered by Slaughterhouse Employees and the Possibility of Redress through Legal Reform." *Georgetown Journal on Poverty Law & Policy* 15 (2): 391–408.

Ditto, Peter H., and David F. Lopez. 1992. "Motivated Skepticism: Use of Differential Decision Criteria for Preferred and Nonpreferred Conclusions." *Journal of Personality and Social Psychology* 63 (4): 568–584.

Doris, John M. 2002. *Lack of Character: Personality and Moral Behavior*. Cambridge: Cambridge University Press.

Dreyfus, Stuart. 2004. "The Five-Stage Model of Adult Skill Acquisition." *Bulletin of Science Technology & Society* 24 (3): 177–181.

Dunning, David. 2015. "On Identifying Human Capital: Flawed Knowledge Leads to Faulty Judgments of Expertise by Individuals and Groups." In *Advances in Group Processes*. Vol. 32. Edited by Shane R. Thye and Edward Lawler, 149–176. New York: Emerald.

Dunning, David, and Jeremy Cone. Unpublished manuscript. "The Cassandra Quandary: How Flawed Expertise Prevents People from Recognizing Superior Performance among Their Peers." University of Michigan.

Dunning, David, Kerri Johnson, Joyce Ehrlinger, and Justin Kruger. 2003. "Why People Fail to Recognize Their Own Incompetence." *Current Directions in Psychological Science* 12 (3): 83–87.

Dutant, Julien. 2015. "The Legend of the Justified True Belief Analysis." *Philosophical Perspectives* 29 (1): 95–145.

Effron, Daniel A., Hazel Rose Markus, Lauren M. Jackman, Yukiko Muramoto, and Hamdi Muluk. 2018. "Hypocrisy and Culture: Failing to Practice What You Preach Receives Harsher Interpersonal Reactions in Independent (vs. Interdependent) Cultures." *Journal of Experimental Social Psychology* 76: 371–384.

Ehrlinger, Joyce, Thomas Gilovich, and Lee Ross. 2005. "Peering into the Bias Blind Spot: People's Assessments of Bias in Themselves and Others." *Personality and Social Psychology Bulletin* 31 (5): 680–692.

Elga, Adam. 2010. "How to Disagree about How to Disagree." In *Disagreement*. Edited by Ted Warfield and Richard Feldman, 175–186. New York: Oxford University Press.

Elga, Adam. Unpublished manuscript. "Lucky to Be Rational." Princeton University.

Evans, Ian, and Nicholas D. Smith. 2012. *Knowledge*. Cambridge: Polity Press.

Evans, Jonathan St. B. T., and Keith E. Stanovich. 2013. "Dual-Process Theories of Higher Cognition: Advancing the Debate." *Perspectives on Psychological Science* 8 (3): 223–241.

Fanelli, Daniele. 2009. "How Many Scientists Fabricate and Falsify Research? A Systematic Review and Meta-Analysis of Survey Data." *PLoS ONE* 4 (5): e5738.

Feldman, Richard. 2003a. *Epistemology*. Upper Saddle River, NJ: Prentice Hall.

Feldman, Richard. 2003b. "Plantinga on Exclusivism." *Faith and Philosophy* 20 (1): 85–90.

Feldman, Richard. 2005. "Respecting the Evidence." *Philosophical Perspectives* 19 (1): 95–119.

Feldman, Richard. 2006. "Epistemological Puzzles about Disagreement." In *Epistemology Futures*. Edited by Stephen Hetherington, 216–236. New York: Oxford University Press.

Feldman, Richard. 2009. "Evidentialism, Higher-Order Evidence, and Disagreement." *Episteme* 6 (3): 294–312.

Feldman, Richard, and Earl Conee. 1985. "Evidentialism." *Philosophical Studies* 48 (1): 15–34.

Feldman, Richard, and Ted Warfield, eds. 2010. *Disagreement*. Oxford: Oxford University Press.

Finocchiaro, Maurice A. 1997. "The *Port-Royal Logic*'s Theory of Argument." *Argumentation* 11 (4): 393–410.

Fitzgerald, Amy J., Linda Kalof, and Thomas Dietz. 2009. "Slaughterhouses and Increased Crime Rates: An Empirical Analysis of the Spillover from 'The Jungle' into the Surrounding Community." *Organization & Environment* 22 (2): 158–184.

Fitzgerald, Scott F. 1936. "The Crack-Up." *Esquire* (February 1936).

Foley, Richard. 1992. "The Epistemology of Belief and the Epistemology of Degrees of Belief." *American Philosophical Quarterly* 29 (2): 111–124.

Foley, Richard. 2001. *Intellectual Trust in Oneself and Others*. Cambridge: Cambridge University Press.

Frances, Bryan. 2010. "The Reflective Epistemic Renegade." *Philosophy and Phenomenological Research* 81 (2): 419–463.

Freemantle, Michael. 2015. *The Chemists' War: 1914–1918*. Cambridge: Royal Society of Chemistry.

Fricker, Miranda. 2007. *Epistemic Injustice: Power and the Ethics of Knowing*. Oxford: Oxford University Press.

Friedman, Jane. 2013. "Suspended Judgment." *Philosophical Studies* 162 (2): 165–181.

Fumerton, Richard. 1995. *Metaepistemology and Skepticism*. Lanham, MD: Rowman and Littlefield.

Fumerton, Richard. 2006. *Epistemology*. Malden, MA: Blackwell.

Fumerton, Richard. 2010. "You Can't Trust a Philosopher." In *Disagreement*. Edited by Richard Feldman and Ted Warfield, 91–110. Oxford: Oxford University Press.

Gaitán, Alfredo. 2017. "The Peculiar Experience of Being a Complete Novice: A Reflection on Supervising Systemic Practitioner Researchers on a Doctoral Programme." *Murmurations: Journal of Transformative Systemic Practice* 1 (1): 45–56.

Galison, Peter. 1987. *How Experiments End*. Chicago: University of Chicago Press.

Garber, Daniel. 2009. *What Happens after Pascal's Wager: Living Faith and Rational Belief*. Milwaukee, WI: Marquette University Press.

Garfield, Jay. 2011. "David Foster Wallace as Student: A Memoir." In *Fate, Time, and Language: An Essay on Free Will*. Edited by Steven Cahn, 219–222. New York: Columbia University Press.

Gaukroger, Stephen. 2001. *Francis Bacon and the Transformation of Early-Modern Philosophy*. Cambridge: Cambridge University Press.

Gawande, Atul. 2009. *The Checklist Manifesto: How to Get Things Right*. New York: Picador.

Gerken, Mikkel. 2018. "Expert Trespassing Testimony and the Ethics of Science Communication." *Journal for General Philosophy of Science* 49 (3): 299–318.

Gettier, Edmund L. 1963. "Is Justified True Belief Knowledge?" *Analysis* 23 (6): 121–123.

Gick, Mary L., and Keith J. Holyoak. 1980. "Analogical Problem Solving." *Cognitive Psychology* 12 (3): 306–355.

Gieryn, Thomas F. 1999. *Cultural Boundaries of Science: Credibility on the Line*. Chicago: University of Chicago Press.

Goldberg, Sanford. 2009a. "The Epistemology of Silence." In *Social Epistemology*. Edited by Adrian Haddock, Alan Millar, and Duncan Pritchard, 243–261. Oxford: Oxford University Press.

Goldberg, Sanford. 2009b. "Experts, Semantic and Epistemic." *Noûs* 43 (4): 581–598.

Goldberg, Sanford. 2016. "On the Epistemic Significance of Evidence You Should Have Had." *Episteme* 13 (4): 449–470.

Goldman, Alvin. 1978. "Epistemics: The Regulative Theory of Cognition." *The Journal of Philosophy* 75 (10): 509–523.

Goldman, Alvin. 1979. "What Is Justified Belief?" In *Justification and Knowledge*. Edited by George Pappas, 1–23. Dordrecht: Reidel.

Goldman, Alvin. 1988. "Strong and Weak Justification." *Philosophical Perspectives* 2: 51–69.

Goldman, Alvin. 1999. *Knowledge in a Social World*. Oxford: Oxford University Press.

Goldman, Alvin. 2001. "Experts: Which Ones Should You Trust?" *Philosophy and Phenomenological Research* 63 (1): 85–110.

Goldman, Alvin. 2018. "Expertise." *Topoi* 37 (1): 3–10.

Grafton, Anthony. 2000. *Traditions of Conversion: Descartes and His Demon*. Berkeley, CA: Doreen B. Townsend Center for the Humanities.

Graham, Peter. 2006. "Testimonial Justification: Inferential or Non-Inferential?" *The Philosophical Quarterly* 56 (222): 84–95.

Graham, Peter. 2010. "Theorizing Justification." *Knowledge and Skepticism*. Edited by Joseph Keim Campbell, Michael O'Rourke, and Harry S. Silverstein, 45–71. Cambridge, MA: MIT Press.

Grasswick, Heidi E., and Mark Owen Webb. 2002. "Feminist Epistemology as Social Epistemology." *Social Epistemology* 16 (3): 185–196.

Greco, Daniel. Forthcoming. "Climate Change and Cultural Cognition." In *Philosophy and Climate Change*. Edited by David Plunkett, Mark Budolfson, and Tristram McPherson. Oxford: Oxford University Press.

Greco, John. 2002. "How to Reid Moore." *The Philosophical Quarterly* 52 (209): 544–563.

Greco, John. 2010. *Achieving Knowledge*. Cambridge: Cambridge University Press.

Greene, Joshua. 2008. "The Secret Joke of Kant's Soul." In *Moral Psychology, Volume 3, The Neuroscience of Morality: Emotion, Brain Disorders, and Development*. Edited by Walter Sinnott-Armstrong, 35–79. Cambridge, MA: MIT Press.

Gross, Neil. 2008. *Richard Rorty: The Making of an American Philosopher*. Chicago: University of Chicago Press.

Grundmann, Thomas. 2009. "Reliabilism and the Problem of Defeaters." *Grazer Philosophische Studien* 79 (1): 65–76.

Haack, Susan. 2015. "Epistemology: Who Needs It?" *Kilikya Felsefe Dergisi* 3: 1–15.

Hadot, Pierre. 1995. *Philosophy as a Way of Life: Spiritual Exercises from Socrates to Foucault*. Edited by Arnold Davidson. New York: Blackwell.

Haidt, Jonathan. 2012. *The Righteous Mind: Why Good People Are Divided by Politics and Religion*. New York: Vintage.

Haldane, J. B. S. 2002 [1927]. *Possible Worlds*. New Brunswick, NJ: Transaction.

Haldane, J. S. 1922. *Respiration*. New Haven, CT: Yale University Press.

Haldane, J. S., A. M. Kellas, and E. L. Kennaway. 1919. "Experiments on Acclimatization to Reduced Atmospheric Pressure." *Journal of Physiology* 53 (3–4): 181–206.

Hanna, Nathan. 2015. "Philosophical Success." *Philosophical Studies* 172 (8): 2109–2121.

Hansen, Katherine, Margaret Gerbasi, Alexander Todorov, Elliott Kruse, and Emily Pronin. 2014. "People Claim Objectivity after Knowingly Using Biased Strategies." *Personality and Social Psychology Bulletin* 40 (6): 691–699.

Hardwig, John. 1991. "The Role of Trust in Knowledge." *The Journal of Philosophy* 88 (12): 693–708.

Hardy, Jörg. 2010. "Seeking the Truth and Taking Care for Common Goods—Plato on Expertise and Recognizing Experts." *Episteme* 7 (1): 7–22.

Harman, Gilbert. 1973. *Thought*. Princeton, NJ: Princeton University Press.

Harman, Gilbert. 1999. "Moral Philosophy Meets Social Psychology: Virtue Ethics and the Fundamental Attribution Error." *Proceedings of the Aristotelian Society* 99 (1): 315–331.

Hatfield, Gary. 1986. "The Senses and the Fleshless Eye: The *Meditations* as Cognitive Exercises." In *Essays on Descartes' Meditations*. Edited by Amélie Oksenberg Rorty, 45–76. Berkeley: University of California Press.

Hawthorne, John. 2004. *Knowledge and Lotteries*. Oxford: Oxford University Press.

Hazlitt, William. 1824. "On the Spirit of Obligations." *New Monthly Magazine* X: 34–41.

Hazlitt, William. 1998 [1827]. "On Reading New Books." In *The Selected Writings of William Hazlitt*. Vol. 9 (Uncollected Essays). Edited by Duncan Wu, 141–151. London: Pickering & Chatto.

Hazlitt, William. 1998 [1831]. "The Letter-Bell." In *The Selected Writings of William Hazlitt*. Vol. 9 (Uncollected Essays). Edited by Duncan Wu, 203–208. London: Pickering and Chatto.

Heath, Chip, Richard Larrick, and Joshua Klayman. 1998. "Cognitive Repairs: How Organizational Practices Can Compensate for Individual Shortcomings." *Research in Organization Behavior* 20: 1–37.

Henderson, David K., and Terence Horgan. 2011. *The Epistemological Spectrum: At the Interface of Cognitive Science and Conceptual Analysis*. Oxford: Oxford University Press.

Hendrickson, Gordon, and William H. Schroeder. 1941. "Transfer of Training in Learning to Hit a Submerged Target." *Journal of Educational Psychology* 32 (3): 205–213.

Hepburn, R. W. 1980. "Wonder." *Proceedings of the Aristotelian Society* (Supplementary Volumes) 54: 1–23.

Hetherington, Stephen. 2016. *Knowledge and the Gettier Problem*. Cambridge: Cambridge University Press.

Hirsch Hadorn, Gertrude, Holger Hoffmann-Riem, Susette Biber-Klemm, Walter Gossenbacher-Mansuy, Dominique Joye, Christian Pohl, Urs Wiesmann, and Elisabeth Zemp, eds. 2008. *Handbook of Transdisciplinary Research*. Dordrecht: Springer.

Hirsch Hadorn, Gertrude, Christian Pohl, and Gabriele Bammer. 2010. "Solving Problems through Transdisciplinary Research." In *The Oxford Handbook of Interdisciplinarity*. Edited by Robert Frodeman, Julie Thompson Klein, and Carl Mitcham, 431–452. Oxford: Oxford University Press.

Hirsch, Jules. 2006. "An Anniversary for Cancer Chemotherapy." *Journal of the American Medical Association* 296 (12): 1518–1520.

Horgan, Terry, and Mark Timmons. 2007. "Morphological Rationalism and the Psychology of Moral Judgment." *Ethical Theory & Moral Practice* 10 (3): 279–295.

Horowitz, Sophie. 2014. "Epistemic Akrasia." *Noûs* 48 (4): 718–744.

Howard-Snyder, Daniel. 2013. "Propositional Faith: What It Is and What It Is Not." *American Philosophical Quarterly* 50 (4): 357–372.

Hu, Xingming. 2017. "Must a Successful Argument Convert an Ideal Audience?" *Argumentation* 31 (1): 165–177.

Infield, Glenn B. 1971. *Disaster at Bari*. London: MacMillan.

Isaac, Joel. 2012. *Working Knowledge: Making the Human Sciences from Parsons to Kuhn*. Cambridge, MA: Harvard University Press.

James, William. 1896. "The Will to Believe." *The New World* 5: 327–347.

Jamieson, Kathleen Hall, Dan Kahan, and Dietram A. Scheufele. 2017. *The Oxford Handbook of the Science of Science Communication*. Oxford: Oxford University Press.

Janis, Irving L. 1972. *Victims of Groupthink: A Psychological Study of Foreign-Policy Decisions and Fiascoes*. Boston: Houghton Mifflin.

Jardine, Lisa. 2000. Introduction to *The New Organon*. Edited and translated by Lisa Jardine and Michael Silverthorne, vii–xxviii. Cambridge: Cambridge University Press.

Jinha, Arif E. 2010. "Article 50 Million: An Estimate of the Number of Scholarly Articles in Existence." *Learned Publishing* 23 (3): 258–263.

John of Salisbury. 1955 [1159]. *The Metalogicon of John of Salisbury: A Twelfth-century Defense of the Verbal and Logical Arts of the Trivium*. Translated by Daniel D. McGarry. Berkeley: University of California Press.

Jones, E. E., and V. A. Harris. 1967. "The Attribution of Attitudes." *Journal of Experimental Social Psychology* 3 (1): 1–24.

Jordan, Jillian J., Roseanna Sommers, Paul Bloom, and David G. Rand. 2017. "Why Do We Hate Hypocrites? Evidence for a Theory of False Signalling." *Psychological Science* 28 (3): 356–368.

Joyce, Richard. 2006. *The Evolution of Morality*. Cambridge, MA: MIT Press.

Judd, Charles H. 1908. "The Relation of Special Training to General Intelligence." *Educational Review* XXXVI: 28–42.

Judson, Horace Freeland. 2004. *The Great Betrayal: Fraud in Science*. Orlando, FL: Harcourt.

Kahan, Dan M., and Donald Braman. 2006. "Cultural Cognition and Public Policy." *Yale Law and Policy Review* 24: 147–170.

Kahan, Dan, Hank Jenkins-Smith, and Donald Braman. 2011. "Cultural Cognition of Scientific Consensus." *Journal of Risk Research* 14 (2): 147–174.

Kahan, Dan. 2016. "The Politically Motivated Reasoning Paradigm, Part 1: What Politically Motivated Reasoning Is and How to Measure It." In *Emerging Trends in the Social and Behavioral Sciences*. Edited by Robert Scott and Stephen Kosslyn. Hoboken, NJ: John Wiley & Sons.

Kahneman, Daniel. 2003. "A Perspective on Judgment and Choice: Mapping Bounded Rationality." *American Psychologist* 58 (9): 697–720.

Kahneman, Daniel. 2011. *Thinking, Fast and Slow*. New York: Farrar, Straus and Giroux.

Kaiser, David. 2006. "The Physics of Spin: Sputnik Politics and American Physics in the 1950s." *Social Research* 73 (4): 1225–1252.

Kaplan, Mark. 1985. "It's Not What You Know That Counts." *The Journal of Philosophy* 82 (7): 350–363.

Keller, John A. 2015. "On Knockdown Arguments." *Erkenntnis* 80 (6): 1205–1215.

Kelly, Daniel. 2012. "Review of *The Meaning of Disgust*, by Colin McGinn." *Notre Dame Philosophical Reviews* (June 23). http://ndpr.nd.edu/news/the-meaning-of-disgust/.

Kelly, Thomas. 2005a. "The Epistemic Significance of Disagreement." *Oxford Studies in Epistemology* 1: 167–196.

Kelly, Thomas. 2005b. "Moorean Facts and Belief Revision, or Can the Skeptic Win?" *Philosophical Perspectives* 19 (1): 179–209.

Kelly, Thomas. 2008. "Disagreement, Dogmatism, and Belief Polarization." *The Journal of Philosophy* 105 (10): 611–633.

Kelly, Thomas. 2010. "Peer Disagreement and Higher-Order Evidence." In *Disagreement*. Edited by Richard Feldman and Ted Warfield, 111–174. Oxford: Oxford University Press.

Kelly, Thomas. 2013. "Disagreement and the Burdens of Judgment." In *The Epistemology of Disagreement: New Essays*. Edited by David Christensen and Jennifer Lackey, 31–53. Oxford: Oxford University Press.

Kelly, Thomas, and Sarah McGrath. 2017. "Are There Any Successful Philosophical Arguments?" In *Being, Freedom and Method: Themes from van Inwagen*. Edited by John A. Keller, 324–342. Oxford: Oxford University Press.

Kelp, Christoph. 2014. "Two for the Knowledge Goal of Inquiry." *American Philosophical Quarterly* 51 (3): 227–232.

Kenyon, Tim. 2014. "False Polarization: Debiasing as Applied Social Epistemology." *Synthese* 191 (11): 2529–2547.

Kidder, Tracy, and Richard Todd. 2013. *Good Prose: The Art of Nonfiction*. New York: Random House.

Kim, Jaegwon. 1988. "What Is 'Naturalized Epistemology'?" *Philosophical Perspectives* 2: 381–405.

King, Nathan. 2012. "Disagreement: What's the Problem? Or a Good Peer Is Hard to Find." *Philosophy and Phenomenological Research* 85 (2): 249–272.

King, Nathan. 2016. "Religious Skepticism and Higher-Order Evidence." In *Oxford Studies in Philosophy of Religion*. Vol. 7. Edited by Jonathan Kvanvig, 126–156. Oxford: Oxford University Press.

King, Patricia, and Karen Strohm Kitchener. 1994. *Developing Reflective Judgment*. San Francisco: Jossey-Bass.

King, Peter. 2007. "Damaged Goods: Human Nature and Original Sin." *Faith and Philosophy* 24 (3): 247–267.

Kitcher, Patricia. 1992. *Freud's Dream: A Complete Interdisciplinary Science of Mind.* Cambridge, MA: MIT Press.

Kornblith, Hilary. 1999. "Distrusting Reason." *Midwest Studies in Philosophy* 23 (1): 181–196.

Kornblith, Hilary. 2001a. "Epistemic Obligations and the Possibility of Internalism." In *Virtue Epistemology: Essays on Epistemic Virtue and Responsibility.* Edited by Abrol Fairweather and Linda Zagzebski, 231–248. Oxford: Oxford University Press.

Kornblith, Hilary, ed. 2001b. *Epistemology: Internalism and Externalism.* Malden, MA: Blackwell.

Kornblith, Hilary. 2002. *Knowledge and Its Place in Nature.* Oxford: Oxford University Press.

Kornblith, Hilary. 2008. "Hilary Kornblith." In *Epistemology: 5 Questions.* Edited by Vincent F. Hendricks and Duncan Pritchard, 211–216. New York: Automatic Press.

Kornblith, Hilary. 2010. "Disagreement in the Face of Controversy." In *Disagreement.* Edited by Richard Feldman and Ted Warfield, 29–52. Oxford: Oxford University Press.

Kornblith, Hilary. 2012. *On Reflection.* Oxford: Oxford University Press.

Kotzee, Ben. 2013. *Education and the Growth of Knowledge: Perspectives from Social and Virtue Epistemology.* Malden, MA: Wiley-Blackwell.

Kremer, Elmar, ed. 1996. *Interpreting Arnauld.* Toronto: University of Toronto Press.

Kross, Ethan, and Igor Grossmann. 2012. "Boosting Wisdom: Distance from the Self Enhances Wise Reasoning, Attitudes, and Behavior." *Journal of Experimental Psychology: General* 141 (1): 43–48.

Kruger, Justin, and David Dunning. 1999. "Unskilled and Unaware of It: How Difficulties in Recognizing One's Own Incompetence Lead to Inflated Self-Assessments." *Journal of Personality and Social Psychology* 77 (6): 1121–1134.

Kruger, Justin, and Thomas Gilovich. 1999. "'Naïve Cynicism' in Everyday Theories of Responsibility Assessment: On Biased Assessments of Bias." *Journal of Personality and Social Psychology* 76 (5): 743–753.

Kuhn, Deanna. 1999. "A Developmental Model of Critical Thinking." *Educational Researcher* 28 (2): 16–25.

Kuhn, Deanna. 2005. *Education for Thinking.* Cambridge, MA: Harvard University Press.

Kuklick, Bruce. 2001. *A History of Philosophy in America 1720–2000.* Oxford: Oxford University Press.

Kunda, Ziva. 1990. "The Case for Motivated Reasoning." *Psychological Bulletin* 108 (3): 480–498.

Kvanvig, Jonathan L. 2011. "Millar on the Value of Knowledge." *Proceedings of the Aristotelian Society* (Supplementary Volumes) 85 (1): 83–99.

LaBarge, Scott. 1997. "Socrates and the Recognition of Experts." *Aperion* 30 (4): 51–62.

Lackey, Jennifer. 2010. "A Justificationist View of Disagreement's Epistemic Significance." In *Social Epistemology.* Edited by Adrian Haddock, Alan Millar, and Duncan Pritchard, 298–325. Oxford: Oxford University Press.

Lakoff, George. 2002. *Moral Politics.* Chicago: University of Chicago Press.

Lamont, Michele. 2009. *How Professors Think: Inside the Curious World of Academic Judgment.* Cambridge, MA: Harvard University Press.

Larrick, Richard. 2004. "Debiasing." In *Blackwell Handbook of Judgment and Decision Making.* Edited by Derek Koehler and Nigel Harvey, 316–337. Malden, MA: Wiley-Blackwell.

Lasonen-Aarnio, Maria. 2010. "Unreasonable Knowledge." *Philosophical Perspectives* 24 (1): 1–21.

Lasonen-Aarnio, Maria. 2014. "Higher-Order Evidence and the Limits of Defeat." *Philosophy and Phenomenological Research* 88 (2): 314–335.

Lazer, David M. J., Matthew A. Baum, Yochai Benkler, Adam J. Berinsky, Kelly M. Greenhill, Filippo Menczer, Miriam J. Metzger, Brendan Nyhan, Gordon Pennycook, David Rothschild, Michael Schudson, Steven A. Sloman, Cass R. Sunstein, Emily A. Thorson, Duncan J. Watts, and Jonathan L. Zittrain. 2018. "The Science of Fake News." *Science* 359 (6380): 1094–1096.

Learoyd, Phil. 2012. "The History of Blood Transfusion Prior to the 20th Century—Part 1." *Transfusion Medicine* 22 (5): 308–314.

Lee, Carole J., and Christian D. Schunn. 2011. "Social Biases and Solutions for Procedural Objectivity." *Hypatia* 26 (2): 353–373.

Lee, Matthew B. 2018. "On Doubt." *Philosophia* 46 (1): 141–158.

Lehrer, Keith. 2000. *Theory of Knowledge*. Boulder, CO: Westview Press.

Leibniz, Gottfried Wilhelm. 1951 [1680]. "Precepts for Advancing the Sciences and Arts." In *Leibniz: Selections*. Edited by Philip P. Wiener, 29–46. New York: Charles Scribner's Sons.

Levin, Michael, and John S. Wilson. 1949. "No Bop Roots in Jazz: Parker." *Downbeat Magazine* 16 (7): 1, 12–13, 19.

Lewandowsky, Stephan, Ullrich K. H. Ecker, Colleen M. Seifert, Norbert Schwarz, and John Cook. 2012. "Misinformation and Its Correction: Continued Influence and Successful Debiasing." *Psychological Science in the Public Interest* 13 (3): 106–131.

Lewis, David. 1973. *Counterfactuals*. Malden, MA: Basil Blackwell.

Lewis, David. 1983. *Philosophical Papers*. Vol. 1. Oxford: Oxford University Press.

Lobato, Joanne. 2006. "Alternative Perspectives on the Transfer of Learning: History, Issues, and Challenges for Future Research." *The Journal of the Learning Sciences* 15 (4): 431–449.

Locke, John. 1975 [1690]. *An Essay Concerning Human Understanding*. Edited by Peter H. Nidditch. Oxford: Oxford University Press.

Locke, John. 1983 [1689]. *A Letter Concerning Toleration*. Edited by James H. Tully. Indianapolis, IN: Hackett.

Locke, John. 1996 [1706]. *Some Thoughts Concerning Education* and *Of the Conduct of the Understanding*. Edited by Ruth Grant and Nathan Tarcov. Indianapolis, IN: Hackett.

Locke, John. 1997 [1660/61]. *Locke: Political Essays*. Edited by Mark Goldie. Cambridge: Cambridge University Press.

Lord, Charles G., Mark R. Lepper, and Elizabeth Preston. 1984. "Considering the Opposite: A Corrective Strategy for Social Judgment." *Journal of Personality and Social Psychology* 47 (6): 1231–1243.

Lycan, William. 2001. "Moore against the New Skeptics." *Philosophical Studies* 103 (1): 35–53.

Lycan, William. 2006. "On the Gettier Problem Problem." In *Epistemology Futures*. Edited by Stephen Hetherington, 148–168. Oxford: Oxford University Press.

Lynch, Michael. 2004. *True to Life: Why Truth Matters*. Cambridge, MA: MIT Press.

Lyons, Jack C. 2009. *Perception and Basic Beliefs: Zombies, Modules, and the Problem of the External World*. Oxford: Oxford University Press.

Machuca, Diego. 2011. "The Pyrrhonian Argument from Possible Disagreement." *Archiv für Geschichte der Philosophie* 93 (2): 148–161.

Machuca, Diego, ed. 2012. *Disagreement and Skepticism*. New York: Routledge.

Machuca, Diego E. 2017. "A Neo-Pyrrhonian Response to the Disagreeing about Disagreement Argument." *Synthese* 194 (5): 1663–1680.

Matheson, David. 2005. "Conflicting Experts and Dialectical Performance: Adjudication Heuristics for the Layperson." *Argumentation* 19 (2): 145–158.

Matheson, Jonathan. 2015. "Are Conciliatory Views of Disagreement Self-Defeating?" *Social Epistemology* 29 (2): 145–159.

McCain, Kevin. 2014. *Evidentialism and Epistemic Justification*. New York: Routledge.

McGinn, Colin. 2011. *The Meaning of Disgust*. Oxford: Oxford University Press.

McGinn, Colin. 2015. "Disgust and Disease." *Emotion Review* 7 (4): 381–382.

McKaughan, Daniel J. 2012. "Voles, Vasopressin, and Infidelity: A Molecular Basis for Monogamy, a Platform for Ethics, and More?" *Biology and Philosophy* 27 (4): 521–543.

McKinnon, Christine. 1991. "Hypocrisy, with a Note on Integrity." *American Philosophical Quarterly* 28 (4): 321–330.

Mele, Alfred R. 2008. "Recent Work on Free Will and Science." *American Philosophical Quarterly* 45 (2): 107–129.

Mele, Alfred R. 2009. *Effective Intentions: The Power of Conscious Will*. Oxford: Oxford University Press.

Mercier, Hugo, and Dan Sperber. 2011. "Why Do Humans Reason? Arguments for an Argumentative Theory." *Behavioral and Brain Sciences* 34: 57–74.

Merton, Robert K. 1938. "Science, Technology and Society in Seventeenth Century England." *Osiris* 4: 360–632.

Midgley, Mary. 2013. "The Golden Age of Female Philosophy." *The Guardian*. https://www.theguardian.com/world/2013/nov/28/golden-age-female-philosophy-mary-midgley.

Mill, John Stuart. 1984 [1867]. "Inaugural Address Delivered to the University of St. Andrews." In *Collected Works of John Stuart Mill, Volume XXI. Essays on Equality, Law and Education*. Edited by John M. Robson, 217–257. Toronto: University of Toronto Press.

Miller, Christian B. 2014. *Character and Moral Psychology*. Oxford: Oxford University Press.

Montaigne, Michel de. 1957. *The Complete Works*. Translated by Donald Frame. New York: Alfred A. Knopf.

Moon, Andrew. 2018. "The Nature of Doubt and a New Puzzle about Belief, Doubt, and Confidence." *Synthese* 195 (4): 1827–1848.

Myers-Schulz, Blake, and Eric Schwitzgebel. 2013. "Knowing That P without Believing That P." *Noûs* 47 (2): 371–384.

Nadler, Steven M. 1989. *Arnauld and the Cartesian Philosophy of Ideas*. Princeton, NJ: Princeton University Press.

National Academies (U.S.)., Committee on Science, Engineering, and Public Policy (U.S.), National Academy of Sciences (U.S.), National Academy of Engineering, and Institute of Medicine (U.S.). 2005. *Facilitating Interdisciplinary Research*. Washington, D.C: National Academies Press.

Nehamas, Alexander. 1997. "Trends in Recent American Philosophy." *Daedalus* 126 (1): 209–223.

Neurath, Otto, Rudolph Carnap, and Hans Hahn. 1973 [1929]. "The Scientific Conception of the World: The Vienna Circle." In *Empiricism and Sociology*. Edited by Marie Neurath and Robert S. Cohen. Translated by Paul Foulkes and M. Neurath, 299–319. Dordrecht: Reidel.

Nichols, Tom. 2017. *The Death of Expertise: The Campaign against Established Knowledge and Why It Matters.* Oxford: Oxford University Press.

Nickerson, Raymond. 1998. "Confirmation Bias: A Ubiquitous Phenomenon in Many Guises." *Review of General Psychology* 2 (2): 175–220.

Nisbett, Richard, and Timothy Wilson. 1977. "Telling More Than We Can Know: Verbal Reports on Mental Processes." *Psychological Review* 84 (3): 231–259.

Nisbett, Richard, and Lee Ross. 1980. *Human Inference: Strategies and Shortcomings of Social Judgment.* Englewood Cliffs, NJ: Prentice-Hall.

Oberman, Heiko Augustinus. 1989. "*Die Gelehrten die Verkehrten*: Popular Response to Learned Culture in the Renaissance and Reformation." In *Religion and Culture in the Renaissance and Reformation.* Sixteenth Century Essays and Studies. Vol. 11. Edited by Steven Ozment, 43–62. Kirksville, MO: Truman State University Press.

Offit, Paul A. 2013. *Do You Believe in Magic?: Vitamins, Supplements, and All Things Natural: A Look Behind the Curtain.* New York: HarperCollins.

Oreskes, Naomi, and Erik M. Conway. 2010. *Merchants of Doubt.* London: Bloomsbury.

Oswald, John. 2000 [1791]. *The Cry of Nature; Or, An Appeal to Mercy and to Justice, on Behalf of the Persecuted Animals.* Mellen Animal Rights Library, Vol. 8. Lewiston, NY: Edwin Mellen Press.

Parker, Ashley. 2008. "At Pundit School, Learning to Smile and Interrupt." *New York Times,* October 24, 2008, p. ST1 of the New York edition. https://www.nytimes.com/2008/10/26/fashion/26pundit.html.

Pascal, Blaise. 2004 [1670]. *Pensées.* Translated and Edited by Roger Ariew. Indianapolis: Hackett.

Peirce, C. S. 1934. *The Collected Writings of Charles Sanders Peirce.* Vol. 5: *Pragmatism and Pragmaticism.* Edited by Charles Hartshorne and Paul Weiss. Cambridge, MA: Harvard University Press.

Peters, Douglas P., and Stephen J. Ceci. 1982. "Peer-Review Practices of Psychological Journals: The Fate of Published Articles, Submitted Again." *Behavioral and Brain Sciences* 5 (2): 187–195.

Pigliucci, Massimo. 2010. *Nonsense on Stilts: How to Tell Science from Bunk.* Chicago: University of Chicago Press.

Pittard, John. 2015. "Resolute Conciliationism." *The Philosophical Quarterly* 65 (260): 442–463.

Plantinga, Alvin. 1985. "Self-Profile." In *Profiles: Alvin Plantinga.* Edited by James Tomberlin and Peter van Inwangen, 3–97. Dordrecht: Reidel.

Plantinga, Alvin. 1990. "Justification in the 20th Century." *Philosophy and Phenomenological Research* 50 (Supplement): 45–71.

Plantinga, Alvin. 1993a. *Warrant: The Current Debate.* Oxford: Oxford University Press.

Plantinga, Alvin. 1993b. *Warrant and Proper Function.* Oxford: Oxford University Press.

Plantinga, Alvin. 1995. "Pluralism: A Defense of Religious Exclusivism." In *The Rationality of Belief and the Plurality of Faith: Essays in Honor of William P. Alston.* Edited by Thomas D. Senor, 191–215. Ithaca, NY: Cornell University Press.

Plantinga, Alvin. 1997. "Warrant and Accidentally True Belief." *Analysis* 57 (2): 140–145.

Plantinga, Alvin. 2000. *Warranted Christian Belief.* Oxford: Oxford University Press.

Plato. 1997. "Apology." Translated by G. M. A Grube. In *Plato: Complete Works.* Edited by John M. Cooper and D. S. Hutchinson. Indianapolis: Hackett.

Plato. 1997. "Meno." Translated by G. M. A. Grube. In *Plato's Complete Works.* Edited by John M. Cooper and D. S. Hutchinson. Indianapolis: Hackett.

Plumptre, James, and Thomas Lantaffe. 1816. *The Experienced Butcher: Shewing the Respectability and Usefulness of His Calling, the Religious Considerations Arising from It, the Laws Relating to It, and Various Profitable Suggestions for the Rightly Carrying It On: Designed Not Only for the Use of Butchers, But Also for Families and Readers in General.* London: Darton, Harvey.

Pollock, John. 1974. *Knowledge and Justification.* Princeton, NJ: Princeton University Press.

Pollock, John. 1986. *Contemporary Theories of Knowledge.* Lanham, MD: Rowman and Littlefield.

Pollock, John, and Joseph Cruz. 1999. *Contemporary Theories of Knowledge.* Lanham, MD: Rowman and Littlefield.

Popkin, Richard. 2003. *The History of Scepticism: From Savonarola to Bayle.* Oxford: Oxford University Press.

Pritchard, Duncan. 2016. "Seeing It for Oneself: Perceptual Knowledge, Understanding, and Intellectual Autonomy." *Episteme* 13 (1): 29–42.

Proctor, Robert N., and Londa Schiebinger, eds. 2008. *Agnotology: The Making and Unmaking of Ignorance.* Stanford, CA: Stanford University Press.

Pronin, Emily. 2007. "Perception and Misperception of Bias in Human Judgment." *Trends in Cognitive Sciences* 11 (1): 37–43.

Pronin, Emily, and Matthew Kugler. 2007. "Valuing Thoughts, Ignoring Behavior: The Introspection Illusion as a Source of the Bias Blind Spot." *Journal of Experimental Social Psychology* 43 (4): 556–578.

Pronin, Emily, Daniel Y. Lin, and Lee Ross. 2002. "The Bias Blind Spot: Perceptions of Bias in Self versus Others." *Personality and Social Psychology Bulletin* 28 (3): 369–381.

Putnam, Hilary. 1982. *Reason, Truth, and History.* Cambridge: Cambridge University Press.

Quine, Willard Van Orman. 1981. "Has Philosophy Lost Contact with People?" In *Theories and Things,* 190–193. Cambridge, MA: Harvard University Press.

Radford, Colin. 1966. "Knowledge—By Examples." *Analysis* 27 (1): 1–11.

Reeder, Glenn D., John B. Pryor, Michael J. A. Wohl, and Michael L. Griswell. 2005. "On Attributing Negative Motives to Others Who Disagree with Our Opinions." *Personality and Social Psychology Bulletin* 31 (11): 1498–1510.

Reich, Eugenie Samuel. 2009. *Plastic Fantastic: How the Biggest Fraud in Physics Shook the Scientific World.* New York: St. Martin's Press.

Reisch, George. 2005. *How the Cold War Transformed Philosophy of Science: To the Icy Slopes of Logic.* Cambridge: Cambridge University Press.

Rhoads, Cornelius P. 1946. "The Sword and the Ploughshare." *Journal of the Mount Sinai Hospital* 13 (6): 299–309.

Rhodes, Richard. 1995. *Dark Sun: The Making of the Hydrogen Bomb.* New York: Simon and Schuster.

Roberts, Robert, and W. Jay Wood. 2007. *Intellectual Virtues: An Essay in Regulative Epistemology.* Oxford: Oxford University Press.

Roberts, Robert C., and Ryan West. 2015. "Natural Epistemic Defects and Corrective Virtues." *Synthese* 192 (8): 2557–2576.

Robinson, Marilynne. 2010. "An Interview with Marilynne Robinson." Interview by Kay Parris. *Reform* (September): 12–15.

Rokeach, Milton. 1964. *The Three Christs of Ypsilanti.* New York: Knopf.

Rosenberg, Daniel, ed. 2003. "Special Issue on 'Early Modern Information Overload.'" *Journal of the History of Ideas* 64 (1).

Ross, Lee. 2018. "From the Fundamental Attribution Error to the Truly Fundamental Attribution Error and Beyond: My Research Journey." *Perspectives on Psychological Science* 13 (6): 750–769.

Ross, Lee, Joyce Ehrlinger, and Thomas Gilovich. 2016. "The Bias Blindspot and Its Implications." In *Contemporary Organizational Behavior: From Ideas to Action.* Edited by Kimberly D. Elsbach, Anna B. Kayes, and Christopher Kayes, 137–145. Boston: Pearson Prentice Hall.

Ross, Lee, and Andrew Ward. 1996. "Naive Realism in Everyday Life: Implications for Social Conflict and Misunderstanding." In *Values and Knowledge.* Edited by Edward S. Reed, Elliot Turiel, and Terrance Brown, 103–135. Hillsdale, NJ: Erlbaum.

Rousseau, Jean-Jacques. 1997 [1750]. "First Discourse." In *The Discourses and Other Political Writings.* Edited by Victor Gourevitch, 1–28. Cambridge: Cambridge University Press.

Rowley, William. 2012. "Evidence of Evidence is Evidence and Testimonial Reductionism." *Episteme* 9 (4): 377–391.

Russell, Bertrand. 1943. *An Outline of Intellectual Rubbish: A Hilarious Catalogue of Organized and Individual Stupidity.* Girard, KS: Haldeman-Julius.

Russell, Bertrand. 1995 [1950]. *An Inquiry into Meaning and Truth,* with an Introduction by Thomas Baldwin. London and New York: Routledge.

Russell, Bertrand. 1997 [1912]. *The Problems of Philosophy.* Oxford: Oxford University Press.

Russell, Bertrand. 1998 [1933]. "The Triumph of Stupidity." In *Mortals and Others: Bertrand Russell's American Essays, 1931–1935.* Vol. 2, 27–28. New York: Routledge.

Russell, Bertrand. 2004 [1928]. *Sceptical Essays.* London: Routledge.

Russell, Bertrand. 2009 [1948]. *Human Knowledge: Its Scope and Limits.* New York: Routledge.

Rysiew, Patrick. 2018. "The Gettier Problem and the Program of Analysis." In *The Gettier Problem.* Edited by Stephen Hetherington, 159–176. Cambridge: Cambridge University Press.

Samuels, Richard, and Stephen P. Stich. 2004. "Rationality and Psychology." In *The Oxford Handbook of Rationality.* Edited by Piers Rawling and Alfred R. Mele, 279–300. Oxford: Oxford University Press.

Sanches, Francisco. 1988. *That Nothing Is Known.* Cambridge: Cambridge University Press.

Saunders, Captain D. M. 1967. "The Bari Incident." *U.S. Naval Institute Proceedings* (September): 35–39.

Schellenberg, John. 2007. *The Wisdom to Doubt: A Justification of Religious Skepticism.* Ithaca, NY: Cornell University Press.

Schellenberg, John. 2014. "Skeptical Theism and Skeptical Atheism." In *Skeptical Theism: New Essays.* Edited by Trent Dougherty and Justin McBrayer, 191–208. Oxford: Oxford University Press.

Schneewind, J. B. 2003. *Moral Philosophy from Montaigne to Kant.* Cambridge: Cambridge University Press.

Schoenfield, Miriam. 2013. "Permission to Believe: Why Permissivism Is True and What It Tells Us about Irrelevant Influences on Belief." *Noûs* 47 (1): 193–218.

Scholz, Oliver R. 2009. "Experts: What They Are and How We Recognize Them." *Grazer Philosophische Studien* 79: 187–205.

Schreiner, Susan E. 2011. *Are You Alone Wise? The Search for Certainty in the Early Modern Era.* Oxford: Oxford University Press.

Schrödinger, Erwin. 1967. *What Is Life?: The Physical Aspect of the Living Cell, with Mind and Matter and Autobiographical Sketches.* Cambridge: Cambridge University Press.

Schrödinger, Erwin. 1996 [1954]. Nature and the Greeks *and* Science and Humanism. Cambridge: Cambridge University Press.

Schwartz, Daniel L., Catherine C. Chase, and John D. Bransford. 2012. "Resisting Overzealous Transfer: Coordinating Previously Successful Routines with Needs for New Learning." *Educational Psychologist* 47 (3): 204–214.

Schwartz, Martin A. 2008. "The Importance of Stupidity in Scientific Research." *Journal of Cell Science* 121: 1771.

Schwarz, Norbert, Eryn Newman, and William Leach. 2016. "Making the Truth Stick and the Myths Fade: Lessons from Cognitive Psychology." *Behavioral Science & Policy* 2 (1): 85–95.

Schwarz, Norbert, Lawrence J. Sanna, Ian Skurnik, and Carolyn Yoon. 2007. "Metacognitive Experiences and the Intricacies of Setting People Straight." *Advances in Experimental Social Psychology* 39: 127–161.

Schwerin, Alan. 1999. "A Lady, Her Philosopher and a Contradiction." *Russell: The Journal of the Bertrand Russell Archives* 19 (1): 5–28.

Segrè, Emilio. 1970. "Enrico Fermi: Physicist." *Bulletin of the Atomic Scientists* XXVI (9): 32, 37–39.

Seneca. 1928. *Moral Essays.* Vol. I. Loeb Classical Library 214. Translated by John W. Basore. Cambridge, MA: Harvard University Press.

Shapin, Steven. 1994. *A Social History of Truth.* Chicago: University of Chicago Press.

Shapin, Steven. 1996. *The Scientific Revolution.* Chicago: University of Chicago Press.

Shapin, Steven. 2010. *Never Pure: Historical Studies of Science as if It Was Produced by People with Bodies, Situated in Time, Space, Culture, and Society, and Struggling for Credibility and Authority.* Baltimore, MD: The Johns Hopkins University Press.

Shapin, Steven, and Simon Schaffer. 1985. *Leviathan and the Air-Pump.* Princeton, NJ: Princeton University Press.

Shope, Robert K. 1983. *The Analysis of Knowledge: A Decade of Research.* Princeton, NJ: Princeton University Press.

Simon, Herbert. 1992. "What is an 'Explanation' of Behavior?" *Psychological Science* 3 (3): 150–161.

Sinclair, Upton. 2001 [1906]. *The Jungle.* Mineola, NY: Dover.

Singer, Daniel J. 2018. "How to Be an Epistemic Consequentialist." *The Philosophical Quarterly* 68 (272): 580–602.

Slovic, Paul, Melissa Finucane, Ellen Peters, and Donald MacGregor. 2002. "The Affect Heuristic." In *Heuristics and Biases: The Psychology of Intuitive Judgment.* Edited by Thomas Gilovich, Dale W. Griffin, and Daniel Kahneman, 397–420. Cambridge: Cambridge University Press.

Soames, Scott. 2003. *Philosophical Analysis in the Twentieth Century.* Vol. 2. Princeton, NJ: Princeton University Press.

Soames, Scott. 2014. "Analytic Philosophy in America." In *Analytic Philosophy in America and Other Historical and Contemporary Essays,* 3–34. Princeton, NJ: Princeton University Press.

Sorensen, Roy. 1988. "Dogmatism, Junk Knowledge, and Conditionals." *The Philosophical Quarterly* 38 (153): 433–454.

Southern, George. 2002. *Poisonous Inferno: WWII Tragedy at Bari Harbour.* Shrewsbury: Airlife.

Stein, Edward. 1996. *Without Good Reason: The Rationality Debate in Philosophy and Cognitive Science.* Oxford: Oxford University Press.

Stevenson, Lloyd G. 1954. "On the Supposed Exclusion of Butchers and Surgeons from Jury Duty." *Journal of the History of Medicine and Allied Sciences* IX (2): 235–238.

Stewart, Coran. Forthcoming. "Expertise and Authority." *Episteme.* doi: 10.1017/epi.2018.43.

Stich, Stephen. 1990. *The Fragmentation of Reason: Preface to a Pragmatic Theory of Cognitive Evaluation.* Cambridge, MA: MIT Press.

Stoljar, Daniel. 2017. *Philosophical Progress: In Defence of a Reasonable Optimism.* Oxford: Oxford University Press.

Stoltz, Jonathan. 2007. "Gettier and Factivity in Indo-Tibetan Epistemology." *The Philosophical Quarterly* 57 (228): 394–415.

Street, Sharon. 2006. "A Darwinian Dilemma for Realist Theories of Value." *Philosophical Studies* 127 (1): 109–166.

Strohminger, Nina. 2014. "*The Meaning of Disgust*: A Refutation." *Emotion Review* 6 (3): 214–216.

Stump, David J. 2007. "Pierre Duhem's Virtue Epistemology." *Studies in History and Philosophy of Science* 38 (1): 149–159.

Sturgeon, Scott. 2014. "Pollock on Defeasible Reasons." *Philosophical Studies* 169 (1): 105–118.

Sullivan, John Jeremiah. 2011. "Too Much Information." *Gentlemen's Quarterly* (March 31). https://www.gq.com/story/david-foster-wallace-the-pale-king-john-jeremiah-sullivan.

Sunstein, Cass. 2017. *#RepublicDivided: Democracy in the Age of Social Media.* Princeton, NJ: Princeton University Press.

Taylor, Shelley, and Jonathon Brown. 1988. "Illusion and Well-Being: A Social Psychological Perspective on Mental Health." *Psychological Bulletin* 103 (2): 193–210.

Thielke, Peter. 2014. "What Would It Take to Change Your Mind?" *Metaphilosophy* 45 (3): 462–472.

Thies, Justus, Michael Zollhöfer, Marc Stamminger, Christian Theobalt, and Matthias Nießner. 2016. "Face2Face: Real-Time Face Capture and Reenactment of RGB Videos." *2016 IEEE Conference on Computer Vision and Pattern Recognition (CVPR):* 2387–2395.

Thune, Michael. 2010. "'Partial Defeaters' and the Epistemology of Disagreement." *The Philosophical Quarterly* 60 (239): 355–372.

Turkle, William J. 2013. *Spark from the Deep: How Shocking Experiments with Strongly Electric Fish Powered Scientific Discovery.* Baltimore, MD: Johns Hopkins Press.

Turner, Marlene E., and Anthony R. Pratkanis. 1998. "Twenty-five Years of Groupthink Theory and Research: Lessons from the Evaluation of a Theory." *Organizational Behavior and Human Decision Processes* 73 (2–3): 105–115.

Tversky, Amos, and Daniel Kahneman. 1974. "Judgment under Uncertainty: Heuristics and Biases." *Science* 185 (4157): 1124–1131.

Van Inwagen, Peter. 1994. "Quam Dilecta." In *God and the Philosophers.* Edited by Thomas V. Morris, 31–60. Oxford: Oxford University Press.

Van Inwagen, Peter. 2004. "Freedom to Break the Laws." *Midwest Studies in Philosophy* 28 (1): 334–350.

Van Inwagen, Peter. 2009. *Metaphysics.* 3rd edition. Boulder, CO: Westview Press.

Van Lier, Jens, Russell Revlin, and Wim De Neys. 2013. "Detecting Cheaters without Thinking: Testing the Automaticity of the Cheater Detection Module." *PLoS ONE* 8 (1): e53827.

Vavova, Katia. 2018. "Irrelevant Influences." *Philosophy and Phenomenological Research* 96 (1): 134–152.

Vazire, Simine. 2010. "Who Knows What about a Person? The Self–Other Knowledge Asymmetry (SOKA) Model." *Journal of Personality and Social Psychology* 98 (2): 281–300.

Vendler, Zeno. 1989. "Descartes' Exercises." *Canadian Journal of Philosophy* 19 (2): 193–224.

Vitz, Rico. 2010. "Descartes and the Question of Direct Doxastic Voluntarism." *Journal of Philosophical Research* 35: 107–121.

Walker, J. Samuel. 2006. *Three Mile Island: A Nuclear Crisis in Historical Perspective.* Berkeley: University of California Press.

Wallace, David Foster. 1997. *A Supposedly Fun Thing I'll Never Do Again.* New York: Little, Brown.

Walton, Douglas. 2008. *Informal Logic.* 2nd edition. Cambridge: Cambridge University Press.

Watson, J. D. 1993. "Succeeding in Science: Some Rules of Thumb." *Science* 261 (5129): 1812–1813.

Weatherson, Brian. 2013. "Disagreements, Philosophical and Otherwise." In *The Epistemology of Disagreement: New Essays.* Edited by David Christensen and Jennifer Lackey, 54–76. New York: Oxford University Press.

Webb, Mark. 2004. "Can Epistemology Help? The Problem of the Kentucky-Fried Rats." *Social Epistemology* 18 (1): 51–58.

Webster, Donna M., and Arie W. Kruglanski. 1994. "Individual Differences in Need for Cognitive Closure." *Journal of Personality and Social Psychology* 67 (6): 1049–1062.

Whitcomb, Dennis, Heather Battaly, Jason Baehr, and Daniel Howard-Snyder. 2017. "Intellectual Humility: Owning Our Limitations." *Philosophy and Phenomenological Research* 94 (3): 509–529.

White, Roger. 2010. "You Just Believe That Because . . ." *Philosophical Perspectives* 24 (1): 573–615.

Whiting, Jennifer E. 2003. "Cultivating Dialectical Imagination." In *Local Knowledges, Local Practices: Writing in the Disciplines at Cornell.* Edited by Jonathan Monroe, 222–231. Pittsburgh, PA: University of Pittsburgh Press.

Wiesner-Hanks, Merry E. 2005. *An Age of Voyages, 1350–1600 (Medieval and Early Modern World).* Oxford: Oxford University Press.

Williams, Bernard. 1970. "Deciding to Believe." In *Problems of the Self.* Edited by Bernard Williams, 136–151. Cambridge: Cambridge University Press.

Williamson, Timothy. 2011. "Improbable Knowing." In *Evidentialism and Its Discontents.* Edited by Trent Dougherty, 147–164. Oxford: Oxford University Press.

Williamson, Timothy. 2014. "Very Improbable Knowing." *Erkenntnis* 79 (5): 971–999.

Willingham, Daniel. 2007. "Critical Thinking: Why Is It So Hard to Teach?" *Arts Education Policy Review* 109 (4): 21–32.

Wilson, David Sloan. 2003. *Darwin's Cathedral: Evolution, Religion, and the Nature of Society.* Chicago: University of Chicago Press.

Wilson, Timothy. 2002. *Strangers to Ourselves: Discovering the Adaptive Unconscious.* Cambridge, MA: Belknap Press.

Wilson, Timothy. 2011. *Redirect: Changing the Stories We Live By*. New York: Back Bay Books.

Wilson, Timothy, and Nancy Brekke. 1994. "Mental Contamination and Mental Correction: Unwanted Influences on Judgments and Evaluations." *Psychological Bulletin* 116 (1): 117–142.

Wilson, Timothy, David Centerbar, and Nancy Brekke. 2002. "Mental Contamination and the Debiasing Problem." In *Heuristics and Biases*. Edited by Thomas Gilovich, David Griffin, and Daniel Kahneman, 185–200. Cambridge: Cambridge University Press.

Wineburg, Samuel. 1991. "On the Reading of Historical Texts: Notes on the Breach Between School and Academy." *American Educational Research Journal* 28 (3): 495–519.

Winters, Barbara. 1979. "Believing at Will." *The Journal of Philosophy* 76 (5): 243–256.

Wittgenstein, Ludwig. 2003 [1922]. *Tractatus Logico-Philosophicus*. Translated by C. K. Ogden. New York: Barnes and Noble.

Wolterstorff, Nicholas. 1996. *John Locke and the Ethics of Belief*. Cambridge: Cambridge University Press.

Wood, Wendy. 2017. "Habit in Personality and Social Psychology." *Personality and Social Psychology Review* 21 (4): 389–403.

Woods, Sean. 2014. "Anthony Bourdain on Writing, Hangovers, and Finding a Calling." *Men's Journal*. Accessed: June 8, 2018. https://www.mensjournal.com/features/anthony-bourdains-life-advice-20140919/.

Woolf, Virginia. 1984. *The Diary of Virginia Woolf, Volume 5: 1936–1941*. Edited by Anne Olivier Bell, assisted by Andrew McNeillie. Orlando, FL: Harcourt Brace.

Woolhouse, Roger. 2007. *Locke: A Biography*. Cambridge: Cambridge University Press.

Wordsworth, William. 1807. "Ode: Intimations of Immortality from Recollections of Early Childhood." In *Poems in Two Volumes*. Vol. 2. London: Longman, Hurst, Rees, and Orme.

Wu, Kaidi, and David Dunning. 2017. "Hypocognition: Making Sense of the Landscape Beyond One's Conceptual Reach." *Review of General Psychology* 22 (1): 25–35.

Wurman, Richard Saul. 1997. *Information Architects*. New York: Graphis.

Yildiz, Ahmet, Abdurrahim Emhan, Yasin Bez, and Said Kingir. 2012. "Psychological Symptom Profile of Butchers Working in Slaughterhouse and Retail Meat Packing Business: A Comparative Study." *Kafkas Universitesi Veteriner Fakultesi Dergisi* 18 (2): 319–322.

Zagzebski, Linda. 2009. *On Epistemology*. Belmont, CA: Wadsworth.

Zeaman, David. 1959. "Skinner's Theory of Teaching Machines." In *Automatic Teaching: The State of the Art*. Edited by Eugene Galanter, 167–176. New York: John Wiley & Sons.

Index

Trout, J. D., 6, 15–16n16, 18–19,
298–99
Twain, Mark, 119
Tyson, Neil deGrasse, 196, 197, 210

Vannikov, Boris, 280n12
Vienna Circle, 2, 8–10, 217

Wallace, David Foster, 150–51, 293–94
Webb, Mark, 6
Wellerstein, Alex, 281n12
Wilco, 150

Wilkins, Shane, ix, 217–18n15, 250n3,
281n13
Wilson, Benjamin, ix, 216–17n14, 238n16,
289n22
Wilson, Timothy, 83–84, 131, 142–43
Wittgenstein, Ludwig, 9, 170, 266
Wollstonecraft, Mary, vi, 61, 151
Wood, W. Jay, 17–19, 27–28n1,
81–82n15, 298–99
Wordsworth, William, 295–96, 295n29

Yeats, W. B., 250n3

Printed in the USA/Agawam, MA
July 15, 2021

777955.008